Clowns &
Tricksters

An Encyclopedia of Tradition
and Culture

Clowns & Tricksters

An Encyclopedia of Tradition and Culture

Kimberly A. Christen

Sam Gill, consulting editor

ABC-CLIO

Denver, Colorado
Santa Barbara, California
Oxford, England

Library of Congress Cataloging-in-Publication Data
Christen, Kimberly A.
  Clowns and tricksters : an encyclopedia of tradition
and culture / Kimberly A. Christen.
      p. cm.
  Includes bibliographical references and index.
  1. Trickster. 2. Clowns—Mythology. I. Christen, Kimberly.
II. Title.
GR524.C48 1998
398.2/09—dc21   98-027562
                                                                      CIP

ISBN 0–87436-936-3

04 03 02 01 00 99 98   9 8 7 6 5 4 3 2 1

ABC-CLIO, Inc.
130 Cremona Drive, P.O. Box 1911
Santa Barbara, California 93116-1911

This book is printed on acid-free paper ∞.

Manufactured in the United States of America

Contents

Preface

No undertaking of this scope is possible without the aid of others. It was a pleasure working with the staff at ABC-CLIO, especially Todd Hallman, in preparing this volume.

I would like to thank Sam Gill for providing me with the challenge and the opportunity to undertake this project. His editing and constant advice kept this project alive through many life changes.

As always, I thank my parents, Bill and Mary, for their love and support for every challenge I undertake.

I dedicate this book to the two most important people in my life: my husband, Chris, and our beautiful son, Jakob. Without their love this project might never have come to fruition. It is to Jakob, however, that I owe the biggest thanks. If it were not for his patience during the first three months of his life and his unselfishness in sharing his mom with the computer, I may never have had the strength to see this project through. His smiles, coos, and laughs have been and will continue to be my greatest accomplishment. Without him, I cannot imagine what else would matter.

Introduction

Tricksters and clowns, found in virtually every culture, are among the most widespread character types in mythology and popular culture throughout the world. However, they vary greatly from culture to culture, revealing distinct social and religious dimensions of the cultures in which they are found. Like any distinctive character, the tricksters and clowns of the world (of which there are an unlimited and always changing number) reveal something about the cultures from which they arose and in which they continue to be perpetuated. These multifaceted characters have been and continue to be sources of entertainment, agents of social change, and mirrors of religious conviction for their audiences.

The characters "trickster" and "clown" are closely related in many ways. Both are found in religious myths, in predominant roles in ritual celebrations, and in common folktales. They are distinguished more through academic categories than through actual indigenous terms. Most of the figures characterized as either trickster or clown are referred to within specific cultures by their individual names, the settings in which they are spoken of, or the activities in which they are involved. Nevertheless, scholars themselves created these categories without specifying clear-cut distinctions, and scholars from various disciplines have attempted to sort out the differences between these two categories with little consensus. Laura Makarius asserts that the difference between tricksters and clowns lies in their mythic (by which she means otherworldly) significance. Makarius designates tricksters as "mythic" figures and clowns as their more "earthly" counterparts. This distinction hinges on both the hierarchical separation of myths and folktales and the assumption that clowns are in

no way mythic figures. Makarius's distinction is meant to counteract the tendency to equate clowns and tricksters and to treat both as the same type of figure.

The terms *clowns* and *tricksters* were popularized when the evolutionary categorization of cultures was dominant in scholarship. Cultures and their specific characteristics were plotted on a linear chart from "primitive" to "civilized." Clown and trickster characters were taken to be signs of primitiveness, signs that a culture was at a childlike stage in development. Clowns and tricksters were seen by early anthropologists as buffoons, merrymakers, and pranksters, all of which were merely entertaining. The ethnocentric view of these figures as primitive was given weight by psychological and functional explanations that saw them as simply "tension-releasing valves" of "lower" cultures. In fact, because they were seen as simple entertainment, clowns and tricksters were not studied seriously for many decades.

Reports of these "grotesque," "savage" characters can be found in the works of early missionaries and settlers dating as far back as the 1600s. But it was not until the mid–nineteenth century with the rise of anthropological discourse in Britain and the United States that the categorizations were developed. In 1868 the term *trickster* appeared in Daniel Brinton's *Myths of the New World*, and in 1893 anthropologist R. M. Stephen reported the antics of clowns at a Hopi ceremony. More reports were to follow from anthropologists studying Native

American cultures, especially those in the U.S. Southwest, where clowns and tricksters are prevalent. At this point, the terms referred mainly to Native American figures portrayed in myths and rituals who acted ridiculously, crudely, and with little regard for social norms.

In the mid-1900s anthropologists began to pay more attention to clowns and tricksters within Native American cultures, focusing on their dual status as pranksters as well as culture heroes. Franz Boas and Robert Lowie, two well-respected anthropologists, defined a trickster as a mythological character possessing "transitional" characteristics. Boas and Lowie discredited the notion that tricksters must be predecessors to culture heroes and that they thus denoted a more primitive cultural stage. Citing several cases in which tricksters embodied the traits of culture heroes and others in which myths of origin contained both characters, Lowie and Boas were the first to study "trickster" characters as an autonomous category.

The ongoing discourse on clowns centered on the "sacred" nature of clowns and their contradictory actions at ritual celebrations. In the figure of the clown, anthropologists saw a character who performed both the most sacred religious rituals and the crudest acts. Ruth Bunzel, Frank Cushing, and Elsie Clews Parsons were among the anthropologists who studied the clown figures at Zuni, Hopi, and Navajo ceremonies. Parsons considered the earlier description of these clowns as "delight makers" to be too simplistic, obscuring their role as ritual specialists and healers. She argued for an understanding of the Hopi and Zuni clowns as "sacred." Along with Ralph Beals, who studied the Yaqui ceremonies, Parsons saw a distinct character type in these clowns; in her terms, they displayed both sacred and profane actions. Parsons and Beals saw these characters as far more than simplistic entertainers; they saw them, rather, as complex representations of cultural and religious ideals.

The trickster and clown categories were not sharply separated as they developed within anthropological circles, except that it was generally agreed that clowns were more visible in actual ceremonies whereas tricksters tended to be identified in myths and folktales. It was not until the appearance of Paul Radin's classic 1956 study *The Trickster* that tricksters or clowns began to be considered cross-cultural phenomena. Radin's work promoted a study of these characters across cultures, especially in Africa, where anthropologists had already noted similar characters. Radin's study is still considered a classic in the field of "trickster" studies. No such work, however, exists for the clown figure. Many scholars tend to lump clowns together as another type of trickster.

Although Radin's work specifically addressed the Winnebago character Wakdjunkaga, his remarks, as well as those of Carl Jung in the concluding chapter, speak to a distinct character type, "the trickster." Radin reinstates the idea that tricksters are precursors to culture heroes; he and Jung reinforce the view that both the cultures who possess these figures and the characters themselves are primitive, inferior, and childlike, that tricksters occur at a primitive stage in cultural development. Working from this assumption, they assert that trickster characters are "primitive" representations of good and evil, and Radin's study has been criticized for his evolutionary view and his simplistic, psychological characterization of the trickster figure.

Scholars like Radin made the "trickster problem" the central focus of their work. Attempting to qualify, classify, and articulate the exact role of these characters, such studies masked many of the qualities of the clowns and tricksters themselves. Recent studies, however, have dismissed tricksters and clowns as "problems" to be solved and have begun studies that place these characters within the worldview of the cultures from which they come. Along with this innovation has come the debate over the general terms *trickster* and *clown*. Some scholars argue that the terms have become so general that they misrepresent and mask the uniqueness of individual characters. Both T. O. Beidelman and Dario Sabbatocci argue for studies that make the categories of trickster or clown secondary to individual cultural standards. In other words, they argue against catchall categories that deny difference and hide the figures' unique cultural aspects. Contrary to Barbara Babcock-Abrahams, whose work focuses on the cross-cultural features of clowns and tricksters, Beidelman argues against any type of general category. He suggests that the category itself has created the misrepresentation of figures around the world. Beidelman calls for strictly cultural studies of trickster or clown figures without the imposition of cross-cultural categories.

On the other hand, Babcock-Abrahams argues that the categories of trickster, clown, jester, and fool are expansive categories that cover the gamut from the town jester in medieval Europe to the coyote character present in many Native American cultures. Relying on Enid Welsford's detailed study of "the fool," Babcock-Abrahams asserts that these types of characters, who reverse order, invoke chaos, and epitomize unpredictability, are found throughout the world with little difference between them except the labels scholars place on them. She denounces strict universal boundaries that are based on the similarities of these types of figures across the world and through time. Instead of attempting to create an all-encompassing category through which to distinguish these characters, Babcock-Abrahams argues for a more thorough study of the ambiguity that clowns and tricksters express in their actions and in the stories told about them.

Drawing on Victor Turner's notion of liminality and marginality, Babcock-Abrahams suggests that the crucial attribute of clowns and tricksters is their *liminal* nature. She sees tricksters and clowns as being part of but at the margins of their cultures, expressing the opposite of their cultures' expected norms; hence their liminal character. Babcock-Abrahams feels that tricksters and clowns around the world express this liminal nature but that scholars, by focusing on psychological explanations, have ignored this aspect of tricksters and clowns. Babcock-Abrahams suggests that these characters present a necessary dualism and paradoxical nature that allows for "pure possibility." The very "messiness" of these characters should be the focus. Instead of attempting to fit characters into a rigid category, Babcock-Abrahams suggests a reevaluation of the categories, such as myth and folklore or trickster and culture hero, from which indigenous figures are judged. In this way she holds on to the categories of trickster and clown but refocuses the attention of scholars on the actions of these characters in light of their cultural settings.

What Beidelman and Sabbatocci, among others, see as the problem of categories others see as a benefit. Babcock-Abrahams is not suggesting overlooking cultural differences; rather, she sees these differences as points for comparison. Instead of denying differences, she argues for an incorporation of those differences within our cross-cultural studies. Without imposing reductive psychological frameworks, Babcock-Abrahams's method would highlight the uniqueness of indigenous characters while at the same time shedding light on the cross-cultural nature of the phenomena.

Another twist in this debate has been explored by Anne Doueihi, who asserts that the representation of tricksters reveals more about Western scholarship than about other cultures or about the specific characters. Doueihi sees scholars' agendas as hampering the study of other cultures. She criticizes scholars and their inclusive, reductive, and ethnocentric categories for hiding and distorting others to fit them into preconceived images instead of attempting to understand them. Doueihi's argument forces us to look at the outcome of our representations of others as well as the methods used to gain such understandings. Similarly, William Doty and William Hynes argue that the inherent seriousness of Western scholarship has led to the misrepresentation and dismissal not only of tricksters and clowns but of a substantial portion of folklore. Doty and Hynes see the "bias against humor" as a longstanding tradition in Western intellectualism. Focusing on the serious nature of intellectualism and especially religion, Doty and Hynes argue that much from other cultures around the world has been mistreated or ignored all together.

Recent studies into play and laughter have made their way into the study of tricksters and clowns. Using classic studies of play by Johan Huizinga and Roger Callois, some scholars have begun to explore the idea of "playing seriously." In the introduction to their collection *Mythical Trickster Figures*, Hynes and Doty suggest that this trend is just beginning in the social sciences and humanities. Scholars exploring a wide range of cultures are reexamining the materials they have at hand in light of the understanding of play as an important and illuminating aspect of culture. Instead of seeing play and playful behavior as frivolous and unimportant, Hynes and Doty suggest that scholars use play as an analytical category through which tricksters and clowns may be examined and interpreted without negative classifications.

In any study employing such general terms there is the possibility of misrepresentation. In this encyclopedia I include figures from around the world who are classified as clowns and/or tricksters by either scholars or indigenous sources. My aim is not to enter into the debate over what is or is not a trickster or clown but to provide the interested reader with an expansive entry into the world of tricksters and clowns. This collection will include such familiar characters as the circus clown and Wile E. Coyote side by side with perhaps less well known characters such as Ture and Yiyi. This inclusiveness is meant to make the unfamiliar more recognizable as well as to cast the familiar in a new light. I have tried to include representations of clowns and tricksters from around the world without exception or cultural bias. The result is an expansive collection of characters as well as an introduction to the cultures in which they are found.

In almost every culture in which they are found, tricksters are identified as ridiculous looking, disobedient, obscene, backward, disrespectful, funny, powerful, or paradoxical characters. Although each of these traits may not apply to every character, they are the generally accepted attributes of these figures. What is distinctive about tricksters is their dual roles. Tricksters are at the same time obscene and powerful, jester and culture hero; their roles are never easily defined. They personify the ability to be both respected and condemned by a society. The Azande of Central Africa have a trickster figure known as Ture. Ture is a spider, but he can take on the form of many animals and humans. Ture is credited with bringing food, water, and fire to the Azande, but he is also seen as crude, incestuous, disrespectful, and selfish. He is constantly tricking people, stealing from them, and doing as he pleases for his own benefit. Like many other tricksters, Ture is not easily confined to one type.

Another example, the coyote, is a common trickster among many Native American cultures; however, within each culture he is named and represented differently. The Navajo call him Ma'ii, the Lakota call him Mica, and the Crow refer to him as

Old Man Coyote. For the Crow, Old Man Coyote made the earth, human beings, animals, and birds. He made First Man and First Woman to begin kinship relations on earth. On the other hand, for the Lakota, Mica is a spirit responsible for thievery, cowardice, and mischief. The Navajo Ma'ii is constantly changing his character and form and is widely known for his offensive sexual behavior. Depending on the context and the culture, the coyote may be trickster, culture hero, creator, and malevolent shape-shifter. As with most trickster figures, his actions are unpredictable and the place he holds in society is tenuous.

Similarly, clowns vary greatly from culture to culture. Although in Western cultures the term *clown* may conjure up images of carnivals and foolish characters running around beeping horns and climbing out of telephone booths, this humor and outrageousness is typical of only one representation of clowns. In other cultures clowns hold privileged positions in religious ceremonies as well as important places in myths of origin. For example, the K'apyo Shure clowns of the Isleta Pueblo in the southwestern United States used their horns to lead the people from the underworld out of darkness and into the upper world of lightness. At Zia, the koshare and kwirena clowns helped people emerge by leading them through four underworlds to this world. These same clowns, however, behave ridiculously and are the source of much entertainment at the ritual celebrations in which they appear throughout the year. The koshare, for instance, talk backwards, run around throwing things—sticks, clothes, dirt, rocks, food—at people, and declare that they "know everything."

Javanese clowns, the panakawan, perform throughout the country in all types of theater, religious and secular. They are fat and ugly, they speak a foul language, and they are sexually ambiguous, having both male and female characteristics. The panakawan are also held to be very powerful, as they are "blood kin" to the highest deities in Javanese religious traditions. Like other clowns, the panakawan are known for their complex roles in society. Clowns around the world hold these paradoxical roles as merrymakers, religious specialists, healers, and frightening thieves.

Tricksters and clowns are most often told about in myths, sung about in songs, and presented through ritual and dramatic performances. Trickster and clown stories and performances are characterized by their impromptu nature. In other words, the characters are well known, but each time the stories are told or performed the scene and plot may change, leaving open the possibility for endless numbers of performances and tales. Clowns and tricksters are forever getting themselves into trouble, causing havoc, and disrupting events. One of the most common themes is the clown's or trickster's complete disregard for social and religious mores. They often do things backward, out of order, or in reverse order. They use deception, illusion, and ambiguity to trick people into following them or doing what they want. Clowns and tricksters often represent "nonhumans" or humans who do not act properly; they epitomize antisocial behavior.

These characters are not merely funny; they are also frightful, using their power to scare people and force people into giving them things. Clowns and tricksters often use their ambiguous status to take advantage of people. In addition, clowns and tricksters often take the role of social commentators. They embarrass people who have broken one of society's rules. They also mock those in power, such as government officials, priests, and ritual specialists. Their mockery is meant to highlight the abuse of power and the role that people can play in reclaiming that power. As entertainers and political commentators, clowns and tricksters have a precarious role in the societies from which they emerge. What sets clowns and tricksters apart in their societies is precisely this ability to hold seemingly paradoxical roles.

The number of trickster and clown figures around the world may be uncountable. In many cultures these figures do not have specific names; any mythic character or animal may be said to take on tricksterlike or clownlike qualities. This is the case among the Ewe of western Africa, for whom any animal can be a trickster. Or, for example, Zuni clowns have group titles, but the clowns themselves do not have specific names. In other cultures tricksters and clowns are easily identified and named. Among the ancient Greeks Hermes stood out as the trickster par excellence; for many Native Americans, the coyote, the raven, and the mink hold the place of trickster; and in Africa the two most widely recognized tricksters are the spider and the hare, who are called by different names depending on the culture.

Surveying tricksters and clowns cross-culturally allows me to present both the similarities and differences among their cultural representations. This process, however, also necessitates boundaries for comparison. In this collection, I present trickster and clown figures that are commonly held to be such, both by the tradition in which they are presented and preserved as well as by academics. The characters are presented in the context of the culture in which they are found. Whenever possible, I indicate what medium these characters are presented through and how they are received by the culture. To narrow the scope of the collection, the tricksters and clowns included are those recognized in the mythic or folktale genre of literature. Some exceptions were made in order to be thorough, but the majority of the characters presented in this work will be those figures who have been incorporated in the popular folktales and myths of the cultures surveyed.

Trickster and clown characters are a result of specific cultural settings, and they themselves change depending on audience, settings, and time of year. As such, tricksters and clowns and the stories about them need to be seen in light of their dynamic nature. Although there are similarities and common themes, the characters and stories set forth here should serve only as a reference point for those interested both in these figures and in their specific cultural representations. The extensive list of references and further reading is meant to provide the interested reader with an opportunity to delve deeper into the richness and complexities of the cultures in which we find these elusive and entertaining characters.

The cross-references and the cultural topic finder will guide readers through the extensive collection of tricksters and clowns. Because the scope of the material collected in this volume is so vast, the entries are meant only as starting points, glimpses into the characters. Although this volume takes the form of an encyclopedia, the entries are not meant to be exact, concrete representations of the characters; given the length of the entries, that would have been impossible. Nor would it have been desirable; to suggest that one can adequately "explain" such complex characters, who depend so much on context, performance, and deep religious insight, would be arrogant. Instead, this volume is meant as a general introduction to both the characters and the people who see the world through their eyes.

Because this volume covers characters and cultures from antiquity to the present, some of these cultures no longer exist. Some of the ritual performances presented herein are no longer performed, and some of the myths are no longer told; but their legacy remains. Nevertheless, most of the cultures represented in this volume continue to flourish. In fact, it is through trickster and clown characters that we see cultures dealing with modernity. Tricksters and clowns are most often the voices of change and the instigators of reform. Although this presentation lacks the richness associated with many of its characters, it is up to the reader to listen to the voices contained in these stories with an interested, open, and sensitive mind.

Entry List by Culture Areas

Africa
Central Africa
Azande
Ture

Bemba
Kalulu

Gbaya
Wanto

Hausa
Dila
Gizo
Zomo

Ila
Fulwe
Sulwe

Lamba
Wakalulu

Ngbaka
To

East Africa
Kaguru
Chibuga
Difisi
Fisi
Sungula

West Africa
Akan
Ananse
Anansesem
Nyame

Bo
Kaka

Dogon
Ogo

Ewe
Yiyi

Fon
Heho

Hwenho
Legba
Yo

Ga
Anaanu

Hausa
Dila
Gizo
Zomo

Kalabari
Ikaki

Limba
Kayi
Wosi

Songhay
Hauka

Yoruba
Ajapa
Eshu-Elegba
Ijapa

Asia and Southeast Asian Countries and Islands
China
ch'ou
Wu'sata

Indonesia
Torajan
Dodong

Malayo
Kantjil

Java
Panakawan
Semar

Japan
Kitsune
Susa-no-o

Korea
ch'angbu
Horangi

Laos
Kammu
Naar
Plaan Thoóy
Púu Raankla

Papua New Guinea
Bimin-Kuskusim
Gabruurian
Kamdaak Waneng
Utuum-khriin min

Lusi-Kaliai
Sega

Mekeo
Ipani

Melanesia
Lelegurulik
Tansa

Tubetube
Talawasi

Umeda
Yaut

Wape
Niyel Carnival

Thailand
Sri Thanoncha
Sug

Tibet
Agu Tomba

Europe and Arabic Countries
Afghanistan
Mullah Nasruddin

Arabic countries
Juha
Khadir
Khezr

England
Gleemen
Scogan

Europe
fool
Harlequin
jester
Pulcinello
Reynard
Saint Peter

Greece
Hermes

Iran
Mullah Nasruddin

Ireland
Bricriu
crosan

Italy
Bertholde

Scandinavia
Loki

Clowns &
Tricksters

An Encyclopedia of Tradition
and Culture

Adúgo
Bororo, *Brazil*

Adúgo is a gullible jaguar constantly being duped by others. See also **Júko.**

Agu Tomba
Tibet

Agu Tomba, a notorious shape-shifter best known for his sexual antics, delights in gaining control over situations and turning them to his benefit, especially if the prize is sex. Stories of Agu Tomba focus on his disruptive and humorous antics. His mischief is rarely aggressive; rather, he tricks people to gain sex, food, or other pleasures. Agu Tomba is also a reminder of the frailty of power, and his best-known adventures are those in which he deceives someone in authority, such as a government official or priest. By undoing the order set by those in power, Agu Tomba demonstrates the chaotic nature of the world.

Agu Tomba's adventures almost always involve sex. It seems as though his sexual appetite is unending. In one story, Agu Tomba disguised himself as a nun and invaded a local convent. After the nuns were asleep, he crept into their beds and had intercourse with all of them. His spree was not discovered until later that month, when several nuns found they were pregnant.

In addition to his own sexual escapades, his pranks often involve helping others gain sexual pleasure. For example, in another story Agu Tomba encountered a discouraged farmer whose crop had been cursed. Instead of producing food, his field yielded hundreds of penises. Agu Tomba cleverly gathered the penises up in a cart and sold them at a local convent. Although the nuns were prohibited from engaging in sex with

men, nowhere did it say that they could not have intercourse with a penis.

Agu Tomba is also known for his association with excrement, often using it to get himself out of dangerous situations, and he delights in offending people with its smell. His use of excrement as a weapon in his bag of tricks highlights the lewd and obscene aspects of society. He treats excrement as if it were a powerful, respected object instead of waste. By doing so, however, he shows the absurdity of rigid categories. That is, he points out the relativity of human understanding of the world and allows us to see that dirt is not always dirt.

In one such story, Agu Tomba was the secretary to a prominent ruler in Tibet who could not read or write and who therefore relied on Agu Tomba to read him Buddhist scripture. One day the ruler got angry with Agu Tomba, thinking he was not reading to him properly. As a punishment, Agu Tomba was sent to the roof of the palace, stripped naked, and made to sleep in the cold. It was so bitter cold that night that Agu Tomba's excrement froze. Agu Tomba covered the excrement with white lime from the palace roof and wrote some words on the bottom of it.

As the ruler was performing his morning meditations, Agu Tomba dropped the excrement through the skylight onto his lap. The ruler believed it to be a sign from the gods, so he ordered his servants to get Agu Tomba to read it for him. After Agu Tomba had a warm breakfast and was clothed again he reported to the ruler. Agu Tomba read the inscription and told the ruler that it was a blessing from the gods and that he should eat some to gain its full benefits. Following Agu Tomba's directions, the ruler broke some off, kissed it, and then ate it. (Dorje 1975)

Ajapa
Yoruba, *West Africa: Southwestern Nigeria; Benin; Togo*
See **Ijapa.**

Ambiguity
The ambiguity, that is, double meaning, of moral, social, ethical, or physical situations may be used by characters in myths or in ritual performances. Some use social and physical ambiguity as a source of comedy or power. Other characters use moral and ethical ambiguity to highlight the ideals within a society by exaggerating their opposites.

Physical ambiguity is commonly portrayed through characters who are not easily characterized by one gender or who embody the elements of both genders. The **vidusaka** clowns of India, for example, are known for their cross-dressing and for their ambiguous sexual nature in performances. They highlight their ambiguity by wearing both men's and women's clothes as well as by their embrace of both male and female activities. By playing on the traditional gender roles of their society, the vidusaka are able to criticize these stereotypical roles and praise the necessity of such divisions at the same time. **Vishnu,** on the other hand, is recognized as a male deity in most cases, but in some instances his earthly avatars are female. Having the ability to take either form, Vishnu highlights the inherent male and female aspects of all of reality.

Moral ambiguity is highlighted by characters who straddle the lines between chaos and order within a society. These charac-

ters delight in turning common social mores upside down, both reinforcing the mores of the culture and in the same breath denouncing them. **Eshu-Elegba,** a Yoruba deity, plays with people's sense of reality by dancing his dance of chaos while at the same time spinning the web of order in the society. Similarly, **Glooskap,** a Native American character, is both creator and deceiver. He brings many things to the world that help people, but he also uses the same powers to trick people, which sometimes results in their death.

The characters who embody the elements of ambiguity, whether it be social, moral, physical, or ethical, do so for multifaceted reasons. Usually some form of ambiguity is used to highlight the many possibilities of the world as well as the idea that people are simply one component in a much larger cosmos. By highlighting the inherent ebb and flow of culture as well as of the universe, ambiguous characters elicit a range of responses from those who hear their tales or see their performances. See also **Ananse, Brhannada, Isáahkawuattee, Nankilslas, Panakawan, Tansa, Ture,** and **Uttuum-khriin min** for more examples of ambiguity.

Anaanu
Ga, *West Africa: Ghana*
The spider Anaanu, a mischievous, greedy, cunning character, enjoys fooling his fellow animals and humans alike. Most Ga stories begin with the storyteller asking the audience, "Shall I tell you a story or not?" and the audience replying, "Yes, tell us!" Ga storytelling is marked by its interactive processes. The audience and the storytellers work together throughout the night of storytelling to create a narrative. Although the storyteller leads the performance, the audience members yell out their suggestions at key moments during the performance, such as when one of the main

characters must make a decision. Audience members are familiar with the general traits of the main characters, and they are therefore able to work with the storyteller to create new plots for each character. (See also **Wakalulu, Wanto, Wosi,** and **Yiyi** for examples of interactive storytelling.)

The Ga know the character Anaanu well. In stories Anaanu is given human characteristics, such as the ability to speak, residing in a home, having a job, and wearing clothes. Anaanu and other animals act out human events and interactions in order to demonstrate a moral, to educate, or simply to entertain. Through Anaanu's tricks and deceptions, children learn the proper ways to act while they are being entertained.

The stories the Ga tell about Anaanu concern other beings in the cosmos and those beings' interrelationships with humans. The Ga recognize several types of beings in the cosmos. The characteristics of Anaanu represent only one set of attributes among a myriad of possibilities. Anaanu's actions demonstrate the clever, humorous, and ambiguous actions that people and other beings may possess.

The Ga say that once people only told stories about *dzemawon* ("powerful beings") and not about Anaanu in particular. *Dzemawon* has been translated by scholars as "god" or "deity." The Ga meaning of the word can be understood by glossing each part of the word: *dze*, "world"; *ma*, "town"; and *won*, "anything that can work but not be seen." Beings who fall in the *dzemawon* category are those beings who are not seen but who work in the world and in specific towns. *Dzemawon* designates not a single being but a class of beings who interact with the Ga people in various ways. In each town the Ga recognize several *dzemawon* who help the people in the town and who never harm well-meaning people. The ritual activity in which the Ga engage is aimed at maintaining beneficial relationships with the various *dzemawon*.

The Kpledzo festival, one example of the Ga's ritual interaction with the *dzemawon*, celebrates the corn-planting and corn-gathering times in Ga towns. During the festival the people sing, dance, and offer food to the different *dzemawon;* wash objects associated with specific *dzemawon;* sing songs that ask for the *dzemawon*'s assistance in healing the sick; and dance in a jovial style. The dancing style throughout the festival is unpredictable, but dances are known to be rowdy and even crude. The humorous pantomime that accompanies the dancing reminds audience members of the antics of some of the *dzemawon*. Although Anaanu is not specifically classified as a *dzemawon*, some of Anaanu's playful characteristics can be seen in the dancing and pantomime of the performers in different festivals.

The Ga account for the numerous stories told about Anaanu through a story that shows that he is thought of as similar to the *dzemawon*. One day Anaanu went to the *dzemawon* in control of the stories and said that he wanted to have all the stories told about him. The *dzemawon* told him that it was a very big responsibility to have stories told about him and that if he wanted stories he would have to pass a series of tests. The *dzemawon* ordered him to collect three things: a swarm of bees, a live python, and a live leopard. For three days Anaanu sat and thought about how to collect the three things. Finally, he figured it out. He got a calabash and went into the forest. He put some honey in the calabash and sat it on his head as he entered the forest. He came to a spot where there was a swarm of bees and took the lid off the calabash. He walked close to the bees and said loudly, "They can fill it; they can't fill it; they can fill it; they can't fill it." The bees heard him and asked Anaanu what he was talking about. Anaanu answered that he had had an argument with a friend who said that with all the honey in the calabash the bees would not fit; Anaanu said they would. The leader of the bees said that they could easily fit, and they all flew into the calabash. As soon as they were inside, Anaanu put the lid on very tightly and took the calabash back to the *dzemawon*.

Next Anaanu set off to capture the python. Anaanu went into the forest carrying a long stick. After scraping all the bark off the stick he went deeper into the forest, saying, "It is longer than he; it is not longer than he; it is longer than he; it is not longer than he." Soon he came upon the python, and the python, who was very proud of his length, asked Anaanu what he was doing. Anaanu told the python that he had had an argument with a friend who said that the python was much shorter than the stick. The python would not stand for this, and he stretched himself out next to the stick. Anaanu asked him if he could tie him to the stick so he could get the correct measurement, and the python agreed. Soon the python was completely stretched out and tied to the stick. Anaanu had accomplished another part of the task.

Anaanu left the python with the *dzemawon* and went after the leopard. Anaanu made his way far into the forest, dug a deep hole in the path of the leopard, and covered it up with sticks and leaves. Soon the leopard came along and fell into the pit; he was trapped. After a little while Anaanu appeared, and the leopard asked for his help. Anaanu asked why he should help the animal, who would surely just eat him and his family. But the leopard made an agreement with Anaanu: If Anaanu would help him out of the pit, no leopard would ever eat a spider again. So Anaanu got his family, and they lifted the leopard out of the hole by tying him to a stick and hoisting him out. Once the leopard was out of the pit, Anaanu dragged him back to the *dzemawon*, who had to honor his word and therefore decreed that from then on all stories would be told about Anaanu. (For similar accounts by the Akan, see **Ananse**.)

Anaanu is known for his greediness and his cunning deceitfulness. Many of the stories about Anaanu tell of his large appetite and his ability to trick people into doing what he wants. In one story, during a great famine, Anaanu gathered all the animals, including the great leopard and the mighty lion, and convinced them all that it would be a good idea for them to work together and plant a crop of yams. After it was harvested they would share the food and nobody would go hungry. All the animals agreed, and they went to work. Once the yams were harvested, the animals stacked them inside a barn and sat outside to rest and enjoy some of their fresh yams. What the animals did not know was that Anaanu had dug a huge hole not far from the barn where the yams were stored. Anaanu had hidden everything he needed to cook the yams in the hole. While the other animals stacked the yams in the barn, Anaanu started from below each night and pulled the yams from the barn one by one.

Soon the animals noticed that their pile was not increasing. Each of the animals blamed another, and the leopard and the lion threatened to eat the others if they did not get their fair share of the yams. Suddenly someone noticed that Anaanu was nowhere to be found. They smelled the scent of cooked yams coming from the hole. They all shouted to Anaanu to come out, but he did not. Several of the animals tried to go down after him, but the hole was too narrow. Anaanu just sat in his hole eating and laughing at the others.

Finally the bush pig decided that he had had enough and that he would retrieve Anaanu. He told the others that he would push his long snout down the hole and bring Anaanu out. Since the hole was so narrow, all the animals got behind the bush pig and pushed. They pushed and pushed, and as they made their final push the bush pig's snout reached close to Anaanu, who sliced off a piece of it with his knife. The flesh fell right into his stew and he cooked it along with his vegetables. The bush pig let out a squeal of pain and tried to back out of the hole. But each time he came up the others pushed him back down. Again and again Anaanu sliced off a piece of the pig's nose. Finally the bush pig was in so much pain that he pushed with all his might and flew out of the hole. When the others saw his face they could not believe it. (This is why bush pigs have red faces.) Anaanu's cunning games got him all the food he wanted, and he was able to make his mark on a member of the animal kingdom, thus showing his power.

Sometimes, however, Anaanu loses at his own games. Once there was a serious famine, and Anaanu, like so many others, was quickly running out of food. Anaanu disliked being hungry more than anything else, so he went looking for food. Anaanu went to one of the animals, showed him his beautifully decorated tongue, and offered to decorate the animal's tongue so that he would be greatly admired in the village from then on. The animal agreed, and Anaanu took him to the forest. He told the animal that the procedure required that he be tied down. After he had the animal tied down, he began to paint a design on his tongue. After Anaanu finished he told the animal that he must lie still with his tongue out for some time so the painting could dry. Then Anaanu disappeared. After a while, when the animal had become weak from lying in the sun, Anaanu appeared with his knife and fork, carved the animal up, and ate him.

One by one, Anaanu went to the other animals in the village and played the same trick, succeeding each time. While everyone else in the village became slimmer, Anaanu grew fatter each day. Finally Anaanu went to the lizard to try his game. He offered to paint the decoration on the lizard's tongue, and the lizard accepted. They went to the forest and Anaanu tied him down, decorated his tongue, and left. The lizard, however, became hot and dry very quickly and decided not to wait for Anaanu to return. Instead, he shed his skin and went into the cool bushes to wait for Anaanu. When Anaanu returned he could not find the lizard anywhere. Suddenly, the lizard rushed out from behind the bushes and ran after Anaanu, chasing him into town. And because of Anaanu's greed, lizards still chase spiders to this day.

Stories about Anaanu demonstrate that greed does sometimes go unpunished. These same stories also show that antisocial behavior can have repercussions for everyone, not just the person committing antisocial acts. In the stories told about Anaanu, the Ga recognize both the negative effects of people's greed and the playful nature of human beings. In the Anaanu stories the Ga incorporate both the possible positive and negative effects of people's actions. In these stories, children are shown that there are choices and that precisely these choices demonstrate one's respect and responsibility toward others. The Ga live in small villages. Although people may move to a different village after marriage, they return to their hometown at least once a year for the major town festival. Thus, even though they move, they always maintain a relationship to their home village, a relationship characterized by their responsibility to the villages, its people, and specific *dzemawon*. The stories of Anaanu remind people of their responsibilities to each other, their towns, and the *dzemawon* to whom they are related. (Berry 1991; Paulme 1977)

Ananse
Akan (includes Ashanti, Brong, Fante), *West Africa: Ghana*

Ananse (whose name literally means "spider") is best known as an ambiguous character who tricks people and *abosom* (powerful beings in the Akan cosmos) alike. The Akan recognize many *abosom* (who are generally thought to be invisible but who manifest themselves through aspects of nature such as wind and rain) within their cosmos: personal, familial, and township. *Abosom* are grouped according to their function and role in society. There is no separation of *abosom* into concrete classes; instead, there are more general groupings based on their actions. For example, *abosom* who are known for their help in fertility matters are seen as similar, yet each individual in that group may also play another role. Thus each *abosom* has a specific function within the society, such as protecting from witches or promoting good health, fertility, or prosperity. There is no hierarchy of power among the *abosom*. To the contrary, different *abosom* relate to each individual or clan on intimate terms based on that individual's or clan's specific needs. The Akan people interact with the *abosom* by feeding their shrines, making sacrifices of food and water to them, and including them in their myths. The *abosom* are fed out of respect, just as a family would feed their human relatives. Akan stories demonstrate the importance of *abosom* presence in the Akan cosmos and describe the proper ways to interact with them by building shrines, making offerings, and participating in ritual celebrations.

Nyame, the male source of power, and Asase Yaa, the female source, are the cocreators of Akan life. All the *abosom* come from this pair, that is, derive their power from them, and the *abosom* take qualities from both. Shrines are constructed both for Nyame and for individual *abosom*. Asase Yaa does not have her own shrines, but offerings are made to her at the shrines of Nyame and the *abosom*. Shrines are usually made of rocks and contain a stool in the center (where, at times of offerings, the *abosom* reside); they exist in homes as well as in community centers.

Ananse is linked closely with Nyame, who is also known as Ananse Kokuroko, the great spider that relates the two by name and by blood. Ananse and Nyame wield two aspects of the same power; Nyame uses it to order the world, and Ananse uses it to cause chaos. Nyame and Ananse together reveal the totality of human possibility by demonstrating the existence of chaos in order and order in chaos. Ananse and Nyame share several characteristics: They are both known as creators, as wise beings, and as messengers to the people. Their relationship, however, is characterized by antagonism. For example, Nyame created the universe and named all the things in it; he is thus venerated by the people with shrines and stories. Ananse, however, wanted all the stories told by the people to be about him rather than Nyame. In his jealousy and greed, he made an agreement with Nyame that if he, Ananse, could capture several wild animals and nature spirits and bring them back to Nyame, the stories would be renamed Ananse tales. Thinking that Ananse could never accomplish such a deed, Nyame agreed. Ananse set out on the challenge. Disguising himself as a beautifully adorned bird he was able to attract and capture the first of the nature spirits. Next he captured a python by having his wife ask to measure the python with a rope and then tying the rope around its neck. He captured a group of hornets by sprinkling water over them and himself, telling them it was raining so they would take cover in the gourd he held. After they entered the gourd, he sealed the end and they were trapped. Slowly, Ananse was able to trick and capture all the animals and nature spirits that he promised he would deliver to Nyame, who then had no choice but to rename the stories *anansesem*, "the stories of Ananse." From then on, all the stories that people told were about Ananse's escapades. (For similar accounts told by the Ga, see **Anaanu.**) By associating all stories, at least nominally, with Ananse, the Akan people demonstrate the importance of humor, chaos, and ambiguity in society. Although Ananse and other characters are often unsuccessful in their endeavors, the stories show that the universe is not rigid, that one might succeed.

Although *anansesem* literally means "Ananse tales," not all *anansesem* are about Ananse. Scholars have classified them as a narrative genre, but unlike other forms of oral history that are remembered and told by specialists, *anansesem* are told by anyone at any time. The stories are generally told at night and by adults to children. Before the storyteller begins, he or she recites a phrase stating that what the children are about to hear is "not true." The stories take on different forms depending on the storyteller and the audience. The storyteller may be directing the stories at a certain group of children, perhaps those close to the age of initiation, or toward a particular theme, such as the importance of obeying one's parents. Generally, the stories address issues of social mores and proper behavior. Ananse is the normal choice for these tales because he epitomizes the antithesis of proper behavior. In his tricks and greediness, Ananse shows the children how not to act, but he also shows them that antisocial behavior does exist in the world. *Anansesem* show children that the world is not entirely right or entirely wrong, completely good or completely bad but, rather, that it is both at once.

There are many stories told about Ananse and his antics. *Anansesem* generally follow one of three patterns: stories about Ananse himself and how he came to be, about Ananse's role in shaping the world, and about how Ananse has affected Akan society. In stories Ananse is most often depicted as sly, selfish, and greedy. The Akan say that Ananse loves trouble so much that his skin hurts if he is not up to mischief. In one story, Ananse stole all the crops from the villagers by faking his own death. As he was buried beneath the fields he had his children put a hoe and a stick into his grave. When the townspeople went to sleep, Ananse took all their crops for himself.

Ananse's physical traits reflect his selfish ways: He is fat, slow, and bald. He also lives on the ceiling, separate from everyone else, because of his deceptive pranks. His selfish actions have made him an outcast in his own society. Ananse shows his disrespect not only to people but to *abosom* as well. Once, after Efu, an *abosom*, had given Ananse water for his crops Ananse beat him to death in order to get even more water. This disrespect is a sign of Ananse's selfishness as well, for in Akan society to be disrespectful of *abosom* or ancestors is to bring the possibility of danger into the world. The *abosom* and the ancestors have the ability to cause disease, storms, and bad crops. Ananse's disrespect puts everyone in danger.

Ananse has many ways of fooling people. One of his most useful powers is his ability to change shape. He shifts forms to resemble animals and people in order to get what he wants. Sometimes he pretends to be a friend or relative in need of food. He tricks children by posing as an elder or scares them by changing into terrible animal forms. Ananse, whose great penis is said to be longer than 77 poles, also tricks married women and young girls into sexual relations. In most stories his trickery is used for his own benefit. Once as he walked home he spotted his neighbor the baboon carrying a bag full of oranges. Ananse went up to the baboon and complained of the foul smell coming from the bag. The baboon, trusting Ananse, decided to give the rotten oranges to the pig. Ananse then rushed ahead of him to the pig's house. When the baboon approached, Ananse began to make pig noises, so the baboon threw the bag of oranges over the fence. Ananse ate all the oranges himself.

Another tale shows that Ananse is not the only greedy character portrayed in *anansesem*. One day, the hyena and his neighbor Ananse took a walk to the river. There they met the king of the river, who gave them some fish to eat. Ananse and the hyena built a fire and cooked the fish, which Ananse then took down by the bank of the river to cool. As he laid them down and went back for more, the hyena ate them one by one. When Ananse turned to eat his fish and noticed that they were gone, he got tears in his eyes, but he told the hyena the tears were from the smoke. That evening Ananse planned his revenge. A few days later the two went for another walk and this time spotted a parrot flying above. The hyena admired the beautiful colors of the bird. Ananse told him that he had given the parrot its beautiful feathers. The hyena begged Ananse to do the same for him. Ananse agreed and tied the hyena to a tree and blindfolded him. He then painted the hyena's body with ugly, dull stripes, and that is the way it remains to this day.

Ananse's greed sometimes helps Akan society. One story tells how wisdom was spread to the people. Ananse stole all the world's knowledge and collected it in one spot. Fearful that someone would find it, Ananse placed it in a gourd and searched for the tallest tree in which to hide it. His son watched Ananse hard at work trying to climb the tree and suggested that his father place the gourd on his back while he climbed. At first Ananse ignored his son's advice, but after many failed attempts to get up the tree, he had no other choice. Strapping the gourd to his back, Ananse began to climb the tree again. This time he made it to the top. Sitting at the top of the tree, Ananse said to his son that he thought he had all the wisdom of the world in his gourd but that some must have slipped out, for his son showed great wisdom. At this Ananse let go of the gourd, and it fell to the ground scattering wisdom throughout the world.

In his quest to reduce Nyame's power, Ananse introduced disease to the world. He told Nyame that he would bring him a beautiful maiden if Nyame would give him his sheep. Nyame agreed, and Ananse found a village full of women. Greedy Ananse wanted all the women for himself, so he married all of them at once. Ananse did not know that Nyame had sent a spy to watch him. The spy reported that Ananse had married all the women and that he was sharing Nyame's sheep with them as well. Enraged, Nyame went to the village and collected all the women for himself, except one who was sick. Being left with only the sick woman, Ananse decided to make her well. He bathed her and fed her, and soon she became the most beautiful woman he had ever seen. The spy then reported to Nyame that Ananse had tricked him by keeping the most beautiful woman of them all, so Nyame took her too. In his anger, Ananse invented an insulting song about her and danced with his sons. Nyame and his harem went to the village to be a part of the dance. When Nyame forced the sick woman to dance, Ananse cracked a gourd over her head and spread disease throughout the world.

Ananse is well known for his playful dances and degrading songs. In Akan society, songs and dances are central to people's interrelations with *abosom*, ancestors, and each other. Through ritual dance performances people are able to interact with other beings in the cosmos. In ritual celebrations, people offer food, dance, and sing in recognition of their ongoing relationship with other beings. The major ritual festivals of the Akan are the Adae, at which many ancestors are recalled and honored through song and dance; the Baya, at which offerings are made to the ancestors for the present rice crop and requests for a successful crop in the next season are made; the

Afahye, at which ancestors are offered the first fruits of the season; and the Odwera, at which the group is ritually cleansed by the ancestors.

As in the previous story, in which Ananse's dance ended with the spread of disease, the Akan show how Ananse's dances and songs can be used in harmful ways. Ananse is depicted in paintings and carvings with his drum, and his diseased gourd is recognized as his companion drum in his wild dances. Drums are a common accompaniment to Akan dances. Special drums are used in different ritual settings; some are painted with designs specific to certain ancestors or themes such as fertility.

Although there are no rituals specific to Ananse, his wild dance style is recognized in ritual celebrations in contrast to the dance styles associated with other *abosom*. The annual Apo festival is an example of a ritual celebration that includes feasting, reversal, and humor reminiscent of the stories about Ananse. The descendant queen mother (that is, the king's wife) is the center of the Apo festival. Each Akan village centers its festivities on its own descendant queen mother (each village has a distinct king, queen, and set of ancestors through which the people trace their genealogies). The king and queen are analogous to Nyame and Asase Yaa in that they share the power in the village and they are considered to be related to all the people of the village. This double base of power can be seen in the king and queen, in Nyame and Asase Yaa, and in the Akan matrilineal system of descent, in which children belong to their mother's clan but their *notro* ("spirit") is passed through their father's clan. Both the male and female sides are represented in each person, regardless of their specific gender.

At the beginning of the Apo festival, an animal is sacrificed (usually a goat or chicken, but some scholars have reported that large animals such as bullocks are also

sacrificed) and the meat is offered to various *abosom* and ancestors. The blood of the animal is sometimes poured over the shrine of the *abosom* as well. These rituals are performed by "priests," that is, those responsible for the *abosom*, and the *abrafo*, or masters of ceremony.

The festival lasts several days. When the shrine of the descendant queen mother is displayed in public, it is time for libations, dancing, and singing throughout the night. Even after the shrine has been returned to its designated place, the people continue to celebrate. The singing and dancing take place throughout the village, in the streets and homes. During the public dancing, the *abrafo* run up and down the streets encouraging people to dance more wildly. Ecstatic dancing is said to please the descendant queen mother and the other ancestors by stimulating sexual energy among the audience-participants. During the festival men dress as women and their dance includes sexual gestures toward other men. Other dancers tease audience members, and on one specific day everyone is encouraged to discharge pent-up anger. People run through the streets screaming, throwing things, dancing wildly, singing loudly, and shaking rattles to the rhythm of several drummers along the sides of the streets. The reversal of dress and the reversal from order to chaos demonstrates the duality of the power base in Akan society, a duality that is reminiscent of Ananse.

Ananse, too, demonstrates the duality of human nature. He shows that both male and female, strong and weak, greedy and unselfish characteristics are always present in the world. Ananse is best known for constantly tricking people, stealing from them, and causing them to break laws and social mores. He is an antisocial character, yet his stories are known by all the Akan. Through the stories told about Ananse, the Akan see the negative effects of selfish behavior and are also reminded of the presence of greed, trickery, and disruptiveness in the world. (Akesson 1950; Barker and Sinclair 1928; Cardinall 1970; Dykstra 1966; Herskovits and Herskovits 1937; Meyerowitz 1958; Pelton 1980; Rattray 1930; Vecsey 1993)

Anansesem
Akan (includes Ashanti, Brong, Fante),
West Africa: Ghana
See **Ananse**.

Appetite
Many characters show their disrespect for their communities through their unending appetites, that is, their focus on sexual or culinary gluttony. Commonly, in fact, these characters' appetites are for both food and sex.

Yiyi, an Ewe spider character, for example, is best known for trickery that gains him food, sex, or both. His gluttony propels him to unthinkable acts, such as sexual intercourse with his daughter. His appetites compel him to lie, cheat, and steal to get what he wants. He even leaves his friends without food so that he can be satisfied. Another African spider character, **Anaanu,** shares Yiyi's love of food. Anaanu's appetite for food is so great that in a time of famine he resorts to killing his fellow villagers so that there will be more food for him.

Stories that highlight sexual gluttony usually provide insight into what the culture considers proper sexual relations. By breaking sexual taboos, the characters show their disrespect for the culture as well as their lack of decency. **Guguyni,** a raven character of the Tanaina, uses his intellect, wit, and charm to manipulate and deceive people, especially when he desires a woman. Guguyni is known for taking advantage of women, even those who are socially forbidden to him, such as married women and his own relatives. By transgressing the restrictions of his culture,

Guguyni actually reinforces those views for the group. By showing how repulsive his actions are, storytellers highlight the necessity of such social and sexual standards. Similarly, the character **Cufalh,** whose sexual antics are the theme of many Nivakle stories, shows his selfishness through his sexual desires. He ignores the social mores that forbid intercourse with young girls, and he heedlessly rapes women. See also **Dahusúi, Eshu-Elegba, Furna, Ganyadjigowa, Gu-e-krig, Horangi, Ijapa, Ikaki, Kaik, Kantjil, Komali, Legba, Mica, Nanabozhoo, Sinkalip, Tatú Bolita, Wanto, Windigo,** and **Yo** for more examples.

Arioi Society
Tahiti
Powerful male and female comedic performers who use their status to frighten as well as entertain, members of the Arioi society are marked by their allegiance to the potent being 'Oro. 'Oro is known throughout Tahiti as a powerful deity of war, although he is also hailed as a peacemaker because he is responsible not only for the onslaught of fighting but for ending it.

Arioi members pledge their allegiance to 'Oro, and their performances do indeed have the effect of stopping fighting, even if only temporarily. The Arioi society, then, highlights 'Oro's peacemaking tendencies. Wherever they travel for performances, peace is expected. Village people stop whatever they are doing and prepare for the week-long festivities of the Arioi. This is no easy task. The people must prepare food, lodging, and ceremonial grounds for the events of the week. Arioi members are accorded the best accommodations and food wherever they stay. Although their performances are humorous, people know that Arioi members can also be dangerous. Because of their association with 'Oro, Arioi members wield a great amount of power. People do not dare offend them by denying them anything they request, including sexual favors. In fact, because of their open sexuality and their exaggerated displays of intercourse, the Arioi society is often seen as a type of fertility group and its members as carriers of life to the communities in which they perform.

Arioi members are segregated into three types: active, parentage, and retired. Belonging to the first or last group is acceptable and honorable, but falling into the second group is seen as a failure of their duty. Because of the time they spend away from their own village as well as the sexual license they are given during their membership, active Arioi members are expected to be childless. If they have a child while they are still active members, they are disgraced and put in the category of "parentage." However, those who serve several years in the group and perform well and who then retire to have a family are honored and considered respectable. Because of their emphasis on being childless, Arioi society members are known for higher rates of infanticide and abortion than other villagers. Retired Arioi members do not enjoy the same sexual license as active members, and in fact the Arioi are an anomaly in Tahitian society, in which one's sexual exploits are not expected to be public.

Arioi members, however, flaunt their sexuality, both in and out of their performances. Members are not secretive about their sexual exploits either with other members of the group or with the men and women of the villages they visit. During their performances, they elicit laughter by exaggerating sexual activity as well as by wearing costumes with large erect penises attached to them. They flaunt their sexuality by taunting audience members and embarrassing them with their open displays. They mock their hosts and criticize chiefs and other authority figures. They insult and demean others through their skits and dances. In fact it is typical for Arioi members to chase chiefs and priests, to throw things at them, and to inundate them with verbal chiding, all the while eliciting laughter from the crowd. Arioi members walk a fine line in their performances. Although they are feared, they can also cross the line of acceptable criticism and fall prey themselves to the wrath of a chief. If they offend a chief, they risk punishment and even death.

Po'o (novices) are initiated into the society during performances. During the lively dancing of the members, the prospective initiates are taken to a state of *nevanera*, a state in which they no longer have control of their bodies but instead have been taken over by 'Oro. By seizing the body of the initiate, 'Oro makes it known that the person is a good candidate for the group. While in this state, the initiate dances wildly, sings, and performs with the others. During this time he or she is judged by the others. One of the hallmarks of the Arioi society is their concern for members' physical appearance; they pride themselves on being physically "perfect." Thus initiates are also weeded out on the basis of physical flaws that would detract from the overall appearance of the group. Once initiated, the new member begins learning dances, songs, and skits and is expected to honor both 'Oro and the traditions of the group. (Oliver 1981; Oliver 1989)

At'pana
Guajiro, *Venezuela; Colombia*

At'pana, a rabbit who delights in playing tricks on others, uses his quick wit and small stature to outrun, outmaneuver, and outthink people and animals alike. He is best known for his ability to steal food from others and then escape without being harmed. Although At'pana is rarely hurt during his pranks, others do not fare as well. At'pana's victims are often hurt, maimed, or even killed. He never shows remorse for his actions and thus is characterized as the ulti-mate deceiver by the Guajiro.

Stories about At'pana and his antics are part of a larger body of Guajiro oral litera-ture that has changed and continues to change with each generation. The Guajiro distinguish between two types of stories, *sukujala alaulayuu* ("what the old people tell") and *nukujalaa wanee wayúu* ("what so-and-so tells"). The former are de-scribed as traditional stories that focus on the origin of the Guajiro and their culture, whereas the latter are an ever-changing array of stories based on personal and group experiences.

Older Guajiro tell their stories in the form of songs that can last anywhere from ten minutes to two hours, but most stories are told in spoken form, and they are mainly told during social gatherings. Often the senior men drink alcohol and tell stories long into the night. Storytelling sessions both entertain and pass on moral teachings. Storytellers educate the youth about their heritage as well as point out any problems that may be occurring in the community or with individuals. Storytellers interact with their audiences throughout their tales. Peo-ple interrupt to ask questions, to get clarifi-cation, or to add to stories. Although there are a wide range of topics, characters such as At'pana make appearances in both types of narratives, depending on the theme and the moral. With familiar characters and personal input, Guajiro stories allow the entire community to come together.

At'pana delights in outsmarting those bigger and stronger than he. For example, knowing that the always gullible jaguar is an easy target, At'pana loves to take advan-tage of him, deceiving the stronger, faster jaguar with his pranks. In one story At'pana saw a jaguar in the forest resting near a tree. Quick to think of a prank, At'pana ap-proached the jaguar, pretending to be out of breath. "Quick," he said to the jaguar. "You must hide." The jaguar was flustered

at At'pana's suggestion, but At'pana told him that a large hunting party was on its way to kill him. Seeing that the jaguar did not know what to do, At'pana suggested that he climb into a sack and let At'pana hoist him up into the tree so the hunters would not see him. The jaguar believed him and climbed into the sack, whereupon At'pana sealed it tightly, attached it to one of the branches, and scampered away, leav-ing the jaguar to meet his demise.

In another story, At'pana took advantage of a hawk and his unsuspecting family. At'-pana heard that the hawk had left his wife and two daughters to work in the fields. Knowing that he could have his way with the girls, he went to the fields and offered to help the hawk work in return for food. The hawk went home and got another shovel so that At'pana could help. After working for some time, At'pana laid his shovel down and complained that he was hungry. The hawk told him to go to his house, and his wife would make him some-thing to eat. Smiling, At'pana made his way to the hawk's house, where he explained to the hawk's wife that her husband had sent him to take the two girls in marriage. At first the hawk's wife was confused, but slowly At'pana convinced her that he had already paid her husband a great sum of money for the girls. Grudgingly, she packed the girls' things and sent them on their way. At'pana and the girls traveled for a few days, and after having intercourse with each of them, At'pana crept away in the middle of the night, leaving them to find their way home. When the girls got home, they told their father what At'pana had done and pointed him in the direction At'pana was headed.

After several hours, the hawk found At'-pana's trail and saw him resting in a small hole. Attempting to deceive At'pana, the hawk convinced a vulture to watch over the hole while he went home to get a tool to get At'pana out. The vulture watched carefully, and At'pana began to talk to him. At'-pana told the vulture that if he would look at him with wide-open eyes, he would come out, and the vulture could eat him himself and not have to share him with the hawk. As soon as the vulture opened his eyes wide enough, At'pana threw urine in them and escaped as the vulture was wracked with pain. As he ran into the forest, At'pana laughed and smiled, for he had once again outwitted the clever hawk. (Métraux and Armstrong 1948; Sullivan 1988; Wilbert and Simoneau 1986)

Aulukuma

Kalapalo, *Central Brazil*

Aulukuma is portrayed as both the younger brother and the twin brother of **Taugi** in Kalapalo narratives. Although Taugi seems to be the more powerful and deceptive of the two, Aulukuma accompanies Taugi during both his creative and destructive adventures. For example, Aulukuma helped Taugi trick the king vulture to get fire and light, thus allowing human beings to obtain them. Aulukuma also accompanied Taugi on his trip to the *ufiti* lizard, from whom they obtained erections for themselves with which to please their wives.

Although occasionally portrayed as twins, Aulukuma is most often characterized as Taugi's younger brother. This distinction parallels the Kalapalo kinship structure, which is ambivalent toward twins because their social roles are less defined. In Kalapalo society, older and younger sibling's roles are structured and formal. The Kalapalo attribute cunning, dignity, and high status to the firstborn, whereas the youngest is thought to be more powerful physically and more obviously sensitive to others. Taugi and Aulukuma demonstrate these roles again and again. Taugi usually carelessly dismisses his actions and their negative effects on society, whereas Aulukuma worries about the effects of their actions. For example, when Taugi and Aulukuma obtained erections from the *ufiti* lizard, Taugi bolted ahead with his plan to capture the erections, while Aulukuma went along but was cautious and worried during their journey.

Yet Aulukuma is not weak, nor does he lack intelligence. In fact Aulukuma is physically more powerful then Taugi. He is able to withstand physical abuse, and even death does not stop him. In many stories Aulukuma dies from his adventures with Taugi, but each time he has the strength to come back to life, often to the dismay of Taugi, who has greedily tricked or killed him. (Basso 1973; Basso 1987; Basso 1988)

Azeban

Abenaki, *Northeastern United States*

The raccoon Azeban is best known for his fanciful pranks that both harm and entertain people. He outwits friends and enemies alike to gain food and other basic necessities. Azeban's behavior stands in stark contrast to Abenaki social norms, which emphasize the importance of harmonious relationships. The basis of Abenaki communities is responsibility to the family. This responsibility is buttressed by an extended kinship system that relates people to many members of their community, including animals and other nonhuman beings in the world.

Stories of Azeban and other Abenaki characters illustrate these basic foundational themes, focusing on one's responsibilities to family and community, on the importance of humility, on the repercussions of the abuse of power, and on the necessity of balance within the world. Abenaki storytelling is a central means by which the community relays its history and values to the younger generations while at the same time incorporating the events of the present. Abenaki stories use well-known characters in a variety of situations to integrate modern-day problems and issues within the boundaries of their oral traditions.

Most stories about Azeban begin with the storyteller placing the character within his or her frame of reference by stating, "Wowigit ndatlokangan wa Azeban [Here camps my story of Azeban]." With this opening statement, Abenaki storytellers place themselves in close relation to the narrative. Each story is the storyteller's own tale about familiar characters; that is, Abenaki storytellers choose their characters from a variety of well-known figures (see **Glooskap,** for example) whom they shape into their own stories.

As one of the more entertaining characters in the Abenaki oral tradition, Azeban demonstrates the importance of maintaining Abenaki cultural values, while at the same time reminding people that the world is an unpredictable place. In one story, Azeban sneaked away from his chores to play in the woods. As he was walking in the woods whistling and humming a tune, he came upon a nest of birds. He called to the birds, telling them that their Uncle Azeban wanted to play with them. But before the young birds could fly toward him, their mother returned and warned them never to play with Azeban. She told the baby birds that Azeban was a nest robber and that he would eat them if he got the chance. Azeban was furious that the mother bird stole his meal. It was not his fault, he thought, that he got hungry once in a while when he played with the birds. In his anger, Azeban called back to the birds saying that he would be back another day for them. Azeban loves to tease the animals, for he knows that he has outwitted them before and can do it again.

After leaving the birds, Azeban came upon a river, which he followed to a large waterfall. The water was rushing over the fall with incredible power. Azeban did not want to be outdone by the loud and raging river. He shouted to the waterfall to quit its loud, obnoxious roaring, for he was the mightiest in the woods. Azeban shouted and shouted, but the waterfall never ceased. Inching closer and closer to the waterfall, Azeban yelled louder and louder for the waterfall to stop. He insisted that he was not to be ignored, but the waterfall did not listen. Angrily, Azeban rushed to the edge of the waterfall and shouted with all his strength, so loud that he became dizzy and fell into the raging water below. He was swept about and thrown out at the bottom of the river. In disgust, Azeban floated down the river, still claiming that he was the most powerful.

Azeban is best known for causing trouble between people simply for his own amusement. He likes best to watch other people argue over something that he has caused to go wrong. As he was floating down the river after having fallen over the waterfall, an old lady snatched him out of the water, believing he was dead. The old lady and her sister were a bit odd in that they shared one eye between the two of them. Consequently, one of them was blind while the other could see. They made their camp near the river and strung rope from their camp to the river, where they fished and drew water to drink.

When the old lady with the eye found Azeban she called to her sister, telling her she had caught a raccoon for their dinner. The second sister was delighted and asked for the eye so she could see the raccoon. The first sister handed over the eye so the second could see their catch, and then the sister who could see skinned Azeban and threw him into a pot of boiling water to cook. When he hit the hot water, Azeban awoke and realized he was being cooked. As he thrashed around trying to get out, the sister with the eye leaned over the pot and was splashed with the water. She cried to the blind sister that their dinner was getting away, and the blind sister insisted that she give her the eye so that she could see for herself. Once she had the eye she leaned over the pot, and Azeban splashed her too and jumped out. Having heard the sisters argue over the eye, Azeban decided to play a trick on them. He sneaked up behind the sister with the eye and imitated the blind sister's voice asking for it. The old woman took out the eye and placed it right into Azeban's paw. Now that both of the women were blind, Azeban sat back on a log and watched them quarrel over who had the eye. Each of the women insisted the other must have the eye. The sisters fumbled over their pot, fell down, and yelled at each other while Azeban had a good laugh. Soon Azeban grew tired of the sisters, so he placed the eye on the ground where he knew they would eventually stumble over it and went on his way to find someone else to trick. (Bruchac 1988; Morrison 1984; Trigger 1978)

B

Bertholde
Italy
See **jester.**

Brer Anancy
African American, *United States*
See **Brer Rabbit.**

Brer Coon
African American, *United States*
See **Brer Rabbit.**

Brer Fox
African American, *United States*
See **Brer Rabbit.**

Brer Rabbit
African American, *United States*
Brer Rabbit, the popular character in slave tales, is known for his disobedience and uncanny knack for fooling even the most clever of his adversaries. The adventures of Brer Rabbit and his friends Brer Coon, Brer Anancy, Brer Fox, and Brer Tarrypin were brought to life by Joel Chandler Harris in his classic Uncle Remus tales in which Uncle Remus tells the stories of Brer Rabbit and his friends to the local children of his small town in Georgia. An American classic, Brer Rabbit's adventures play on the racial tensions between the North and South in the United States.

Harris immortalizes Brer Rabbit and his friends in his stories centered on pre–Civil War African American experiences. Using a dialect true to the people he represented, Harris broke ground with his novels by focusing on issues of slavery, poverty, and racial identity at a time when mainstream

Brer Rabbit chatting with Brer Fox in an illustration for the book Uncle Remus and Friends *by Joel Harris (1848–1908). (Corbis-Bettmann)*

culture ignored these problems. Although the main character is a rabbit, the tales highlight the plight of African Americans and the trials of that period in U.S. history, and even though the stories are called "children's tales" they often cross into adult themes, dealing with social and moral issues.

Brer Rabbit's antics reflect his mischievous nature. He teases and taunts his friends and loves to take advantage of others with his quick wit. His cunning ability to trick others is his most powerful tool. Although Brer Rabbit and the other characters are depicted as animals, they have human characteristics, face human dilemmas, and deal with human emotions: greed, jealousy, selfishness, and anger.

Brer Rabbit is most often associated with the "tar-baby" prank. In this story, Brer Rabbit and Brer Fox were engaged in their usual game of chase, with Brer Fox once again failing to catching Brer Rabbit. Frustrated that Brer Rabbit always got the best of him, Brer Fox mixed some tar and turpentine and covered a molasses jar with the mixture to make a "tar-baby." He set his tar-baby by the side of the road and waited for Brer Rabbit, who soon came by. Brer Rabbit was intrigued by the small baby. He went over to the tar-baby and struck up a conversation. "Mawnin mam," Brer Rabbit called to her, but he got no response. Brer Rabbit continued his one-sided conversation as Brer Fox patiently waited to make his move.

Brer Rabbit shouted at the tar-baby, "Is you deaf?" "You're stuck up, dat's what it is," he finally concluded. Meanwhile Brer Fox was doing all he could not to laugh out loud and give himself away. Brer Rabbit got madder and madder, shouting at the tar-baby, telling her he would "learn her how to talk to respectable folks." Still nothing from tar-baby, so Brer Rabbit pulled back and smacked her on the face. When he touched the molasses jar covered with tar, his hand stuck. He wiggled and pulled but could not get loose from the grip of the tar-baby. The madder he got, the more he tried to hit the tar-baby and the more he got stuck. Soon every part of Brer Rabbit was stuck to the tar-baby, and Brer Fox sauntered out of hiding. Brer Fox rolled on the ground laughing at Brer Rabbit. "I spect I got you dis time, Brer Rabbit" said the fox.

Finally Brer Rabbit spoke to Brer Fox very humbly, saying that he had been wrong. Brer Fox was so upset with all the pranks the rabbit had played on him time and again that he told Brer Rabbit he was going to barbecue him. Brer Rabbit played along, admitting to Brer Fox that he deserved it but pleading "for de Lord's sake, don't throw me in the brier patch." Brer Fox went through the list of possible ways to get rid of the rabbit—hang him, cook him, drown him, skin him—and Brer Rabbit agreed to all of them but pleaded with him not to be thrown in the brier patch. Soon his manipulation worked, and Brer Fox angrily flung him into the brier patch. A few moments later, when Brer Fox saw Brer Rabbit sitting upon the hill combing the tar out of his fur and laughing at him, the gullible fox realized he had been duped again. (Brown 1941; Harris 1972; Lester 1990)

Brer Tarrypin
African American, *United States*
See **Brer Rabbit.**

Brhannada
India
Brhannada, an androgynous clown, appears in the fourth book of the Indian epic poem the Mahabharata, the Virataparvan. This portion of the Mahabharata deals with the exile of the powerful Pandava family. Exiled from their home, the Pandavas assume disguises to hide their true identity. One of the main characters of the story is Arjuna, one of the king's sons. Arjuna is a heroic figure throughout most of the text, but in this section his heroism is tempered by his comedic role as Brhannada.

As Brhannada, Arjuna hid his true identity as a charioteer and a future king and lived in the king's harem as the women's dance teacher. In such a ludicrous role for royalty, Arjuna highlights the plight of the Pandava family during their exile. Inverting his normal royal status, Arjuna takes on the role of Brhannada, and his comedic performance brings out the humor and absurdity of life. As the harem's dance instructor, Arjuna spent his days dancing among the beautiful women and exploring the lighter side of life. In his androgynous role, Arjuna dissolved gender boundaries. He played with his appearance, voice, and posture to keep his true identity hidden, yet King Virata was nevertheless suspicious when he saw him for the first time. Looking at Arjuna as Brhannada, the king exclaimed that she/he appeared to be an "archer wrongly attired." Of course the king's suspicions were correct, but his wives liked Brhannada so much that the king allowed him to stay.

From the moment Arjuna appeared at King Virata's court as Brhannada the incongruous elements of life are played upon. Brhannada's appearance is grotesque, not true of either a male or female. He has long braided hair but sharp masculine features. He is a graceful dancer, yet clumsy at everything else. Attempting to accentuate the feminine, Brhannada distorts female characteristics and bungles even the simplest activities. Yet the king's wives were entranced by his dancing. Enjoying his disguise, Arjuna nevertheless found it hard not to be sexually attracted to the beautiful women. Playing his role as Brhannada did not allow Arjuna to express his true lustful feelings for the women. Part of the story, then, focuses on the tension Arjuna feels as Brhannada, an ambiguous character caught in a disguise and a way of life.

At a pivotal point in the story, Arjuna is discovered for who he is. As the king's men were leaving for war, Princess Uttara saw through Arjuna's disguise and convinced him to be her brother's charioteer. Playing his role as Brhannada, Arjuna accepted the role of charioteer, but in a comedic light.

First he had trouble finding the chariot. Then he put on his armor upside down. Finally, as he climbed into the chariot he pretended not to know that he was heading into battle, telling the king's wives that he would bring them back fine fabric. When the king returned and found out who was taking his son into battle, he worried openly because the "eunuch is his charioteer." Once in battle, however, Arjuna showed his true colors as he led the charge, and it was the prince who became afraid and sought the advice of the effeminate Brhannada.

In a delightful comic twist, Brhannada plays upon the fuzziness of self-imposed boundaries in life. In exile, the Pandavas are able to explore different aspects of their humanity, and in Arjuna's role as Brhannada the epic poem highlights the androgyny in many aspects of life. Similarly, popular puppet shows throughout India portray Brhannada in a light-hearted look at the possibilities of life. As a eunuch or a transvestite, Brhannada uses sexual ambiguity to distort all common roles in life. Brhannada uses wordplay, inverted roles, and comic slapstick to show audiences that life is not always what one expects. (Dumezil 1968; Hiltebeitel 1980; Shulman 1985)

Bribal
India
Bribal was a poor northern Indian writer, a Brahman (a member of the priestly ruling elite class), who used his skills of wit and satire as a court jester to show the foolishness of the monarchy (see also **Tenali Rama** for a similar figure from southern India). Bribal is best known for his tenure as court jester during the reign of King Akbar in the late 1500s. As Akbar's constant companion, Bribal was able to make light of even the most serious situations. Bribal's activities have been made famous throughout India in popular books, comic strips, paint-

ings, and poems. Although the truth behind all the stories cannot be verified, Bribal's antics in Akbar's court survive as a testament to those who challenged the rigid class system in India and stood up to the power of the kings.

Bribal was a preeminent joker. He delighted in showing the king and his advisers the error of their ways through practical jokes, word play, satire, and outright mockery. Part of Bribal's power was his ability to make his point to the king while still being entertaining. The position of a court jester is notoriously tenuous, since he is always under the scrutiny of the king's court and if his joking went too far he could be put to death. Bribal, however, had mastered the art of joking without offending Akbar. In one story, Akbar commanded Bribal to bring the ten biggest fools to the court to entertain him. Bribal left for the surrounding villages, and when he returned he brought eight men to stand before Akbar. Akbar asked Bribal where the other two were. Bribal smiled and politely said that he and the king were surely the other two! Pointing out his own foolishness as well as the king's, Bribal is able to show that there is humor and foolishness in all positions and classes within India.

In another famous story, Bribal showed the king that his whims were not always possible. Akbar had been watching the Brahmans in his court and decided that he too wanted to be a Brahman. Not satisfied with his power as a king, he wanted to be privy to divine matters as well. Summoning Bribal, Akbar asked him to arrange a ceremony to make him a Brahman. After several days, Bribal told Akbar that he had arranged for the ceremony but that it was to be held at a nearby temple. Akbar and Bribal walked along the country roads toward the temple. As they were walking, they passed a man who was washing his horse. Akbar asked the man, who was scrubbing furiously, what he was doing.

The man replied that he was trying to change his horse into a donkey. Shocked, Akbar lectured the man on the ways of the universe, telling him that something born one way cannot be made another. As he spoke he looked at Bribal and realized that the meeting had been set up to teach the king that very same lesson.

Part of Bribal's appeal and his legendary status is his ability to use pranks and foolish behavior to show the absurdity of societal norms and values. Bribal uses humor to reverse situations, challenge the powerful, and stand up for equality. He is a master of disguise and can change his appearance, voice, and posture to make himself unrecognizable to the king and his court. In one story, the king called to the people for the finest poet. The poet who won would receive many rewards. Bribal realized that one of the guards was demanding bribes to allow poets entrance when they came to the court. To expose the guard's corruption, Bribal disguised himself as a poet and approached the palace gates. When the guard demanded money for his entrance, Bribal told him he had none but that he would give the guard all the rewards the king bestowed upon him. Accepting his bargain, the guard let him pass. When he came before Akbar, he spoke eloquently and charmed Akbar as well as the rest of the court. Impressed, Akbar told him he could have any reward he wanted. Without hesitating Bribal looked at Akbar and said he wanted 100 lashes for his reward. The king was stunned but granted his request. When the guard heard that Bribal had won, he made his way to Akbar and told him that the young poet had promised his rewards to him. The guard was taken away for his reward, and he soon learned that he had been fooled by Bribal.

Akbar is said to have cherished Bribal's companionship, wit, and intelligence and to have rarely made a move without consulting him. In the final chapter of his life with

Akbar, Bribal went into battle in the north-east with the king's men. After several weeks of the battle, Akbar received word that Bribal had been killed. Devastated at the loss of his companion, Akbar did not eat or sleep for days. In a tribute to Bribal he wrote: "When I was melancholy Bribal gave me everything except more sorrow to bear. That he bestows now. And so it may never be said that Bribal did not give me all." Bribal's body was never found, and many believe that he went to Bengal under the name of Gopal. The stories told about Gopal bear a striking resemblance to the tales of Bribal's pranks and jokes. Although the tie has never been proven, most Indians believe that Bribal and Gopal were one and the same. (Siegel 1987)

Bricriu

Ireland

Bricriu is a devious, deceptive, and disrespectful troublemaker who tries to turn any situation to his own advantage and prides himself on his ability to get the best of anyone. Bricriu has been a popular character in Irish literature since the early ninth century, when the tale *Bricriu's Feast* spread throughout the country. Prior to that Bricriu had been known through oral tales in which he was pitted against many Irish nobleman in struggles for power.

Bricriu is a character who embodies disorder. He tricks people into quarreling with their neighbors, he causes royalty to fight among themselves, and he is destructive for no other reason than to prove how powerful he is. Yet however chaotic his actions seem, he often straddles the line between order and anarchy. Although he loves to incite riots and generally cause mischief, his pranks also stress the importance of solidarity and cohesion among those not in power.

Bricriu is disruptive and intrusive and makes himself the center of attention through his foolish and disrespectful activi-

ties, but he also calls attention to the absurdity of the power held by the king, warriors, and other nobility. His antics are often focused on showing the enormous inequality between classes in Ireland. Bricriu's comedic pranks and squabbles often create a sense of order and stability by uniting common people in their distrust of authority.

Tales of Bricriu's adventures are related with great fervor. Storytellers do not simply tell the stories; rather, they enact them with all of Bricriu's intensity, using exaggerated gestures to highlight his ability to get the best of people. They often use a burlesque style to focus attention on the highly comedic and often lewd aspects of his tricks. In both oral and written literature, Bricriu stands as a paradox to the line between chaos and order by showing that one can be changed to the other in the blink of an eye. His actions do not allow him to be rigidly characterized, and thus, because he has no sharply defined limits, his character is always in a process of being invented.

In the tale *Bricriu's Feast* Bricriu incited a riot among a group of noblemen and their wives. Bricriu invited the noble warriors to a feast that he had prepared, but because of his bad reputation they were hesitant to accept. Finally, after he pleaded with the warriors and told them that he had built a sunroom especially for the feast, they agreed on the condition that Bricriu would not enter the dining hall. Bricriu agreed to the warrior's request because he knew that he could cause his chaos from the outside.

As the men and their wives arrived, Bricriu told each one separately that he was the most powerful and deserved the hero's portion. Once they were all seated for the feast, a fight broke out over who should have the hero's portion, since each believed that he was entitled to it. Bricriu sat outside and watched the chaos unfold.

To add to the mess, Bricriu told each of the wives that if she was first to enter the house she would be guaranteed the privileges that came with the hero's share. Trying to be as ladylike as possible, the wives attempted to make their way to the main house, but once they realized they would have to fight to be first, they pushed and shoved each other, lifted their skirts to run, and engaged in a battle of words unbecoming their status. Both the warriors and their wives fell prey to Bricriu's prank, allowing themselves to be made fools of. (Evans 1957; Gantz 1981; Harrison 1989; O'Suilleabhain 1973)

Bugs Bunny
United States

Bugs Bunny, the "wascally wabbit" who loves to trick and taunt his enemies, became one of the most loved animated characters in the United States soon after his first appearance, in the Warner Brothers 1940 cartoon *A Wild Hare.* Like other popular rabbit characters, Bugs embodies cleverness, wit, and ingenuity. He is not a hero, but the fact that he is constantly pursued by others allows him to showcase his intellect, cunning, and comic wit.

Bugs skillfully thwarts his adversaries' attempts to kill or eat him, often turning the tables on them and making them the victims of their own aggression. Bugs's calm and cocky demeanor, as well as his use of physical comedy, borrows heavily from vaudevillian humor and the comedy of early film stars Charlie Chaplin and Groucho Marx. Bugs gracefully turns a corner or shuts a door just in time to knock down a trailing villain.

In a similar vein, Bugs uses disguise and impersonation to fool his pursuers, tricking others into believing he is an old man, a policeman, a fox, a turtle, or, on numerous occasions, a woman. In *Now Hare This,* Bugs dresses up like Little Red Riding Hood to fool the hungry wolf and ultimately convinces the wolf that the only way to have a rabbit for supper is to cook *for* him, not to cook him.

Bugs faces a number of antagonists, but the one who appears most frequently by far is Elmer Fudd, the bungling hunter who pursues Bugs with his double-barreled shotgun. Elmer is the quintessential fall guy whose overzealous nature always gets the best of him. He repeatedly tries to catch Bugs, but he can never seem to get the rabbit to fall into his traps. He either makes a mockery of his own plan by calling attention to himself accidentally or falls into Bugs's trap unknowingly. In *A Wild Hare* Elmer set a box-trap for Bugs, baited with a carrot and a neon sign advertising "carrots." After setting the trap and fixing an alarm to it, Elmer hid behind a tree and waited for his prey. When he heard the alarm sound he ran to check the trap. In his

Bugs Bunny's enormous popularity has caused the cartoon character's image to appear in a wide variety of places. Here a Bugs Bunny balloon is shown in the Macy's Thanksgiving Day Parade in New York, 1986. (Joseph Sohm; ChromoSohm Inc./Corbis)

excitement, he reached into the trap and grabbed his quarry without looking at what he had caught. He walked away from the trap, thinking he was holding the wild hare, when suddenly he ran into Bugs himself. It was only then that he realized he was holding a skunk, placed in the trap by Bugs.

Bugs Bunny often gets the best of others by playing on their own stupidity. In a typical plot, Bugs thwarts Daffy Duck's attempts to fool Elmer Fudd into shooting Bugs instead of Daffy. For example, in *Duck! Rabbit! Duck!* Elmer had cornered Bugs and was about to shoot him when Bugs declared, "I'm not a stewin' rabbit. I'm a Fricasseein' Rabbit! Have you got a license to shoot a Fricasseein' Rabbit?" "Why, no," answered Elmer. "Do you happen to know the penalty for shooting a Fricasseein' Rabbit, without a Fricasseein' Rabbit license?" asked Bugs. "What is this,

a cooking class?" exclaimed Daffy Duck, coming out of hiding, "Shoot him! Shoot him!" "But I haven't got a license to shoot a Fwicasseein' Wabbit," explained the befuddled Elmer. The frustrated Daffy then tried to get the upper hand by writing Elmer a proper license, but he did not know how to spell *Fricasseeing*. When he asked Bugs how to spell it, Bugs replied, "F-R-I-C-A-S-S-E-E-I-N-G-D-U-C-K." Daffy handed the license to Elmer, who read it and then looked at Daffy in confusion. Daffy responded, "Hurry up. The fine print doesn't mean a thing." Elmer shrugged and shot Daffy.

According to Chuck Jones, "We love Daffy because he is us, we love Bugs because he is as wonderful as we would like to be." It is Bugs's ability to prevail in the face of adversity that endears him to so many people. (Adamson 1990; Jones 1989)

C

Caracara
Caduveo, *Brazil*

Caracara is a deceitful counterpart to the creator Go-noeno-hodi in Caduveo stories. He spoils Go-noeno-hodi's plans, tricks him into changing things he has created and even the shape of the world, and is always making improper suggestions. Although Caracara is often portrayed in stories as a bird, he has human characteristics, including the ability to speak and to affect humanity through his manipulations. His actions are always motivated by a desire to be in control and to see how far he can distract the creator from his plans.

The Caduveo tribe is smaller than other native tribes in the region, which puts them at a disadvantage for food and other natural resources. Stories about Go-noeno-hodi and Caracara demonstrate how the Caduveo have dealt with and continue to deal with their surroundings. Caracara demonstrates the chaotic, deceitful characteristics of the world, and Go-noeno-hodi represents the positive aspects. Together, the two highlight the tentative nature of the Caduveo's world. Stories focus on near cataclysms at the beginning of time, diseases and floods that killed thousands, and more recently their encounter with missionaries and government officials, who have attempted to relocate them and change their traditions. In the character of Caracara, the Caduveo incorporate all the negative traits of those who are seen to have ill effects on Caduveo culture.

Caracara is responsible for bringing death and hard work to the Caduveo, but he is also partially responsible for their creation. After Go-noeno-hodi had created many of the native people in the region he decided he had enough, but Caracara appeared as a bird and convinced Go-noeno-hodi to pull one more group of people, the Caduveo, from the underground to the upper world. Once they were in the upper world Go-noeno-hodi wanted to give them all the food and supplies they would need, but Caracara convinced him that people and animals should have to work for their food and shelter, that they should have to harvest cotton and search for honey. Caracara told Go-noeno-hodi that the people were already lazy and that if he didn't make them work the world he had created would fall apart.

In a similar story, Caracara observed that after people died they had the power to resurrect themselves. Not liking the fact that humans had so much power, Caracara went to Go-noeno-hodi and told him that people were taking advantage of him, that they were not working hard, and that they should not be rewarded with the power to resurrect themselves after death. Believing Caracara, Go-noeno-hodi was upset that the people he had created would take advantage of him, so he took away their power of resurrection, and when people died they could no longer come back to life. (Hopper 1967; Métraux 1946a; Oberg 1949; Wilbert and Simoneau 1990)

Ch'angbu
Korea

The ch'angbu is a humorous female clown character and is one of the most popular of the ancestors who appear in the *kut*, a common Korean women's ritual. Traditional Korean religious practices include women's rituals that range from daily practices to annual celebrations. In the *kut*, ancestors are summoned, reveal themselves, and are spoken to through a *mansin* (female shaman). The ch'angbu is not only a humorous character but also carries with her the spirits of dead actors, singers, and acrobats. As such, she brings with her a wide range of skills to enhance the *kut*.

A *kut* is meant to bring one's deceased relatives back into harmony with one's living relatives. In traditional Korean society one's relatives, whether alive or dead, must be cared for and shown the proper respect. Illness, strife, economic hardship, and other misfortunes are thought to be caused by lack of respect and honor for one's deceased relatives. During a *kut* offerings are made to ancestors in the hope that they will help an ill person or bring luck to a family who is in need. The *kut*, however, is not always successful.

The ch'angbu is only one of many relatives summoned during a *kut*. The *mansin* in charge of the *kut* calls the ch'angbu when she wants to lighten the mood or when she wants to embarrass some of the guests. By calling the ch'angbu the *mansin* ensures that people will make more offerings, and thus help ensure a successful *kut*, because no one wants to be chastised and embarrassed by the ch'angbu.

Once the ch'angbu is summoned the *mansin* takes on the voice, gestures, and actions of the ch'angbu. As a humorous entertainer, the ch'angbu pokes fun at relatives, especially those who are not participating by offering money. She chides people for being lazy or greedy and will even physically attack people. Oftentimes the ch'angbu will grab women's breasts, chase them from the yard, or pull at their clothes. Anything she does is aimed at motivating people to participate or at telling people why their deceased relatives are angry.

Although her actions are amusing and oftentimes somewhat vulgar, the ch'angbu also advises people. For example, she may remind a wayward daughter that it is her obligation to make offerings of rice cakes to her father-in-law. Or she may tell a widow that she is not properly acknowledging her late husband with offerings. Her advice, however, does not come without a price. If the women at the *kut* do not pay her properly, her humorous antics may turn more violent. (Harvey 1979; Janelli 1975; Kendall 1985; Mattielli 1977)

Chapayeka
Yaqui, *Southwestern United States and Northwestern Mexico*

The chapayekas are masked performers who both protect and entertain during ritual performances. The Yaqui say that the chapayekas are committed to "acting two ways." That is, they perform their ritual activities with a vow to Jesus, but their foolish and obscene actions and their merciless persecution of Jesus in the Easter ceremony puts their vow in jeopardy. To counter their obnoxious and dangerous behavior, all chapayekas recite silent prayers to themselves as they hunt for Jesus, and they hold the cross of the rosary that hangs around their neck in their mouths at all times while they don their masks. They thus are always reminded that they work in service of Jesus even if their behavior seems contradictory to a peaceful community life.

The chapayekas mock performers by standing next to them, imitating and exaggerating every move they make. Sometimes they will sit directly behind a performer and smoke a cigarette, showing their disrespect and calling attention to themselves. The chapayekas play with one another; they tease each other with their swords, pretending to cut one another's hair off or to kill one another in violent attacks. They do everything left-handed and never face the audience fully, always standing either with their backs to them or half-turned. The chapayekas power is so great that to face one fully is to open oneself to harm.

Within Yaqui society, there are several religious societies that serve at different ritual performances throughout the year. One such, the Fariseo society, is dedicated to upholding the Yaqui community through their vows to Jesus. Members of the Fariseo society oversee and perform in ritual activities and act as protectors to the Yaqui community, and the chapayekas are recognized within the Yaqui community as the common soldiers of the Fariseo society. Chapayekas are also referred to as *chapayeka ya'ura* (Fariseo officers), *chapayeka alpes* (flag bearers) because of their use of flags in the Easter ceremony (see **Pascola** for more detail on the Easter ceremony) and *naka'aram* (long-eared) because of the style of their traditional masks. Chapayekas are masked dancers, distinguished from other Fariseo society members by their playful actions, rude behavior, and masked appearance. Despite these distinctions, however, chapayekas are full members of the Fariseo society, taking a vow to Jesus. Jesus is regarded as the head of the Fariseo society, knowing all that the members do and say. Fariseo society members make their vow to Jesus for at least three years, but many remain for life. In fulfillment of their vows, the chapayekas perform ritual work that is both physically draining and dangerous.

The chapayekas surround themselves with danger by participating in the crucifixion of Christ. By playing the role of Christ's enemies, the chapayekas open themselves to retribution by Yaqui spirits. The chapayekas lead in the search for and persecution of Christ in the ritual dramatization of Christ's death each year. But the work of the chapayekas is necessarily a precursor to their eventual downfall on Holy Saturday morning. The chapayekas, as well as the other Fariseo society members, are eventu-

ally captured by the Yaqui people and ambushed in the central dance plaza. Once cornered, the Fariseos are showered with flowers that symbolize all that is good and proper in Yaqui society. The Yaqui tell that at Christ's crucifixion, his blood turned to flowers as it hit the ground, and as symbols of Christ's blood these flowers serve as protection for the community. Using flowers of good as their weapon, the people ritually kill the chapayekas and maintain the balance of their community for another year.

During the Easter ceremony and other fiestas the chapayekas dance, pantomime other performers' activities, and clown around as the crowds gather. They chase people, throw things at them, and even hit them with sticks if they see someone being lazy during a ceremony. One of the chapayekas' main roles is to ensure that people do the work that is necessary to bring harmony to the Yaqui community. Although their rude behavior seems to be at odds with bringing harmony, it actually prompts people to work and reminds them of the consequences of inactivity.

Chapayekas must stay active the entire time they wear their masks, ready for any problems that might come up during the Easter ceremony. As they parade around during fiestas, they watch over the crowd, maintain order, and keep their vow to Jesus to protect the Yaqui community. Although their actions seem negative or wrongheaded, they maintain the balance within the society and are able to prevent misfortune because of their connection with the community. For example, when it is time for the audience to go inside the church to pray or offer gifts, the chapayekas run behind them, pushing them into the church or swatting them with sticks to obtain offerings. The chapayekas thus ensure the necessary participation by the community in ritual performances.

The chapayekas are most often associated with their masks, which are often referred to as *chapayeka sewa. Sewa* is a term that designates the reward or fulfillment one attains from performing work for the community. The concept captures the reciprocity of the world in which the Yaqui live. A person gains *sewa* through good deeds, including prayer and ritual activity, and through the fulfillment of vows, duties, labor, and all activities that benefit the community. *Sewa* is further related to the Yaqui concept of flowers as protective agents by embracing the actual behavior that results in *sewa*. For example, the flowers that are used to symbolically kill the Fariseos on Holy Saturday are said to be taken by angels to heaven as a record of the good deeds the Yaqui have performed. Thus the chapayekas receive *sewa* from their participation in the Easter ceremony. Moreover, the masks of the chapayekas are called flowers as well, showing that their actions and symbols reflect their devotion to their community and that their community recognizes their actions as necessary.

The chapayekas' masks are made of cowhide or goathide. The masks cover the entire head and neck, like a helmet, and have two small holes, barely recognizable, for the performers to see through. Each man makes his own mask, in whatever shape and style he likes, and cares for it throughout the year. The men decorate the masks themselves, and only other chapayekas may see the masks when they are not being worn. When they are not in use, the chapayekas' masks are kept in sacks out of view of the public. The danger involved in the chapayekas' activities is embodied in the masks themselves. The masks stand as symbols of the chapayekas' dangerous work and the harm that may befall them from their disruptive activities and associations with the negative forces in the cosmos. A person who comes into contact with a mask alone could harm himself or herself or the community. In fact, after a mask is made, all materials used to make and decorate it are burned so that nothing remains with which people may come in contact. The masks are so dangerous that photographing or sketching them is forbidden.

There are generally two types of masks, those that resemble a human with long ears and a slim nose, and those that resemble animals, birds, or butterflies. Masks are generally painted with white, red, and black; other colors are rarely used. The masks change with new members and historical time periods. Most masks typically have flowers drawn on the outside and a painted cross on the inside, so the performers are always reminded of their vows and the reasons for their behavior. The men who take this vow to be a chapayeka do so understanding the danger and power involved in being associated with the evil in the world. Nevertheless, they take the risk in order to maintain the Yaqui world. By associating themselves with the dangerous and destructive forces of the world, they allow themselves to maintain some control over it. The seemingly negative actions of the chapayekas are part of the cosmic balance that ensures the continuation of the Yaqui world. (Handelman 1981; Lutes 1983; Montell 1938; Painter 1986; Parsons and Beals, 1934; Spicer 1984)

Chibuga
Kaguru, *East Africa: Tanzania*

Although Chibuga may refer to any small creature, it is most often the hare character within Kaguru folktales. Although *Sangula* is the Chikaguru word for rabbit, the word *Chibuga* is used to indicate the rabbit's physical traits, namely, his size. He is also referred to as "the little one." In addition, the prefix "ch" designates the rabbit's status as one who is amiable and beloved. In the majority of the Kaguru stories, Chibuga plays a positive role. Although he tricks **Difisi** (the hyena) and others, it is because he was provoked or because he was acting in the best interest of the community. In some stories, Difisi and Chibuga are friends, but inevitably Difisi takes advantage of this relationship and Chibuga is forced to retaliate. In the bulk of the folktales told about Chibuga and Difisi, Chibuga's actions are presented as well respected and justified, whereas Difisi's are seen as harsh and exploitative. The two characters exemplify the choices people must make between using their positions of power for their own ends or for the benefit of the community.

Chibuga is known to be clever, swift, and agile; he is the shrewdest animal in the bush. He is also known for his ability to sweet-talk others and outwit even the cleverest of people and animals. Chibuga is further admired for his ability as a diviner and a medical expert. Diviners are well respected within Kaguru society because they are responsible for the physical well-being of individuals and the collective well-being of the community. Diviners are consulted in order to heal physical illnesses, to help with fertility, to help produce good crops, and to maintain peaceful relations. Diviners are also consulted to curb the powers of antisocial beings such as witches. In this way there is a parallel between Chibuga acting to challenge Difisi's antisocial behavior and that of diviners acting to challenge the antisocial behavior of witches and the like.

Chibuga shows his positive social role by challenging Difisi's negative actions. Chibuga is paired with Difisi in order to demonstrate that the misuse of power can be challenged. In Kaguru society people follow rules set down by elders and enforced by relatives. In many stories, the main characters are uncles and nephews, an important relationship in Kaguru society because the uncle's role is one of educator and provider. In stories about kinship relations, the uncle is usually depicted as misusing his power and thus unfairly taking advantage of his status. Chibuga, as the nephew in many stories, shows that a mis-

use of power is grounds for behavior that is normally considered disrespectful. Or Chibuga may trick Difisi, his elder, but the trickery is deemed necessary because Difisi is improperly using his status. In one story, Chibuga tricked Difisi into starving himself after Difisi had tricked others into giving up their food. In another story, Chibuga pelted Difisi with stones and broke his teeth in order to teach Difisi that he should not steal from others and take advantage of his kinship relations. Chibuga turns others' tricks around on them by being more clever than they are at their own games.

Chibuga is not always portrayed in a positive light. For example, in one story, Chibuga and his friend Chitukwa (the mongoose) set out to get some food. After searching for hours without any luck, Chibuga proposed a plan: They would take a chicken from the coop at the end of the village. First they had to make sure no one would catch them. Chibuga told Chitukwa that the next day they would play a trick on the people of the village so they would be fighting and not notice that Chitukwa and Chibuga were stealing the chickens. The next day, Chibuga replaced the game in each villager's trap with the game of his neighbor. First he went to the guinea fowl trap and took it to the river where the fish trap was. Then he took a fish and put it in the guinea fowl trap. He continued through town switching the game around. When the people awoke, each one found another's game in his trap. Each went to the other and blamed them for the switch. By midday the entire town was quarreling. Chibuga and Chitukwa listened at the edge of the village and when they heard the people fighting they took all the chickens they wanted.

Unlike the stories in which Difisi appears, this story shows Chibuga's potential to use his cleverness for mischief. Many Kaguru folktales depict situations in which people must decide whether to use their power, whether that power be position in society or intellect, in either harmful or helpful ways; the Kaguru use these stories to teach children proper ways to behave. Proper behavior is defined in relation to the group: What benefits the group is probably the best way to act. Tales about Chibuga and Difisi are told almost exclusively to children, in the evening in a leisurely setting. Children are surrounded by their mothers, uncles, and other relatives as they listen to the stories about Kaguru social values. The setting is playful and entertaining. Kaguru storytellers are known for their active performances, especially in the case of the popular characters. Since there are only a few main characters, the children know their attributes well. It is up to the storyteller to bring the story to life through action. Often the storyteller fumbles, stumbles, and sneaks around in the bushes while enacting his stories. In addition, storytellers will change their speech patterns and pronunciation for different characters, often using this technique to identify the deviant characters by their inappropriate use and pronunciation of the language. Although the Kaguru's economic situation has changed with European contact, the stories reflect the ideal social relations of a people who rely on group interaction to sustain themselves (see the stories of Difisi for further explanation of the Kaguru social system). (Beidelman 1961; Beidelman 1963; Beidelman 1975b; Beidelman 1976; Beidelman 1980)

Ch'ou
China

The ch'ou, a clown figure, is the most popular of the four main character types around which Chinese theater revolves. Although the ch'ou is said to be the lowest of the four main character types, in the actual performances he plays a significant role. Because of the element of improvisation within Chinese theater, the role of the ch'ou is always expanded from the script. In most performances, the ch'ou takes the stage as a minor character but embellishes his role through physical comedy and improvised humor to become one of the main characters. For example, in the play *Hung-li-chi*, the ch'ou plays a drunken servant. In the script he is given no more than two or three minutes of performance. But normally the ch'ou enlarges the scene to a half hour of nonstop comedy.

The role of the ch'ou in Chinese theater dates back to antiquity. There are even indications that the Tang emperor played the role of the ch'ou in palace performances. However, the popularity of the ch'ou comes from regional theater throughout China. There are two types of clowns in Chinese theater, the *wen ch'ou* and the *wu ch'ou*. The *wen ch'ou* are distinguished by their verbal humor, and the *wu ch'ou* are known for their physical comedy based in skillful acrobatics. Depending on the performance, the ch'ou wear different costumes and use face paint to accent their humor. Typically they use black and white paint, the extremes of color, to highlight the extremities of their roles.

The role of the ch'ou offers the actor the opportunity to voice social commentary. Although there are varying degrees of political wit, the ch'ou performances in regional theaters are known for their overt irreverence. Clowns often mimic the emperors or local officials, and their interaction with other performers highlights their rude and even obscene nature. In their actions, the ch'ou satirize many of the highest-ranking political and religious characters in the culture. As an accepted vehicle for voicing protest and frustration, the role of the ch'ou is highly regarded. (Towsen 1976)

Chunga
Toba, *Argentina*

A small, birdlike creature who uses his intellect and small size to outwit others,

Chunga is able to hide easily from enemies and escape troublesome situations quickly. He is often the instigator of trouble, but he hides his part in pranks by leaving the scene or accusing others of foul play. Although Chunga is described in Toba oral literature as a bird, he is portrayed as having the ability to speak, disguise himself, and interact with people, and he plays his tricks on both humans and animals.

Stories about Chunga demonstrate the physical contact between animals and people as well as the moral association the Toba have with animals. That is, the Toba refer to people using animal characteristics. People can be swift and strong like a jaguar or clever and small like Chunga. Living in the Gran Chaco region of Argentina, the Toba have constant contact with animals of all shapes and sizes. This contact has made its way into their literature, art, and history. The Toba, like other native groups in the area, rely on both hunting and agriculture to support themselves.

Animals are frequent characters in Toba stories, taking on human characteristics and interacting with humans. In addition, some human characters have the ability to change shape and take on the characteristics of animals. One of the most common scenarios is a shaman turning into a jaguar. The Toba recognize two types of jaguar: those who live above ground and those who live underground. The jaguars who live underground communicate with shamans and advise them on healing techniques. Often shamans take on the characteristics of these jaguars to heal a patient or to seek advice from other jaguars. The opposite of these helpful and powerful underground jaguars are the jaguars who live above ground. Gullible and stupid, these jaguars are the butt of many pranks by Chunga, **Wayay-qaláchiyi** (the wily fox), and other animals such as the deer and even the tiny tick (see **Keyók** for stories about the laughable jaguar). Characters like Chunga demon-

strate the tenuous and reciprocal nature of animal and human relationships.

Chunga outsmarts others by using his power to manipulate objects and people without them knowing it. For example, once Chunga fell in love with a beautiful young girl. He watched the girl for days trying to figure out how to take advantage of her. Finally he flew ahead of the girl and her sisters as they walked along a path and dropped a ball of honeycomb in her path. The girl picked up the honey and ate half of it and then decided she would give the rest to her sisters. As she walked with the ball of honey it shrank, just as Chunga had instructed it to do. Since it was so small the other girls did not want it, so she put it in her pocket and continued on her way. Later that evening, as the girl slept soundly from the tainted honey, Chunga had sexual intercourse with her and the girl became pregnant.

Chunga often accompanies Wayayqalá-chiyi on his escapades and even outwits him on occasion. In one story, Chunga and Wayayqaláchiyi were out hunting when they got bored and decided to bet on who could stay underwater the longest. They walked down to a small lagoon and waded into the water at the same time. Chunga's tail feathers stuck out of the water as the two submerged themselves. After some time, Wayayqaláchiyi cheated and emerged to see Chunga's feathers still sticking up. Diving back under, Wayayqaláchiyi thought he could certainly outlast the bird. Again and again he came up, only to see Chunga's tail feathers still sticking out of the water. Finally he dove deep down and swam around to find Chunga, but he was nowhere to be found. Wayayqaláchiyi emerged again and again, growing more and more tired, until finally he grabbed what he thought was Chunga, only to find a pile of feathers. (Karsten 1923; Métraux 1946b; Miller 1980; Wilbert and Simoneau 1982b; Wilbert and Simoneau 1989; Wright 1986)

Circus Clown

United States

The circus clown, a comedic performer in U.S. circuses, took shape in the United States soon after its separation from England. The first clowns relied heavily on their European counterparts, but with time the circus clown became a distinctly American character.

Taking hold of U.S. audiences early in the nineteenth century, circuses included equestrian exhibitions, theatrical performances, acrobatics, and clowning. The earliest U.S. circuses took their cue from the most popular circuses in London, those of Philip Astley and Charles Hughes. Astley pioneered the modern-day circus. Although the circus began mainly as an equestrian exhibition, it soon became populated with clowns, and Astley was responsible for clowns becoming more than comic entertainers. In his circus, the clowns were acrobats, equestrians, and actors as well. By demanding such well-roundedness of his clowns, Astley set the mark for all clowns to perfect their craft within the entirety of the circus.

The Latin word *circus* means "circle," and it was Astley's equestrian exhibits that gave rise to the round shape of the circus ring. Equestrian clowns were the earliest form of circus clowns. They rode horses and performed daring feats of bravery along with their comedic endeavors. In one of the most common skits, a clown dressed as a tailor tried in vain to get his horse to take him to his appointment. The clowns had to be in good physical shape for their performances, as much of their comedy was based on physical humor, especially falling off the horse. Slowly, however, with the circus's birth in the United States, the clown became an orator as well as a physical comedian.

Following some of their French counterparts, American clowns painted their faces white and wore baggy clothes, either striped or dotted. Most clowns also donned a tipped hat, a thin hat with a drooping top, reminiscent of the costumes of early European **jesters** and **fools.** The first U.S.-born clown was John Durang. Durang carried the art of clowning into a wide range of activities. He took his act on horseback, in the ring, in the air, and on the stage. Playing a part in all the components of the circus, Durang set the stage for the popularity of the modern-day circus clown. Durang was even one of the first U.S. clowns to include comic songs in his repertoire.

By 1862 circus clowns had become so popular that one clown, Dan Rice, nicknamed "Yankee Dan," earned $1,000 a week, more than President Abraham Lincoln! In a country torn over social and economic issues, the circus clown was something everyone could rally around. President Lincoln considered Rice a personal friend, and some even saw him as the president's personal jester. In fact, Rice brought clowns into the political arena with his political sarcasm and one-man speeches on local issues across the country. Yankee Dan's act was popular because he would incorporate the local politics and gossip of the towns in which he performed. Early in the day Dan would walk around town listening to conversations and picking up the local stories. To the amazement of the townspeople, Dan would incorporate local people and scandals in his act each night.

Today, as in the early days of U.S. circuses, clowns are expected to entertain audiences between other acts as well as in performances of their own. One of the clowns' main adversaries is the Ring Master. Because the Ring Master stands at the center of the ring and is always present, he makes a perfect target for their pranks. Clowns engage the Ring Master in tongue-twisting debates and dialogues that usually turn into the clowns' own satirical monologue. In a one-sided monologue, the clowns poke fun at audience members, the Ring Master, and anyone close to their show. Although clowns do have some stock jokes, their repertoire is based mainly on their ability to improvise. (Chindahl 1959; Durang 1966; Fox and Parkinson 1969; Greenwood 1898; Towsen 1976)

Coyote

The coyote is a popular, multifaceted character found within many Native American folktales whose most recognizable characteristics are his flaws: The coyote is selfish, disrespectful, and gluttonous; at his worst he is a murderer and thief. The coyote shares with other tricksters a total disregard for cultural mores and laws. In order to teach young people the proper way to act, stories about the coyote often focus on his greed and wrongheadedness

The Lakota coyote **Mica** has an unending sexual appetite, he steals, and he is greedy and generally disrespectful. Mica disregards all Lakota social mores by being selfish and rude. Mica takes advantage of his friends' wives, he steals food from his neighbors, and he lies to get whatever he wants, never working at all. Mica outwits people using lies, tricks, and any other means possible. He challenges people, animals, and other powerful beings to contests that he is sure to win; if necessary he cheats to make sure that he will be victorious. Similarly, **Yogovu,** the Ute coyote, is best known for his unending sexual appetite and his pranks, which often result in harm to others.

But although the coyote is rude, disrespectful, and even harmful to people, he is also a creator and hero in many Native American cultures. **Italapas,** for example, is a cocreator of the Chinook people, and **Isáahkawuattee** was responsible for the creation of people and many social systems for the Crow. Coyote characters often walk

The coyote appears in the mythology of many Native American tribes. His image is an ancient one, as can be seen in these petroglyphs near Galisteo, New Mexico. (North Wind Picture Archives)

the fine line between creator and deceiver, and in fact most embody traits of both. It is their ability to weave social messages of fidelity, reciprocity, and generosity into their comical and disruptive activities that makes them such popular characters. See also **Ma'ii, Sendeh, Sinkalip,** and **Yenaldlooshi,** for more examples.

Creator

Creator characters—that is, those responsible for bringing life or life-sustaining goods to a community—are found in myths throughout the world. Creators range from all-powerful gods to animals and take all shapes and sizes. They are usually known for benevolent actions that create the physical world, usher in a new age, begin life, or provide the necessities of life. Trickster characters, however, often divert this image of creators by bringing about change through unsanctioned, violent, and oftentimes selfish ways.

Myths about the creation of the world, communities, and social structures are the most popular mythical genre in the world. People are fascinated with stories of origin. Trickster characters are no less popular in stories of creation than they are in those of destruction. As creators, tricksters and those characters who enjoy deception often lead the way to new worlds and societies, sometimes by accident, sometimes unwittingly as

This depiction of the Tewa creation myth illustrates the many characters—both benevolent ones and tricksters—that participate in the myth cycle. (National Geographical Society)

a result of selfish acts, and sometimes by choice. Tricksters' power lies in the very fact that they can be at one and the same time creators and destroyers.

Isáahkawuattee is known both for his role in the creation of the Crow people and world and for his comic behavior, which is disruptive and entertaining. The Crow creation story tells of a time when the earth was wet and cold. No one lived on the earth except Isáahkawuattee. Isáahkawuattee roamed the cold, damp earth, traveling wherever he wanted to. But he was lonely and finally decided that he would create human beings out of the mud so he would have some companions.

Not all creators directly create or make the world. Some tricksters are part of creation by their very nature as tricksters. That is, they incite creation because of their pranks or negative deeds. For example, two African tricksters, **Ogo** and **Legba,** are not sole creators but are part of the cosmic forces that created the world. Both acted as the agents or catalysts for creation, but they themselves did not create the world.

The **Susa-no-o** of Japan and the **Maui** of the South Pacific represent another type of creator, those who bring necessities to humans. Although Susa-no-o's parents were the actual creators of the world, Susa-no-o was responsible for bringing food to humans. Maui, on the other hand, used his considerable power to bring the Hawaiian islands to their present shape and form. See also **Ananse, Caracara, Furna, Iktomi, Italapas, Kwatyat, Legba, Mbudti, Taugi, Tokwaj,** and **Yetl** for more examples.

Crosan
Ireland

Like other **jesters** in other parts of Europe, crosans provided entertainment in chieftains' courts throughout medieval Ireland.

Crosans exhibited their comic wit, acrobatic skills, and obnoxious behavior in festivals and local rituals. In Ireland the focus on crosans is linked with the impact of Christianity in the fifth century. The priests and bishops considered crosans to be antichurch, believing that they maintained the Irish people's link to their traditional Druid religious traditions and festivals, and therefore sought to suppress them. Instead of replacing Druidic characters with Christian characters in jokes and performances, the crosans turned their jokes on the church powers.

Prior to Christian influence, the crosans were one among many classes in Irish society. The laws of Ireland recognized the crosans as a distinct group with specific rights and responsibilities. For example, others could not imitate their appearance by letting their hair grow. During festivals they would blacken their faces and wear shabby clothes as part of their performances. Living together, groups of crosans wandered about the countryside performing for local towns. Unlike the drúths, "natural" fools whose absurdity was based on their lack of intelligence, the crosans were "professionals." That is, their comedy was inspired by their intellect and their keen observations.

Crosans were branded as outcasts by Christians because of their lack of respect for power. Their comedy always walked the line between acceptable humor and abuse. They were known for their gluttony both for food and for sex. Their costumes were stretched in the stomachs to highlight their unending hunger, and their pants were worn in the crotch; sometimes they had mock penises hanging out.

In their performances they chastised the church by shouting at the priests and mocking their rituals. But in an ironic twist, the crosans were often hired by the churches to act in the churches' ritual performances, which required battles between good and evil. Not wanting to play the evil roles, the church authorities would hire crosans instead, which may have been why Christians so often referred to them as devils. (Harrison 1989; Hughes 1966)

Cufalh
Nivakle, *Paraguay*

Cufalh is an unethical, multidimensional shape-shifter, neither human nor animal, who indiscriminately ignores social and moral codes. He rapes women and young girls, and his extremely long penis kills most of his sexual partners. His sexual appetite is matched by his deceptive pranks. He is notorious for his ruthless tricks and deceptions, which serve only to hurt people and animals alike. One of his favorite games is disguising his excrement as honey and tricking people into eating it.

Cufalh's ability to change his appearance is his most potent attribute. By disguising himself from his unsuspecting victims, Cufalh is able to satisfy all his needs. His sexual appetite is at the center of many stories. He changes into a man or a woman depending on his needs, and he will take advantage of anyone. However, he usually preys on young girls. In one story, Cufalh changed into a young girl and went to a neighboring village. When he arrived he saw a group of young girls gathered at the edge of the village. The girls were just about to start a dance when Cufalh arrived. He approached them as another young girl, and they unsuspectingly invited Cufalh to join them. When night fell and the dance ended, Cufalh suggested to the girls that all of them who were virgins should sleep together in one area. After the girls fell asleep Cufalh lifted their dresses and had intercourse with them one by one. When the girls awoke they all had a pool of blood underneath them, and they realized that Cufalh had been among them.

Cufalh's sexual antics are the theme of many Nivakle stories. He ignores the social mores that reject the notion of intercourse with young girls, and he casually rapes women. In stories about rape Cufalh always succeeds. Although he may be chased or chastised, he is never stopped. In one story, a group of women encountered Cufalh as they were gathering food. Cufalh threw himself on the women one after another and because of his strength the other women could do nothing to help. One of the women tried shoving a stick in his eye, but Cufalh just laughed, unharmed. Cufalh raped all the women one by one, telling the others as he did not to "worry," that their turn was coming soon.

Cufalh's violence sets him apart from other characters in Nivakle oral tradition because he cannot be stopped. Even when he appears to be dead, he revives himself and returns. In one story, he fought with neighboring warriors and they beheaded him, but he brought himself back to life and killed them. Another story tells of a jaguar catching Cufalh and trying in vain to kill him. Each time the jaguar thought Cufalh was dead he would spring back to life. Finally the jaguar gave up, realizing he could never kill Cufalh.

In Nivakle oral tradition Cufalh is the opposite of Fitzokojic, the creator. Unlike Fitzokojic, Cufalh does not help people, and stories about him emphasize the unpredictable nature of the world, whereas stories about Fitzokojic focus on the ordered nature of society and the world. Yet at the end of his life Cufalh grows remorseful for the wrongs he has done and asks the Thunderbirds to kill him. After his apparent death, he is revived, but this time as a more humanlike creature who takes away the pains of the elderly. Even with this twist, the majority of stories about Cufalh deal with his unending trickery and destructive adventures. (Métraux 1946a; Wilbert and Simoneau 1988b)

D

Dahusúi

Ayoreo, *Bolivia; Paraguay*

Dahusúi, a crafty tapir who both aids and deceives people, is known for his gluttony and his humorous ways of acquiring food. In one story, each time Dahusúi broke wind a new type of food was created for him to enjoy. As he walked through the forest he created honey, yucca plants, and fruit, all staples for the Ayoreo. But not all Dahusúi's actions are humorous. In another story, a man approached Dahusúi's fruit tree trying to get some food for himself. But as he reached for the fruit, Dahusúi lured him into the forest by promising him more food; once there, however, Dahusúi killed him instead. Stories of Dahusúi, then, focus not only on his pranks but on his deception and greed as well.

Not only does Dahusúi let his appetite rule his actions, but he is also greedy and lazy and will lie, cheat, and steal to get what he wants. At the beginning of human existence, people had to decide whether to follow the moon or Dahusúi. Wanting to have human beings on his side to aid his quest for food, Dahusúi falsely promised people that if they followed him they would all be fat. The moon, on the other hand, promised them immortality. The people chose to follow Dahusúi; consequently they often experienced famine, and death was introduced into the world.

Stories about Dahusúi reveal the distinctive worldview of Ayoreo culture. The Ayoreo have a seven-clan kinship system in which not only every person but also every animal, physical object, and natural phenomenon has a place. Interweaving human and nonhuman, the Ayoreo kinship system bridges the gap between the animate and the inanimate by placing everything in relation to everything else. That is, each person

in the society is responsible not only to and for other people but also to what non-Ayoreos might consider inanimate objects, such as material goods, rocks, mountains, the sun, and clouds. Ayoreo oral narratives depict this interdependency by highlighting the interaction of human, animal, and non-human characters without distinction. For example, the moon showed people how to act morally, bravery is taught by the sun, and the tobacco worm brought humans both tobacco and healing powers.

Ayoreo storytellers weave the actions of animals and humans together with those of natural phenomena such as thunder for a narrative collection that relies on the interaction of several sources to produce a convincing story. In Ayoreo narratives, animals are portrayed with human characteristics, and humans are depicted changing shape into animals or taking on the appearance of water, thunder, sun, or rain. In one story the lake was responsible for killing a woman who swam in it while she was menstruating. In another, a man changed to a jaguar to catch a thief, and in another an armadillo changed into a tree to outwit an approaching jaguar and avoid death.

In a similar fashion, the story of Dahusúi's origin as a tapir highlights the transformative nature of the Ayoreo world. At one time, Dahusúi was a man with a very large appetite that he could never satisfy. He was lazy and did not like to hunt for himself, so he always schemed to get others to do the work for him. He was a glutton, and he thought that if he changed to an animal he would be able to eat whatever he wanted by stealing crops from people and killing other animals. He tried this for a while and it worked. He was successful in stealing from his neighbors. Soon, however, his wife became suspicious and watched as he left the house and transformed himself. Angry at his behavior, she told the rest of the village what he had been doing, and they forced him to turn into a tapir for good. But before he did he warned them that if anyone ate his meat they would go mad. This is why Dahusúi is safe from human hunters, and people do not eat tapirs.

Once Dahusúi was transformed into a tapir he satisfied his unending appetite by stealing from people and animals alike. In one story, he tricked the jaguar into thinking he was near death from hunger so that the jaguar will give up his food. In another, Dahusúi hid in the town's pumpkin patch, and the morning before the townspeople were to harvest he stuffed himself with the pumpkins. (Bórmida 1978; Briggs 1973; Sullivan 1988; Wilbert and Simoneau 1989)

Death

Many tricksters' pranks and deceptions result, intentionally or not, in the death of the unknowing victim. Although many tricksters are harmless, causing only embarrassment, others purposefully hurt, maim, and kill. Restrictions on murder are almost universal, but tricksters exist just to break those taboos. In one display of greed and disregard for kin, **Difisi,** a hyena character of the Kaguru, killed his own mother in a time of famine in order to sell her flesh and get rid of the burden of feeding her. In another case, **Ture,** the spider character of the Azande, set fire to an entire village when he carelessly fell asleep after cooking some meat he had stolen from his neighbors. When Ture awoke, all the villagers were dead because of his greed. In a similar display of greed, **Kaik,** the Salish mink character, pretended to befriend a hungry wolf, but once the wolf fell asleep Kaik cut his throat, skinned him, and ate him.

Myths about death also revolve around the existence of death itself in the universe. Often a trickster's prank is responsible for bringing death to humanity, or death may be the unwanted result of human involvement with a trickster. Sometimes, however, tricksters show their positive side by revealing the mysteries of the universe to humans. The Navajo coyote, **Ma'ii,** is one such character. Although he is known for his selfish behavior and his love of pranks, Ma'ii also explained to the first Navajo the necessity of death in the world so that the people would not be frightened by their loss. Because the Navajo had not known death in their prior existence in the underworld, Ma'ii is credited with helping people begin their new life on earth. In a different tale of death, **Odosha,** a deceptive character of the Makiritare, brought death and disease to earth because he did not want his adversary Wanadi to have all the power. Odosha saw that Wanadi had discovered how to revive people after death, but before Wanadi could teach the people how, Odosha stole his power and hid it for all time.

Another common theme is the power that many trickster figures have over death. Often tricksters are immortal; others are at least able to evade death through their cunning intellect. **Tenali Rama,** a jester from India, has the ability to outwit death even when he appears to have no chance. Time and time again he is sentenced to death by a king whom he infuriates with his jokes, but his clever wit are always enough to gain him his freedom. Similarly, **Lelegurulik,** the trickster known as the little orphan from Papua New Guinea, constantly puts himself in situations in which he risks death, but he always emerges unscathed.

See also **Ananse, Aulukuma, Caracara, Cufalh, Dahusúi, Ipani, Juan Pusong, Júko, Kai-Palaoa, Kantjil, Konehu, Koshare, Kumarxúo, Mbuduvrire, Méri, Niyel Carnival, Palu, Punia, Shodieonskon, Sulwe, Susa-no-o, Talawasi, Tokwaj, Txamsem,** and **Wayayqaláchiyi.**

Deception

One of the stock character traits of both tricksters and clowns is their love of deception, their willingness and ability to deliberately mislead others for the trickster's or the clown's own benefit. Tricksters deceive people in multiple ways and in varying degrees, anything from changes in shape or form to elaborate schemes that end in death or injury. Most often a trickster's deception results in his own benefit. **Iktomi,** the spider, loves to use his power to deceive to gain food from anyone he can. He will take advantage of friends, neighbors, and even relatives to satisfy his appetite. **Eshu-Elegba,** the Yoruba trickster, uses his deceptive tricks to gain sex from unsuspecting women. He uses multiple disguises and his sensational speech to lure women to him. A trickster's use of deception is endless; almost every adventure they embark on is either fueled by or ends up in deception at some level.

The art of deception is well crafted by comedic characters throughout the world. Often it is the unknowing dupe who is the butt of others' laughter. The one on the receiving end of the jest is frequently someone in power, such as a government official, priest, or parent. **Plaan Thoóy,** a trickster from Laos, loves to deceive monks and government officials. As social commentary, his actions highlight the inequality of power. His antics show the corruption or abuse of power, and he is an excellent role model for the young men to whom his stories are most often directed. Although deception is not condoned for selfish reasons, it is al-

lowed when it results in freeing the common people from abuses of power.

Deception can occur at many levels and with varying degrees of response, from laughter and embarrassment to anger and even death. The Japanese trickster deity **Susa-no-o** deceives his creator father and commits incest with his sister to produce a divine offspring that he can control.

Sometimes deception actually benefits society. Although most tricksters are selfish, oftentimes their antics lead to the creation of something beneficial for a society, such as food, fire, and shelter. The Cree master of disguises **Wesucechak** creates the world and the Cree people as a result of his deceptions. Other times, trickster's deceptions lead to permanent changes in the form or shape of the world, society, or other animals. The armadillo trickster **Kakxó,** for example, tricked the jaguar into helping him by pretending to be ill, but when the jaguar tried to help, Kakxó bit his nose and from that time on all jaguars have had shorter, flatter noses. See also **Anaanu, At'pana, Cufalh, Dahusúi, Furna, Ganyadjigowa, Glooskap, Gu-e-krig, Guguyni, Isáahkawuattee, Kaik, Keyók, Legba, Maui, Nanabozhoo, Nowarera, Shodieonskon, Sinkalip, Sri Thanoncha, Sulwe, Taugi, Tokwaj, Wayayqaláchiyi, Yiyi,** and **Yo** for more examples.

Difisi

Kaguru, *East Africa: Tanzania*

Difisi is a hyena character in Kaguru folktales. In Chikaguru, the language of the Kaguru, *fisi* means "hyena." Hyenas are considered to be dirty, coarse animals who have an unpleasant smell and who eat bones and other substances that the Kaguru find repulsive. The prefix *di* added to *fisi* designates the hyena's status as an inhuman creature, one who does not follow the social and moral codes of Kaguru society. This prefix is used most commonly to refer to witches or to people who behave as such. The hyena Difisi is an antisocial character who is greedy, self-interested, disruptive, gross, and foolish. Difisi's antisocial behavior includes not sharing his food with those relatives who have a legitimate claim, incest, cannibalism, murder, and the abuse of ritual authority. In the stories told about Difisi, he breaks the rules of the Kaguru society time and time again.

Stories about Difisi's escapades are told almost exclusively to children and in most cases are their first exposure to the difficulties and possible problems involved with different social relations. Often a storyteller will mix up the words Difisi says or pronounce them improperly to demonstrate Difisi's foolishness. Difisi is just one character among many who interact in order to demonstrate both the positive and negative effects of power (see **Chibuga** for an example of the positive side of power). In a society like that of the Kaguru, in which social relationships also include power relationships, the abuse of power is a relevant topic. In Kaguru society, power is demonstrated through one's ability to act in ritual ceremonies, one's knowledge of ritual behavior, and one's rights over land.

The Kaguru have a matrilineal society in which political rights over land and rights to perform ceremonies are passed to men through women. The relationship between a man and his sisters' children is crucial for the maintenance of this system. Stories encourage the members of a maternal clan to support one another socially, economically, and ritually. Stories often highlight proper behavior by focusing on negative acts and their harmful repercussions. Many stories are told about people in power who use their positions to manipulate and trick other people; Difisi usually plays this role. Difisi, a hyena, is a large, powerful animal and is thus normally cast in the role of an elder (most commonly an uncle). As an elder, Difisi commands respect from his junior kinsmen. However, he uses his status for his own ends, not holding up his end of the reciprocal relationship with his kinsmen.

Difisi is notorious for taking advantage of reciprocal kinship relations, especially the important *bulai/mwihwa* (uncle/nephew) relationship. Uncles demand respect and labor from their sisters' sons, and in return the nephews can expect economic benefits later in life as well as education into the social and religious systems of the Kaguru. Difisi continually takes advantage of this relationship by selfishly asking for assistance from his *mwihwa*. In one case, Difisi decided to take a journey to another village. He asked his *mwihwa*, Genet, to accompany him to help him carry his bags and cook for him. Difisi warned Genet to be mindful of their provisions, reminding him that on a long journey one's food supply is crucial. He also told Genet that on the journey they might run into creatures or malevolent spirits who would demand food, which must be given to them at all costs so as not to bring on danger. Genet believed everything his uncle told him. Once they were on there way, Difisi went ahead of Genet, saying he would keep an eye out for any danger. When Genet reached a pond he heard a loud voice from the bushes calling for bread. So Genet threw bread into the bushes just as Difisi had ordered. What Genet didn't know was that it was Difisi behind the bush eating all his food. Further down the road, Genet met up with Difisi and asked when they would eat. Difisi told him they should travel further before they ate and that they should not waste their food. The next day, Difisi played the same trick on Genet. This happened throughout the journey, and when they returned home Genet was very skinny.

The next week Difisi asked his *mwihwa*, Civet, to accompany him on a trip. The same thing happened to Civet, and he too returned hungry and tired. When Difisi's nephew Chibuga heard of this he decided to find out what Difisi was up to. Chibuga accompanied Difisi on his next journey. Difisi gave Chibuga a sack with provisions, as well as medicine for his teeth and stomach, which had been troubling him. Difisi showed Chibuga the trees from which the medicines came in case he needed more. Once on their way, Difisi went ahead and again called for bread from behind a bush. Knowing that it was Difisi calling, Chibuga threw stones instead of bread at the bush. Later that night Difisi told Chibuga to get him some medicine, but Chibuga had already dug up the roots needed to prepare the medicine, so he did not have to leave Difisi alone with the food. Knowing that Chibuga had caught on to his plan, Difisi became flustered and told Chibuga to go ahead and eat without him. Throughout the rest of the journey Difisi tried to distract Chibuga with errands, but Chibuga turned every trick around on him, and when they returned to the village Difisi was the skinny one, not Chibuga. Difisi was able to take advantage of his relationship with Genet and Civet, but he was not able to outsmart the clever Chibuga. Although Chibuga was obligated to obey his *bulai*, since Difisi had acted selfishly he forfeited his right to expect reciprocity from his relatives. By acting antisocially, Difisi had opened himself up to abuse and disrespect that is warranted by the community.

The Kaguru distinguish between those who use trickery and cunning to take advantage of people and those who use the same skills against those who have taken advantage of others. For example, Chibuga (the rabbit) often appears in stories with Difisi. Chibuga is known to be clever, cunning, swift, and shrewd. He is also known for his ability to trick and manipulate, but his trickery is normally in defense or to revenge actions taken against him or his relatives. For example, once Chibuga and Difisi took a trip together. On their trip, Difisi tricked Chibuga into giving up his food by playing an unfair game in which Difisi fooled Chibuga into thinking that he could turn wild plantains into edible bananas and wild vegetables into edible tomatoes. Difisi told Chibuga to pick wild plantains and say the magical words "wild plantains wild plantains become bananas," assuring him that this would turn them into a wonderful meal. Chibuga did not know the game Difisi was playing, and that night, as Difisi ate the bananas he had picked, Chibuga went hungry, having only picked inedible wild plantains. Later that night, Difisi told Chibuga to get him some medicine because he did not feel well, but when Chibuga left, Difisi ate all the dinner and once again Chibuga went hungry. The same thing happened the next day. After much thought, Chibuga figured out that Difisi had fooled him, so he decided to turn the tables.

The next night he kept medicine with him at the table, and when Difisi asked for it, he did not have to leave. When they went to bed, Chibuga placed shining pebbles on his eyes to make it appear that he was awake all night, not allowing Difisi to sneak out and eat all the food. The next morning at breakfast, Chibuga mixed their gruel with stones. When Difisi woke and demanded to eat, he broke all his teeth on the stones and could not eat for several days. Although both Difisi and Chibuga may trick people, Difisi's behavior is seen as antisocial because it is premeditated and manipulative, whereas Chibuga's behavior is usually interpreted as positive and warranted because he is reacting to Difisi's malicious behavior. Although Chibuga's actions might be judged unacceptable in other situations, in this context his actions are justified.

Although Difisi can trick and cheat people, his foolishness often gets in his way and he ends up harming himself. In one story, Difisi was killed by a pack of lions because he could not keep quiet about the method he had used to gain entrance to their cave.

Difisi had discovered the lion's hunting schedule. Thus he could enter the cave and take the meat they had collected while they were out hunting for more. Instead of keeping his secret and continuing to consume the lion's meat, Difisi gloated to the other hyenas that he knew a way to get all the meat he wanted. Difisi and his friends entered the cave and began to eat the meat and bones the lions had collected and to beat the small cubs. They were causing such a ruckus that the other lions heard it even from the forest, and they were so loud that they did not hear the lions returning. Once the lions entered the cave, the hyenas had no chance for escape and they were all killed. In his foolishness and longing for acceptance, Difisi revealed a secret that led to his demise and the demise of his friends.

In another display of greed and disregard for kin, Difisi killed his own mother in a time of famine in order to sell her flesh and relieve himself of the burden of feeding her. Difisi stabbed his mother to death so that he would be more comfortable. In doing so, Difisi showed himself to be a wicked relative, unworthy of the benefits of the community. After the food that he obtained from the sale of his mother's flesh was gone, he was hungry once again. Only now he had no one to turn to because his remaining relatives would not help him because of his unspeakable act. Slowly Difisi withered, as he had no food and no kin to help him. He was soon dead because of his selfishness. (Beidelman 1961; Beidelman 1963; Beidelman 1975a; Beidelman 1980)

Dila

Hausa, *West and Central Africa*

A cunning and mischievous yet generally sagacious jackal, Dila is a character within the Hausa's *tatsuniya* genre of oral narrative.

Tatsuniya stories are classified by scholars as folklore. This genre is typified by its use of animals in human roles; that is, animals are given human characteristics. The stories are generally entertaining and educational; they contain morals and demonstrate socially acceptable ways of behaving in Hausa society. In addition, the Hausa have several other categories of oral narrative and prose: *kirari*, the praise-epithet; *yabo*, the praise-song; *labari*, history and biography; and *waka*, poetry. Each of these genres was established prior to outside contact. Under the influence of Islam, changes can be seen in each genre. For example, after several years of contact with Muslim leaders, both religious and secular, the *labari* genre began to incorporate stories about Islamic saints and heroes. This did not mean the end of Hausa cultural history; to the contrary, each of these genres expanded to include Muslim stories, while at the same time keeping traditional Hausa tales. In addition, Hausa tales were expanded, modified, and created anew to take into account this new stage in their history. The Hausa seem to embrace not a static notion of history or literature but rather a view of narratives as flexible, thus accounting for change in their society over time.

Stories about Dila are generally set in the *daji* (bush), away from town and less concerned with the new urban centers developed by the Muslims. *Tatsuniya* stories tend to focus on rural life and the effect of Islamic rule on rural life. Another indication in these stories of Islam's influence is that oftentimes an Islamic proverb is added to the ending of a story, whether it "fits" the story or not.

Tatsuniya stories also reflect the highly stratified nature of Hausa society. Prior to Islamic presence, Hausa society was organized along a clan basis and was essentially agrarian. As the society grew, a number of centralized states were formed, and by the twelfth century each state had a central *birni* (walled city) surrounded by small towns, villages, and isolated homesteads. This spatial stratification mirrored a social and economic stratification. Scholars have characterized Hausa society by the large gap between the ruling class and the peasantry. Before the strong Muslim presence in their country, Hausa society was stratified on the basis of hereditary occupational classes. At the top were the *sarakuna na asali*, the aristocracy by birth, which included the royal family and the *sarki* (king). Next were the *masu sarauta*, which included the appointed officeholders, the traders, and the small merchants; and, finally, there were the farmers and peasants at the base.

Traditionally the rural, or farmer, class told *tatsuniya* tales. Early in their rule Islamic leaders tried to discourage these stories by saying they were "lies" and distractions from the "truth" of Islamic law. But the stories have persisted as a way for rural people to account for and challenge the rule of the Muslims and the urban classes. *Tatsuniya* stories are replete with themes of economic and power imbalances and the exploitation that takes place between the rulers and those who are ruled. The stories, however, are not grim. Instead, they mock the rulers with characters such as Dila and **Gizo** (a spider character), who continually outwit those in power. In addition *tatsuniya* stories develop themes of the social values of the working class. Although these have changed over time, the stories reflect the needs of farmers, traders, and slaves.

In *tatsuniya* stories, Dila and Gizo play similar roles—both are very cunning and mischievous—yet Dila is generally thought of as sagacious. Whereas Gizo is depicted as simply immoral, Dila is shown to be wise and clever. He is commonly referred to by his nickname, *malamin dawa*, "the clerk of the jungle." One story demonstrates the extent of Dila's cunning abilities. Dila went to a Muslim *malam* (spiritual adviser) and asked him to say prayers so that Dila would become more cunning. The *malam* agreed but said that first he must pass a test: He must get the milk calabash of a Fulani

woman. Dila agreed. He left the *malam* and went out to the road, laying down as if he were dead. Soon a Fulani woman came by and saw the dead jackal. After she passed, Dila jumped up, ran ahead of her, and threw himself down again. The woman was surprised to see another dead jackal in the road and thought that this would be a good opportunity to sell the pair at the market, so she set down her calabash and went back to pick up the first jackal. While she was walking back, Dila hopped up and drank her milk and then ran off with the calabash. He took it to the *malam*, who sent him on another trial, this time to collect the milk of a bush cow.

Dila set off again, this time into the bush. As he walked he repeated the sentences "I tell you it could be split" and "I tell you it couldn't." Soon he ran into a bush cow. Dila told her that he and a friend were having an argument about whether she could or could not split a baobab tree with her horns. Wanting to prove her strength, the bush cow stood back a distance and charged full speed at a baobab tree. When she hit the tree her horns sank in and stuck so that Dila was able to milk her. He returned to the *malam*, and the *malam* gave him one more challenge, to retrieve a black-hooded cobra.

Dila thought of a plan. First, he stitched together a goatskin bag, and then he set out to find the cobra's hole. As he made his way to the cobra's home, he repeated all the while "I tell you he'd fill it" and "I tell you he wouldn't." When he saw the cobra he told him that he and a friend were debating whether or not he was big enough to fill the bag. So the cobra asked Dila to let him try the bag out. The cobra coiled himself up inside the bag and as soon as he was completely inside Dila tied it tight. When he returned, victorious again, to the *malam*, he asked him to teach him more cunning. The *malam* agreed and told Dila to sit down on the calabash by the tree. As Dila turned his back the *malam* picked up a rock, but Dila heard the noise and turned around before he could be struck with it. Dila asked the *malam* whether this was how he taught cunning. The *malam* answered that Dila had enough cunning, that if he had any more he would be dangerous to society, and he sent Dila on his way. Thus Dila is thought to be the wisest and most cunning of all the animals. (See also **Anaanu** for similar accounts by the Ga.)

Dila's escapades are seen in a different light from those of Gizo or other mischievous animals. Because he uses his intelligence to get the best of people, Dila's tricks are seen as wise and clever instead of mischievous and deliberately malicious. Dila's intelligence is a positive attribute, even if used negatively; Gizo's mischief is a result of his ignorance and stubbornness, which are negative character traits.

Some of Dila's antics, however, cross the line into malicious trickery. In one tale, Dila was out of money and had no food to feed his family. He went to his neighbors to borrow some money. First he went to the cock's house and asked if he might borrow 10,000 cowries until the second of the month. The cock agreed and gave him the money. He asked the same question at the house of the wildcat, the dog, the hyena, the leopard, the lion, and the hunter. Each one gave Dila 10,000 cowries and expected to be paid back on the second of the month. Dila bought what he needed for his family. When the second of the month neared, he cleared a space in the bush large enough to be able to see who was approaching from any direction. In the middle of the space he built a grass hut with a doorway at the front and a small entrance in the back.

Soon the second day of the month arrived, and the cock showed up to collect his money. As he spoke with Dila he saw the wildcat approaching. The cock got nervous and asked if there was another way out. Dila told him of the back door, but said it

was the children's and that they charged 20,000 cowries for the privilege of its use. No matter, thought the cock, and he paid the price, telling Dila that he would pay him the 10,000 that he now owed him the next time he came to his house. As soon as the cock had escaped, the wildcat came to the front door. As they were speaking, the wild cat noticed the dog approaching. He asked if there was another exit he might use to flee from his enemy, the dog. Dila told him of the back door and the price. The wildcat said he would gladly pay and slipped out the back before the dog had a chance to see him. In this same manner, the dog, the hyena, and the leopard all came and went, with Dila collecting a tidy sum. Finally the lion showed up, and upon his arrival he saw the hunter approaching. The lion questioned Dila, asking if he knew the hunter was coming. Dila said that the hunter must have seen the lion and followed him in hopes of a kill. So Dila told the lion he could hide inside until the hunter had gone. When the hunter came in, Dila signaled to him that the lion was hiding nearby. So the hunter drew his arrow and shot the lion dead, and then Dila paid his debt to the hunter and kept the rest of the money and the lion carcass to feed his family. In this case, Dila's prank is not warranted. Although Dila is normally portrayed in a positive light, even his antics can be harmful. (Johnston 1966; Rattray 1969a; Sigel 1982; Skinner 1969)

Dodong
Torajan, *Indonesia: Sulawesi*

Stories about Dodong, a clever slave who outwits those in power using his quick wit and cunning, focus on the ways in which people can escape and manipulate their social status. The rigid Torajan social system allows for little variation. In characters like Dodong, however, the Torajan express their animosity toward this system.

Stories about Dodong highlight the absurdity of the master-slave relationship, as well as other prescribed roles through humorous descriptions of Dodong's trickery. The stories delicately interweave social commentary into their comedic plots, shedding light on sensitive issues without directly placing any blame, therefore allowing them to be accepted by officials.

Although Dodong is a fictional character his escapades have taken on mythic proportions throughout Sulawesi. People are said to resemble Dodong, and some even take his name. Similarly, businesses and publications use his name to underscore their understanding of the social inequalities among the Torajan in their modern situation. For example, one man named Dodong runs a tourist restaurant in Sulawesi and is known for his charm, cunning tongue, and comedic antics.

The most widely known story of Dodong tells of his cleverness at the expense of his master Parengan, a young nobleman. Parengan and his young lover Lebonna decided that if either should die the other was to commit suicide so that they could be together in the grave. Soon after their vows Lebonna became ill and died suddenly. Ignoring his promise, Parengan went about his regular business. One day he sent his young slave Dodong to collect some wine for him. On his way to the vineyard, Dodong passed through the graveyard where Lebonna was buried. As he passed, her spirit called to him, asking him to remind his master of his promise.

When Dodong went home, he did not say anything to his master about Lebonna; instead, he asked him to come to the vineyard with him. As they passed through the graveyard, Parengan heard the cry of his young lover and was overcome with grief. Without hesitation he killed himself immediately. After his death, the villagers gave him a fitting burial in his familial plot. His spirit, however, followed the villagers and haunted them day and night. Although Dodong knew that Parengan wanted to be buried with his lover, he said nothing to the villagers. Instead he watched them try unsuccessfully to appease the wayward spirit. Finally Dodong announced that he knew how to calm Parengan's spirit. The nobles promised him all Parengan's wealth and his freedom if he was able to stop the haunting. Dodong smiled and told them to rebury Parengan next to Lebonna and they would be rid of him forever. After they followed Dodong's instructions, Parengan stopped plaguing the village, and Dodong became free and wealthy.

Dodong's success in becoming a free man hinges on his clever manipulation of his situation. Stories of Dodong show his cleverness at the expense of others, especially those with power and wealth. (Adams 1988; Ness 1992)

Eshu-Elegba

Yoruba, *West Africa: Southwestern Nigeria; Benin; Togo*

Eshu-Elegba, one of many *orisha* (usually translated in English as "gods" or "deities") with whom the Yoruba interact, is set apart from other *orisha* by his pranks and disruptive behavior.

The Yoruba cosmos is inhabited by many beings in addition to humans, including *orisha*, ancestors, and spirits. Each of these groups is a part of the Yoruba life-ways; each interacts with humans and is found within ritual and social settings. *Orisha* may be local beings, specific to a certain village, or they may be communal beings, known by all of the some 25 million Yoruba-speaking peoples. Eshu-Elegba is one of the latter, commonly referred to as either Eshu or Elegba, and his activities and characteristics are depicted in art, story, and ritual.

Eshu-Elegba is said to be responsible for the troubles among people, constantly causing fights and disputes at the marketplace. He also steals from people and tricks them into giving him what he wants, especially sexual favors. Indeed, Eshu-Elegba is best known for his playful eroticism. He dances erotically around women and is able to transform himself into anything or anyone he wants in order to deceive a women into having sexual relations with him. Eshu-Elegba is known for imitating sexual intercourse in his dances as well. During ritual celebrations for Eshu-Elegba, dancers enact Eshu-Elegba's erotic nature through their dance styles and their interaction with the crowds, especially the female audience members, dancing wildly around them while mimicking sexual actions.

Phallic imagery dominates Eshu-Elegba's shrines. Most shrines are constructed at the entrances of compounds, crossroads, and

An elaborately carved ceremonial staff depicts the Yoruba orisha Eshu-Elegba, with a curved object indicative of the character's phallic nature. (Seattle Art Museum/Corbis)

marketplaces, where Eshu-Elegba is typically found, and consist of a small image of Eshu-Elegba, usually made from red rocks or mud. Some shrines also contain an *igba* Eshu, which is a large closed calabash painted with three black concentric circles. The calabash is placed on a pot decorated with figures of Eshu-Elegba and serves as the seat for Eshu-Elegba when he comes to receive his offerings of food and palm oil.

In fact, Eshu-Elegba is given offerings at every festival, whether the festival is particularly for him or not. Because Eshu-Elegba is known for making trouble, people make daily offerings to him in order to avoid falling prey to his pranks. Eshu-Elegba not only causes trouble himself, he also tricks other people into causing trouble by picking fights or stealing. The Yoruba hold that if Eshu-Elegba becomes "dry," that is, if not enough palm oil offerings are made at his shrines, then trouble will break out all over town.

The decorations on the shrines and the carved images of Eshu-Elegba reflect his phallic nature. He is commonly pictured holding a flute or having his thumb in his mouth, and his long curved headdress is one of the most commonly seen images of Eshu-Elegba. In other wood carvings and on calabashes, Eshu-Elegba's phallic nature is depicted by the long curved object he holds in his left hand.

The Odun Elegba, a large festival devoted to Eshu-Elegba, is held annually in December or January. Lasting seventeen days, the festival demonstrates the many sides of Eshu-Elegba. The festival begins with a figure of Eshu-Elegba being unwrapped from red-and-black cloth coverings and washed in cool water containing the leaves of several plants known for their medicinal properties. The figure is then painted with black paint, cowries of medicine are attached, and a tricolored cap is placed on his head. Eshu-Elegba is then placed in a whitened calabash and situated in a prominent position in his normal shrine in the village center. On the second day, a goat is sacrificed in the shrine area and the blood is poured on the permanent mud image of Eshu-Elegba, which remains in the shrine area. The skull and the lungs of the goat are left for Eshu-Elegba as an offering, and the rest is roasted for the next

day's feast. People also bring nuts and yams as offerings to the shrines. On the sixth day of the festival, people dedicated to Eshu-Elegba (Bale Eleshu) form a procession from the main compound to the central marketplace. The figure of Eshu-Elegba is carried on the head of the third-highest-ranking Eshu-Elegba priestess, the arugba. Along the way the people sing of Eshu-Elegba's long hair, his club, and his mischievous powers as the *bata* drummers keep the beat. The people announce his arrival with the following song:

> People of the market, clear the way!
> We are coming through the market gate.
> My Lord is coming to the market.
> My husband, I have arrived.
> Baraye, Baraye, Baraye!

Once in the market, the Eshu-Elegba statue is placed on a mat and devotees sing and dance around it to the rhythm of the *bata* drummers. The celebration is in no way as solemn as those for other *orisha*. Instead, it is festive, with people singing and dancing and making offerings to Eshu-Elegba continuously. Many songs tell of his mischief and his phallicism. For example, one song, repeated many times, states:

> We are singing for the sake of Eshu.
> He used his penis to make a bridge.
> Penis broke in two!
> Travelers fell into the river.

The dancing connected with this celebration is spirited and playful as well. Dancers enact scenes from tales told about Eshu-Elegba and imitate his playful, mischievous nature with the audience and other dancers. The dancers wear carvings of Eshu-Elegba strung together over their left shoulders. The figures are alternately male and female. The female figures are usually depicted grasping their breasts and the male figures are shown holding swords and fly whisks over their shoulders. These vestments are said by the priests to be Eshu-Elegba; all the other adornments are simply decorations. The dancers use high steps and kicks as well as a whirling step that is not found in any other Yoruba dances. One song tells of Eshu-Elegba's connection to wild, erotic types of dancing:

Eshu is a snail-shell dancer
he spins rapidly
he knows dancing well
he doesn't join the singing
If there are no drums
He will dance to the pounding of the
    mortars.

The festival is also a time when priests demonstrate the powers that Eshu-Elegba has given them. These men lie on the ground and have mortars filled with stones pounded into their stomachs without any outward signs of pain. They also carry a heavy mortar wrapped in cloth held between their teeth. Each of these activities is aimed at showing the audience that they have received the power of Eshu-Elegba and that they are able to use it. Like the shrines to Eshu-Elegba, these priests or diviners are the outward manifestations of Eshu-Elegba. Although the priests are not said to *be* Eshu-Elegba, they have the power to call on him and they become the transmitters of his power.

In stories told about Eshu-Elegba, he is best known for causing trouble and for tricking people, especially friends. He causes fights between neighbors at the market, and he allows people to steal from each other. Eshu-Elegba also steals from the market when he is hungry or when he wants to cause a commotion in the already chaotic marketplace. One story tells of two men who had neighboring farms and were the best of friends. They dressed alike and helped each other in any way they could. Just for fun, Eshu-Elegba decided to cause

trouble between the two. One day, he walked the path between the two farms wearing a multicolored hat. He also had a pipe at the nape of his neck and he let his staff hang over his back instead of his chest where men usually wear it. He greeted the two men, already busy at work, and passed on. Later that day when the two men were discussing Eshu-Elegba's unusual outfit they began to argue over what exactly he had been wearing. Soon they came to blows. Seeing their fight, one of the townspeople called the authorities.

When the two men went before the king, Eshu-Elegba showed up and admitted to starting the fight for sheer pleasure. When the king tried to bind Eshu-Elegba, he fled quickly, started a bush fire, and threw the fire back on the town. A large ruckus began as people flew out of their homes, running for safety, and Eshu-Elegba was seen running out of town, laughing uncontrollably. Eshu-Elegba is known for this kind of destructiveness not only toward humans but also toward animals and other *orisha* as well. Eshu-Elegba is notorious for killing people, causing calamities, and tricking other *orisha* into fighting. One of the songs sung to Eshu-Elegba at his shrines demonstrates his destructive side:

Eshu fought on Iwata street like a
    hundred men.
My father comes with his club.
Eshu is a wicked child, who has inherited
    a sword.
Eshu swings a club, as *Ifa* priest diving
    chain
Eshu, do not deceive and harm me;
    deceive another.

As a child Eshu-Elegba was the ultimate experimenter and broke all the rules. As an old man he has wisdom that takes him far beyond the rules. He does not conform to any of Yoruba regulations, whether they are laws against stealing or social mores that see adultery and fighting with one's neighbors as disruptive. One of the biggest problems for the Yoruba people is Eshu-Elegba's unending appetite, which benefits not only Eshu-Elegba but the other *orisha* as well. Eshu-Elegba's appetite is a concern to people because they are responsible for feeding him; if they do not he will steal food or trick people out of their own food. Feeding Eshu-Elegba takes up not only a great deal of time but also a lot of food resources. In addition, people must be constantly aware of Eshu-Elegba's presence.

Eshu-Elegba satisfies his great appetite and that of other *orisha* by tricking people into sacrificing to different *orisha* and thus into making offerings to him along with the others. In order to get people to sacrifice to the *orisha*, Eshu-Elegba must first fool them into doing something wrong or doing things without consulting the proper *orisha*. Eshu-Elegba uses his powers of transformation to persuade people to steal, to commit adultery, or to refrain from consulting the proper diviners. He may turn himself into a woman and seduce a man, or he may turn himself into a diviner and instruct people to offer more to himself. He may also use special powders, his staff, or the clapping of his hands to illicit the desired response from people. After Eshu-Elegba has tricked a person he may reveal himself to the community to show his power and ensure that others continue to make offerings to him daily. There are several indications in Yoruba culture of the power of Eshu-Elegba's appetite; for example, a popular Yoruba saying is that without Eshu-Elegba the other *orisha* would starve. In carvings and drawings, Eshu-Elegba is regularly depicted with a spoon, which represents both his unending hunger and the necessity of make offerings to him of food and oil.

Although Eshu-Elegba is known for his debauchery, he is also credited with bringing *Ifa*, the Yoruba system of divination, to the world. Without Eshu-Elegba people would not be able to communicate effectively with other *orisha*. Once all the *orisha* were hungry because people had stopped making offerings to them. In order to stop the disrespectful activities of the people and ensure that he and the others would be fed properly, Eshu-Elegba asked Yemaya (another *orisha*) how to set things right. Yemaya said that many *orisha* had already tried to rectify the situation and had failed. Yemaya believed that the situation was doomed. But Eshu-Elegba was not convinced. He decided that he would give people something so good that they would always yearn for more. So he set out in search of this wonderful object. Orungan (another *orisha*) told Eshu-Elegba of a large object made of 16 palm nuts. Eshu-Elegba went to the palm trees, and the monkeys he met gave him 16 nuts, telling him to go to 16 places and hear 16 sayings. Eshu-Elegba did as he was told and returned to the other *orisha* with his new wisdom. The *orisha* decided that they should tell the people of the palm nuts and of the proper way to know the *orisha* and escape evil through the system of *Ifa*. Thus Eshu-Elegba took *Ifa* to the people and ensured that they would always make offerings to the *orisha*.

Eshu-Elegba plays a dual role in Yoruba society; he demonstrates both raw chaos and the importance of order. Eshu-Elegba is both social and antisocial, harmful and helpful, trustworthy and deceptive, entertaining and dangerous. In the character of Eshu-Elegba the Yoruba express the duality of their cosmos; they show that "right" and "wrong" do not exist apart from each other, but that there exists a delicate balance between the two. Eshu-Elegba embodies this constant duality in everything he does, and the Yoruba people celebrate this ambiguity in the shrines, songs, myths and rituals dedicated to Eshu-Elegba. (Bascom 1969a; Bascom 1969b; Pelton 1980; Pemberton 1975; Pemberton 1977; Westcott 1962)

Fai Fale Aitu

Samoa; Hawaii

During the Samoan comedic performances known as *fale aitu* certain performers, the fai fale aitu, become the mediums for *aitu* (ancestors and ghosts), for whom they speak and act. During these performances, the *aitu* speak their wishes, air their grievances, and cause trouble for their living family members. In addition, the fai fale aitu may act spontaneously at weddings, dedications, and other public events, commenting on social values or specific community problems. These informal performances normally take place outside of a public forum and are directed at specific events or toward one certain group. For example, at work or during harvesting, people may spontaneously engage in a comedic performance to make light of the task at hand or to comment on the boss. Unlike scripted performances, these spontaneous ones are mainly performed to elicit laughter and to entertain. The formal *fale aitu*, in contrast, are more concerned with airing grievances and social commentary on a community level.

Both performances are part of a comedic genre of criticism in Samoan society. In fact, these types of performances are the only avenues for social, political, or relational criticism in traditional Samoan society. In Samoan society those in power, or authority figures in general, are accorded great respect and are not confronted directly with grievances or criticism. Instead, public and private comedy sketches, as well as impromptu informal comedic performances, are used to voice criticism. These performances are steeped in the Samoan understanding of relatives, both deceased and living, and of one's obligation to honor and respect those relatives. Therefore, during *fale aitu* performances, the fai fale aitu is seen not as the individual him- or herself but as the ancestor who has chosen to speak through him or her.

In addition to providing internal social commentary, *fale aitu* performances are an avenue for addressing *fengaiga* (respect relationships), especially those between men and women. In addition, these performances are known for their criticism of Western institutions and culture. Since Samoa has been divided since 1962 into Western Samoa and American Samoa, the impact of colonialism has been a constant source of commentary. Western Samoans are politically independent, yet they feel the impact of U.S. and European culture and values on their traditional practices. The *fale aitu* are one way to deal with the impact of outsiders while at the same time avoiding direct conflict.

For example, one performance in the late 1970s dealt with Western medicine and its opposition to Samoan traditional healing practices. During the performance, the actors mimicked the sterile environment of Western medical offices and exaggerated the pains of surgery to demonstrate the differences between the two practices as well as the Samoan opinion that Western medicine is detached, brutal, and involuntary. Through their comedic roles, the performers stressed the differences between medical practices and advocated that Samoan traditional practices be favored. The public forum of these performances allows people

51

to focus on issues but does not force a confrontation. Instead, people are forced to think about the societal issues at hand and the direction of their community. In a society based on small clan groups who are represented by a chief at larger council meetings, these performances are a way of demonstrating to those in power what the important issues are and how people feel they should be dealt with.

The scripted *fale aitu* are rehearsed for weeks before a performance. Actors are chosen, songs are composed, and dances are choreographed around each specific performance. Yet despite this formal preparation, each performance has an element of improvisation. Performers are allowed to improvise during performances and embellish their scenes within certain limits of acceptable behavior, a boundary that performers must learn one performance at a time. Those skilled in the art will be asked to perform again and again and will eventually be involved in the layout and song-writing aspects of the performance. Although women perform, the main performers are normally middle-aged men, with younger males taking the smaller roles while they learn the craft. Women take the lead roles in all-female productions. In contrast to the public male productions, female performances are normally performed only for other women.

As the lead character in a performance, the fai fale aitu is seen as a deceased relative or ghost. That is, his or her humorous commentary and rude antics are not seen as the actor's own but as those of an ancestor. The fai fale aitu delivers the "punch lines" during the performances and from time to time steps out of character to interact with the audience and direct their attention to what the ancestor is saying. At other times, the fai fale aitu will perform as a *fa'afafine*, or transvestite. Dressed as a member of the opposite sex, the fai fale aitu mocks sexual behavior and exaggerates the roles of the opposite sex. As either an *aitu* or a *fa'afafine*,

the performer is not regarded as him- or herself and thus can deliver his or her commentary safely without fear of punishment. (Shore 1977; Shore 1978; Sinavaiana 1992)

Fisi
Kaguru, East Africa: Tanzania
See **Difisi.**

Fool
Europe
Costumed fools entertained European audiences through comedic wit and physical bumbling. The modern day term *fool* comes from the Latin word *follis*, meaning "windbag." The Latin term was applied to these performers both because of their tendency to blow wind and because of their proclivity toward boisterous outbursts.

Fools abounded in the early centuries throughout Europe. By the thirteenth century they were reported entertaining at king's courts and theater squares and had taken on a typical style and dress. Most wore a turned-up or horned hat, carried a bauble or staff, and wore a multicolored robe (see **Harlequin** and **Pulcinello** for examples). Some fools' robes were one color on one side and another on the op-

A seventeenth-century woodcut depicts a traditional European fool on horseback distributing nuts and other goodies to a crowd. (Corbis-Bettmann)

posite side to denote their character as having one foot in the real world and one in the imaginary. Often fools' baubles or staffs were mounted with bells or mirrors, and some of the more offensive ones had pig's bladders attached to them. The fools' staffs were seen as phallic symbols, as the fools themselves used them to imitate sexual acts and exaggerate the size of their penis. Adding to the eroticism of the fools' dress were their hooded hats, which gave them the appearance of a cock. During performances the fools delighted in teasing women, flirting with them, and making mock sexual gestures. Because of their status as fools, they even flirted with the wives of kings, knowing that for fools such behavior was acceptable.

Two of the events in which fools first appeared in Europe were mummers' plays and Morris dances. Mummers' plays were popular in England through the eighteenth century. *Mumming* means to wear a disguise, and in mummers' plays the actors dressed up as many characters, with one of the most popular being the fool. The fool often played the part of the comedic doctor coming to save the people after a battle with their rivals. The fool would appear as the two sides were about to give up and would spout nonsensical dialogue about his travels and the two rival groups. His wordplay and his bumbling movements brought audiences and performers together. In fact, one of the marks of a good fool was his ability to interact with other performers as well as with the audience members.

Morris dancing usually accompanied mummers' plays. The dances got their name from the term *moorish*, referring to anything pagan in medieval Europe. The Morris dance was usually performed by a group of men costumed much like fools. The men danced at many holiday occasions, as well as at local community gatherings. One of the most prominent characters in the dances was the fool. He was set apart from the other dancers by his hat, which was usually made of an animal skin or tail. His job was not only to entertain but to be the master of ceremonies as well. He would entertain the audiences between dances. His antics included lewd dancing, chasing people, and nonsensical singing.

Fools in the mummers' plays and Morris dances set the stage for the popularity of fools, **jesters,** and other clowns throughout medieval and Renaissance Europe (see **Gleemen** for an English example). Not only were fools funny, but they were actors, dancers, jugglers, and acrobats; they further added to their popularity by being a voice of social commentary. One of the most popular tricks of the fools was to come up with rhymes on a whim. They used wordplay to entertain and confuse audiences. In fact, almost any type of wordplay was popular among fools. They delighted in their ability to confuse and manipulate people with their tongue-twisting rhymes, nonsensical prose, and witty songs.

Although most fools were male, there were some popular female fools in Europe. The wife of the Roman philosopher Seneca had a female fool as one of her companions. Another famous female fool was Mathurine, who presided in the French court for many years. She delighted the courts in the late 1500s and early 1600s. She dressed as an Amazon warrior and walked the streets of France jibing people. She also tried vigorously to convert people to Catholicism, sometimes carrying her fun to the point of ridicule.

One of the most famous celebrations accompanying the mass acceptance of fools and their activities was the Feast of Fools. Predating the wide array of fools across Europe, the Feast of Fools was a celebration in which the minor clergy of the Catholic church engaged in roguish clowning, much of it at the expense of their superiors. During the feast, the subordinate clergy would overturn the normal rules of etiquette and respect they showed for the priests. The celebrants wore masks and bright costumes, and some even dressed as women. The laity also got involved by dressing up and joining in on pranks with the clergy. One of the most popular costumes was a hooded robe with donkey's ears. Playing the ass, people were able to embody the spirit of the celebration by turning every situation around. Nothing was left untouched in such celebrations. The boundaries were limitless, and people took advantage of the chaos to use sarcasm and wit to voice their frustrations.

The Feast of Fools flourished throughout Europe as a celebration of the New Year, as a time for reversing the status quo. The participants would run through the streets singing wildly, jeer and chase officials, and even ransack churches. The feast was usually capped by a parade through the main streets of town. Some processions ended with people filling the local church and saying a mock mass. These celebrations persisted throughout Europe into the 1600s. But with many bishops and higher clergy demanding the end to such blasphemous actions, the celebrations waned. Finally, with the Protestant Reformation, the Feast of Fools died out, but the character of the fool remained in carnivals, local plays, and celebrations.

One offshoot of the Feast of Fools was the amateur fool societies whose participants performed skits called *sotties*. Every character in the play was depicted as fool, including the highest-ranking clergy and statesmen. The fools engaged in physical comedy as well as verbal humor to entertain audiences. Their skits satirized the clergy and government officials. Anyone and everyone who held any power was a target for the fools, whose dialogue was harsh. One of the most famous troops was the French Mère Folle. They were known for their caustic social commentary, which often led to reform. In fact, by the second half of the sixteenth century they had over 500 members, including

lawyers and princes and other noblemen. The troop became so popular that it became a voice of reform throughout France. The performers were known for their brilliant comedies that combined wit and ridicule. Their performances were so powerful that those being ridiculed were often subjected to public humiliation and punishment. (Billington 1984; Davidson 1996; Fuller 1991; Welsford 1935; Willeford 1969)

Fulwe
Ila, *Central Africa: Zimbabwe*
See **Sulwe**.

Furna
Sikuani, *Eastern Colombia*
Furna, also known as Furnaminali, Kúwei, Matsuludani, Purna, and Purnaminal, is a creator character who uses his powers to deceive, manipulate, and trick people and animals. He is also responsible for the creation of birds, fish, hunting techniques, fire, the Milky Way, and much else. Although many of the things he creates are beneficial to the Sikuani people, they are usually the byproducts of one of Furna's selfishly motivated escapades.

One of his most important powers is his ability to change his appearance anytime he likes. He often takes the form of animals to satisfy his appetite or to take advantage of unsuspecting females. Furna can change from a man to a turtle to a bird in minutes in order to achieve his goals. He often takes the form of small animals such as ticks, turtles, or birds in order to appear harmless. In the form of a small bird he calls to women to come to him, in the form of a turtle he can crawl down snakes' holes and steal their prey, and as a tick he is known to attach himself to the genitals of a young girl to later take advantage of her.

In Sikuani oral tradition, many animals take on human qualities to demonstrate the negative effects of certain types of behavior without using specifically human characters, which allows the Sikuani to avoid characterizing human beings as the proponents of deception and ill will. Instead, animals with human characteristics demonstrate the same societal concerns. Sikuani oral tradition, then, provides a framework for proper behavior as well as the general order of the world. Characters such as Furna and **Palu** (the rabbit) demonstrate how certain features of the world came into being, as well as the proper and improper use of power or status.

In human or animal form, Furna uses his powers to take advantage of people, to change shape, and to create in order to benefit his own desires. In one story, in which Furna's sexual antics are highlighted, he turned into a tick and attached himself to a snake's vagina in order to marry her. After their marriage, the snake's mother found out who her daughter had really married and attempted to kill him. But Furna changed his brother's flesh into two eagles who carried his mother-in-law off to be eaten by piranhas.

In another story, emphasizing creation, Furna was alone in the world without any women. He wanted to have intercourse with a woman so he created one out of the trees and married her. However, even though married, Furna ignored Sikuani social mores and continued to attempt to have intercourse with his mother-in-law. In one story, Furna changed himself into several handsome looking men and animals in order to gain the love of his mother-in-law, but nothing worked. Finally, Furna laid next to her, pretending to be asleep. Once she fell asleep, he directed his large penis into her and impregnated her without her knowing it.

Almost without fail, stories about Furna end with him on top. Although he deceives people and takes advantage of their weaknesses, he is also respected as a beneficial creator. (Wilbert and Simoneau 1992)

Furnaminali
Sikuani, *Eastern Colombia*
See **Furna.**

G

Gabruurian

Bimin-Kuskusim, *Papua New Guinea*

A wily boy-man being who can take on female and animal attributes and forms, Gabruurian is known for his lack of respect for Bimin-Kuskusim culture. His disrespect is portrayed by his constructing drums improperly, disobeying ritual restrictions, and ignoring sexual taboos. Gabruurian uses his ability to change form to deceive people, and he is not afraid to break any rule to get what he wants. He uses his trickery for selfish ends, ignoring the outcome of his pranks. He is often paired in stories with his female counterpart **Kamdaak Waneng,** whom he tricks as well.

Stories about Gabruurian are moral tales told to young boys during their initiation into adult male societies. These tales stress the importance of following societal rules by highlighting the negative effects of Gabruuian's actions. Although the tales are entertaining, the young boys who hear them are left to ponder the moral dilemmas they pose. Characters such as Gabruurian illuminate the antisocial and immoral traits of human beings. By focusing on characters such as these, the Bimin-Kuskusim allow their youngsters to begin seeing the consequences of their actions at an early age. By the time a boy has reached the age of initiation, he is expected to know right from wrong. In Gabruurian, the boys have a shining example of the "wrong." (See **Utuum-khriin min** for more on Bimin-Kuskusim literary styles.)

In one story, Gabruurian sat in his forest home picking up *tiinba* leaves (sacred leaves used in rituals) and wrapping them around his penis. After he finished, he began to dance and play his drum wildly. After a while Kamdaak Waneng heard the commotion, and she followed the noise to the clearing. Gabruurian saw her immediately and yelled at her to leave. As she ran she tripped and fell against a stone and began bleeding into the stream from which the *dapsaan* marsupial drinks. The *dapsaan,* which is crucial to ritual celebrations and especially initiation ceremonies, was poisoned by the polluting blood. Reviving herself, Kamdaak Waneng ran away to the edge of the clearing, while Gabruurian raged in the distance, angry that he had been discovered.

After he calmed down, Kamdaak Waneng offered him something to eat. Refusing, he ate moss, which the Bimin-Kuskusim consider a dirty food. Ignoring Kamdaak Waneng, Gabruurian began to make another drum from the *kuutok* tree. Not skilled in the art of drum making, Gabruurian made the drum improperly. After making the drum, his giant penis moved beneath Kamdaak Waneng's skirt and she cried, "No I am your *naa-kunum* [kin, literally, 'same person'],'' but he ignored her. After taking advantage of her, Gabruurian went back to making his drum. Gabruurian showed his disrespect for Bimin-Kuskusim society by ignoring social rules that prohibit sexual intercourse between kin and the making of ritual drums by the uninitiated.

Looking for a skin to complete his drum, he used the skin from a *dapsaan* marsupial. Again ignoring proper etiquette, Gabruurian offered nothing to the *dapsaan* in return for his skin; instead, he simply took what he needed. After he was finished, Kamdaak Waneng stole the drum and ran into the forest. Gabruurian looked everywhere for her and for his drum but could find neither. Returning to the clearing, Gabruurian began to eat, and then he danced wildly again. As he did, the *tiinba* leaves fell from his penis showing his gigantic sores. He called for Kamdaak Waneng, but she had fallen into a hole and was covered with rocks. As he sang of death, he turned into a bird and flew into the deep forest.

The story is meant to illustrate the socially unacceptable exploits of Gabruurian. From raping his kin to his improper drum construction, Gabruurian is constantly violating Bimin-Kuskusim social norms. He is punished with the sores on his penis, but he remains powerful, keeping his ability to transform himself into a bird. The boys in the initiation are left to interpret the story themselves and find the moral. (Poole 1983; Poole 1987)

Ganyadjigowa
Seneca, *Northeastern United States*
The mud hen Ganyadjigowa uses her trickery to kill animals to feed her huge appetite. She is also known for naming several things in the material world and planting trees throughout many forests. Ganyadjigowa's activities place her in a curious position in Seneca oral history; she is both a creative and destructive force. Yet stories told about Ganyadjigowa mainly focus on her negative behavior and her ultimate demise at the hands of Gaasyendietha, a fire dragon. By eating Ganyadjigowa, Gaasyendietha showed the Seneca that her deceitful powers were no match for his strength and wit.

Ganyadjigowa deceives and manipulates animals and people alike in her travels throughout the world. She distracts or diverts her unsuspecting prey's attention long enough to trap them. By disguising her appearance and voice, she fools everyone with her tricks; everyone except Gaasyendietha.

It is not simply Ganyadjigowa's appetite that leads her to kill and maim; it is also her *orneda*, a powerful force within her. People, animals, and other beings in the Seneca community have *orneda*. A person's *orneda* can be manipulated in various ways: It can be used for antisocial and destructive activities as well as beneficial and proper actions. Ganyadjigowa chooses to abuse her *orneda* by ignoring Seneca social mores that favor actions that benefit the community. Ganyadjigowa, then, appears in stories as a reminder of the negative repercussions of abusing one's power. (Fenton 1987)

Gidji
Havasupi, *Southwestern United States*
The comedic performer Gidji performs at the Havasupi annual summer dance, which brings people together to celebrate the harvest and to offer their thanks to many members of their community. During the celebration, the man chosen to embody Gidji dresses and acts like his mentor. His body is painted in black and white horizontal stripes, and he wears a headdress with long horns. During the celebration, Gidji forces people to dance by poking and prodding them and pretending to whip them. He plays with the audience throughout the performance, sometimes distracting the other performers. Gidji is similar to the Tewa's **Koshare** performers. Because the Havasupi have no stories about his origin, many scholars believe they adopted the character after many years of contact with the Tewa. See also **Paiyakyamu** for a similar Hopi character. (Spier 1928; Steward 1991)

Gizo
Hausa, *West and Central Africa*
The spider character Gizo (the term *gizo-gizo* means "spider") speaks with a lisp,

lies, cheats, is maliciously cunning, and delights in tricking people, especially those more powerful than himself. His stories are found in the *tatsuniya* genre of oral narratives (see **Dila** for description of this and other genres of Hausa oral narratives). Gizo is usually set against a *zaki* (lion) or a *sarki* (emir or king) in his adventures, both of whom are more powerful than he. *Zaki*, the king of the bush animals, presents a physical challenge for Gizo, and *sarki*, the king of the social and political world in town, presents an ideological challenge for Gizo. The obstacles presented by the *zaki* and the *sarki* exemplify the grand challenges that Gizo enjoys facing. These economical, political, and social challenges are the same as those faced by the Hausa people. Because of the stratification of Hausa society, rural people are constantly under the control of the elite rulers. The stories of Gizo demonstrate the frustrations of the rural Hausa people with the imbalance of power in their society.

Although Gizo often challenges and tricks human beings, the majority of *tatsuniya* tales are set in the bush and portray other animals with human characteristics. The Islamic morals tacked onto the endings of these stories show the effects of Muslim contact. Because many of the Hausa's stories were recorded prior to Muslim contact, scholars have been able to demonstrate the effects of Islamic rule through the stories told by the Hausa.

The storytellers are generally women, and the tales of Gizo are usually told to children. The tales focus on action rather than description because the children are already quite familiar with the character's traits. The *tatsuniya* stories have other deceptive characters such as **Zomo** (the rabbit) and Dila (the jackal). Gizo, however, is the most popular character. Gizo, nicknamed *mai wayo*, the "clever one," lives up to his reputation by continually getting what he wants from others. Often he provokes conflict among others to get food or gifts, but sometimes his pranks are purely for revenge. Gizo can be cruel, killing and maiming to demonstrate his power.

Once when Gizo was cooking fish, a lion came and asked for one to eat. Intimidated by his size, Gizo gave him a fish. After eating the first fish, the lion asked for another and another until Gizo had none left for his wife and children. As they sat in the bush, a bush fowl paraded by, ignoring them both. Gizo said, "How dare she ignore me? I am the one who gave her that beautiful spotted plumage." The lion asked if it was true. "Oh yes," said Gizo. The lion then asked if Gizo would make the same beautiful plumage for him. Gizo hesitated, but the lion persisted so he agreed. However, he warned the lion that it would be a long and difficult process and that he needed a big bush cow and a *kazaura* tree for the process. This was no problem for the big, strong lion, and he set off to get what Gizo requested. The lion came back quickly with a large bush cow, and the two of them killed and skinned it. Then Gizo instructed the lion to find a strong *kazaura* tree, one strong enough that if he hit it, it would not fall over. The lion searched until he found such a tree and then returned to the camp to get Gizo. When they arrived at the tree, they kindled a fire to cook their meat, and the lion broke sticks for a cooking rack. When they were finished eating, Gizo said it was time for the lion to get his beautiful plumage. He told lion to lie down. The lion flung himself down next to the *kazaura* tree. Gizo began to tie him up with the hide from the bush cow. Gizo would occasionally stop and ask the lion if he was bound tightly, and the lion would show Gizo the spots he had missed. Finally, the lion was secured. Gizo went to the fire and picked up the red hot skewers and pressed the skewers one by one into the lion's chest, saying, "That's for my fish." Again and again Gizo repeated the phrase, and again and again he stuck the red-hot skewer into the lion until he was completely covered with spots. Then Gizo left with the meat from the bush cow, leaving the lion behind in agony. In this story, Gizo shows his relentless ability to avenge any wrongdoing and also his ability to trick the strongest of the bush animals.

Another Hausa story reveals Gizo's more mischievous side. Gizo was very hungry but was too lazy to get any food for himself, so he called on his animal friends to help him. He promised them each a share of the food in return for their help. The dung beetle arrived first, followed soon after by the cock. As the cock arrived he saw the beetle's spear and asked Gizo whom it belonged to. Gizo answered that it belonged to the dung beetle and sent the cock inside to wait along with the beetle. When the cock went inside, he killed the dung beetle and sat down to wait for the others. Next, the wild cat arrived. Seeing the spear, he asked whom it belonged to. Gizo said it was the cock's. So the cat went inside and killed the cock. In a similar fashion, the dog arrived and killed the cat, the hyena arrived and killed the dog, and the leopard arrived and killed the hyena. So far, Gizo's plan had worked. He managed to have each of the animals kill their foes and leave the meat for him. But now, he awaited the lion for the big kill.

Soon the lion appeared at Gizo's gate and asked if the others were there. When Gizo replied that only the leopard was inside, the lion went in and attacked him. As soon as they were locked in battle, Gizo grabbed some pepper he had already prepared and sprinkled it in their eyes. When they could no longer see, Gizo grabbed his club and beat them, muttering as he did, "Have you no shame, fighting like this." Soon they were dead, and Gizo and his wife collected all the slain animals, amassing enough meat to last several months. Through his cunning, Gizo was able to stock his cupboard without actually killing many animals himself. He took pride in beating the lion and leopard, for they were supposed to be the strongest animals. Gizo also showed his disrespect and mockery when he chastised the lion and the leopard for fighting in his house.

Gizo is well known for his cunning ability to trick those in power. Some stories depict Gizo as a servant or aid of the king or some other in power. However, he always acts to benefit himself. He reveals the secrets of his employers or of his friends in exchange for gifts. When Gizo is portrayed as working for the *sarki*, he tells the *sarki* about those who have not paid taxes, knowing that he will receive a reward. Gizo's actions both mock the power of the *sarki* and gain rewards for himself. In one story, Gizo secretly made the *sarki*'s son sick and then sought a magical cure. Upon his return with the elixir, the *sarki* rewarded him for saving his son's life.

Gizo does not always prevail in his trickery. Stories in which Gizo fails or is punished for his wrongdoings demonstrate that, like humans, Gizo inevitably will suffer the consequences of his antisocial behavior. In several stories Gizo receives the same treatment that he inflicts upon others. In one story Gizo failed to deceive the half-human ogre of the bush and was branded with hot pokers, just as he had done to the lion. In another story, Gizo entered a contest proposed by the *sarki*: Whoever could harvest the *sarki*'s crop of fruit without eating any of it would be permitted to marry his daughter. Gizo was able to win the contest using underhanded tactics, but after he received his prize, a little bird who had watched the entire event told the *sarki* about Gizo's antics, and Gizo had to give back his bride and face the wrath of the *sarki*. Although the stories of Gizo relate his mischievousness and cunning ability, he is held accountable for his actions. (Johnston 1966; Rattray 1969a; Sigel 1982; Skinner 1968; Skinner 1969)

Glaskap

Algonquian, including Micmac, Passamaquaddy, Penobscot, Ojibwa, and Abenaki, *Northeastern United States; Southeastern Canada*

See **Glooskap.**

Gleemen

Saxon England

Among the many types of **fools** found throughout Europe were gleemen, wandering entertainers known for their seemingly magical abilities as well as their merriment. Known as "wise fools," they wandered from town to town performing skits, singing songs, playing instruments, and telling fortunes. Gleemen were multitalented men who were normally outcasts in their own towns because of their uncanny combination of wit and wisdom. Some gleemen traveled with "glee maidens," women who added acrobatics, sex appeal, and musical performances to the gleemen's shows. However, many women were included in the cast simply for their sex appeal, which led to their being shunned by religious and government authorities. (Billington 1984; Fuller 1991; Towsen 1976)

Glooskap

Algonquian, including Micmac, Passamaquaddy, Penobscot, Ojibwa, Abenaki, *Northeastern United States; Southeastern Canada*

The giant being Glooskap, both a creator and a deceiver, is known among several Native American cultures of the woodlands in the northeastern United States and parts of Canada. He is known for his large stature and stone eyebrows and for his ability to perform superhuman feats. He is known as the preeminent liar, as well as the source of human life. Glooskap loves to use his power, speed, and strength to get what he wants. Even more, however, he uses his wit to trick people into doing what he thinks they should do. Glooskap fashioned people and animals in his quest to populate the world after he killed his malevolent twin brother.

Stories about Glooskap tell of his unpredictability. Glooskap is known for aiding people when they are in need, especially when they are in danger. In one story Glooskap heard that a giant beaver was killing people by causing a flood. Glooskap quickly intercepted the beaver and with his mighty ax cut down several trees to stop the flooding and save the people. Once the water ceased to flow, the beaver had nowhere to hide. Glooskap called the beaver, but the beaver ran the other direction. This so enraged Glooskap that he

This undated illustration of Glooskap shows him defeating a wolf character. Glooskap is a trickster/creator figure in the mythologies of several tribes of the northeastern United States and southeastern Canada. (Werner Forman/Art Resource)

began to swing his giant ax in circles above his head as he raced after him. The beaver swam upstream under the ice hoping to outwit Glooskap, but Glooskap ran beside the stream, and each time he saw the beaver's shadow he would crack the ice with his ax. Glooskap finally caught the beaver. He was so furious when he captured him that he beat him and swung him over his head, throwing him off into the woods. Today, there is a hill that marks the spot where the beaver landed.

In a similar story Glooskap caught a giant moose who was disrupting several villages. For four days Glooskap tracked the moose and finally caught him outside of the woods. When he caught him, Glooskap killed him and threw his insides across a river, where stones now sit marking the spot. Glooskap is known for his savage pursuit of giants and other negative forces in the community. He uses any means necessary to rid the communities of danger and restore harmony.

Some of Glooskap's actions are driven by selfish motivations. Although the end result helps people, he often uses his strength and size to retaliate for what he sees as actions against himself and his creations. For example, after Glooskap created tobacco, a giant grasshopper seized the tobacco for himself. The people called on Glooskap to help them retrieve their tobacco. Glooskap was so outraged that the grasshopper would take what he had intended for the people that he made himself a canoe to reach the island where the grasshopper lived. It was not hard to find the island, for the smoke rising above it was endless. Once Glooskap arrived, he captured the grasshopper without much trouble. He placed the grasshopper underneath his foot and pushed him down to the size grasshoppers are today. Before he left the island he put a pinch of tobacco in the grasshopper's mouth, enough to last a creature of his size for his whole life. Glooskap then returned to the

people with the tobacco he had promised. Although the people were in no immediate danger, Glooskap attacked the grasshopper and changed his size because he saw the grasshopper as being outside of his control and breaking the order he wanted in the community.

Glooskap also uses his skill, intellect, and power to deceive people for purely selfish reasons. Glooskap is notorious for using his superhuman strength to get what he wants from people and animals. He overturns boats, uproots crops, and uses his powerful breath to blow birds and others away from what he believes he should have. He uses his strength and speed to move throughout the world taking what he wants from people. Once Glooskap was annoyed by the wind blowing over his canoe. The wind was not causing any harm; it was only keeping Glooskap from doing what he wanted. Glooskap ran toward the wind bird atop a hill, and when he reached him he told him he wanted to help the bird by moving him to another spot. Trusting Glooskap, the bird allowed him to approach his nest atop the hill. Once Glooskap had the bird in hand, he threw him down the hill, breaking one of its wings and slowing the wind. In another story, Glooskap altered the seasons by tricking the keeper of summer. He approached the keeper and distracted him with a grand story. While telling the story, he used his long arms to steal the box with the mixture for summer weather. With the potion in hand, he went to the keeper of winter and threatened to melt him if he did not reduce the amount of cold. The keeper of winter had no choice but to succumb to Glooskap's wishes, and so winter was shorter from that point on.

Part of Glooskap's association with pranks and deception is his friendship with the skunk. Once, the skunk was a beautiful and witty animal who loved playing tricks on others just to entertain himself. The skunk also held Glooskap in the highest regard. He wanted nothing more than to be with Glooskap all the time and to accompany him on his adventures. The skunk begged Glooskap to allow him to be his cook. Finally, Glooskap agreed, and he had the best meals of his life. The skunk created wonderful meals for Glooskap every night. Then, one night, Glooskap received a message that the snow bird was endangering people with the snowfall. Glooskap needed to leave immediately. The skunk begged and begged Glooskap to let him go with him. Finally, Glooskap gave in and allowed the skunk to accompany him.

Once they reached the snow bird, Glooskap cleverly sweet-talked the bird into dropping less snow. The skunk was so amazed by this that he too wanted to do something great. The next day as they traveled home, the skunk came upon the day bird, who gives light to the world when he spreads his wings. The skunk tried to speak as smoothly as Glooskap had, but the bird would not listen. In haste, the skunk grabbed the bird and tied his wings together. Glooskap saw the scene and went to help the bird, but he could only untie one of his wings. Glooskap was furious with the skunk, so he blew his pipe on him, making him smell bad and defacing his white fur.

Glooskap allowed the skunk to stay with him, and some of the skunk's love of trickery rubbed off on Glooskap. For even though he helps people, Glooskap delights in using tricks to get what he wants from people, monsters, or whomever he encounters. (Beck 1966; Bruchac 1988; Fisher 1946; Helm 1981; Hill 1963; Morrison 1984; Skinner 1914; Speck 1915; Speck 1935; Thompson 1966)

Gluskabe
Algonquian, including Micmac, Passamaquoddy, Penobscot, Ojibwa, Abenaki, *Northeastern United States; Southeastern Canada*
See **Glooskap.**

Gopal
India
See **Bribal.**

Gu-e-krig
Caduveo, *Brazil*
The crafty Gu-e-krig is known for his insatiable sexual appetite and theft. Unlike **Caracara,** whose pranks and improper suggestions are motivated by his desire for power, Gu-e-krig's deceptive activities are always driven by his appetite for sex or food. He is cunning and irresponsible. He never takes care of his family, and he ignores his responsibilities to work and contribute to the community. With such qualities, Gu-e-krig is a model of what Caduveo culture considers inappropriate. The Caduveo are a small community who rely on the cooperation and support of each member of society to sustain themselves (see **Caracara** for more on Caduveo society). Because of his indolence and lack of respect for women, other people's property, and others' diligent work habits, Gu-e-krig represents the antitheses of proper behavior.

Gu-e-krig is most often described as a man. Although human in form, he has the ability to change his appearance and disguise himself in many ways, and changing his appearance is his most common way of deceiving people. But he also uses his creative intelligence to deceive people with "smooth talk." He has the ability to convince people of things they would normally never believe simply by his artful way with words and his soothing gestures. People are continuously driven to accept his false claims and to accept his unbelievable stories without question.

In one story, Gu-e-krig heard that a man had died in a nearby village. Knowing that the widow would be vulnerable, he went to the village and convinced her and her relatives that he was her dead husband's brother. According to Caduveo tradition, such a status would put Gu-e-krig in the position to marry and take care of the woman. Gu-e-krig showed up at the village wailing and mourning in the customary fashion. He approached the widow and immediately began to take care of her, as a brother-in-law should. He hunted for her and took care of her land and then after a few days he wanted to have intercourse with her. The woman was still in mourning, but Gu-e-krig convinced her that he was her rightful husband now and that she should have sex with him. Unsure of her proper duties, the woman asked her mother. Her mother, not able to see through Gu-e-krig's deceptions, told her that it was the proper thing for her to do. Finally the woman gave in and had sex with Gu-e-krig. That night while the woman slept, Gu-e-krig left the village, having succeeded once again.

Although Gu-e-krig is usually successful in his adventures, he also gets caught and is often beaten up by women, men, and animals whom he has deceived. In one story, Gu-e-krig heard a group of girls working in a small building. The girls were busy sewing for their day's wages when Gu-e-krig waltzed into the building, sat down in a corner, and began to tell stories. The girls did not notice him at first. But he began to laugh out loud and wave his arms around while he told his fanciful stories. Slowly the girls peered in his direction, and one brave girl asked if she could sit and listen to his tales. "No" shouted Gu-e-krig. He never allowed people to listen to his tales. The more he denied their plea, the more interested the girls became, and they gathered at a distance to listen. Gu-e-krig laughed to himself as his plan for seducing the girls came together. One by one the girls gathered in a circle around him, listening to his fantastic tales. As night fell, the girls became sleepy and laid down on the floor. After the last one fell asleep, Gu-e-krig went to each one, took off her clothes, had

intercourse with her, and left a small stick in her vagina. After he had taken advantage of all the girls, he switched their clothes around and sneaked out, smiling and singing quietly to himself.

When the girls awoke, they knew something was wrong because they all had on the wrong clothes and as each stood up she felt the stick break in her vagina. Knowing that Gu-e-krig had taken advantage of them, the girls were furious and plotted revenge. Knowing the girls would be upset, Gu-e-krig ignored them in the village and went about his business pretending nothing had happened. A few of the girls approached him, but he ignored them. The girls begged him to tell them more stories. They heaped praise on him and sobbed. Gu-e-krig tried to ignore them, but finally the leader of the girls came up to him and asked him to join her in her private room. Fighting his desire, Gu-e-krig declined, but the girl persisted and was able to seduce Gu-e-krig. Once he was in her room and in bed with her, the door was flung open and the other girls attacked him, beating and scratching him until not one bit of his body was left unharmed. (Hopper 1967; Métraux 1946a; Oberg 1949; Wilbert and Simoneau 1990)

Guguyni

Tanaina, *Alaskan Subarctic Region*

The raven Guguyni is notorious for outsmarting people. Guguyni is able to disguise himself and to transform himself into many different characters in order to get the results he desires from any situation. Guguyni uses his intellect, wit, and charm to manipulate and deceive people, especially when he desires a woman. Guguyni is known for taking advantage of women, even those who are socially forbidden to him, such as married women and his own relatives. Guguyni takes advantage not only of women but his male relatives as well.

Totem poles often depict a variety of characters from tribal mythology, such as Guguyni, the raven-trickster of the Tanaina people of Alaska. (Corbis-Bettmann)

Stories about Guguyni tell of him stealing from and breaking confidence with those with whom he entered into a *slocin* (that is, "blood-brother") relationship. For the Tanaina, a *slocin* is a relationship of mutual respect and reciprocity that one does not enter lightly. Guguyni, however, perverts the *slocin* partnership by lying to, cheating, and even harming those to whom he has pledged his support and respect.

Guguyni steals, lies, cheats, and manipulates at will. He disregards Tanaina cultural norms by imposing his will on the community without taking into consideration the needs of others. The Tanaina social organization is based on the interworking of two clans. The Tanaina clan system follows the female family line, meaning that children inherit land, wealth, and social status based on their mother's family. The mother's family, then, determines the relationships with-

in a clan. Being in good relations with one's clan members includes sharing and contributing to clan-owned property, assisting in funeral and other ceremonies, and entering into arranged marriages.

Although some of these practices have been abandoned or changed in the last 100 years with European settlers in the area, the Tanaina social system remains focused on reciprocal relationships as the basis for their lifestyle. The area of southwestern Alaska they occupy is rich in berries, plants, fish, and wild game, which means that the Tanaina face relatively few hardships, as compared to their neighbors in the interior regions. When the Russians brought the fur trade to the Tanaina in the early 1800s the Tanaina joined the fur trade, incorporating the Russians into their social system. The Russians, however, much like Guguyni, took advantage of the Tanaina, and the result was animosity, war, and strife. Stories of Guguyni encompass the Tanaina's conflicts with the Russians and others by focusing on the negative effects of irresponsible and socially unacceptable behavior.

Guguyni uses his powers to create and destroy at will. He mixes any number of potions to distract people, to disorient them, or to manipulate them into doing what they know is wrong. In one story, Guguyni changed his appearance to that of a very wealthy, handsome man. Upon meeting a beautiful young woman, he turned his powers to winning her affection and marrying her. Knowing that her father was very rich, Guguyni intended to have intercourse with her and then steal her father's wealth. After spending the night with his new bride, he changed back into a raven to steal her riches. As he was collecting the money, the girl's mother awoke and saw his long, black beak sticking out from underneath the blanket on his head. She screamed, and her husband grabbed Guguyni to ring his neck, but the crafty Guguyni slid from his grip and was not hurt.

Guguyni is normally directed by his appetite in harmless pranks and manipulations. For example, when walking in the forest he will shrink food that is too large or make fruit fall from branches that are too high. In one story Guguyni persuaded some villagers that he would catch enough fish by himself for all of them. Caught in his spell, they lent him their equipment and sent him off. After catching and eating the fish, Guguyni rubbed blood and entrails on his body and returned to the village telling the people that all the fish had gotten away; the people were left hungry.

At times Guguyni's actions are beneficial to the Tanaina. His course of action, however, is normally a result of his selfishness, egotism, and destructiveness. In one story, Guguyni tricked the man who had stolen the sun and moon into dropping them into his trap. Although he had wanted the sun and moon for himself, when he threw them into the sky they lit the entire world. With his manipulative ability, however, he directed the sun and moon to change the seasons according to his own wishes. (Osgood 1937; Turner and Edmonds 1968; Vaudrin 1969)

Hagondes

Iroquois, *Northeastern United States*

Hagondes, commonly known as "Long Nose," is a humorous member of the False Face society, a masked medicine society that focuses on healing "red diseases," including nosebleeds, paralysis, and muscular disorders. One becomes a member of the False Face society by dreaming about a particular mask one may wear or a ritual one may perform, or one may be invited by current members to join. The False Face society members, as well as members of other masked societies, are united by their powers to heal through their masked ritual performances.

The Society of Faces to which these performers belong originates from Iroquois hunters who encountered humanlike beings in the forests on their hunts. These beings were known for their strange bodies and disfigured faces. They hid in trees and preyed on unsuspecting hunters. Once the hunters were able to speak to the beings, they agreed to leave the hunters alone if the hunters gave them offerings of tobacco and cornmeal. These "faces of the forest" also held the power to cure and control disease. Through dreams the faces of the forest instructed the Iroquois to carve masks in their likenesses and to perform ritual dances to heal the sick among the Iroquois. In addition the faces of the forest showed the Iroquois how to burn tobacco and sing curing songs to invoke the faces' power. In the grip of such power, the False Face performers are able to scoop up white-hot ashes during their performances without being burned.

Hagondes is a well-known False Face character who is said to reside in tall trees in the forest and scare people as they walk beneath him. One story tells of a young boy

This Native American mask collected in 1913 represents Hagondes, a humorous member of the False Face society. (Werner Forman/Corbis)

who did not believe in Hagondes. Although his mother warned him of Hagondes's pranks, the boy did not believe her. To prove to her that Hagondes did not exist, he went to the tree where Hagondes was supposed to live. He climbed high in the tree and waited for someone to pass by. Soon two boys walked beneath the tree, and he heard them say, "There are two of them," as they ran away. The boy could not figure out why the others had said that until he felt some branches falling on him. He looked up and there was Hagondes, with his long nose and crooked smile, laughing at him. The boy scampered down the tree and ran home, possessed by Hagondes. He got a nosebleed and was very sick for days. When he awoke, he told everyone what Hagondes had done.

In ritual performances, Hagondes maskers wear a buckskin mask with an elongated, slim nose, oblong eyes, and a crooked smile. Each False Face mask is carved by a performer and worn only by that person. Masks are carved in response to dreams in which a person is shown the mask by a specific False Face ancestor. However, individual maskers do have some freedom in how their masks are adorned. It is common for a person who is sick to dream of a mask and then perform wearing the mask. After a person dreams of a False Face, he must make the mask and wear it in ritual performances to avoid any negative reactions from the False Faces.

Hagondes is best known for his comedic actions during ritual performances and his ability to provoke fear in children. During ritual performances, Hagondes performers dance ecstatically, out of step with the other performers, they chase people, and they act obscenely. Hagondes's activities during rituals coincide with his classification in myths as a comedic and malevolent character. Parents threaten their children with the wrath of Hagondes if they misbehave. Stories about Hagondes describe him taking naughty children away from their parents to his dark home in the forest. If children act up, it is said that a kinsman will appear with a large basket, scoop up the children, and take them to Hagondes's home in the forest. At other times Hagondes uses his power to make adults sleep while he chases young children in the dark and mimics their cries for help. Stories about Hagondes also tell of him eating children and maiming adults in his tirades. (Fenton 1941b; Fenton 1987; Isaacs and Lex 1980; Parker 1909)

Han mane 'ak su
Rotuma, *South Pacific*

Han mane 'ak su means "the woman who plays the wedding." A han mane 'ak su is invited to all Rotuman weddings. She is normally an elderly woman affiliated in some way with the bride's family. She is said to "play" the wedding because of her merrymaking antics and humorous pranks on the groom's family and guests. As an invited performer, the han mane 'ak su is free to do as she pleases in regard to the groom's family and guests. She is expected to tease, chase, chastise, and mock the people during her performance, which begins prior to the actual ceremony and continues throughout the night. (See also *Sega* for an example of female comedic performers in Lusi-Kaliai society.) Her performance highlights the division between the two families as well as the union that the wedding signifies.

In Rotuman society comedic performers are part of many ceremonies, yet none plays such an integral role as the han mane 'ak su. She illuminates the values and traditions of Rotuman society through her caricature of and disrespect for those values. In Rotuman society people are grouped together through common ancestral bonds that link them to a specific kin group, land, wealth, and inherited titles such as chief. Although many of the roles are only ceremonial today, the importance of one's kin group and the affiliations it creates can be seen in Rotuman weddings.

Even before the introduction of Christianity in 1839, Rotumans valued female chastity highly, and they expected virginity of a bride. During her performance, the han mane 'ak su inverts the ideal of female chastity by engaging in sexual burlesque, and she calls attention not only to the bride's chastity but also to the sexual exploits of the groom. The people of Rotuma value proper relationships that hinge on a monogamous family unit and a larger extended familial group. At Rotuman weddings the bride's and groom's families enter into an agreement of cooperation and mutual respect. Upon his wedding the groom and his family enter a formal relationship with the bride's family, and with the union comes many new responsibilities. By mocking the sexual nature of their relationship, the han mane 'ak su brings to the fore a touchy subject that is not otherwise openly talked about.

During her performance the han mane 'ak su stretches the bounds of the bride's family's respect by inverting the respect relationship and dispensing with tradition and proper behavior. Normally, the guests at a wedding show the utmost respect for the bride and her family. The han mane 'ak su mocks that respect by dressing as a man and performing mock sexual antics. In addition, she chases the groom's family and beats them or cons them out of money. She may order a chief to dance or a group of men to drink. She uses her power in this setting to highlight the division of power in normal everyday life. Dressed as a man she exaggerates the male attributes of powerfulness by shouting orders and using her stick to get people to do what she wants. The han mane 'ak su is at her best when she gets the most powerful of men to wait on her, dance with her, and carry out her wishes. By inverting the normal power roles, the han mane 'ak su both entertains and calls attention to the possibility that power might be abused. That is, she highlights the flexibility in the seemingly inflexible "norms" of society.

The han mane 'ak su must see that the guests are entertained and that the groom's family and guests are mocked without taking her antics too far. There are no written rules of conduct; her relationship with the bride's family and her understanding of Rotuma values guide her performances. The line she treads is thin. If she is to be paid well for her services and asked to perform again, she must not cross over into offensive behavior, but she must always be entertaining.

Relatives and other guests chime in with their commentary, helping the han mane 'ak su in her pursuits or bantering with others in the audience. While most of the banter and entertainment is going on, the people ignore the bride and groom, who sit quietly watching the antics. The newlyweds are exempt from the ridicule of the han mane 'ak su. Their role is to acknowledge both families and concentrate on their new responsibilities as members of a larger kin group.

Rotuman society values harmony, extended family units, sensitivity, and polite, nonjudgmental behavior. The han mane 'ak su and other comedic performers provide an outlet for social criticism and a way to bring about changes in values. While inverting the normally accepted values of the culture, the han mane 'ak su are engaged in an ongoing revival of their values as a society. Even European influence has not diminished the role of comedic performers, especially of the han mane 'ak su, who not only entertains but forces people to look at the choices they are making and the impact of those choices on others to whom they are related. (Andersen 1969; Hereniko 1992; Hereniko 1995; Malo 1975; Rensel 1991)

Harlequin
Europe

The heroic prankster Harlequin was one of the precursors to the court fools as well as to the modern-day circus clowns. His name is derived from Hellequin, a figure from German folk legend who was known as the leader of a horde of ghosts and pranksters. The character was popular in the Italian commedia dell'arte, where he was known as Arlecchino, between the sixteenth and eighteenth centuries. (See also **Pulcinello** for another popular character of this time.)

One of several Harlequin paintings by the nineteenth-century French artist Paul Cézanne illustrates the traditional diamond-patterned costume. (Francis G. Mayer/Corbis)

Once his style and characterizations became popular throughout Europe, he became known as Harlequin, a popular pantomime, fool, and all around merrymaker.

As a performer Harlequin not only poked fun at others with his humorous antics but was also an acrobat, singer, dancer, and juggler. He wore many disguises and was one of the first of this type of performer to wear the multicolored costume with patches and diamond shapes that later became a trademark for **fools** throughout Europe.

Harlequin played the part of the hero in performances. He had magical powers that allowed him to transform himself at a moment's notice and swoop in acrobatically to rescue others. His acrobatics were among his most popular feats. On stage he would swoop through fire, leap across swords, and perform other daring acts. He would almost always rescue the damsel in distress, carrying her away to safety.

In addition to his heroics, however, Harlequin was also a prankster. He delighted audiences with his bumbling dances, humorous songs, and precarious juggling. Playing the fool, he would rouse audience members with his follies. Harlequin was known as a character who would race about the stage dodging balls, laughing in the face of "normal" characters, and jeering at the audience, lunging at them with canes, sticks, and so on. The Italian plays that featured the Harlequin character were the most popular of that era. His magical feats made him seem invincible, and indeed he never ended up the dupe. (Billington 1984; Fuller 1991; Mayer 1969; Oreglia 1968; Towsen 1976)

Hauka
Songhay, *West Africa: Niger*

The Hauka are a family of ancestors of the Songhay. The Hauka movement began in Niger with the French invasion. Prior to French rule the Songhay had recognized five families of ancestral spirits with whom they interacted during ritual performances; the Hauka are the sixth. During Hauka performances, ancestors take over the bodies of people whom they use as mediums to let their wishes be known and to request certain actions of the Songhay. Through these communications with their ancestors the Songhay maintain their communities.

With the French invasion that began in 1898 the Songhay, along with other native peoples of Niger, were forced by the French to give up their traditional governments, economies, educational systems, and religious practices. Although the Songhay attempted a rebellion, the French were too powerful to resist. The Hauka movement represents one of the lasting ways in which the Songhay have dealt with their French colonizers and other outsiders.

Songhay *holey hori* ("possession dances") are those in which ancestors take over the bodies of people to let their wishes be known. The first instance of a Hauka performance was in 1925. Prior to that, the Hauka ancestors had not revealed themselves to the Songhay. However, since their appearance in 1925 they have never left. The Hauka ancestors are both horrific and humorous; they imitate generals, government officials, missionaries, and other recent arrivals during their performances.

The Hauka mock the actions, intentions, speech, and mannerisms of all their French invaders. Government officials and educators are among the most popular targets because they are the most disruptive to traditional Songhay culture. Government officials forced the Songhay to give up their system of government, which rendered the chiefs mute and disrupted their whole system of societal checks and balances. Further, educators took the children out of their homes and taught them French customs and language. As a result children were cut off from the traditional way of learning their culture—through the informal instruction of their parents and relatives—and generations of Songhay were deprived of their traditions.

The Hauka mock officials' intentions and actions by exaggerating their importance and parodying their authority. For example, a Hauka member may carry a large stick and pretend to write in French on a chalkboard. All the while he may speak in a broken Songhay dialect to show the actual inferiority of the French. Another popular Hauka is a doctor. The Hauka mimic doctors by carrying large syringes and chasing around audience members, holding them down and injecting them with medicine. Their actions bring the crowds to laughter and encourage social criticism. Although the Song-

hay won their independence from the French in 1960, the Hauka continue to perform as the voice of ancestors who do not want to see foreign ways take over tradition.

The Hauka relatives have taken it upon themselves to be the voice of social commentary for the Songhay. Speaking and acting through individual Songhay, the Hauka have continued to be a powerful voice in Niger. Typically the Hauka perform in public places. During their performances they foam at the mouth, their bodies are contorted, and they convulse (the word *hauka* literally means "craziness"). This sight horrified French officials, who attempted, with no success, to outlaw the Hauka performances.

Once an ancestor has taken over a person's body, he or she mocks anyone and everyone. A Hauka performance includes interaction with audience members, especially if there happen to be any foreigners in the crowd. The Hauka's favorite activity is to mock the ways of outsiders and make them feel uncomfortable. They engage them in wordplay, mock their dress, and mimic their speech. The Hauka are at times terrifying because their mockery can be physical. They hit people, throw things around, and directly chastise outsiders. The Hauka inspire fear and laughter by their complete disrespect for any authority and their willingness to say or do anything. They are not awed by authority figures. In fact, they delight in making authority figures uncomfortable by getting the audience involved in their mockery. (Courtney 1974; Kanya-Forstner 1969; Stoller 1977; Stoller 1984)

Healing

Although tricksters and clowns are best known for their destructive tendencies, many go beyond trickery and also have the ability to heal people or animals through their own actions or through the use of natural powers. Although it may seem ironic that the same characters who mock society and cause trouble also heal others, it is part of the multifaceted nature that makes tricksters and clowns powerful. The power that they have to deceive, in other words, can also be used in a positive manner if they so choose.

Several clown societies possess the power to heal along with their role as comedic performers in ritual celebrations. For example, the Zuni **Newekwe** clown society uses several different types of medicines; they dance and sing over the sick person rubbing medicine onto the painful area or spitting the medicine into their patient's mouth in order to heal him or her. In addition to their healing, however, they are notorious for running around during ritual performances eating bits of refuse, small insects, and rodents and drinking dirty water. The Newekwe show the balance between their power to heal and their power to shock and entertain during performances in which they do both.

Horangi, the Korean tiger, aids village shamans, who communicate with him when they need to heal an ill person. It is through Horangi's power that the shamans are able to heal the sick. Similarly, the coyote **Ma'ii,** one of the chief protectors of Navajo people, appears in Navajo myths as a master of pranks and shape-shifting and in rituals as a healer. Navajo singers call on him to cure the ill, and the Navajo pray to Ma'ii to bring forth his power. See also **Anaanu, Dahusúi, Fai Fale Aitu, Hagondes, Heyoka, Nanawitcu, Niyel Carnival, To Ninilii,** and **Yenaldlooshi** for more examples.

Heho
Fon, *West Africa: Benin*
See **Legba; Yo.**

Hermes
Greece
Hermes, the clever, deceitful, erotic, and paradoxical messenger and interpreter in Greek mythology, is known both as "the god most loving of human beings" and as "the shameless one." He represents the continuity between the human and the divine within ancient Greek mythology. The son of Zeus and Maia, he is descended from the original triad of Greek gods, Chaos, Eros, and Gaia, and is the most human of the gods. He acts as an intermediary between humans and gods, and as such he lives between the human and the divine realms, not quite belonging to either.

Hermes plays a multifaceted role and is known for his many creations benefiting human beings. He is responsible for bringing the art of astronomy to humans, as well as the musical scale, hunting techniques, diving, libraries, fire, and sacrifice, just to name a few. His positive side is that of creator and restorer. A fight between his two giant arms helped humans understand the benefit of cooperation over individualism. He assists in births and is known as the "male midwife." He is a physician, a master of herbs, and a healer; as a healer he is not limited to medicines: He improved Charon's sight by singing a powerful song. Hermes also acts as the prototype for human physicality. His unusually long penis is shortened so it does not have to be carried in a box, and his intestines are tucked neatly into his body.

The list of Hermes' creations, however, can be equally matched by the list of his pranks, deceptions, thefts, and masquerades. His sense of humor was apparent from his birth, for he came into the world laughing. He teases Aphrodite, he steals his mother's clothes while she is bathing, and he mocks the great god Zeus. Not even family members are spared his jokes and pranks. He especially loves to tease his brother Apollo. He steals his brother's cat-

A depiction from a late-fifth-century wall of the Greek god Hermes with the infant Dionysis. (Corbis-Bettmann)

sexual liaisons with gods and goddesses as well as human beings. In fact, it is through phallic images that Hermes was most often represented in Greek society. In ancient Greece the first representations of Hermes were a single erect phallus. The classic image expanded upon the early representations by adding wings and the head of Hermes on top of the erect phallus. Herms, as they are known, were found throughout ancient Greece, especially as markers of boundaries, such as entrances to homes and villages, and as mile markers along roadways. In addition, many festivals revolved around Hermes as the erotic. People celebrated his sexual freedom by leaving their inhibitions behind and engaging in sexual encounters with others. Either literal or symbolic, the sexual freedom is usually accompanied by the reversal of standard social roles, during which time people mock those in power.

As both a creator and a deceiver Hermes rests at the margin of society. He uses humor and wit to gain control over others, while at the same time using his ability as an interpreter to aid others. As a master interpreter Hermes shows the quality most useful to human beings. He guides people by using his insight into the deeper meanings of actions, events, and relationships. He directs people in social activities, he shapes the boundaries of politics, and he defines the limits of military power. In fact, his association with interpretation leads to his common association with speech and language. He brought speech to the world by giving human beings tongues. Because of this association, on ritual occasions people take the tongues of those who have died and sacrifice them to Hermes.

In Greek mythology Hermes is depicted as a paradoxical member of the Greek pantheon. He is at once an old man and a baby, a thief and a lawyer, a man and a woman; he resides in the country as well as the city. As a god who can be found in any and all parts

tle and turns their hooves around. Then he uses his power to turn himself into dust and squeeze back into his home through the keyhole so he can say he never "walked" out of his home. Hermes steals from everyone and then claims not to have committed the theft, thus perjuring himself.

Sometimes Hermes' comedic side goes hand in hand with his creative abilities. For example, in one story Hermes disguised himself to trick the goddess Hera into believing he was her son. When Hera believed Hermes to be her son, he drank from her breast. But she knew something was wrong, and she pulled him away from her. When she fled, the milk that sprayed out became the Milky Way.

In addition to his trickery and humor, Hermes is notorious for his playful eroticism, which connects his humorous nature with his lustful tendencies. He has many of Greek life, Hermes represents the entirety of the cosmos. His pranks and deceptions and his creations and interpretations make him a symbol of the many different aspects of the universe. (Athanassakis 1976; Doty 1978; Doty 1991; Doty 1993; Godolphin 1964)

Hero

Hero characters are those who deliberately help the community. One of the most paradoxical aspects of tricksters and clowns is that they are often both the most destructive and the most creative and beneficial of beings. With powers to deceive as well as to heal, tricksters and clowns cross the line from merely being pranksters to ushering in harmony, well-being, and happiness.

The hero aspect of clown and trickster characters highlights their multifaceted, complex natures. They are never what one thinks they are, and just when they seem to be predictable they break the monotony by overturning everything they have previously done. A hero stands above the crowd and defends a community against outsiders, natural disasters, and internal strife. Tricksters do just that.

Nanabozhoo, the Algonquian giant, helped in the creation of the Algonquian people and brought them fire. He saves them from outsiders and protects them from floods. He is continually using his superior strength and intellect as well as his ability to change shape to help his fellow tribesmen. In return, the Algonquian people honor him through ceremonies and sacrifices.

Maui, the trickster hero of the South Pacific, is also known for graciousness. Maui saves islanders from the wrath of an evil monster and brought the sun and moon to their present courses. Without Maui the people would have never survived the darkness and cold.

Heroes are plentiful in cultures the world over. But trickster and clown heroes shed new light on the meaning of that role. Far from being perfect members of the community, they walk the line between hero and malicious pranksters. By showing the flexible nature of the hero role, tricksters and clowns show the unpredictable nature of the universe itself. See also **Brhannada, Glooskap, Kalulu, Koyemshi, Ma'ii, Sri Thanoncha, Tenali Rama,** and **Wanto** for more examples.

Heyoka

Lakota, *Plains Region of the United States*
The term *heyoka*, meaning "foolish," "silly," or "contrary to nature," takes on several connotations for the Lakota. It can refer to a state of being, to one incarnation of Wakinyan, and to those human beings who dream of Wakinyan and act ridiculously in ceremonies. *Heyoka* refers to any person or being who acts ridiculously or out of the ordinary. People are deemed to be heyoka only when their behavior warrants the label, not forever. In addition, however, the Heyoka society is composed of people who have dreamed of Wakinyan (the Winged One, or Thunderbird) and who are forever different from other Lakota.

Wakinyan was given a double personality by Inyan (the Rock), the creator of much of Lakota life. Inyan made Wakinyan a terrible-looking creature with a harsh voice, a large beak with sharp teeth, and eyes of lightening. His normal state is anger, although he loves to contradict himself and be pleasant when he looks furious and furious when he looks pleasant. When Wakinyan is amiable, he is known as Heyoka, his other personality. As Heyoka, he restores people to a normal state after he has frightened them as Wakinyan.

Heyoka society members are associated with both Wakinyan and his alter ego Heyoka, and they are considered to be heyoka. They live their lives apart from and in contradiction to the rest of Lakota society. They follow the direction of Wakinyan, in that they are frightening and powerful, as well as of Heyoka, in that they are silly and foolish and delight in pulling pranks. During ritual activities members of the Heyoka society perform normal actions backward; for example, they walk or talk backward, they wear no clothes in the winter and dress fully in the summer, and they eat dog food or other things not usually consumed by humans. People who are not members of the Heyoka society avoid looking at the sky during thunderstorms so as not to see Wakinyan, because anyone who sees Wakinyan or any of his followers is in danger of becoming heyoka.

Heyoka members perform a ceremony called *Heyoka Woze*. During this ceremony the members dance clumsily around a fire with a large pot in the middle. Two of the heyoka *wowaxi* (helpers) strangle a dog, singe it completely, and cut it up. The dog meat is then placed in the large pot of boiling water; the dancers plunge their hands into the boiling water, commenting on how cold it is, and pull out the meat without being burned. They dress in rags, scare children, and call out crude and obnoxious remarks to the audience. In their role as heyoka the members enact the ridiculous side of Lakota life, entertaining people but also showing that their power can be used to manipulate and bring about disaster.

Members of the Heyoka society are united by their connection to Wakinyan. Each member has been visited by Wakinyan in a dream or vision, and they must perform that vision to the community or they will become sick and may even die. Dreams and visions are an important part of the Lakota way of life. In English both the term *dreams* and the term *visions* have been used to name the state that one is in when one receives information and guidance from other beings in the cosmos. The difference is that a vision is something that one seeks, either through fasting or prayer,

and a dream is something that one is given or receives without effort. People gain knowledge and instruction from people, animals, and other beings they meet in their dreams or visions. People become connected or related to the other beings in their dreams and visions by enacting what they have been shown for the community. If a person dreams of a buffalo or a dog, then he becomes part of the buffalo or dog society; by acting out his dreams or visions a person brings forth the power of another being in the universe, and from that point on he is associated with that other being.

Heyoka society members enact their dreams or visions in a ritual called *Heyoka Kaga*. What a member does during the ritual depends on his dream or vision. A member who dreamed of healing or medicine from a certain animal must kill that animal and carry it or wear it on his body to show his connection with the animal and his power to heal. Heyoka members share the power to heal with other animals and beings in the Lakota universe. (See **Iktomi.**) Because of their association with Wakinyan, all Heyoka society members share in the power to heal, although not all hold the same power. Heyoka members are well respected because of their healing power and because they are able to perform dangerous feats without being harmed. Their humorous and crude activities display one half of their personalities; like Wakinyan, they also possess the power to destroy or harm what they have healed. (Buechel 1978; Deloria 1932; Feraca 1963; Jahner 1977; Powers 1975; Walker 1980; Walker 1982; Walker 1983)

Horangi
Korea

Horangi, the tiger, is an ambiguous character in Korean folktales and religion. The ambiguity is reflected in his name, which derives from the Chinese character *ho*,

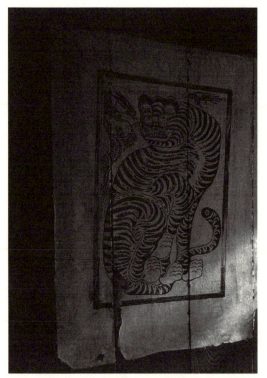

Like many other tricksters, the character of the tiger in Korean folktales is an ambivalent one. Here its image is used as a guardian, protecting a farmhouse in Kyonggi-do, South Korea. (Michael Freeman/Corbis)

"tiger," and *rang*, "young boy." The name *Horangi* thus contains the contradictory notions of the playfulness and harmlessness of a young boy and the power and danger of a tiger. As a character in folktales Horangi pushes social and cultural norms to the edge, challenging all that is proper in Korean society. He can be foolish, greedy, vengeful, fierce, cunning, or idiotic depending on the situation. His many different faces are part of his appeal. In addition, within Korean traditional religious activities he is found as a companion to powerful shamans and is a master of healing himself and others.

Stories of Horangi emphasize his ambiguous nature. He is seen as a mockery both to traditional life and to the accepted cosmic order. He tricks and manipulates people, but oftentimes his pranks also result in beneficial outcomes for Koreans. For ex-ample, Horangi acts as a mediator between humans and deities, allowing people to pay their respects and honor their deities without harm. He helps shamans in their quest to heal and to free people from bad spirits. In many stories Horangi is paired with the mountain spirit *san sin*. Horangi mediates between *san sin* and humanity and thus helps people with funeral rites and other religious events. Horangi and *san sin* are depicted together in Korean sculptures, paintings, and shrines. Together the two depict the reciprocal aspects of the relationships among humans, nonhumans, and spirits within the cosmos.

Part of Horangi's association with power comes from Koreans' interactions with tigers. According to tradition, Korean villagers once came face to face with tigers in their everyday lives. Many tigers lived in the forests surrounding Korean villages, and they were known for night raids in which they would carry people off. In fact, Korean parents would scare their children by telling them that if they did not behave a tiger would carry them into the woods. Only the fiercest of hunters were able to catch tigers, and those who did were seen as powerful, brave, and wise. A hunter needed to be wise to outsmart the tiger, but once he did he could tap into the tiger's powers. A hunter helped by a tiger was almost unstoppable. The power, cunning, and strength he acquired from the tiger enabled him to challenge any animal in the forest and almost guaranteed victory.

Stories about Horangi tell of his many powers. He is able to transform himself into a human or to disguise himself as another animal or some other natural feature in order to trick people. He has the ability to fly, hurl lightning, and throw fire to get out of any situation. Typically, storytellers begin their tales about Horangi with the introduction "Long ago, when tigers smoked long pipes." People know that the story will mix human and animals traits and focus on the cunning adventures of Horangi.

Korean folktales pit Horangi against villagers, Buddhist monks, other animals, and powerful shamans. His antics are used both as social and personal commentary. Storytellers use Horangi to air their grievances about societal issues, such as problems with government officials, young people, or neighboring villages. In one story, Horangi's tricks revealed a hypocritical Buddhist monk to villagers. In another, he outwit the deity *hananim* to allow the sun and moon to take their present courses. However, in the same story he was duped by two children into believing that their reflections in a pond were the children themselves. Chasing the reflections, he allowed the children to get away, and he looked the fool. His actions, however, are not always without negative outcomes. He is notorious for his fierce appetite, which propels him to devour human beings and unsuspecting animals. In one story, he changed his appearance and coaxed an old woman into his den only to spring on her and devour her whole when she entered.

Another story, in which Horangi helped a farmer that he met, shows not only his compassionate side but his powerful insight into human nature as well. The farmer was a kind man, but unfortunately he was married to a mean woman. One day the woman threw him out of the house, and he met Horangi as he wandered about. Horangi, disguised as an old man, ran into the farmer on the road. The old man told Horangi his troubles with his wife, and Horangi gave him one of his eyelashes and told him to put it on his own eye and look at his wife with it. Horangi told the man the eyelash was magical and that it would reveal his wife's true nature. Taking the eyelash the farmer went home and discovered that his wife was really a pig. The farmer left immediately and went to the next village, where he found a beautiful, kind woman to marry.

(Canda 1981; Hynes and Doty 1993; Pyun 1946; Zong 1952; Zozayong 1972)

Huckleberry Finn
United States

Huckleberry Finn, a character created by Mark Twain, is a young boy who finds his way into trouble over and over again on his adventures down the Mississippi River. Huckleberry Finn has come to symbolize children's loss of innocence during the formative years of the United States as the nation struggled with questions of freedom, slavery, and creating a united nation. Huckleberry Finn stands as a quintessential American folk hero who uses only his wit to survive in trial after trial.

Twain's 1885 classic *The Adventures of Huckleberry Finn* is set in the Mississippi

An 1884 illustration by E. W. Kemble from Mark Twain's Huckleberry Finn *shows Huck holding a dead rabbit, with a particularly mischievous look on his face. (Corbis-Bettmann)*

Valley with Huck; his companion, the runaway slave Jim; and his friend, Tom Sawyer. Huckleberry Finn sets out on his own to get away from his abusive father and from the Widow Douglas who "adopts" him. The power of Huck's character is that as a young boy he sees the stark reality of the world and still maintains his sense of humor. He is a smart aleck prankster who gets himself into trouble just trying to survive.

In his adventures Huckleberry Finn tries to avoid becoming "sivilized"; he sees civilization as the downfall of his free-spirited lifestyle. The Widow Douglas brought him into her home to try to "sivilize" him. But Huck found it was "rough living in the house all the time." He preferred the freedom of roaming the streets, alleys, and river bottoms around town. Along with other vagabonds, the 14-year-old Huck enjoyed teasing the local townsfolk and generally offending them with his smell, worn clothes, and raw language.

Finally breaking free from the widow, Huck sets out on an adventure to find freedom from the "sivilized" world. Huckleberry Finn and his companions represent the lowest class of U.S. society, then and now. As a drifter, Huck lived day to day by the seat of his pants. He begged, borrowed, and stole to get what he needed. Often he tricked people out of their food or money by causing a diversion or sneaking into their goods while they were away.

As Huck describes himself, "I go a great deal by my wits"; we see his reliance on his wits to get him through. Huck is a quick thinker and can talk himself out of almost any situation he cannot run from. He even disguises himself as a girl at one point to divert attention away from his antics and sleep peacefully for at least one night.

Although Huck is portrayed as a boy on the run, he makes friends with many people along the river. He befriends not only those in his own position but others better off than himself as well. As a testimony to his charm, Huck wrangles his way into many homes, including a judge's, a widow's, and a middle-class spinster's. Huck embodies the spirit of freedom, but he always reminds us that there is a price for it. With his companion, the slave Jim, Huck is constantly reminded that neither are really free.

First and foremost, Huckleberry Finn is a clever young boy whose pranks are motivated by boyish curiosity and the will to survive on his own. Whether he steals, lies, cheats, or disobeys, Huck is always prepared to flee his surroundings at a moment's notice. He is not attached to anyone or any place. Huck's travels make his deceptions and pranks necessary. In order to get from one place to the next, he must cooperate with some of the seediest elements of society. In doing so, Huck calls on his cleverness to bring him through safely. (Twain 1965)

Hwenho
Fon, *West Africa: Benin*
See **Legba; Yo.**

Ijapa

Yoruba, *West Africa: Southwestern Nigeria; Benin; Togo*

The Yoruba characterize Ijapa, a mischievous tortoise, as one who tricks and cheats those larger and more powerful than he with his clever wit. He is selfish and greedy, especially when it comes to food. His large appetite is never satisfied, and his gluttonous eating habits are matched by his indolent behavior. He is disrespectful both of people and of social mores. He ignores proper ways of acting in public by being loud and self-indulgent; nor does he share with his relatives or friends. Ijapa is shrewd, however, and his cunning makes him ambiguous because even when he seems to be helpful and reliable one cannot know what is up his sleeve.

The Yoruba stories about Ijapa demonstrate the inherent flexibility both of the narratives and of Yoruba relationships. Ijapa, like other characters, is recognizably an animal, but he acts like a human. Yoruba tales use animals to demonstrate the qualities and attributes of human nature that are most beneficial to their society, which is characterized by the expectation that each individual's actions will benefit the group. For example, in ritual activity no single person can carry out the proper responsibilities of feeding an *orisha* or dancing for an ancestor. (See also **Eshu-Elegba.**) Yoruba society is based on a communal model in which individuals' actions have repercussions for the rest of the community. Ijapa demonstrates the chaos that can be introduced into the community when one member acts solely for his or her own benefit. In addition, Ijapa, like Eshu-Elegba, demonstrates that chaos is not far removed from order.

Ijapa is happy to trick anyone, family, friend, or foe. In one story, Ijapa and his wife, Yanrinbo, found themselves with no food during a drought. Ijapa had never tended his crops, relying on the generosity of others and on his cunning to feed his family. Ijapa knew that his neighbor, Bamidele, had a storage house full of yams. Telling his wife that it was not right that Bamidele had so much food and they had none, Ijapa thought of a plan to get the yams. Early one morning, Ijapa told his wife to get on his shoulders, and they went to Bamidele's storage house. Ijapa carried his wife as they walked through the storage house. Yanrinbo collected the yams and put them in the basket on her head. The next day they went back for more, and they went again and again until they had plenty of yams.

Bamidele soon figured out that a large amount of his yams had been stolen. He saw the footprints leading from his house to Ijapa's and Yanrinbo's house, and he accused them of taking the yams. Next, Bamidele reported Ijapa and Yanrinbo to the chief, and they were called to appear before his shrine to stand trial for the crime they were accused of committing. There the priest prepared a drink for them; either they were to confess their misdeeds or drink the medicine, which would sicken anyone who lied. The two sat before the shrine, drank the medicine, and declared their innocence. Ijapa said, "If I, Ijapa, the husband of Yanrinbo, ever stretched my hand to remove yams from Bamidele's storage house, may I fall sick instantly and die." Then Yanrinbo said, "If I, Yanrinbo, wife of Ijapa, ever used my legs to carry me to Bamidele's storage house to steal yams, may I fall sick instantly and die." They drank the medicine, and neither of them fell sick. They were let go and Bamidele was left with no food.

Ijapa's adventures appear not only in Yoruba tales but in their songs, proverbs, and moral sayings. The Yoruba have several sayings that allude to his antics as examples of what not to do or of what might happen if one does do what is forbidden. Other sayings hail Ijapa's cunning; for example: "It is a meticulous person like the tortoise who can see a tortoise in the bush," which states that an alert person will always be aware of the trickery of others. Most of the tales concerning Ijapa deal with his mishaps, tricks, and wrongdoings. They are told as examples of how not to act, but they are also told to show that sometimes bad behavior prevails and sometimes it fails. Ijapa's activities are used as a yardstick against which others can measure the appropriateness of their behavior.

Sometimes Ijapa's tricks fail miserably. One day Ijapa went to visit his mother-in-law with two of his friends. Ijapa's mother-in-law made them some porridge, and they sat down to eat. Even though the food was hot, the three ate quickly. Ijapa, however, was still hungry, so he left his friends and sneaked into the other room to find the remainder of the porridge. Ijapa took off his cap, poured the hot porridge into it, and placed it back on his head. He then went back and sat with his friends, but the heat of the porridge began to make him restless. Soon he told his mother-in-law that he and his friends had to leave. She told him to wait while she wrote a note to her daughter. Ijapa sat back down to wait, trying to ignore the hot porridge on his head. When he bid his mother-in-law good-bye, his hat fell off his head and his crime was exposed. Not only was he caught stealing, but his hair had been burned so badly that it never grew back, and that is why tortoises have no hair.

That the Yoruba refer to Ijapa as *ologobon ewe*, that is, "one who deals in a myriad of little mischievous tricks and stratagems," shows his position in the society. Ijapa is always an unpredictable character; he may appear to be helpful and respectful, but he changes quickly if it suits his needs. When Ijapa's father-in-law died he was obliged to go to his in-laws' house and perform the funeral rites. Part of the rites include wailing and crying for the deceased. Because of his contempt for everyone, especially his father-in-law, Ijapa could not muster the tears needed. However, he thought of a clever trick to fool the others. He boiled a vegetable and put it in his cap; when he neared his father-in-law's house, he put the cap on his head with the boiled, watery vegetable inside. As they entered, Ijapa told the others it was time for the wailing. Soon Ijapa appeared to be weeping the most and the loudest. As he cried, he would put his hands on his head and squeeze the vegetable so the large drops of water would run down his face. Everyone was impressed by Ijapa's wailing, which demonstrated the love and respect he held for his father-in-law.

Ijapa is a premier exhibitionist. His actions are always meant to make him the center of attention, even in the situation of a death in the family. Ijapa's behavior demonstrates the delicate balance between chaos and order. When he does as he pleases and disregards Yoruba social mores, he puts everyone in danger. By ignoring the *orisha*, not making offerings to ancestors, and mocking funeral rites, Ijapa sets the community up for retaliation. Ijapa's selfishness is a warning to all that the deeds of one may affect everyone. (Berry 1991; Courlander 1957; Lawuyi 1990; Owomoyela 1990)

Ikaki

Kalabari, *West Africa: Nigeria*

Ikaki, a tortoise character known as the "old man of the forest," is generally the protagonist in the stories and ritual celebrations in which he appears. The myth of Ikaki's origin and the origin of the Ikaki dance-drama show his cunning, disruptive qualities. Ikaki was first seen in a village that is no longer inhabited, the village of Oloma. He lived at the edges of Oloma and rarely came into the town. The villagers had heard of him and knew that he was a very powerful being. When he felt like it, Ikaki would come from his home at the back of the village and dance wildly about, singing and entertaining the people. The people loved his dancing and always asked him to stay longer or come back more often, but Ikaki always did as he pleased.

One day, after much prodding by the people, Ikaki showed up to dance, and this day he danced his finest dance yet. As he danced he sang a special song in which he told the people how he loved human meat: "human meat, yum, yum, human bones, yum, yum" he sang to the crowd. As he danced ecstatically for the people he lifted one leg toward a section of the audience. As he did so, the people were struck dead immediately. He then lifted up his other leg toward another section of the crowd, and they were killed immediately. Ikaki returned to the forest and was never seen again. Eventually, the surviving people thought they would like to imitate Ikaki's dance, but they were afraid that they might die if they did. They consulted an oracle and were told of a few changes to make to the dance so it would not inflict harm. To this day, Ikaki masquerade dance-dramas are an annual part of the *ekine* societies' dances.

The dances of the *ekine* societies are many, but the Ikaki dance-drama is one of the most popular. The *ekine* societies are all-male societies also known as the *sekiapu*, the dancing people. Each village has its own *ekine* society, which performs several masquerade dance-dramas throughout the year. Each dance-drama is dedicated to one

of several water beings (also called spirits). The *ekine* society traditionally performed 40 to 50 dance-dramas a year. Since European contact the number has been reduced, but the dance-dramas are still an integral part of the Kalabari culture. Each performance includes singing, dancing, and offerings to the water spirit being honored. Normally the dance-drama begins at the water in order to bring the being into the festivities. At this stage the dancers are said to be walking with the being. During the dance-drama, people request aid from the being, both for general health and well-being and for the specific performance. For example, people ask that the dancer's legs be nimble, his ears wide so he can hear the drum, and his arms light. The performances are directed at the water beings, but they are also for entertainment. The beings who are represented in the dance-dramas are beings who are malevolent, rude, and marginal figures in Kalabari society. Other societies perform rituals and dances for other types of beings. The *ekine* society represents a side of Kalabari culture that is concerned with the antisocial and comedic side of life.

The *ekine* society dance-dramas are an end in themselves; they are not performed to "get" anything from these particular beings. Although people make offerings before performances, the performers' actions are directed at the performance itself. The performers practice weeks ahead of a performance (which is not the case with other rituals), and the dancers are judged by their ability to move with the drummer and for their accuracy, timing, and rhythm. Not only are the dancers judged as a group, but each performer is judged for his own performance.

In *ekine* dance-dramas, the drummer serves as the focus for the mood of the performance. Changes in drumming signal a change in scene or plot. Each drum rhythm is specific to a certain being; that being is said to "own" that rhythm. The drummers and dancers hold respected places in Kalabari society; through their performances they give life to the many beings in Kalabari society. That is, they embody the very attributes of those beings and thus become literally associated with them. When a dancer becomes associated with the character he embodies in a performance, he then has the exclusive right to perform that dance-drama. This raises not only the performer's own status in society but also that of his kin, who will be the heirs to the performance.

During the Ikaki dance-drama, one performer dresses in a headdress and hunchbacked tortoise costume. He is flanked by two dancers known as his children, Nimite Poku (knows all) and Nimiaa Poku (knows nothing). The Ikaki dance-drama lasts a full day, with the whole village participating toward the end of the performance. During the dance-drama the Ikaki performer demonstrates his cunning, greedy, and deceptive ways. Because the audience is familiar with the stories surrounding Ikaki, the dancer's gestures are interpreted in terms of the canon of Ikaki stories. Everyone knows of Ikaki's complete disregard for morality; his insatiable appetite for food, money, and women; and his selfish, devious pranks. Ikaki is especially notorious for his incestuous sexual activities and his theft of food from his neighbors. He tricks even the most clever and powerful, such as the king and his court. In one story, Ikaki posed as a great friend of the king's as he came to mourn his untimely death. Ikaki came into town wailing and mourning loudly as if he had been a great friend. But once he got close to the family he cheated them out of their inheritance by claiming that the king owed him money.

In the Ikaki dance-drama the dancers relate the stories of Ikaki in song, dance, gesture, and mime. For instance, Ikaki dances around, pokes his head into the bushes, and comes out with his knapsack completely stuffed, showing how he steals from his neighbors. Throughout the performance, Ikaki dances in sexually explicit ways. He dances a pelvic dance called the *egepu* during which he claims his son's wife for himself and makes sexual gestures toward her and the other women in the audience. He dances wildly, pulls out his large, overgrown testicles, made from wood, and lunges toward the women. All the while the drummer plays a rhythm especially for Ikaki called the Ikaki Ada. The drummer jibes at Ikaki, calling him a rapist and one who sleeps with his own daughter. The crowd, too, takes part in the name-calling. Throughout the performance Ikaki pleads that he is innocent, all the while showing his guilt. His dual role adds to the comedy of the play.

In another portion of the dance-drama, Ikaki shows that his selfish ways get the best of him too. In one of the final sequences, known as the "palm tree climbing," Ikaki climbs to the top of palm tree; he is showing off, as he is the only animal in the forest who can do so. Once he reaches the top, he boasts and calls everybody's attention to himself. Ikaki dances and sings and is so proud of his accomplishment that he does not notice Nimiaa Poku slashing at the bottom of the tree with an ax. When he does notice it is almost too late, and the crowd cheers as they think he is going to come tumbling down. Nimiaa Poku, however, is too clumsy and cannot finish the job. Once again Ikaki comes out on top. Throughout Ikaki's showing off, the drummer and the audience sing and yell at him about his wild ways and his disrespectful behavior. But this only makes Ikaki dance with more fervor. He runs at the women in the crowd and teases one and all. The women shout back at him, making fun of his enlarged scrotum, which is attributed to his large sexual appetite. Throughout the performance, the audience and the performers interact with one another, both enacting the episodes they are familiar with and improvising others on the basis of Ikaki's character.

Ikaki performances demonstrate the crude, obnoxious, and comic aspects of Kalabari life. *Ekine* society performances like this one are performed in opposition to the more serious rituals directed toward ancestors and other powerful beings. The *ekine* society demonstrates, through their performances of different characters, the playful side of life. In addition the *ekine* society gives its members a way to improve their status within the society. The *ekine* society is directly related to the Kalabari political organization; its member make decisions that affect the entire community. The *ekine* society is called upon to act as judges in cases of wrongdoing, and they are consulted, along with other societies, on matters of economics and war. The *ekine* society (and its members) is one of many groups that act together in the political system. Like Ikaki, the *ekine* society represents one set of skills and characteristics among many. (Finnegan 1970; Horton 1962; Horton 1963; Horton 1967)

Iktomi
Lakota, *Plains Region of the United States*

Iktomi is a mischievous spider character who uses his comical adventures to teach Lakota values and morals. Iktomi has a spider's large round stomach, thin arms and legs, and powerful hands and feet. But he was hatched from an egg already full grown. He is the size of a human being, he can talk, he interacts with other humans, and he dresses in clothes made of buckskin and raccoon.

The Lakota universe is peopled by many different types of beings who share with humans the responsibility for the maintenance of the world. The Lakota distinguish between several types of beings based on their power and their physical place in the universe. Certain beings are associated with each of the four cardinal directions and others are associated with specific colors. Further, there are beings specific to the water, land, sky, forest, and lodge. By being associated with certain directions and colors, each being in the Lakota cosmos has specific responsibilities, duties, and powers. None holds all the power to control or manipulate the community. Instead, because the roles are interconnected, each plays an important part in the continuation of the culture.

There are both friendly and dangerous beings in the universe; one must learn from one's kin the proper ways to interact with each type in order to maintain harmony, although it is not always achieved. The Lakota camp circle can be seen as a metaphor for their social system. In the camp circle, the Lakota form an interactive group of kin who rely on each other for survival. Each member of the group must act responsibly in his or her duties in order for the group to survive. Similarly, the traditional political system was based on the ideal of an interrelated community. A governing council and seven elected chiefs worked together to make decisions for the group. Each chief directed a certain part of Lakota life in council with the others. Decisions were made based on the interworking of the entire group. Like the camp circle and the governing body, the many beings within the Lakota universe work together and are related through kinship ties in the common goal of maintaining the Lakota cosmos.

Iktomi is a being within the Lakota cosmos who takes on many characteristics; he is both a creator and a destroyer, human and nonhuman, playful and dangerous. Iktomi was the firstborn son of Inyan (the Rock), the source of all things in the universe. Inyan created Wakinyan (Winged-One, or Thunderbird) to be his companion, and it was Wakinyan who brought

Iktomi forth from an egg full grown. Wakinyan is so terrible to look at that anyone who sees him is frightened into being **heyoka,** foolish or silly. Having begun his life in an unnatural manner and being in close contact with Wakinyan, Iktomi was destined to live life the opposite of others. Iktomi was first named Ksa, or wisdom. But he was disfigured and not very attractive. In his vanity, he enlisted the help of the demon Gnaski, who was very handsome. The two set out to change Ksa's appearance, and in doing so they shamed two powerful beings in the universe. Because he used his wisdom to scheme against others, Ksa was renamed Iktomi and became known as the "imp of mischief." Even with his playful nature, Iktomi maintained his wisdom. He is a master of languages; he is able to speak to all types of animals and spirits in the universe. He was the first to reach maturity in the western part of the Lakota universe, and so he named all the animals and watched them grow. He delighted in teasing and playing jokes on the animals and spirits alike. He was always getting into trouble, cheating, and lying. Although he looked somewhat like a man, everyone knew he was not an ordinary human being.

Iktomi's influence on the Lakota way of life can be seen in the spatial design of their camps. The Lakota always camped near one another to protect against raids, to share the responsibilities of hunting, and so on. Once, however, Iktomi convinced the people to scatter and live at a distance from each other. When the Lakota's enemies learned of their new placement, they quickly took advantage of the situation and began to raid. Without a strong defense, the Lakota were defeated, and Iktomi laughed at their foolishness. After the raid, the elders came together in a council and decided that from then on the Lakota would always camp in a circle, with the door of each lodge facing the door of the next. With this arrangement the Lakota were more secure and could easily fight off enemies; they could also watch for Iktomi trying to enter the village and cause problems.

Iktomi is best known for his trickery. He manipulates, cheats, steals, lies, and changes shape in order to get what he wants. He tells people of great hunting lands where there is only barren earth. He confuses people with his smooth talk and cheats them out of food and clothes. One story tells of a young Lakota man who set out for the chief's camp with gifts for the chief's daughter, his future bride. The young man's oldest sister warned him before he left to keep watch for Iktomi while he traveled alone. After a day in the woods, the young man encountered Iktomi. He was leery of him at first, remembering his sister's warning. But Iktomi was cleverer than he. Iktomi flattered him, remarking on his great strength and his ability as a hunter. The pair walked together through the woods with Iktomi complimenting the young man. Soon Iktomi talked the young man into give him his clothes and the gifts he had for his future bride. The young man waited for Iktomi to return, but soon Iktomi's spell wore off and the young man realized he had fallen prey to the smooth-talking Iktomi. In shame, he returned to his home without his bride.

Once Iktomi took the shape of a buffalo by asking the buffalo to "make me like that." The buffalo ran at him and crushed him, but Iktomi emerged as a buffalo. Having turned himself into a buffalo he wandered the plains taking food from others. Iktomi can take the form of anyone or anything he wants in order to deceive others. He is so notorious for appearing as an old man in the lodge that if an old man comes into the lodge and asks to play a game he is said to be Iktomi. If it is Iktomi and the people do not recognize him and they feed him, he will relieve himself on the floor, leaving a pile of dung behind to mark his spot.

Iktomi's actions are not always destructive. Once Iktomi killed the monster Iya, who ate entire villages of people. When Iktomi heard of Iya's actions he tricked him into revealing his fears, and then in his moment of weakness Iktomi slew Iya and freed the people from his stomach. In another story the lark, the turtle, and the wolf were arguing over the merits of the gifts they had given to the wizard. Each had helped the wizard regain his wife by giving him a gift. Iktomi came upon the three arguing and suggested that they run a race to determine the value of their generosity. They all agreed, and Iktomi set out a course through a plum thicket, across a marsh, and up a hill through white clay. During the race, each animal was physically marked by a part of the course, and today each animal bears the mark of the race they were destined to lose. None of the animals won the race because they encountered so much hardship during their journey. Iktomi purposely made the course so challenging that no one could win; rather, they had to help each other in order to survive. By making each animal help the others Iktomi showed them the necessity of cooperation and the futility of their argument.

Stories about Iktomi are part of a larger storytelling practice among the Lakota, who distinguish between two major categories of narratives, the *ohunkakan* and the *woyakapi*. *Ohunkakan* stories are those that have a fictional element to them, whereas *woyakapi* stories are concerned with actual events. There are also subcategories within these two main categories that refer to specific time periods and types of stories. For example, within the *ohunkakan* category stories are distinguished as either happening before, during, or after the creation period and are further distinguished as pertaining either to amazing events or to more mundane events such as hunting. Whichever category a story falls into, the tale itself changes with the storyteller. Oral performances are marked by the signature of the teller. Storytellers use different pitches, pauses, and other vocal techniques to set their tales apart and to entertain the audience. Stories are usually told at night, and in the days prior to reservation living they were told around the campfire of the main lodge. Although there are many common stories and characters, Lakota storytellers weave new elements and problems into their stories depending on the situation. Even traditional tales that relate historical events and social customs are told differently by different people; that is, the structure of the tale remains, but the details are created anew by each individual storyteller. Individuals also create their own stories based on characters such as Iktomi whose traits are familiar to the Lakota. (Black Elk and Giago 1980; Buechel 1978; Deloria 1932; Feraca 1963; Hymes 1981; Jahner 1977; McLaughlin 1916; Powers 1975; Walker 1980)

Incest

Taboos against incest, that is, against having sexual intercourse with an immediate relative, exist almost universally, and any such far-reaching restriction is sure to be at the top of the list of restrictions that tricksters and clowns break. By their very nature clowns and tricksters delight in shocking people, inverting social norms, and abusing any and all power they have. Committing incest is a sure way to highlight their roles as outsiders and comics. Although some of their incestuous activities are literal, oftentimes clowns mock sexual intercourse so as to highlight these restrictions. That is, they actually reinforce the taboos by showing the absurdity of the affair in a public forum.

The Zuni comedic performers known as **koyemshi,** or "mud heads," revel in the opportunity to break sexual taboos. The koyemshi get their association with incest from their connection with Shiwelusiwa, a hero, and his nine children. Shiwelusiwa committed incest with his sister in order to have his children, and as a result he became disfigured. To hide his disfigurement he covered his face and body with mud, as the modern-day koyemshi do. The koyemshi do not literally perform incestuous actions during rituals; instead, they mock sexual behavior in crude and obnoxious ways.

Incest is commonly associated with one's relatives. In many communities, however, the spectrum of relatives is enlarged so that intercourse with uninitiated members of the opposite sex are restricted as well. By expanding the scope of incest, many communities ensure the balance of reciprocity with neighboring tribes or other clans. That is, they facilitate outside marriages by making internal ones immoral. In doing so, communities ensure trade, reciprocal offerings, and protection from their neighbors. **Gabruurian,** the wily boy-man being of the Bimin-Kuskusim, ignores such social restrictions and is constantly seducing young, uninitiated girls into having intercourse with him. By doing so, he not only puts himself in danger but he potentially alienates many young girls from their families. (See also **Difisi, Ikaki, Kaik, Kumarxúo, Ma'ii, Odosha, Susa-no-o,** and **Yiyi** for more examples.)

Ipani
Mekeo, *Papua New Guinea*
In ritual mourning rites the focus of ipani, which literally means "to eat," is to gorge oneself on food and to burlesque the activities of others. Among the Mekeo one's spouse's relatives are normally respected and honored; a person would not mock or make fun of his or her spouse's family. But at funeral rituals *bakau,* or humorous playing, is acceptable between affinal kin, and this societal norm is inverted through ipani, in this context meaning the hilarious and gluttonous eating of massive amounts of food.

The Mekeo live in seven villages scattered along a river surrounded by rain forest and swampy areas. People make a living farming, gardening small vegetable plots, and hunting. The Mekeo divide their society into two sections, or moieties. Each of these moieties is also divided between two clans. One must marry someone from the opposite moiety and from the opposite clan. The Mekeo marriage system is the basis for their funeral rites, which serve to bring the deceased back to his or her clan. An exchange of food is used to symbolize the returning of one's blood back to one's maternal grandmother's clan. The funeral rites culminate with the workers (*ipangaua,* "ritual laborers") gorging themselves on the food obtained from the opposite moiety, the family (*ina ngome,* "ritual owners"). Thus both groups aid in sending the deceased to a state of rest, one by collecting and preparing the food, the others by eating it.

The purpose of the mortuary feast is to bring the family's mourning to an end. During the mourning period, beginning right after the death, family members are prohibited from doing anything considered "sweet." Mekeo society divides life's activities into those that are "sweet," including normal daily activities such as work, eating, sleeping, and sexual intercourse, and those that are "unsweet," including crying, mourning, and going without food, sex, or bathing. For days following a death, the family is rendered unsweet. All of their time is taken up by mourning. Their normal duties of working, cooking, and cleaning are performed by the opposite moiety. The laborers work daily taking care of all the business in the village. During this time the workers must comply with all the mourners' requests.

The trigger for the ipani portion of the mourning ritual is a statement by one of the workers that they need more of a certain type of food. This statement is seen as a greedy remark, since all the while they have been working they have been fed generous portions of food. Greed is one of the most serious charges in Mekeo society. Once it is leveled it is not easily escaped. Having made the charge of greed, the owners demand that the workers collect large amounts of the food specified as well as other foods.

After that request the workers spend up to two days collecting and cooking a wide variety of food. All of the work is done as part of their *kaua*, or duty to the deceased and his or her family members. Once the food has been collected and cooked, the workers assemble in the middle of the village in a circle. While they sit, the owners bring out piles and piles of food and command the workers to eat. Not accepting the feast would be a sign of great disrespect. The humor of the ipani is in the way in which the workers eat. They gorge themselves, all the while pretending not to have enough. They call out for more food and comment on how little there is to go around. Their humorous eating and mockery are meant to liberate the owners from their mourning by bringing them to laughter and thus back into the "sweet" existence of life. The workers inevitably cannot eat all the food prepared. If any is left over, they are "fined" by one of the chiefs. The fines go to help the deceased's family.

The burlesquing of the workers, that is, one's affinal kin, is meant to provide a socially acceptable way for the mourners to return to normal daily activities and at the same time ensure that the deceased has been properly taken care of. The humorous behavior, mocking gestures, and exaggerated greed highlights the connection as well as the separation between the two moieties. Without the separation there would be no one to do the work, and without their connection in marriage the society would diminish. The reciprocal relationship of the two is mocked in the funeral rites to demonstrate their inherently symbiotic nature.

Joking relationships among the Mekeo follow strict kinship rules. Funeral rites are one of just a handful of situations in which one is able to mock one's relatives. This affinal joking, or *ipaipa*, is one way that the Mekeo both honor their kinship system as well as critique its shortcomings. Ordinarily one would not order around one's spouse's family, nor would one laugh and make fun of them. Ipani during funeral rites is an obligatory act that all affinal relatives owe to their spouse's family. This performance humor on their part fulfills their duty and ensures the proper passage of the deceased. (Hau'ofa 1981; Mosko 1992; Stephen 1987)

Isáahkawuattee

Crow, Northwestern United States: Montana

Isáahkawuattee, also called Old Man Coyote, is known both for his role in the creation of the Crow people and the world and for his disruptive and entertaining comedic behavior. The Crow creation story tells of a time when the earth was wet and cold. No one lived on the earth except Isáahkawuattee, who roamed the cold, damp earth, traveling wherever he wanted to. When he wanted to sleep he would lay down in the water and float on his back. He was lonely traveling by himself, and his journey was difficult. But one day as he was traveling, he saw four ducks flying overhead. He asked the ducks if they would plunge below the water and bring up some earth so that he could make land. The first three ducks failed in their attempt to retrieve the earth for Isáahkawuattee, but the fourth duck succeeded, and Isáahkawuattee traveled west, following the sun, spreading this mud as he went. As the mud hardened, Isáahkawuattee used it to make mountains, hills, and valleys across the earth. After he finished making the land, Isáahkawuattee made animals, trees, and plants. But he feared that something was missing, so he rolled and molded some mud into an image that he liked, the first Crow people. Isáahkawuattee gave the people a language and land and taught them how to behave responsibly toward all the things he had created.

For some time the people lived peacefully, but one day there was a disturbance outside the camp. Two boys were fighting, and each mother came to her son's defense. Isáahkawuattee stepped in and decided that the people would be split up into separate lodges. In recollection of the driftwood that gathered along the side of the river, he called these "driftwood lodges." Now each member of the Crow village would be part of one of a group of separate but interconnected driftwood lodges.

The Crow clan system is based in one's affiliation in the driftwood lodge system that Isáahkawuattee created. There are eight clans and each person belongs to one clan. Each clan has a name assigned by Isáahkawuattee. For example, one group was known for eating the fatty portion of their meat, so Isáahkawuattee named them "Greasy Mouth." The members of each clan today are the descendants of the first clan members. Each clan works as a unit tied to the village through their ceremonial and economic responsibilities. Each member of a clan is part of the same lodge. As a group, the lodge participates in gift exchanges with one another to maintain their close ties and ensure their reciprocal relationship with their kin. Each clan is also associated with different plants, animals, and natural phenomena, from which they acquire certain powers to aid in hunting and in the general maintenance of their lodge. In return for the help of the other members of the cosmos, the Crow hold ritual celebrations and gift exchanges that demonstrate their close relationship to and respect for the members of their community. In gift exchanges, each lodge gives another

items, such as blankets and food, that they need to live. By each lodge giving another their basic necessities, every family is taken care of. To show their respect for other members of the cosmos, the Crow also include animals and other beings in their gift exchanges and reciprocal relationships. For example, prior to contact with Europeans and the impact of colonialism, the Crow relied on the buffalo as a source of sustenance in many aspects of their lives. They hunted the buffalo for food, shelter, and clothing. But in return they offered the buffalo gifts and ritual performances. The Crow took the advice of Isáahkawuattee as a directive for living their lives through the interconnected lodge system that unites each clan with each other and the world in which they live.

But Isáahkawuattee is an ambiguous character; although he created the Crow and their way of life, he also uses his power to unravel the threads of the driftwood lodge and to cause the opposite of what is desired to happen. His tricks show the Crow that life does not always follow the patterns they want. Instead, through Isáahkawuattee's antics the Crow see that the world is made up of many varied components that do not always act as they wish. Isáahkawuattee's character traits as they are revealed in stories are used as reference points to characterize people's behavior. For example, if someone is telling of the improper behavior of another person, he or she may refer to a story about Isáahkawuattee or to an episode from a story about Isáahkawuattee to illustrate the point. Stories about Isáahkawuattee are told during sweat lodges while people are purifying themselves. By sharing stories of negative and improper behavior during a sweat lodge, people open themselves to understanding the negative repercussions of improper behavior.

People do not simply retell the stories about Isáahkawuattee; they act them out and incorporate modern-day situations in them. Adults act out stories for their children, exaggerating Isáahkawuattee's disruptive behavior. By using the stories of Isáahkawuattee's escapades as entertainment, Crow adults impress upon their children the importance of proper behavior and emphasize the repercussions of Isáahkawuattee's actions.

In stories Isáahkawuattee is portrayed as greedy, self-centered, assertive, and deceptive. He deceives people to get what he wants, and he is never satisfied. He lies, cheats, and steals from his own clan and does not respect the gift-giving ideals of the Crow. He almost never shares his food or money with his kin, and he uses whatever means necessary to obtain the best for himself.

Once when Isáahkawuattee was very hungry he came across two buffalo grazing in the open. He approached the fatter of the two and challenged him to a race. The buffalo was sure he would win and asked Isáahkawuattee where he wanted to run. Isáahkawuattee pointed to the place he had just come from, knowing that there was a cliff in that direction. He knew that if the buffalo fell off the cliff he would surely die, and Isáahkawuattee could have a feast. As they started the race, Isáahkawuattee bolted ahead, shouting at the buffalo, teasing him, claiming to be faster. This enraged the buffalo, and he ran even faster. At the top of the hill Isáahkawuattee slowed down and turned off to the side as the buffalo raced into the sun, which blinded him, and ran over the edge. Isáahkawuattee gloated that he could now eat back fat until he was full, and he jeered at the buffalo's stupidity for not knowing his own country well enough.

In another story, Isáahkawuattee showed that he will go to any lengths to obtain what he wants. He scratched himself with twigs and branches until he was bleeding, then threw himself on the ground near some geese yelling for help. The geese heard the commotion and flew over to help Isáahkawuattee. But as they approached, Isáahkawuattee caught them in the trap he had set and he ate them for dinner.

Beyond deceit, Isáahkawuattee uses his power to change form to catch animals and people off guard. Isáahkawuattee can turn himself into anything or anyone he wants. Sometimes he changes himself into a little girl to pretend that he is lost and in need of assistance in the woods. Other times he will turn himself into a mouse and sneak up on people in order to hear their plans just so he can sabotage them. He will often take the form of a buffalo to fool hunters. No matter what form he takes, Isáahkawuattee always uses his power to change appearance to get what he wants for himself.

The only one who can outwit Isáahkawuattee is the whirlwind witch, who sleeps during the day and flies to village after village at night. Once Isáahkawuattee decided he wanted to marry the most beautiful woman in the village. Not knowing who she was or how powerful she was, he picked the whirlwind witch and announced to everyone that he was the most intelligent and handsome man in the village, so he could claim her as his wife. He took her to a village near a stream. They camped there for a day, and then the whirlwind witch moved them that night. For several nights the whirlwind witch moved them at night. Soon Isáahkawuattee was so tired and worn out from the moving and hungry because the whirlwind witch did not cook for him that he decided to leave her. He tried each night to sneak out, but she always caught him. Finally he left one day to go hunting and did not return. He went to the mouse lodge and changed himself into a mouse so she would not find him. That night she came looking for him, but seeing only mice she left. From then on, Isáahkawuattee decided that she was the only one he would not try his tricks on.

Isáahkawuattee plays two roles in the life of the Crow. As a creator he is credited with creating life and with giving the Crow their culture. He instituted the driftwood lodge system and showed people the proper ways to act and live in the world. But his role as a mischief maker, deceiver, and comic plays against his role as a creator. He is rude, disruptive, greedy, and selfish—all the things he warned people against when he created them. The two sides of Isáahkawuattee demonstrate the balance and the ebb and flow of all life. In his actions as a creator and a deceiver, Isáahkawuattee displays the many sides of Crow life. (Frey 1987; Hathaway 1970; Linderman 1932; Lowie 1918; Lowie 1935; Lowie 1993)

Italapas
Chinook, *Northwest Coast of the United States*

The Chinook consider Italapas, a coyote, to be both a menace and a necessity. Italapas is a cocreator, along with Ikanam, of the Chinook people; he is also a foolish prankster who disrupts Chinook society. The Chinook creation story begins before there was anyone on the earth, when Italapas and Ikanam lived by themselves. One day the earth was flooded and Italapas climbed a great tree to escape the flood. When the water had subsided, he threw some sand in the water to make land, and then he and Ikanam made human beings out of the mud and showed the people how to catch salmon, weave, and maintain themselves. Italapas also showed the people how to get along and the proper ways to act toward one another. Although Italapas showed people the proper ways to act, he constantly breaks those same rules by acting selfishly. Italapas delights in taking advantage of people by tricking them into giving him their food or fulfilling his endless sexual desires. This dual role makes Italapas a multifaceted character within Chinook oral history.

Chinook society is based on small family units that traditionally hunted and lived together throughout the year. Families were bound together through kinship ties that extended beyond their own siblings. Men and women within a community worked together, men hunting and fishing and women gathering roots, berries, and other foods to maintain the community. Although today there is not the same emphasis on hunting and gathering, people maintain their kinship ties through other community interactions. People come together in the evenings and during the winter months to share in large feasts and ceremonies. Families pool their resources to provide for both boys' and girls' puberty ceremonies or in competitions to both display and give away their wealth to others.

During the evenings and during the cold of winter the community often gathers for storytelling. Storytellers in Chinook society tell of characters that are already well known to the community. Stories usually announce specific places, names, and characters through both action and words. Storytellers are very animated, as is the audience, who join in or encourage the storyteller in one direction or another. There are several well-known plots and characters, but each storyteller tells stories differently, and storytellers are known for their own distinctive styles and actions. Thus, although stories of Italapas and others are familiar, they are never the same.

Italapas is a favorite among the children because of his wild and humorous antics. Storytellers relate stories of the creation to children, but they also use the character of Italapas as a way to stress the importance of proper behavior within the community. Stories of Italapas deal with both his creative and his destructive roles, showing him as both a benefactor and a disruption to

Chinook life. Whatever the case, stories of Italapas are always entertaining.

Italapas loves to play pranks on people, including friends and family. He takes advantage of his younger kinsmen by convincing them that his misbehavior is acceptable. Often Italapas appears in stories as the uncle or the headman of a group. As such, he deserves respect from others, especially the younger kin. Often he is paired with the skunk in stories. Italapas is seen as the skunk's older brother and thus as being in the position of control. Because Italapas is lazy and does not possess adequate hunting skills he is often in need of food. One of his favorite games is to convince the skunk to steal food for them on the grounds that the food rightfully belongs to them. Or Italapas will wait until the skunk has gone hunting. Of course, while the skunk is away Italapas always eats his food. Italapas has no shame when it comes to taking advantage of the skunk or any other of his younger kinsman. In fact, he delights in seeing how far he can push his younger kin; he is never content.

In one story Italapas and the skunk were at the skunk's home in the woods when Italapas decided that he was hungry. Being too lazy to hunt for himself, Italapas convinced the skunk to allow him to tie the skunk's anus together. Once the skunk was tied, he fell to the ground in pain and blacked out. Italapas called to the village for help. "Who will come?" he asked. "My younger brother is dying." Soon a doe came to help him. Italapas told the doe that his younger brother was dying of a great stomach pain and that he must be moved inside. The doe took the skunk's hind legs and Italapas picked up his torso. Just as they had started to move the skunk, Italapas loosened the tie around the skunk's anus, which released a terrible odor and knocked the doe out. When the doe was helpless, Italapas killed, skinned, and ate her. By the time the skunk woke up Ita-

lapas had eaten all the food, and the skunk never knew what trick Italapas had played on him. (Boas 1894; Jacobs 1959; Jacobs 1960; Ray 1938)

Iwa
Hawaii

Iwa, "the crafty one," is one of the many characters in traditional Hawaiian oral literature who compete with kings, chiefs, monsters, and malevolent forces to overcome their abusive power. His intellect, wit, and cool temperament enable him to overpower and outmaneuver even the strongest of opponents. (See also **Kamapuaa** for another similar Hawaiian character.) Iwa is best known for confronting his aggressors and laughing at their inability to outdo his tricks. Rather than bowing to the ruling elite, Iwa demonstrates the ability of common people to overcome tyrannical rulers and other obstacles. In Iwa Hawaiians have a character who represents the power that people have to prevail in difficult situations and who shows that intellectual prowess is necessary to do so.

In traditional Hawaiian society some considered thievery an acceptable profession. The bounds of the thievery were not absolute; people known for their ability to steal, especially from chiefs and outsiders, were praised. Stories about Iwa suggest that thievery can be an honorable and even necessary act, showing that stealing is not always bad; in fact, his thievery is often rewarded.

Iwa relies on his intellect to outmaneuver his opponents, whatever their size or position. In one story, Iwa and a friend were out fishing when they saw the chief's men diving one by one from his fishing boat. The two stood on the shore and watched; after a while one of the chief's men came to them asking for their assistance. The chief's fire shell, which normally brought all the squid to his line, was missing. None of his divers could retrieve it, and the chief was becoming furious. When asked who was the best diver in the village, Iwa's companion said that Iwa was indeed the best. Iwa returned with the chief's assistant to the boat and faced the chief, who inspected him and asked about his abilities. After a brief conversation, the chief instructed Iwa to dive for the fire shell. Iwa just laughed and said that there was no need for him to dive, for the shell was not in the water. "What!" exclaimed the chief. Still laughing quietly, Iwa told the chief that he had removed it that morning himself and hidden it to make fishing a fair endeavor for all the villagers.

Again battling the chief, Iwa was challenged to retrieve the chief's prized stone ax from the nearby temple of Pakaalana. The chief was sure he had outwitted Iwa this time because his ax was watched day and night by two guards. The ax actually hung between the two guards, attached to their necks with rope. The village that surrounded the temple was under *kapu*, strict laws. People were forbidden to come out of their homes at night, and no animal was permitted to make a sound once the town crier called the night to rest. People would only leave their homes if they heard a bell sound. Entering the village after nightfall, Iwa went to the town crier, out of breath, and told him that he was to relieve him of his duties, for the chief requested his immediate presence. Knowing the chief was prone to whims, the town crier departed quickly, leaving Iwa with the bell to alert the town of any wrongdoing.

Iwa went to the temple and called out to the guards, asking them if they were awake. "Indeed," they replied, knowing they were not permitted to sleep on duty. Iwa approached them and told them he wanted to feel the ax to make sure it was intact. Once he had hold of it, Iwa slipped the knot from the ax and ran away with it. Because the town crier had left, despite hearing the commotion the people were slow to leave their homes for fear of the chief. Once they realized what had happened it was too late, and Iwa made it safely from the village with the ax. Stealing the ax showed that Iwa was not intimidated by the chief or his power. Iwa's actions highlight the plight of many of the early islanders' struggles with authority figures. (Beckwith 1970; Green 1926; Thompson 1990; Westervelt 1915)

Jaguar

The jaguar is a popular character in South American folk literature, in which he is most commonly depicted as a gullible dupe. He is constantly embarrassed, taken advantage of, hurt, and even killed by the jokes and pranks of others. Set up as the ultimate fool, jaguars are the butt of jokes throughout South America. Although a second class of jaguars associated with shamanic powers is also recognized, the most common representation of the jaguar is less than flattering. In fact, when the jaguar does attempt to flex his muscles and trick someone, the prank normally backfires making him look even more foolish.

The Toba of Argentina call **Keyók** the gullible jaguar in their folktales. Storytellers invoke tales of Keyók as an entertaining character who never fails to fail. He allows animals smaller and weaker than he to get the best of him in almost every situation. As a testament to his powerful nature, Keyók also has the ability to heal, but even that ability does not help him in all situations. For example, in one story, Keyók agreed to help an armadillo, all the while planning to kill him for his supper. He so fumbles the attempt to kill the armadillo that the armadillo ends up overpowering and killing Keyók.

Although the jaguar is strong and fast, he never ceases to fall prey to smaller but cleverer animals, especially the rabbit. **At'pana,** the Guajiro rabbit from Argentina, is one nemesis to the jaguar. Boasting a sharp intellect and a love for pranks, At'pana delights in fooling the jaguar. Similarly **Chunga,** a small birdlike character of the Toba, continually tricks the jaguar into giving up his food, shelter, and even his life for the small bird. See also **Adúgo, Cufalh, Dahusúi, Júko, Kakxó, Kumarxúo, Nowarera,** and **Palu** for more examples.

Jester
Europe

Jesters, licensed buffoons whose outrageous pranks entertained royal courts across Europe, became popular in Europe in the early sixteenth century. These jesters were contemporaries of the **fools** throughout

A carved jade depiction of a jaguar spirit, probably from pre-Columbian Olmec culture. (Werner Forman/Corbis)

An undated lithograph shows a traditional European court jester. (Corbis-Bettmann)

Europe at the time, setting themselves apart by being recognized as part of the official court of their king. In fact, the jesters' repertoire became somewhat standardized by being published as jest books beginning in Germany. Jest books contained the popular rhymes, word games, satirical comments, and practical jokes of jesters throughout the continent.

Jesters differed from other comedic characters in that their purpose was to entertain only the king and his court, not the common people. Their humor, however, was not limited by their role. They indulged in social commentary, and the most daring even played practical jokes on their kings. (See also **Bribal,** a court jester in India.)

One of the most famous jesters of his time was **Scogan,** the jester of England's

Edward IV. Like his contemporaries, Scogan used clever witticisms, sarcasm, and physical comedy to entertain the king. His wit, however, had a decidedly vulgar slant, and oftentimes he offended the king with his lewd jokes and offensive acts. Scogan, like other jesters, was allowed a certain license as a comedian. Jokes and pranks that would usually land someone in jail or worse were laughed off as part of the jester's job.

Scogan, however, liked to test his limits. Once, after a practical joke had failed, Scogan failed to pay back a large sum of money he owed to the king. Scogan was sentenced to death by the king as the only solution to his insolence. Before he could be executed, Scogan faked his own sudden death and funeral. At the funeral rites, the king said glorious things about Scogan and even forgave him his enormous debt. Upon hearing those words, Scogan jumped up from the casket and thanked the king. Another time Scogan was forced to leave the country. He was forbidden by the king to ever set foot on English soil again, or he would be put to death. After a short time in France, Scogan returned to England with French soil in his shoes, again escaping death through his clever wit.

Jesters throughout Europe relied on standard pranks to entertain. One of the most common stunts was to forge a disparaging letter to the king and read it to him in front of his court. The jesters walked a fine line between entertainment and remarks that could lead them to death. Many jesters were considered brilliant. Unlike their counterpart the fool, jesters were clever. Their jokes and pranks relied on subtle social commentary and provocative satires. But even court jesters were not above the physical comedy that brought laughter to all. Many jesters were known for their acrobatics, juggling, and miming. A favorite joke of the jesters, presented frequently at court, was to pretend not to know how to ride a horse, to try in vain to mount the horse, and then to be bucked off.

One famous Italian dwarf jester, **Bertholde,** combined physical humor and cleverness to outwit the king. After embarrassing the king he was exiled from the court. But before he left he told the king that he could not rid his court of jesters because they were like flies. The king answered that he could return safely to the court if he did so in the company of flies. Bertholde purchased an old, sick mule and rode into the king's court on the ass swarmed by flies.

Court jesters were most notorious for their foolish disrespect of authority. They mocked the power of the king, bringing the first brand of free speech to the continent. Although they were part of the official courts, most jesters had lived as commoners before they were accepted as court jesters. Bringing with them a sense of the problems facing the ordinary people of the country, many jesters acted as liaisons between the common people and the ruling elite. More than one jester was put to death for his social commentary, and rival political factions would often use jesters as their mouthpieces for social change. (Hazlitt 1864; Towsen 1976; Wardroper 1970; Welsford 1935)

Joker, The
United States

The crafty Joker appeared in the Batman comics and television series. From his first appearance in the comics in 1939, Batman was a symbol of freedom, hope, and all that is good. In contrast his arch rivals, such as Two-Face, Cat Woman, and the Joker, represented the evil, dark side of humanity. With the television series in the 1960s, however, Batman and his nemesis the Joker became symbols of U.S. culture. Batman and the Joker epitomized the duality felt in the U.S. consciousness of the battle between right and wrong. The line,

however, was not always so clear. Although Batman was clearly the "good guy" and the Joker the "bad guy," the Joker's tricks, humor, and slow-wittedness endeared him to audiences.

Batman and the Joker are intertwined in the mythos that surrounds them. It is Batman's apparent triumph over an eager criminal that leads to the appearance of the Joker as we come to see him in the comics, television shows, and the movies. In the television episode "The Man behind the Red Hood," the Joker, an ordinary criminal, botches a million-dollar heist, and in an attempt to escape Batman he dives into a tank of noxious chemicals and is forever transformed. The chemicals turned his face white, his hair green, and his lips a dark red. With his new physical appearance, the Joker takes on the persona of an "evil clown," out to get revenge for what Batman has done to him.

Realizing that his new persona gives him power over ordinary people, the Joker turns

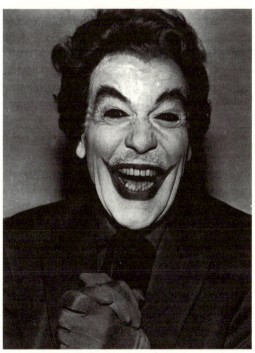

Caesar Romero as the Joker from the 1966 television series Batman. *(Corbis-Bettmann)*

to a life of crime and thus cements his future as the arch rival of Batman. Although both Batman and the Joker had life-changing experiences (Batman's parents were killed before his eyes), the Joker chose to avenge his tragedy through crime, whereas Batman chose to pursue justice.

The "game," as the Joker refers to his relationship with Batman, is a volley of wrongdoings and social ineptness by the Joker and corrections by Batman. In fact, it is the game that drives the Joker to his evil ways. In one comic, as he stands over the limp body of Batman, seemingly victorious, he laments the fact that "without the game that the Batman and I have played for so many years, winning is nothing." The Joker's cunning and clever deeds keep the game alive, while Batman's endless goal to rid Gotham City of crime keeps him in pursuit of the Joker. Batman and the Joker each plays his own role in the cosmic duel between good and evil that is at the heart of American culture. (See also **Kesey, Ken, and the Merry Pranksters** for more on U.S. culture.)

Basing his violence on his role as the "evil clown," the Joker mixes dark humor with violence, crime, and chaos to try and outwit Batman. The Joker is a classic thief, attempting to rob banks, kidnap people, and subvert the normal order of the city. In the 1950s and 1960s, especially on the television series, the Joker's attempts were bumbling; he looked a fool in contrast to the cool Batman and his sidekick Robin. The Joker's pranks were lighthearted, harmless, and always easy to see through. But when Batman and the Joker reemerged in the 1980s and 1990s, after 50 years of their "game," the stakes were raised.

With the fiftieth anniversary of Batman, a major motion picture and a renewal of the original comic series, along with other offshoots, introduced a more savvy and ruthless Joker. Like other evil counterparts of the 1990s, the Joker turned from a fool to a cool killer, with his "jokes" ending in murder, mayhem, and destruction. In fact, the 1990s Joker is portrayed as a "madman," and whenever Batman does catch him he is put away in Gotham City's insane asylum, the Arkham Asylum. A novel by the same name—*Arkham Asylum*—depicts the Joker as a combination of a "mischievous clown" and a "psychotic killer" because he has no real personality of his own. The therapist explains to Batman that the Joker has "no control over the sensory information he receives from the outside world." Because of his lack of control, the Joker is unpredictable. Nobody, even Batman, knows what he is going to do next. And it is that element of chaos that endears the Joker to his many fans. (Collins 1991; Marriott 1989; Morrison 1989; Pearson and Uricchio 1991a)

Juan Pusong
Philippines

Juan Pusong, a dishonest and cunning young boy who delights in deceiving others, is known variously throughout different regions of the Philippines as Juan Osong, Suan, or simply Juan. Despite the different names his escapades remain the same.

Juan Pusong is a clever, witty, and oftentimes obscene prankster who never misses an opportunity to poke fun at someone or some situation. Most of his pranks are harmless; only occasionally do his antics cross over to the malicious. Usually Juan Pusong can be found swindling a trader at the market, manipulating children out of their food, or convincing strangers that they would be better off following his directions than the ones they had already received. Juan Pusong is a favorite character in Filipino folklore because of his wit and charm. His jokes remind everyone of the lighter side of life.

Filipino folklore addresses a wide range of subjects, from the most personal experiences, such as childbirth, to cosmic events, such as the creation of the world. Characters like Juan Pusong are popular because of their humor. (See also **Pilandok** for a similar Filipino character.) Storytellers use tales about Juan Pusong to cover a range of subjects. They may focus on his negative behavior for local communities, as in stories in which he attempts to steal food from others in the market. In other tales storytellers show Juan Pusong outwitting a government official, king, or teacher. In these stories the moral may be twofold: first, that those in power are not always right, and second, that sometimes one needs to stand up to those abusing power. Most commonly, however, storytellers use the character of Juan Pusong to entertain. Although there may be a moral to the story, Juan Pusong is first and foremost a jokester whose antics always elicit laughter.

Juan Pusong is notorious for his manipulation of people, and he is known especially for his lies. Even the king knew that Juan was an infamous liar. In one story, the king saw Juan passing by his palace, and he called to him to tell him a lie. Juan disregarded the king's wish, telling him that he was in a great hurry to catch all the fish that had washed ashore. But Juan told the king if he sent his cook down to the shore he would share the fish with him. Later that day the king sent his cook to meet Juan, but Juan was nowhere to be found and neither were the fish. Angry at his lies, the king called Juan to his court. Juan protested that the king had asked him to tell him a lie and that he had just done as he had been told. Perturbed by his manipulations, the king ordered Juan to leave and told him never to set foot on his soil again. A few days later, as the king was looking out over his court from his balcony, he saw Juan Pusong standing on a *pa-baba* (sled) outside the palace. Juan had crafted the sled himself, placing sand on the floor before he drove to the palace. When the king yelled at him for

his disobedience Juan showed him that he was not on the king's soil; he was standing on sand from the beach.

Juan's disregard for the king's power and prestige are common themes. In addition, his use of people's own words and actions against them is a common source of humor. Juan prides himself on being able to trip people up by their own actions. In another version of the previous story, after Juan showed up at the palace in his sled the king ordered his guards to place him in an iron cage to be cast out to sea three days later. On the second day of Juan's incarceration, however, a student saw him and asked him what his crime was. Juan told the young man that he was imprisoned because he refused to marry the king's daughter and that he had decided to accept death rather than honor the king's wishes and say yes. "What a fool," cried the student, and he begged Juan to let him take his place so that he could marry the princess. Juan gave in to the student's pleas, and the young man freed Juan and climbed inside the cage.

A few days later Juan showed up at the palace, and the king was amazed that he had survived being thrown out to sea. Juan told him that there was a great city under the sea and that the king's deceased grandparents lived there. "They wish to see you," Juan told the king. He showed the king some jewels and fish that were part of his grandparents' great wealth, a wealth they wanted to bestow upon the king. Believing his story, the king followed Juan to the sea and had his subjects cast him into the sea in an iron cage; he plummeted to his death while Juan stood smiling on the shore.

Storytellers use Juan's antics as a way to show the fallibility of those with power. In similar stories, Juan is found tempting the king's daughters, stealing his food, and tricking his guards into leaving their posts.

Even Juan is occasionally a fool, sometimes being duped by those smaller and less intelligent than he and sometimes simply acting foolishly. Although he is normally clever, Juan's senses take leave of him at times and he plays the part of a numskull. In fact, stories of Juan Pusong the fool are almost as plentiful as those of Juan Pusong the clever prankster. For example, in one story his mother told him to bring home a quiet bride, and he showed up with a dead woman. Another time he was told to cook some bamboo shoots, but he cooked the bamboo ladder instead. In the story that perhaps shows him at his most foolish, Juan's mother told him that dead things stink; after she passed gas he buried her, thinking she must be dead. (Alburo 1977; Eugenio 1982; Hart 1964; Maxfield and Millington 1906; Maxfield and Millington 1907; Ness 1992; Nimmo 1970)

Juha
Arab Countries

Juha, as he is most commonly called, is a popular clever fool in folktales throughout many Arab countries from Morocco to Syria. He is based on the poet Abu-Nawwas, who is said to have been a member of the court of Abbasid calif Haroun al-Rasheed in the ninth century. Known for his drunkenness, homosexuality, eroticism, satire, and racism, Abu-Nawwas took on the title Juha (*Juha* comes from the term *goha*, meaning "one who walks hurriedly and without rationality"), and tales about him have flourished ever since.

Juha is best known for his ability to gain insight where others see only laughter. His cleverness is matched by his unrelenting wit, from which no one is safe. In fact, Juha and his wife are common characters in tales. Trading tricks back and forth, Juha and his wife strive to get the best of each other.

In one story, Juha returned from the market with a pair of calf's legs and asked his wife to cook them. As she began to prepare the meat, Juha went to the market to

get the rest of their meal. As she cooked the calf's legs the aroma overtook her, and she began to eat one of them. Overwhelmed by the wonderful taste, she ate one whole leg. When Juha returned and asked for his calf's legs, his wife brought out the one remaining. "Where is the other?" Juha demanded. "What?" his wife replied in disgust. "You only brought me one." Juha was furious, and in his anger he declared that he would prove her wrong. But before he had a chance he grabbed his chest and fell to the ground. Juha's wife called the undertaker, and as the funeral procession ran through town the butcher asked who had died. One of the people told him it was Juha. The man sobbed, declaring that he had just seen Juha healthy that morning when he sold him a pair of calf's legs. When Juha heard the butcher say that, he leaped from his casket and told his wife he had been proven correct.

Stories about Juha do not discriminate. They challenge both secular and religious authority, and through his comedy people call attention to disputes, inequality, and abuse. Although his antics are well known, there is not a core set of tales that chronicle his activities. Instead, Juha's antics vary from town to town and region to region. Each town takes Juha as a character of its own, spinning tales to suit its own particular situation and communities. Lore about Juha is not limited to stories; proverbs, poems, songs, and even chants revolve around this paradoxical character. (El-Shamy 1980; Magnarella and Webster 1990)

Júko
Bororo, *Brazil*

Júko, a monkey, uses his cunning wit to exploit people and animals, especially **Adúgo** (the jaguar), and to obtain food and other resources for himself. Bororo stories relate that Júko was one of the four animals remaining after a cataclysmic flood early in Bororo history. Although the Bororo people were created soon afterward, Júko decided that they should not be alone in the world, so he created several other races of people. Since Júko populated the world, the Bororo consider him indirectly responsible for the negative interactions and many of the hardships they have faced since contact with outsiders. Several stories tell of the time before Júko created others, when the Bororo lived alone, peacefully. Júko's actions demonstrate the negative aspects of contact with outsiders.

The Bororo have been forcibly relocated several times since European contact. In addition, their relationship with neighboring groups competing for the same resources have led to fighting and devastation. Unlike other groups in the Central Brazilian highlands, the Bororo are a relatively small group who live along several small rivers. Each camp along the river interacts with the other members through trade and marriage. Bororo stories focus on aspects of their social order, such as their dual kinship system and marriage arrangements, as well as descriptions of interactions that have led the Bororo to sickness and hardship. As an antisocial character, Júko represents the negative aspects of the Bororo world. (See also **Méri** for a similar Bororo character.) In a small society dependent on community, Júko ignores social mores and steals, lies, and cheats to get what he wants. He takes advantage of those weaker than he is, and he even tricks people and animals stronger than himself because of his sharp intellect.

Stories about Júko demonstrate his power over several types of animals as well as over humans. He is afraid of no one, and he is infamous for his dealings with Bororo hunters. He lures them away from their catches and steals their equipment. He often hides in the trees and scares away their prey just for fun.

Even though Júko's actions have negative effects, he is looked up to for his ability to get out of even the most difficult situations. In one story, Júko and a small cavy (guinea pig) were traveling together in his canoe. The cavy began to chew on the canoe, and even though Júko warned him to stop the cavy continued to gnaw on the canoe until he had chewed a hole in the bottom and the boat sank. Once in the water, Júko grabbed onto a fish and was dragged to shore. Not as cunning as Júko, the cavy was eaten by a larger fish.

Taking the fish with him, Júko went in search of a place to cook him. Before he found enough wood to make a fire he met Adúgo, the gullible jaguar. Adúgo begged Júko to share the fish with him. Júko pointed at the sun, which was low on the horizon, and sent him to retrieve this "fire" to cook the fish. When Adúgo returned without any fire, Júko scolded him and sent him on another fruitless chase. Laughing at his friend's stupidity, Júko found some wood and cooked the fish for himself. When Adúgo returned the second time he could see the fish had been eaten. Angry, he jumped on Júko, surprising him, and swallowed him whole. Inside Adúgo Júko took out his knife and cut through his stomach to escape unharmed, while Adúgo bled to death. (Cook 1908; Hopper 1967; Kietzman 1967; Wilbert and Simoneau 1983)

K

Kaik
Salish, *British Columbia, Northwestern Coastal Region of North America*

Kaik is best known for his sexual antics, his multiple marriages, and his deceptions. He is normally portrayed as a mink, but he has the power to transform himself to get what he wants, which is usually a sexual favor. Stories of Kaik demonstrate the negative and deceptive qualities within the Salish community. (See **Sinkalip** for more on Salish culture.) Kaik lies, maims, kills, and rapes to get his way. He has no shame and no respect for Salish values.

Kaik delights in marrying as many women as he can. His sexual appetite drives him to marry and leave women at an alarming rate. One story tells that Kaik married fog and then took advantage of her sisters at the celebration. Ignoring Salish social mores about incest and respect for one's partner, Kaik took advantage of all the women at the ceremony one by one. He married eagle, salmon, gum tree, and sea kelp in turn. Each time he married he would curb his sexual drive for a time, but inevitably he moved on to another person because of his selfishness and disregard for his responsibilities.

In another story the Salish show Kaik's destructiveness. Kaik took his canoe out to go fishing on a nearby lake and came across a wolf who had been out hunting and fishing for several days. When the wolf saw Kaik from the shore, he called to him to come over, but Kaik ignored him. Finally, after the wolf had cried and cried for Kaik to come over, Kaik paddled to the shore and let the wolf in the canoe. Once the wolf was in the canoe, Kaik was very hospitable. He offered the wolf some sea urchins, and after the wolf had eaten he made a place for him to sleep. Once the wolf was asleep Kaik

cut his throat; then he paddled back to shore, skinned him, and went to the wolf's house to cook the meat and dry the skin.

After many hours the wolf's grandmother grew concerned about her grandson and went to look for him. After checking in the forest, she stopped at the wolf's house, only to find Kaik. Kaik showed her the wolf's skin and gloated about killing him. Horrified, the wolf's grandmother ran home. She told the other wolves what Kaik had done, and they decided to invite Kaik to a potlatch (feast ceremony; see **Nankilslas** for more information). When Kaik heard about the potlatch he knew it was a trick to avenge the wolf's death. To protect himself, he went to see his grandmothers, Knothole and Mouse. He told the first to grow in size if he needed to escape and told the latter to chew through all the wolves' paddles and bows so they could not chase him. When Kaik arrived at the potlatch the wolves trapped him as he had expected, but he called to his grandmother Knothole, jumped through her, and ran to his canoe. The wolves chased him, but when they tried to row, their paddles broke. The wolves were so angry that they swam to shore, got new paddles, and returned to chase Kaik.

When Kaik saw the wolves coming a second time he tried to paddle faster, but they overtook him and carried him to shore. He asked if he might have one last dance before they killed him. Agreeing, the wolves untied him and let him perform. He danced

101

with one foot in each canoe, jumping between two canoes until finally he flung himself deep into the lake. Once at the bottom of the lake, he took out the entrails from the wolf he had killed and pushed them to shore. Believing he was dead, the wolves began to go home. But just as they did, they heard Kaik gloating, "Here I am." The wolves chased him in the water, but he again used the entrails of the wolf to trick them into thinking he was dead. Again, as they retreated, he popped up, gloated and mimicked the wolves cries. This continued for several hours until the wolves gave up, knowing they could not outwit Kaik. (Ashwell 1978; Hill-Trout 1978; Smith 1940)

Kai-palaoa
Hawaii

Kai-palaoa is the character in Hawaiian folklore whose skill at riddling won him status and elevated riddling to an art form as well as simple entertainment. In traditional Hawaiian society, the ability to riddle was looked upon as a great achievement. Traditional Hawaiian society centered around a hierarchy based on family blood; because riddling was not only seen as entertainment but also as the sign of high intelligence and deserving of a high status, it was one of the only ways for a peasant to improve his standing in society.

Stories about Kai-palaoa tell of his expert ability to concoct riddles even as a baby. From a very young age Kai-palaoa and his father, Halepaki, would practice riddles and chants for hours every day. Halepki wanted more for his son and knew that riddling was one of the only ways to improve his standing. Riddling represents one of the few instances of a member of the common people mixing with and being considered part of the upper class. In the character of Kai-palaoa, Hawaiians show their respect for the intellectual and humorous art of riddling and their desire to climb the social ladder.

As Kai-palaoa grew, his father could tell that his ability to form and answer riddles was beyond that of a child. Halepaki told his son of Kalani, the chief of the island of Kauai and the champion riddler. Kai-palaoa practiced every day, hoping one day to challenge Kalani and become the champion. One day Kai-palaoa's father decided that he would challenge the chief himself, making way for his son to be next. Halepaki went to Kauai, leaving his wife and son behind. After several days, Kai-palaoa and his mother became worried. They had not heard from Halepaki and feared the worst. Wanting to save his father and become the champion himself, Kai-palaoa learned all he could from his mother and then went to stay with his aunt, whose husband was an excellent riddler. After weeks of training, Kai-palaoa felt confident that he could beat Kalani.

When he reached the island of Kauai, Kai-palaoa asked about his father. Another youngster told him that Halepaki had challenged the chief and lost. His bones now lay in the chief's house of bones. Saddened, Kai-palaoa knew he must challenge the chief and avenge his father's death. Kai-palaoa went to the chief's flag pole, tore down the flags, and replaced them with fish and thus announced his challenge. The chief quickly summoned the young riddler, and the contest was on; the winner would take home the loser's bones. Before they began, the chief and Kai-palaoa were both asked to compose a chant telling of the wonders of their own island homes. After each had given his chant, the riddling began. Round after round the two engaged in a battle of wits, but each round was deemed a tie. Finally, on the last round, Kai-palaoa defeated the chief and won the match. Watching the chief being taken to his death, Kai-palaoa became the new riddling champion, and he and the new chief decided that the stakes would never again be so high. From then on riddling would be an art and a source of entertainment, not a battleground. (Beckwith 1970; Green 1926; Thompson 1990)

Kaka
Bo, *West Africa: Sierra Leone*

The kaka, that is "shit-devils," are one of four types of "devils" performed by the members of Alikali, a multiethnic group of 8- to 12-year-old boys who perform in street masquerades. Throughout Sierra Leone there is a long tradition of masking groups who perform at religious and social events. The Alikali is distinguished by the youth of its members.

The group, a source of camaraderie and power for the boys, is sponsored by several urban associations, but each boy contributes to the group by helping construct the *igberre*, or devil house, in which they make their costumes, practices their performances, and write accompanying songs and skits. The Alikali are a modern outgrowth of the changing social climate in Sierra Leone. Since contact with Europeans Sierra Leonean culture has been changed in several ways, most obviously in the ways that people make a living and in the education system. With more parents now living in urban areas instead of villages, the status of young boys has changed. Whereas traditionally young boys would accompany their fathers on hunts or in the fields, now they are expected to attend school. They remain dependent on their families longer than before and thus reach "adulthood" at a later age. The Alikali group is one way in which boys show their independence and power.

The Alikali have four types of "devils" who perform. The kaka is the antithesis of the other three—rainbow, jolly, and talabi—which are seen as heroes. The kaka, on the other hand, is seen as a slow-witted, antisocial misfit. Whereas the other three are neat and clean, with costumes that never show wear, the kaka purposely wears torn clothes, rolls in the dusty streets, and lets himself get dirty to entertain the audiences. While the kaka performs his antics, the other boys sing songs pointing out his antisocial ways. "Ah de fall down [oh, they fell down]" or "e no fine [he's not fine]" the boys sing in the Creole language of Krio. As they sing, the kaka will fling himself onto the street, chase people, foam at the mouth, and do anything else he can think of to elicit a response.

The kaka portrays the undesirable side of life among the Bo, especially as conceived by the younger generation. It is desirable to be "fine," that is, for one's clothes to be neat and for one's physical appearance to be spotless. In the kaka the boys reverse the acceptable and show the unacceptable. As a comedic performer the kaka delights audiences and is rewarded by the money people pay to see him perform. The kaka represents the boys' struggle with what they know they should do, which is shown in the other masked performers and which they cannot always achieve.

As a masked performer, the kaka brings out the unthinkable, the grotesque, and the crude in society. By throwing himself at the audience or spouting profanities at them, the kaka reverses the acceptable, and for that performance, at least, the unacceptable is what is expected. Eliciting laughter from young and old, the kaka shows that the world is not always the way people expect it to be. (Bockarie and Hinzen 1986; Cannizzo 1983; Clarke 1971)

Kakxó
Nivakle, *Paraguay*

Kakxó, a cunning and mischievous armadillo who changes form and deceives others to get what he wants, is at the center of many Nivakle stories. He makes fun of people and animals, lies, cheats, and outwits others, especially the jaguar. He manipulates people and gets them to do things that they know are morally wrong. Using Kakxó to illustrate negative behavior, Nivakle storytellers entertain audiences with humorous stories of his tricks and adventures. He is well known for leaving talking excrement in his trail to fool people and for steering them in the wrong direction. Unlike **Cufalh,** however, Kakxó is not intentionally violent. Although people may get hurt from his antics, that is not his intent. Normally Kakxó's adventures are purely selfish outings in which he dupes others out of their food, clothes, and other material goods to satisfy his unending desires.

Kakxó is notorious for tricking others out of their food. In story after story he leads hunting expeditions and cunningly convinces the others to listen to his suggestions so that he gets most, if not all, of the catch. In one story Kakxó convinced the jaguar to build a fire away from their camp while he cleaned the prey they had caught. While the jaguar was building the fire, Kakxó sneaked away with the meat and left his excrement behind to throw the jaguar off his trail. Before he left with the meat he told his excrement to answer "over here, over here" when the jaguar called his name. The jaguar returned from building the fire and could not find Kakxó, so he called him. Kakxó's excrement called out "over here, over here." The jaguar turned in every direction but could not find Kakxó or his food anywhere.

Some of Kakxó's deceptions and trickery lead to permanent changes in the world and in Nivakle society. One story tells how the jaguar came to look as he does because of Kakxó's antics. One day Kakxó pretended to be very sick and called on the jaguar, who was then known as a very powerful healer, to aid him. One of Kakxó's friends went to the jaguar's house and told him about Kakxó's illness. At first the jaguar was leery of Kakxó, but when he saw him writhing in pain he decided to help. Leaning over Kakxó, the jaguar blew onto Kakxó to get

rid of the illness. He blew over him and tried other remedies, but still Kakxó called out in pain. Finally the jaguar leaned close into Kakxó and blew as hard as he could; just at that moment Kakxó grabbed the jaguar's long nose and began to squeeze as hard as he could. Kakxó held onto the jaguar's nose and retreated into his shell while the jaguar cried out in pain. Kakxó finally let go, and the jaguar left embarrassed and with a much smaller nose; it has remained that way ever since. (Métraux 1946a; Wilbert and Simoneau 1988b)

Kalulu
Bemba, *Central Africa: Zambia*

Kalulu, a cunning hare, represents an honored characteristic in Bemba society; the term *kalulu* is used of any person who is cunning, clever, and wise. The Bemba recognize wisdom, rewarding it with status in social institutions, including the chieftainship and the familial structure. Kalulu uses his wisdom to transmit cultural, social, and historical information to others in the society. Like the Citimukulu (the chief), Kalulu directs people's attention to the wrongdoings of others, to proper activities, and to beneficial ways of dealing with antisocial behavior.

The Bemba divide the world into two spheres, the *mushi* (village) and the *mpanga* (bush). The village represents an orderly existence in which people live, and the bush represents disorder. Kalulu bridges the gap between these two spheres by showing that one can bring order to the bush and also that disorder can be found in the village. In addition the Bemba distinguish between two types of beings who inhabit these spaces, *mipashi* (deceased relatives, usually of the matrilineal line) and *fiwa* (malevolent ancestors). The *mipashi* help their living Bemba relatives, and in turn the living relatives make offerings at their shrines. The *fiwa*, however, wreak havoc on the living

Bemba; they cause illness and misfortune, either because they themselves died a violent death or because they committed misdeeds while they were alive.

These two types of relatives are brought to life in the folktales told by the Bemba, especially those concerning Kalulu. Tales with Kalulu as the main character present the Bemba with a meeting between those relatives who wish to help and those who wish to do harm. Kalulu demonstrates that vengeful ancestors do not always succeed in their destructive behavior. He also shows that cunning and skill can be used to one's advantage when dealing with an angry relative. Kalulu, therefore, embodies the positive, helpful attributes of Bemba society, whereas his counterparts represent the negative side. Kalulu himself, however, also shows that constructive and destructive elements may be characteristic of a single individual. Kalulu does not always succeed, and at times he is tempted to use his wisdom for negative ends. The folktales of the Bemba capture the various types of relationships the people have with their surroundings (*mushi* and *mpanga*) and their relatives (*mipashi* and *fiwa*), as well as the interaction between place and people; that is, the folktales capture the interaction between order and disorder.

Kalulu is generally portrayed in folktales as a hero who uses trickery to help others or to expose the misdeeds of others, especially the hyena, who plays the malicious, villainous character, or the elephant, who is characterized as lazy and dumb. For example the Bemba tell a story about the lion and Kalulu. Once, the lion, head of all the animals, decided that all the old animals were taking up too much space and eating too much food, and he therefore decreed that they were useless and should all be killed. They were all killed mercilessly, except for the old hare, Kalulu. Kalulu escaped from the forest, and only his son knew where he was. Soon all the old animals were dead,

and the others were going about their normal routines, having forgotten about lion's cruel actions. One day, as the lion slept with his mouth wide open, a snaked crawled by and mistook his mouth for a hole and went in. The snake curled up inside the lion's mouth and went to sleep. When the lion woke up he felt a bit of discomfort in his throat, and he could not roar at all. Once the snake started moving the lion felt terrible pain and was upset. He went to the others and, using sign language, told them that whoever could get the snake out of his mouth would be rewarded greatly. One by one the young animals came forward, but none of them had the wisdom to coax the snake from his warm shelter, and in turn the snake became even angrier and more restless.

The son of Kalulu had an idea about how to get the snake out. He went to the lion and told him that he had recently heard tell of a wise person in a cave who might be able to help the lion. The young hare went to his father in the cave and explained to him all that had happened. Disguising himself, Kalulu set off for the lion. Kalulu decided he would act like a medicine man, so he dressed himself with shells around his neck and a skin cap on his head and he carried a mouse with him. When Kalulu arrived, he did not speak but began to dance around the lion, chanting as if to invoke the assistance of the spirits. As Kalulu sang, the snake inside the lion's mouth began to smell the odor of the mouse, and at once he slipped out of the lion's mouth to go after his prey. Roaring with joy, the lion hugged Kalulu and told him to name his reward and it would be his. But Kalulu was modest and requested a boon for the sake of others. Kalulu requested that the lion let the older animals live, telling him that in times like these it is important to have the wisdom and knowledge of the elders. Seeing the error of his ways, the lion granted his wish, and, because of Kalulu, from then on all the older animals lived peacefully in the forest.

Kalulu's wisdom also demonstrates to others the error of their wrongheaded behavior. Leading by example, Kalulu shows others the proper ways to act in order that they might live peacefully. Kalulu's intelligence helps him out of many situations in which others would be lost, and even if he tricks others or acts improperly it is always in response to others' negative actions. For example, once Kalulu had just finished planting rows of cabbage, carrots, lettuce, and other vegetables in his garden. His was the biggest garden in the forest, and because he was so smart it was the most profitable as well. Kalulu always had food year-round. This year Kalulu decided he would plant pumpkins as well. While he was hard at work in his garden a large elephant came by. The elephant looked with envy at Kalulu's great garden and congratulated the hare on his magnificent garden as he passed by. Kalulu thanked him and told him that as it was pumpkin season he was busy planting. The elephant said that he enjoyed pumpkins as well and wondered if Kalulu might help him plant some. But Kalulu politely declined, as he knew that the elephant was lazy and that he would end up doing all the work himself. Instead, Kalulu lent the elephant his hoe and gave him some seeds to get him started.

The elephant went home and tried to plant the seeds, but he became very winded and tired and did not end up doing much work at all. As the days passed Kalulu's garden grew magnificently. The elephant's garden, on the other hand, was very poor and did not look as if anything was growing properly. The elephant grew more and more jealous of Kalulu every time he passed his garden. Soon Kalulu's garden was ready to harvest, and he decided to start early in the morning, but when he arrived all the pumpkins were gone. He was angry and knew that the elephant was the culprit. He

decided to teach him a lesson. As the smaller pumpkins began to come up, Kalulu thought of his plan. When they were large enough Kalulu went to the garden very late one night and cut a hole in the side of one of the large pumpkins. He scooped out all the seeds and climbed inside to wait for the thief. But the pumpkin was so warm that Kalulu fell asleep, and the next thing he knew he had been swallowed whole by the elephant. Thinking quickly, Kalulu climbed out of the pumpkin and started loudly beating a drum and jumping about violently inside the elephant. The elephant was in terrible pain and frightened. Kalulu kept up the racket, and the elephant ran around trying to figure out what was wrong, but soon he was so tired that he fell asleep. While he was sleeping, Kalulu crept out of his stomach and went home. From that day on, the elephant had a great dislike for pumpkins and stopped his stealing immediately.

Although Kalulu is usually portrayed as the cunning hero, once in a while his ego gets the best of him and he fails. Once when all the water holes had dried up, the lion ordered everyone to help dig the holes deeper. The animals set up a rotation shift so that some worked during the day and the others at night. The hyena, however, was lazy and did not want to help, so he tricked the others by telling those who were on the day shift that he had worked on the night shift and vice versa. It took several days for the others to figure out his ruse, but when it was found out the lion decreed that the hyena would not be allowed to drink from the water hole when it was finished.

Soon the water hole was deep enough, and the lion posted guards so the lazy hyena would not get any water. However, every night the hyena sneaked into the well and cheated the rest out of their water. Though they were angry they did not know how to stop the crafty hyena. Kalulu thought of a plan. He went to the king and bragged that he was the only one who could stop the hyena, and he asked if he might guard the well that night. The king agreed. Around midnight the hyena showed up, but he did not see anyone guarding the water hole. He thought it might be a trick so he announced himself, asking if anyone wanted any of his potion, which allowed him to go for days without water. Kalulu was watching the hyena's every move. Kalulu called to the hyena to show him the potion. The hyena went over and greeted Kalulu and sat down with him. The hyena showed Kalulu the special potion and told him that he need not guard the well anymore, as he had this potion for thirst. Kalulu became intrigued and questioned the hyena. Soon Kalulu decided to give it a try, and he tilted his head back very far as the hyena had instructed him. But as he stretched further back he fell over, and the hyena tied him up and got his fill of the water. In the morning the other animals saw Kalulu and laughed because he had boasted so much. In the end it was the tortoise who captured the hyena, and the lion punished the hyena by putting him in jail. Even Kalulu with his intelligence and willingness to help can be tricked at times. (Raman 1979; Rattray 1969b; Richards 1982; Roberts 1973; Werner 1968)

Kamapuaa
Hawaii

Kamapuaa is a mischievous child who is also known as "hog-child" because of his appearance: He has the face of a hog and short hair all over his stout body. Not only is he a gifted prankster, he also has the ability to change form; he has unending strength and an intellect that is almost unmatched.

At his birth Kamapuaa's family was ashamed of the creature that lay before them. Not realizing his power, the family's eldest son, Kahiki, took Kamapuaa to his Kupuna (grandmother). Peeling the blankets back from the baby's face, Kupuna saw the wily hog-child but did not flinch. Instead, she scolded Kahiki for being ashamed, telling him that Kamapuaa was her grandson just as he was. She took the baby from his arms and chided him. "Stupid one," she scolded, telling Kahiki that the youngster was a *kupua*, a powerful one. That night Kamapuaa's grandmother wrapped him tightly in *kapa* (sheets made from bark), and he slept well. She knew that he would one day wield great power.

Over the next month Kamapuaa grew quickly. Kahiki brought food for him every day, but he soon grew tired of all his hard work and complained that it was Kamapuaa's turn to collect the *taro* for the meals. Kamapuaa heard Kahiki's complaint, and that night he uprooted the neighbors' garden and stole all their food. The next day the neighbors complained, and Kahiki scolded Kamapuaa for stealing from them, saying he had caused him great embarrassment. That night Kamapuaa raided the high chief's garden and stole four hens, leaving two for Kahiki and his grandmother and the others for himself.

By successfully tricking the chief's guards and stealing his hens, Kamapuaa quickly called attention to himself. Angered, the chief sent his men to capture Kamapuaa. The chief's men saw Kamapuaa sitting on a hillside feasting on the chief's hens, and they rushed toward him. But as they did he disappeared, and in his place were hundreds of hogs of all colors and sizes. Not knowing which was Kamapuaa, the men left defeated while Kamapuaa laughed at their ignorance.

Kamapuaa's power lies in his ability to change form and in his superior strength. He can change from a man to a wild pig to any other animal form that may aid his adventures. He ignores the chief's laws and mocks the chief's power by tricking him time and time again. Kamapuaa shows that even the chief is not above being tricked and that while he may claim power he is not the sole possessor of it. Traditionally the chief held control over the Hawaiian people. Stories like those about Kamapuaa come from a time when the chieftainship was being challenged. (See also **Iwa** for another example of this type of Hawaiian character.)

Kamapuaa represents the people's ability to overcome abusive power, while at the same time reminding them that power comes in many different forms. Although Kamapuaa defeats the chief, he also steals, lies, and deceives to do so. Kamapuaa and other Hawaiian crafty characters represent the range of choices people are faced with every day. The entertaining stories are meant to be more than humorous; they are also moral tales showing the dangers of improper behavior and the abuse of power. (Beckwith 1970; Green 1926; Thompson 1990; Westervelt 1915)

Kamdaak Waneng
Bimin-Kuskusim, *Papua New Guinea*

Kamdaak Waneng, a wandering woman being, is a common character who tricks people simply for the pleasure of it. Although she is generally depicted as female, she can take on male and animal characteristics and forms to deceive and trick people into doing what she wants. Kamdaak Waneng is often portrayed as having no *finiik* (socially proper aspects of personhood), and thus she is constantly breaking social rules and sexual taboos, especially by seducing her male relatives. She is usually paired with her male counterpart **Gabruurian** in the tales of her antics. Kamdaak Waneng is very powerful, and she is feared for her ability to trick men, especially during male rituals.

Kamdaak Waneng is one of several antisocial characters used in Bimin-Kuskusim stories to educate their youth on the perils of immoral behavior. Topics such as stealing, lying, cheating, misusing ritual objects, or attempting activities beyond one's knowledge are all dealt with during times of *weeng keeman*, or moral instruction. *Weeng keeman* may occur during initiations or other ceremonial events, or it may occur during social gatherings at which children are present. (See **Utuum-khriin min** for more on Bimin-Kuskusim literary styles.)

Stories about Kamdaak Waneng focus on her deliberate neglect of social mores and taboos. In one story Gabruurian was involved in a male ritual when he saw Kamdaak Waneng wearing the *siriik* headdress associated with the ancestral underworld. Gabruurian knew the power associated with the *siriik* and ran from the ritual area, leaving all the men open to danger by interrupting the ritual process. Kamdaak Waneng tricked Gabruurian into leaving the ritual by creating an illusion of power, whereas in reality Kamdaak Waneng's appearance posed no threat to Gabruurian or the other men because the headdress was only an illusion.

In another story Kamdaak Waneng showed her ability at trickery by luring Gabruurian into eating women's food and thereby polluting himself. In Bimin-Kuskusim society males and females properly have different actions, food, roles, and responsibilities. In her disregard for these rules, Kamdaak Waneng demonstrates the dangers associated with breaking societal rules, but she also shows that they can be broken. Another one of Kamdaak Waneng's favorite tricks is to entice men, including Gabruurian, into her garden to copulate with her. The men are unaware that in her garden Kamdaak Waneng has ultimate control and can use her power to seduce men into actions they would normally never undertake.

Through her antics Kamdaak Waneng shows her ability to interfere in all aspects of society. However, she is most often portrayed together with Gabruurian. The two engage in a back-and-forth type of trickery with each other, showing both the humorous and the dangerous aspects of humanity. (Poole 1983; Poole 1987)

Kantjil
Malayo, *Indonesia*

Kantjil is a mouse-deer (a small, nimble, mobile mammal) portrayed in Indonesian folklore. Tales about Kantjil focus on his ability to trick people and animals, even those quite a bit larger than he. Kantjil loves to take on tigers, kings, and pythons in his adventures across the Indonesian terrain.

A favorite among Indonesian storytellers, Kantjil exposes the weakness of those who seem powerful. In his tricks he manipulates the wise and the brave into awkward and dangerous situations. The humor in his adventures is matched by the moral dilemmas he poses. With the influence of Islam in Indonesia, many stories also include Muslim characters, such as prophets. In fact, Kantjil often portrays himself as an aid to the prophets in order to get out of negative situations. Invoking the name and power of the prophets is a more recent characteristic of Kantjil, but the innovation fits his traditional role as a quick thinker ready to do anything to get what he wants.

Storytellers present Kantjil as an example of both antisocial behavior and a quick intellect. That is, although Kantjil indulges in trickery, he also shows the benefits of such trickery in dangerous situations. For example, in one story, Kantjil found himself face to face with a large python. Knowing that the python could strangle him at any moment, Kantjil quickly spoke up and caught the python's attention. Kantjil told the python that a tiger would soon cross his path and that he should save his appetite for the much larger tiger. Convinced by Kantjil's smooth talk, the python coiled himself up and awaited the tiger, leaving Kantjil to roam freely.

Kantjil delights in playing pranks simply for the sake of entertainment. Although he does not intentionally set out to hurt anyone, his tricks usually end up with someone being hurt. In a story about Kantjil and a tiger, Kantjil again used his quick wit to keep from being eaten by the tiger, but the tiger did not fare as well. Kantjil was in the forest when he heard the deafening roar of a mighty tiger. Before he could run for safety, the tiger was upon him. Thinking quickly, Kantjil picked up a leaf and laid it over a pile of water buffalo dung, and he began to fan the pile with another leaf. When the tiger saw him, he asked what he was doing. Kantjil did not answer, but simply continued to fan the pile. Angered, the tiger asked why Kantjil was standing there and not running away in fear like a monkey (in Indonesia it is an insult to compare someone to a monkey in such a situation).

Looking up from his work, Kantjil told the tiger that he was fanning a special portion of a feast to be given to the new prophet. The tiger was enraged that the prophet trusted such a job to the small Kantjil. He asked Kantjil why the prophet had not picked him, with his size and strength. Kantjil took advantage of the opportunity to answer the tiger's question with a cannon of insults. Telling him that he was ugly and had no self-control, Kantjil enraged the tiger even more. Finally, when the tiger was about to strike him, Kantjil agreed to let the tiger have some of the prophet's feast, but only on the condition that Kantjil be allowed to leave so that the prophet would not be angry with him. The tiger agreed, and Kantjil scurried off into the forest leaving the tiger to eat the dung. Believing it to be a delicious dish prepared for the prophet, the tiger dug in and ate it without haste. After he ate it, his stomach became enlarged and he vomited. Realizing that Kantjil had tricked him, he set out for revenge.

The tiger found Kantjil in the forest again and approached him angrily. This time Kantjil was fanning a large bulb-shaped object with leaves over it. Curious, the tiger asked what the noise from the object was. Kantjil told him that the object was the prophet's ceremonial gong and that it was still reverberating from its last use. Intrigued, the tiger wanted to strike it himself to hear its sweet sounds. At first Kantjil denied his request, saying that the prophet would be angry if he heard the gong being struck. The tiger threatened him again, and Kantjil backed off, telling the tiger he would go ask the prophet for permission. Kantjil ran off, and after a short while he called to the tiger that the prophet had agreed to let him strike the gong. Happy, the tiger swiped at the object with his paw, and, to his surprise, a swarm of hornets came out from under the leaves and surrounded him, stinging his entire body until he was completely swollen.

Laughing to himself, Kantjil knew the tiger would be back for more, but he loved teasing the gullible beast. The next time the tiger came upon Kantjil he was fanning a coiled-up python. The tiger asked what it was. Kantjil told him it was the prophet's ceremonial garments. Wanting to try them on himself, the tiger pleaded with Kantjil until he left to ask the prophet. Again calling to the tiger from a few feet away, Kantjil told him the prophet had given him permission. The tiger grabbed the pile, thinking it was a beautifully adorned scarf, and the python struck out at him and strangled him to death.

Kantjil's pranks teach that even he can go too far to avoid danger. Although using one's intellect and quick thinking are praised in Indonesian society, Kantjil's zest for tricking unsuspecting victims crosses the boundaries of acceptable behavior. By taking his pranks too far, Kantjil puts himself and those around him in danger, and he ultimately hurts and even kills those he set out to trick. As a popular character, Kantjil demonstrates both the positive and nega-tive effects of manipulating one's situation. (Dixon 1916; Laidaw 1906; McKean 1970; Winstead 1958)

Kayi
Limba, *West Africa: Northern Sierra Leone*
See **Wosi.**

Kesey, Ken, and the Merry Pranksters
United States

As counterculture pioneers during the 1960s, Ken Kesey and his band of merry pranksters came to symbolize the free spirit ushered in by the youth of the late 1950s and early 1960s in the United States. As the Merry Pranksters' ringleader, Kesey, along with other counterculture gurus like Allen Ginsberg, Timothy Leary, and the Grateful Dead, shared in the experience of uniting a generation around a message of freedom, love, and peace. In addition to group freedom, however, Kesey and the Pranksters also offered personal insight through LSD.

Kesey and his Pranksters were known best for their "acid tests" in which LSD was handed out freely. Tom Wolfe immortalized the antics of Kesey and the Pranksters in his book *The Electric Kool-Aid Acid Test.* Kesey popularized acid tests in and around the San Francisco area during the early 1960s. With bands such as the Grateful Dead as their entertainment and with acid flowing in the Kool-Aid, young people across the country flocked to the Bay area to be a part of the new culture. Promising a new outlook for a generation tired of their parents' America, Kesey and the Pranksters delivered.

Huge parties at which anyone and everyone was accepted and praise of free love, free speech, and freedom from authority were the hallmarks of any good acid test. Crossing social and gender boundaries, Kesey and the Pranksters

Author Ken Kesey, a leader of the psychedelic movement, speaks to the Merry Pranksters in San Francisco in 1966. (Ted Streshinsky/Corbis)

opened their ideas of a good time to everyone. Hell's Angels, lawyers, journalists, and anyone who would participate was welcome. Taking the acid was not the only aspect of a "good" test. Bringing a crowd in tune with each other was always the goal. Once the tests were banned in San Francisco, the Pranksters moved their tests to a small farm outside of the city. There Kesey and the Pranksters filmed and taped their tests to ensure they would be recorded for posterity.

Kesey and the Pranksters promised not just a good time but a new vision of the world. This vision included an end to the authority that promoted the nine-to-five workaday lifestyle. It was for their denunciation of U.S. culture as it was then that the Pranksters got their name. Causing trouble for police, loitering in the streets and in restaurants, ignoring social mores about sex, love, and hygiene, the Prank-

sters represented everything that the United States of the 1950s loathed. Troubled by war and by the feeling that the government was out of control, Kesey and the Pranksters pecked away at the social fabric of America with their pranks, acid tests, and literature.

One of Kesey's and the Pranksters' most famous escapades was their cross-country bus trip, which highlighted freedom, love, and the spirit of the moment in their motto of being "on the bus" or "off the bus." "On the bus" referred to a state of mind more than a physical presence. Being on the bus meant that one was in tune with the feeling of the moment and living only in that moment, free from trivial squabbles and external responsibilities. Boarding a multicolored school bus in 1964, Kesey and some of the more infamous Pranksters, Babs, Neal Cassady, Mountain Girl, and Hassler, set out to cross the country with their message, or nonmessage, as it had come to be known.

The Pranksters' touchstone was experience. Whether through the use of LSD or not, Kesey and the Pranksters saw experience as the only way to usher in the new culture. The bus, named "Further," and the trip symbolized the awakening of a generation and the possibilities for living in the "now" without outside pressures. Traveling across the country, the Pranksters lived up to their name. Just by their physical appearance they drew attention, in large cities as well as small towns. Mocking the police, bathing in mud, and taking what they needed, the Pranksters' biggest prank was their denial of authority. (Kesey 1990; Roszak 1969; Wolfe 1968)

Keyók
Toba, *Argentina*

Keyók is a gullible jaguar who attempts to outsmart others but who normally fails. Unlike Chunga, the crafty bird, Keyók fails in his attempts to deceive and trick people and animals. Like other jaguar characters of the region (see also **Kumarxúo, Nowarera,** and **Palu**) Keyók is portrayed as a slow-witted, predictable dupe who is the butt of many jokes and pranks. Despite his seemingly low intelligence, Keyók, along with other jaguars, is known to have the ability to heal others. (See **Chunga** for more on Toba understandings of jaguars.) Keyók's power to heal is his only asset. Although he is normally perceived as an easy catch, both animals and humans come to him in times of need. Keyók succeeds at times, but storytellers portray him as an entertaining character who never fails to fail.

Although Keyók attempts to outwit others he is easily distracted and slow to catch on to subtle deceptions by others. (See **Wayayqaláchiyi** for more on Toba oral literature.) In one story a weak goat

frightened the stronger Keyók by pretending to have killed a much larger puma. Keyók and the goat were working when Keyók tried to use his size to his advantage by telling the goat that if he did not get Keyók some food he would eat him. The goat went into the forest and found a puma who had already been killed. Bringing the puma back to Keyók, the goat stood tall and declared that he was the stronger and that Keyók should get food for him from then on. Frightened, Keyók ran off to get the goat more food.

Keyók's adventures place him in awkward situations in which he is either embarrassed, taken advantage of, hurt, or killed. In one story, an armadillo was ill and called on Keyók to heal him. The armadillo's wife went into the forest and told Keyók of her husband's situation. Keyók agreed to help, all the while planning to kill the armadillo for food. Keyók arrived at the armadillo's house and began to blow on the armadillo's stomach where his pain was. He got closer and closer, blowing on the diseased area, until he was close enough to try to take a bite. Sensing Keyók's intentions, the armadillo jumped up and grabbed Keyók's snout and held it shut. Keyók wiggled around and tried to free himself, but he could not break loose. Soon Keyók died, and the armadillo threw him into the woods.

There is no animal too small or too insignificant to outwit Keyók. One story pits a tick against Keyók in a race with several other animals. All the animals in the forest decided to have a race to see who was the fastest. Throughout the race Keyók was able to outrun the other animals. But just as he was approaching the finish line, the tick jumped off his eyebrow, where he had been riding, to win the race and humiliate Keyók. (Karsten 1923; Métraux 1946b; Miller 1980; Wilbert and Simoneau 1982b; Wilbert and Simoneau 1989; Wright 1986)

Khadir
Islamic Arab Countries
See **Khezr.**

Khezr
Islamic Arab Countries

Khezr, the green man or the hidden prophet, is also referred to as Khadir, which literally means "green." Khezr is associated in Islam with esoteric knowledge and the shock of paradoxical statements, actions, and visions. Khezr is not indigenous to Islam, but by the early Middle Ages Khezr had clearly been assimilated into Islamic traditions. Stories of Khezr link him to Moses and Alexander the Great, as well as to modern-day Sufi mystics (a sect within the Islamic tradition). In fact, Khezr is most clearly associated with Sufi traditions that highlight his ambiguous, paradoxical, and cunning nature. Khezr is called the one with "crazy wisdom" because his seemingly odd actions and jumbled words always lead to a richer understanding of the world.

Khezr is known to be immortal and also a master of disguise; therefore one is never sure when or where he will be found. Because of his ability to be anywhere at anytime, when people speak the name of Khezr they follow it by saying "Salaam aleikum" [Peace be unto you] to properly acknowledge his presence and prestige. Khezr reveals himself to people by showing his green clothes or by revealing some esoteric knowledge. He speaks in rhymes and is known for his love of wordplay and other games. He loves to indulge himself by twisting his words about to the point where they are almost unrecognizable. But that is where his power lies, in his ability to see through ordinary reality, beyond words and language to the pure experience of life. Through his play, people learn lessons of the world.

Khezr reveals the existence of hidden knowledge in the Koran (Islamic holy book). Although orthodox Muslims may disagree with Sufi interpretations of the Koran, the Sufis hold up Khezr as an example of the secret knowledge of Allah (God). Sufis point first to the story of Khezr and Moses as a prime example of this hidden knowledge.

In that story Moses met an unidentified figure, not named but commonly accepted to be Khezr, at the borderland between two oceans and asked to travel with him. After much thought, Khezr agreed but stipulated that Moses must not ask any questions about Khezr's actions on their journey. As a sign of the mystical quality of their adventure, Moses saw a cooked fish leap into the sea and swim away. In addition, the borderland where the two met is commonly understood to be the intersection of the real and visionary worlds, one of which is tangible and the other of which is only accessible to those who have been shown parts of the hidden knowledge of the world.

Moses agreed, and the two set off on their journey. During their travels Khezr sank a boat, killed a boy, and repaired a wall for a village of disreputable people. Each time he performed one of these seemingly negative acts, Moses broke his promise and asked why he was acting in such an immoral way. Each time, however, Khezr ignored him and went about his business. Finally they reached an appropriate destination, and Khezr decided to answer Moses. He told him that the ship would have been seized by force by the king so it was better to sink it first; that the youth whom he killed had been destined to become an outlaw and that by his death his parents were given another chance at having a pious son; and finally that although the townspeople were unworthy of his help the two boys who owned the wall were orphans, that underneath it was a treasure meant for them when they were older, and that by repairing the wall Khezr ensured that the townspeople would not get the boys' wealth.

Sufis point out that although Khezr's actions seemed negative, unpredictable, and nonsensical, because of his visionary powers he was able to see past the reality of his actions to the way they would ultimately affect the world. Khezr's activities are notoriously paradoxical. He is always pointing out things that seem banal or discrediting those who seem respectable, but the power of his escapades lies in his ability to shed light on the invisible aspects of reality. (Arabi 1989; Wilson 1991)

Kitsune
Japan

Within Japanese literature, both written and oral, there are three distinct portrayals of Kitsune: as the messenger of Inari, a Shinto (traditional religion in Japan) deity; as a spirit who takes over people's bodies and makes them crazy; and as a master of pranks, a trickster, and shape-shifter.

Kitsune brings with him the physical characteristics of his animal counterpart, the fox: He is stealthy, quick, and crafty. In Japanese folklore and popular culture Kitsune is the messenger of the Shinto deity Inari, who is a symbol of prosperity and fertility and who in his modern incarnation is often revered as the patron of prostitutes. Always accompanying Inari, Kitsune is also associated with his powers. There are public shrines and statues in Inari's honor throughout Japan. The shrines are normally red and gold and are flanked by a pair of foxes. Inari is a prominent feature of Japanese culture: His shrines range from large stone structures to small carvings one can buy in the market; in rural Japan almost every house has a small shrine dedicated to him; and roadside shrines with statues of foxes at the gates can be found at the entrances to most villages. Along with Inari, the fox is praised for his power and is seen as a boon to the community, to which he brings prosperity and fertility.

Another side of Kitsune, however, is his association with people who act irrationally or who have gone crazy. Possession of one's body and mind by Kitsune was a common diagnosis for irrational behavior in traditional Japanese culture. Even today when children act up or a person displays odd behavior because of alcohol or for other reasons, people will associate their actions with Kitsune. Traditionally, if one was diagnosed as possessed by Kitsune, a ceremony would be held to get rid of him. More than one person has died from the cures meant to drive Kitsune out, which can range from songs and incantations to scarring and burning.

Probably the most popular characterization of Kitsune, however, is as an adventurous shape-shifter who outwits others for his own pleasure. Although his actions may at times cause problems or hardships, the majority of his pranks are harmless. In Japanese mythology one of the traits of all foxes is that with old age they acquire the ability to change their shape at will. Most commonly they take on human form, especially that of a beautiful young woman, but they may also transform themselves into other animals or inanimate objects.

Stories about Kitsune often tell how to recognize him in another form. Japanese folklore tells that a fox always emits a slight glow, even when he is not in the form of a fox. Another sign of a transformed fox is his appearance as a human with eyebrows that grow together. Any human being with such a trait is always suspect. Dogs are not fooled by the transformation of Kitsune. They will bark, chase, and relentlessly hound a person who is really a fox. Another hint that a person is a fox in disguise is his or her inability to pronounce certain words accurately. Finally, a fox will never pass up a fried rat, whatever state he has transformed himself into.

Kitsune can be found in Japanese literature from the eighth century onward, and it has been argued that oral accounts of his escapades appeared even earlier. Whatever the case, stories of Kitsune abound in Japan. One of Kitsune's favorite transformations is into a beautiful woman. In one story, an old farmer lived without a wife. He had been waiting his whole life to find the perfect woman to marry. On his way into town one day he passed a beautiful woman on the roadside. After a few moments of conversation he realized she was not married, and he quickly asked her to marry him. After the couple was married, the woman gave birth to a son, and on the same night their dog had puppies. One of the puppies despised the woman; he followed her barking relentlessly, and one day he attacked her mercilessly until she changed back into a fox and scampered away. The farmer was heartbroken at her departure and wanted her back. But Kitsune had gone for good, the prank having been revealed.

In another popular story Kitsune is said to have turned himself into a train. In 1889 a story surfaced about a train on the Tokyo-Yokohama line. The engineer saw another train in the distance heading straight for his. He blew his whistle and tried everything to alert the other train to his presence, but it kept coming. The engineer braced for the impact but felt only a slight bump as the train came to a stop. When he opened his eyes there was no other train, and all that remained was the dead body of a fox on the tracks.

In another story, Kitsune reveals his vengeful side. A farmer in a rural village was tired of the foxes stealing his food. So one night the farmer smoked one of the foxes from his den and killed him, selling his fur at the market. The next night, several men stormed the farmer's home demanding money. After he gave them all his money the men left, and the farmer went to town to get the police. When the police returned with the man, his money was in his house but there was no food, the place had been ransacked, and a fox's paw prints were on everything.

Even the wily foxes, however, can be caught at their own games. In one story, a group of foxes decided to play a trick on an old lady so that they could get all the food they wanted. They saw the woman in her garden bending over revealing three warts. Upon seeing the warts the foxes thought of a plan. The next day they appeared as policemen at the woman's door and said they had to escort her to town to have the warts removed. Before they left, however, the woman offered them lunch. The woman prepared their favorite dish, red beans and fried bean curd. After they had eaten, the foxes told the woman it was too late to take her that day and that they would be back the next day. For days the foxes continued to trick the gullible woman, until one night a neighbor passing the nearby shrine heard the foxes singing and gloating of their tricks. The next day when the foxes showed up at the woman's house as policemen, the neighbor showed up with his dogs, who became enraged at the sight of them and attacked and killed them all. (Dorson 1962; Johnson 1974; Johnson 1990; Nozaki 1961)

Komali
Tamil Nadu, *India*

Komali, comedic performers in south Indian theatrical performances, are common characters in folk plays in Tamil villages. The komali always wear a conical hat tipped at the end to show they are comedians. Their actions and gestures are similar to those of their counterpart in Sanskrit plays, the **vidusaka,** except that the komali rely in part on their association with inauspicious forces for their power. The komali always appear with a wild grin on their faces. They are described as grotesque, and part of their humor lies in their juxtaposition with ritual and theatrical participants who highlight the serene and beautiful.

The komali appear as comedic performers in two main venues in Tamil villages: in small village plays and on ritual occasions. During both types of performances, the komali act as rude, even obscene, commentators. In plays they act like "madmen," running and jumping about, mocking singers and dancers with their exaggerated mimicry, and forcing the audience's attention to them and away from the main characters.

The komali satirize village life with verbal play and mimicry. They point out the absurd in everyday situations. For example, one of the mundane aspects of life the komali focus on is eating. The komali are known for their unending appetite and their bizarre and disgusting way of eating food. They stuff themselves with food, leave it lying about, and mock those who attempt to clean up their messes. The komali love a mess. Highlighting the chaotic, they delight in trampling clean areas, leaving garbage behind everywhere they go. In addition to their fascination with food and their unending appetites, the komali startle audiences with their graphic sexual dialogue and mimicry. They are embarrassed by nothing and do not show any restraint in their portrayal of the sexual lives of villagers. In fact, they delight in embarrassing audience members with their sexual imagery, which includes elongated penises. Running about and taunting people, the komali make public what is normally always private. Their role as comedians highlights the inverse of normal village life.

Similarly, during ritual performances the komali invert the roles of the participants by being loud, obnoxious, and rude. They taunt the audience and follow the participants around attempting to distract them from their duties; all the while they tease the dancers with their outrageous dance styles. The komali appear as a reminder that the world is not as it is always perceived. Their association with inauspicious forces makes them feared by spectators even though their crazy antics highlight their playful side.

The komali are intentionally ambiguous. In their performances they dress as a member of the opposite gender or as both genders, and they purposely jumble their speech, trip over unseen objects, and confuse simple directions. In this way the clowns focus attention on life as *maya*, or illusion. That life is *maya*, that nothing in life is permanent but in fact that it is all flexible, is a traditional Hindu tenet. The komali highlight the idea of *maya* by focusing their antics on ambiguity. They are never quite what they seem to be. This Hindu philosophy finds an expression in their performances.

The komali also have a representative in the popular puppet shows of south India. Puppet shows have common clown characters who act similarly to the komali, in this case focusing on the slapstick side of the comedic. For example, they take awful beatings and emerge unscathed, always coming back for more. They highlight the humor in all aspects of life, even those that appear to be tragic. The puppets themselves resemble the komali. They wear their trademark tipped hat and crooked smile. Often the puppets are misshapen, their limbs are not aligned, and their appearance is dirty and often grotesque. The puppet clowns take up the same themes as their human counterparts. They mock the power of the elite, highlight sexual tension, and generally poke fun at any subject they desire.

In an ironic twist, the komali represent both the harmful and the helpful sides of the world. By focusing on the comedic, they show people the absurdity even in religious rituals, yet at the same time their presence deflects any unsuspected inauspicious forces from entering the village. By reversing the norm, the komali challenge the everyday interpretation of the world. Their playful satire and forceful performances direct attention to the chaotic nature of the world. (Kunjunni Raja 1969; Shulman 1985; Siegel 1987; Zvelebil 1973)

Konehu

Warao, Orinoco Delta of Venezuela

Konehu is described as a rabbit, but he is certainly no "ordinary" animal. He takes on the characteristics of both a rabbit and a human. He is sometimes portrayed as a man who changes into a rabbit, and other times he is described as a rabbit with the ability to talk and disguise himself. Konehu is lazy; he exploits others, steals, and disguises himself to elude work and outwit others; he tricks and even kills out of spite; and he often steals other men's wives.

Stories about Konehu highlight the Warao emphasis on proper behavior. Through Konehu's exploits the Warao show the ill effects on the community of deceptive and cunning behavior. The Warao depend on fishing as well as agriculture to sustain themselves in their camps along the Orinoco river. They plant large tracts of bananas, plantains, sugar cane, and rice to sustain themselves. The community uses their agricultural skills cooperatively to survive. Stories about Konehu reflect the negative aspects of Warao society in a humorous way.

Konehu is always up to no good. No matter whether he is walking through the forest or sitting idly by the river, he is always planning his next prank. One of his most powerful deceptive tools is his ability to make even the wildest schemes sound prudent. His tricks are unprovoked and unpredictable, and he carries them out purely for his own amusement. He is notorious for catching people off guard as they walk through the forest or near the river. In one story, a traveler passed Konehu on a path in the brush and saw him eating *kokerite* nuts. Hungry from his journey, the man asked Konehu where he got the nuts. Without

hesitating, Konehu claimed to be eating his own testicles and suggested that the man do the same; he suggested that he should pound his own testicles against a rock. The traveler believed Konehu's outrageous story and began to hit his own testicles against a large rock. He hit them so hard that they burst, and he died alongside the road.

Konehu is well known for his ability to sweet-talk himself out of trouble through his amazing storytelling. Konehu convinces people that he is in the right even when they know he is wrong. The Warao most fear this sweet-talk because they know it is so powerful that even intelligent men can be deceived by it. For example, in one story Konehu met a man carrying yams from the village to sell in another settlement up the river. As he passed Konehu the man heard him say, "Those are very fine yams." Proud of his crop, the man stopped to show his yams to Konehu, who poured on the praise and told the man that he knew a of village where he could get double the price for such fine yams. Convinced, the man allowed Konehu to take the yams with him. As he left, Konehu told the man he would bring him the money the next day. Later that night, Konehu sat in his hut with his wife and they enjoyed the foolish man's yams all for themselves.

The next day the man realized he had been duped and went to Konehu's house to seek revenge. When he arrived Konehu once again sweet-talked the man to calm him down and told him he would give him some pepper-pot (a sweet dish) for his trouble. As the man waited, Konehu went into his house and told his wife to yell and shriek as if she was being hurt. Then Konehu arrived back outside with the food for the man. After eating it, he asked Konehu how he made such a fine dish. Konehu answered without hesitation, "from my wife's breasts." When the man got home he cut off his wife's breasts with a knife attempting to make the pepper-pot, but he had been tricked again by Konehu; his wife bled to death, and he remained hungry. (Osborn 1960; Roth 1915; Wilbert 1970)

Koshare

Tewa, *Southwestern United States: Arizona; New Mexico*

The Koshare, black-and-whited striped, horned comic performers, comprise one-half of a pair of Tewa comedic performers, the **Kwirena** being the other. (See also **Paiyakyamu** for a similar Hopi character.) Together they are known as kossa, and the pair share ceremonial duties divided by their association with summer (koshare) and winter (kwirena). Both are part of the Made People group within Tewa society. The Tewa cosmos is divided into several groups of inhabitants. The Made People include the kossa as well as the *kiva* (ceremonial building) chiefs, the members of the two moiety societies, all ritual healers, and the Hunting, Scalping, and Women's societies. The Made People interact with other members of the Tewa cosmos, including the Dry Food People, who serve no ritual capacity; the Dry Food People Who Are No Longer, who are the souls of the Dry Food People living apart from the Made People; and the Dry Food People Who Never Did Become, who are all the people who did not make it to the upper world during the emergence. Each group makes up an important and necessary part of Tewa life. They interact within the society in specific roles that ensure that everyone is taken care of and all work is fulfilled.

According to the Tewa creation story, the kossa were created to entertain and amuse people on their journey to this world. Prior to their existence above the surface of the earth the Tewa lived in the underworld, beneath a lake called Sandy Place Lake. The Tewa underworld is similar to this one but it is dark and cold. The Tewa lived in the

An artistic depiction of a Koshare, the horned comic performers associated with summer ceremonies in Tewa society. (AINACO/Corbis)

underworld with all members of their society, and death was unknown. One day the corn mothers asked one of the male leaders to look for another place to live. The man looked and looked but could not find a place. Then, after several attempts, he came upon a group of animals; he was frightened and ran, but the animals spoke to him, telling him they knew a way to the upper world and would help him. Giving him his power, they made him into the Hunt Chief. The Hunt Chief then took an ear of white corn and handed it to another man, making him the Summer Chief, and with another ear of white corn he made another man the Winter Chief. These were the first three Made People of the Tewa. Along their journey to the upper world, the three made others, including the kossa. In addition, they were flanked by six pairs of twins known as *towa é* (literally "persons"). When they reached their departure point, the Made People went to the upper world, the original corn mothers stayed behind, and the *towa é* went to live as the six mountains that mark the boundaries of the Tewa world. Like the Winter and Summer Chiefs, the Tewa divide themselves as Winter and Summer People through moiety affiliation. In their travels and emergence to

Four Kossa clowns. The term Kossa *refers both to the koshare (seen above) and the kwirena (winter) performers.* (*Museum of New Mexico*)

the upper world, one kossa traveled with the Summer People (koshare) and the other with the Winter People (kwirena). Thus, the koshare are known as "hot" and the kwirena as "cold." Each group performs at ceremonies associated with their respective seasons.

Today the koshare play a more active ceremonial role than do the kwirena. One explanation is given through a Tewa story. Long ago the kwirena challenged the koshare to a contest to see who could make the people of the village laugh the most. Each performed in front of the village, singing, dancing, and carrying on with their usual antics. After each segment, the audience cheered and laughed louder and louder for the koshare. In disappointment, the kwirena left the plaza, only to return once a year.

One of the duties of the koshare is to bring the *Oxua* (cloud beings) to ceremonial performances. The *Oxua* are represented by masked dancers who bring with them the power of the *Oxua*, the relatives of the Made People who live in the clouds. The *Oxua* emerged with the Made People but went to live in the clouds to protect the others. The *Oxua* are divided into Summer, Winter, and "middle time" *Oxua*. The Summer and Winter *Oxua* perform at ceremonies during the appropriate seasons, and in the "middle time" the koshare and kwirena work together to bring the four middle *Oxua* to the Tewa pueblos.

During ritual performances the koshare speak and act in a manner opposite to the way people act in everyday life. They invert not only their appearance but also their speech and actions. They run quickly around as they say they are standing still; they eat excrement and delight in its wonderful taste; they are hot when it is cold, loud when all is quiet; and happy at even the most solemn occasions. They come to the dance plazas dressed shabbily, usually in rags, their bodies are painted black and white, and they have horns rising from their heads. With their odd appearance as their background, the koshare play with the audience and each other. They pretend to urinate on each other, they chase women in the audience, and they make sexual gestures toward everyone. They mimic the actions of the *Oxua* and delight in throwing things at them and chasing them. In some performances, such as the Squash Dance, the koshare appear dressed as women. They engage in mock sexual intercourse with each other and tease the male audience members, making sexual gestures toward them as they pass.

Appearing at the change of seasons, the koshare are associated with the inversion of the seasons at each equinox and the flow from one to the next. Inverting the characteristics and social mores of everyday life, they represent both the differences between the seasons and the variety of the cosmos, while at the same time reinforcing the balance within the cosmos. Because the Tewa Made People are already divided into Summer and Winter People and *Oxua*, the koshare's antics parody the inherent differences of each group of people, including the *Oxua*. In their satire of everyday life and the change of seasons, the koshare show that although their world is distinguished by several seemingly opposite pairs, the pairs flow together and are intimately bound. The koshare bring the *Oxua* into the dance plaza and explain their role to the crowd, they offer prayers to them and aid in their performance, yet as soon as the *Oxua* are gone they mock them, exaggerate their performance, and call them names. Their

behavior toward the *Oxua* reflects their view of the cosmos. They show that there is not just one way or one type of being, but that together, the Winter and Summer People comprise the Tewa world and together they maintain the cosmos. (Handelman 1981; Laski 1959; Ortiz 1969; Ortiz 1972; Parsons 1930; Wright 1994)

Kossa
Tewa, *Southwestern United States: Arizona; New Mexico*
Refers to both the **koshare** and the **kwirena** comedic performers.

Koyemshi
Zuni, *Southwestern United States: Arizona and New Mexico*
The term *koyemshi*, a general title given to a group of ritual performers commonly referred to as "mudheads," is used not only by the Zuni but by neighboring peoples as well. The Hopi, for example, use the term *koyemshi* to refer both to a similar ritual performer within their society and to the Zuni character. The Zuni, Hopi, and other native peoples of the southwestern United States came in close contact with each other upon the arrival of Europeans. Many shared aspects of their cultures with their neighbors, adopting new characters into their own society. The koyemshi are one type of character that can be found within several pueblos of the southwestern United States. They share common features of costume, activities, and behavior, but each remains a distinctive part of its own culture. (See **Tachukti** for a similar Hopi character.)

The koyemshi perform at ceremonies throughout the year; they disrupt dancers, throw things on people, and generally cause chaos. Koyemshi take their place alongside other ritual performers during annual Zuni ceremonies, including *Shalako* (a celebration

An artist's rendering of the koyemshi *ritual performer.*
(Museum of New Mexico)

ritual objects. Although they appear to be only entertaining to outsiders, the koyemshi make ritual activity possible through their dedication to the Zuni community.

Zuni people live surrounded by mountains, lakes, and paths that hold stories of their ancestors and remain important sites for ritual activity and sacrifices throughout the year. The Zuni year begins on the winter solstice, *itiwan'a*, translated as the "middle time" or "middle place." The summer solstice is referred by with the same word. Throughout the year, under the direction of Zuni ritual leaders, people make offerings of "prayer sticks" to their ancestors. Prayer sticks are usually made from six feathers tied to a carved and painted cottonwood stick. The prayer sticks are offered to the Zuni ancestral beings known as "raw" or "soft" people. In contrast to living Zuni people, who are classified as "cooked" or "ripe" people, the "raw" or "soft" people include the sun, moon, stars, deer, rainstorms, rainbows, corn plants, snakes, and the dead. All of these beings are given offerings throughout the year by their living relatives. These two types of people were created by *Yatokka Tacchu* (Sun Father), who sent his twin sons on a rainbow to the interior of the earth. Prior to this all people lived together under the earth's surface. When the twins emerged from the earth the Zuni people followed them, and when they reached the surface and were exposed to the sunlight, the Zuni were transformed into the "cooked people," as they are known today.

Upon reaching their home on earth the Zuni people instituted several of their traditions. They set up social organizations, political structures, and social restrictions. During this time, the koyemshi came to be known as the personification of Shiwelusiwa, a hero, and his nine children. Shiwelusiwa and his sister were the parents of these children. After committing incest, the two performed extraordinary acts, cre-

of Zuni creation), celebration of the summer and winter solstices, and initiation ceremonies. As part of their ritual work koyemshi perform dances, aid in the building of ceremonial houses, make prayer sticks, and attend prayer meetings. The activities of the koyemshi are central to the survival of the Zuni and the continuation of their ceremonial cycle. Without the koyemshi, the other ritual performers would not have time to perform their duties, since the koyemshi aid in the transition between ritual performances, the building of ceremonial structures, and the construction of

ating rivers, mountains, and lakes. They built a village at the bottom of one lake, which became the home of the *kokko* (Zuni ancestors and the masked performers who become the ancestors in ritual activity; they are also referred to as *kachinas*). However, Shiwelusiwa became disfigured after his incestuous act; his eyes swelled out, his mouth filled with blisters, and his skull became covered with scars; he rolled on the ground and covered himself with mud, trying to hide his hideous body. From then on he was set apart by his mud-covered appearance (from which comes the koyemshi's title "mudhead"). After the incestuous act, Shiwelusiwa also spoke a strange language and was always shouting and laughing. No one could understand Shiwelusiwa, and everyone laughed at him. To counteract their laughter, he displayed his awesome powers by hurting people, creating rainstorms, and other disruptive acts.

Like Shiwelusiwa, the koyemshi are ugly, disfigured characters who are both feared and accepted. They wear horrible masks and dress in black kilts and scarves. They ridicule people by throwing things at them and shouting obscenities, such as telling the people to go "copulate with rams." Koyemshi also act out explicit sexual scenes in front of crowds, exaggerating the size of their penises, drinking each other's urine, and throwing urine onto the crowd. (See also **Newekwe,** a society of ritual healers who use humor and obscenity.)

Although the koyemshi are known collectively as a group, each has a distinctive appearance, character traits, and name, which is the opposite of what it implies. For example, Eshotsi, the bat, is afraid of the dark, running at the sight of even the smallest shadow. Posuki, the pouter, laughs hysterically at everything and everyone, and Itsepasha, the Glum One, is equally cheerful. Each of the ten koyemshi embody a different aspect of Zuni life. Although most of the time their outward appearance signifies

their tendency toward mockery, disruptive behavior, and ignorance, they play an equally strong role as ritual leaders. The koyemshi are knowledgeable relatives who are respected and even feared because of their powers. They embody the duality of childlike and even crude play as well as wisdom and power.

The koyemshi bring together seemingly disparate parts of the Zuni cosmos in their activities and appearance. This can best be seen in the integral role they play in the most elaborate of all Zuni ceremonies, *Shalako*. *Shalako* celebrates the creation and migration of the Zuni to the "middle place," their home. For most of *Shalako* the mudheads act in the most obscene ways and ridicule people. The koyemshi arrive in the Zuni pueblo on the first day of *Shalako*. They are covered with clay, ears and genitals stick out from their masks, the eyes and mouth on their masks are turned inside out and express surprise, they are naked except for kilts, and they have neither noses nor hair. Upon entering the village at nightfall, they make a circuit of all four dance plazas announcing the coming of the other *kokko*. They run from place to place, joking with people and calling them names, and then they finally go into their ceremonial home for an eight-day retreat before the other *kokko* arrive. Prior to the last day of *Shalako*, the koyemshi behave in crude and obnoxious ways. They scare children, demand food, and interrupt dances. On the last day of *Shalako* they act as ceremonial elders, performing sacred duties. They retreat from the rest of the group to fast and perform purifying acts that aid in the community's celebration and the maintenance of their society for another year. With these actions the koyemshi show their role as responsible members of the Zuni world. They bring together their playful antics with their solemn quest to maintain the Zuni world. Although the antics of the koyemshi remind people of the social restriction against incest and of the negative effects of improper behavior, they are referred to as both "grandsons" and "grandfathers," demonstrating their dual role as both uneducated youth and knowledgeable elders.

People show their respect for the koyemshi by taking care of them throughout the year while they aid in the year-long preparations for *Shalako* and other ceremonies. Ten men are chosen at the close of each year to act as the koyemshi for the following year. Because of the demands on their time that go with being a koyemshi, these men are not able to work for a year; therefore the responsibility to provide for them falls on the hosts of *Shalako* and their family. During the ceremony and at its close, people give gifts of food, money, and other useful objects to the koyemshi to show their appreciation. In fact, oftentimes the mudheads demand gifts during ritual performances, and because of their great powers they are never refused. Simply touching one of the koyemshi puts one in danger of their great power. They are feared and respected for their abilities to interact with humans, *kokko*, and other members of the Zuni cosmos. (Bunzel 1932a; Bunzel 1932b; Bunzel 1932c; Cazeneuve 1955; Cazeneuve 1956; Cushing 1891–1892; Gonzales 1966; Handelman 1981; Hieb 1972; Makarius 1970; Tedlock 1975; Tedlock 1983; Wright 1985)

Krishna

India

Krishna, a playful deity in the Hindu pantheon, invokes laughter and entertains with his tricks, wordplay, and lack of sexual inhibitions. His most notorious escapades are those of his childhood and early adulthood. Stories about this part of Krishna's life focus on his jovial attitude toward life and his complete disregard for rules and boundaries. The stories about Krishna only hint at his popularity as an Indian deity.

Throughout India his image can be found in temples, shrines, statues, and paintings. Although there are many images of the playful Krishna, the most popular depict him in his youth, usually with blue skin, holding a flute, and wearing his trademark smirk. Because of his sexual exploits, the flute is often interpreted as a phallic symbol. Indeed, in many stories Krishna calls women to him by the hundreds using his magical flute and unending charm.

The stories of Krishna's life on earth begin with his birth in a small Indian village. The precursor to the story, however, shows Krishna's true origins as an avatar (incarnation) of the powerful deity **Vishnu.** As an avatar of Vishnu, Krishna is sent to earth to destroy Kansa, an evil demigod. Before Krishna's birth Kansa found out about Vishnu's plan to destroy him through the child. Kansa stalked the cities waiting eagerly, but Krishna's birth was concealed from Kansa. As soon as he was born he was whisked away to the small forest village known as Braj. Once in Braj, Krishna lived with his foster parents Yasoda and Nanda.

A miniature painting of the Hindu deity Krishna with his consort Radha. (Philadelphia Museum of Art/Corbis)

As a baby Krishna began to establish his playfulness along with his role as a preserver. In many instances Krishna's innocent, childlike appearance fooled and thus defeated enemies and demons. The people of Braj recognized his mischievous nature, yet they applauded and venerated him for his ability to protect them and the village. People only objected to his pranks and mischievous acts for a moment before his presence overwhelmed them and they forgot his mischievous and stupendous acts. In the midst of his childish pranks Krishna revealed his extraordinary powers to his foster parents, as well as to the others in the village.

Even in the early antics of his childhood Krishna is portrayed as acting outside the norm. He is constantly upsetting the women of Braj with his butter stealing and his disruption of their chores. In one story, his foster mother realized her son's power through his pranks. Krishna wandered off while his mother hung the laundry. Sitting in the sunshine he grabbed handfuls of mud and hurled them at the passing women. As his mother ran to stop him he committed a final act of disobedience by shoving the dirt into his mouth. While his mother scolded him she pried his mouth open to get the dirt out. In his mouth she saw the entire universe. Awestruck, she set him down, and he went about with his antics.

As a baby and in early childhood Krishna showed his power by fighting off demons and warding off evil from the village. Amid his duties as a protector and preserver of the village his role as a lover also emerged. The *gopis* (girls who herded cows) were consistently intrigued and enticed by Krishna. He played his flute, and the women could not help but fall under his spell. Leaving their husbands, they flocked to Krishna to sing, dance, and make love with him in the forests. He delighted in their company and was content to spend his days entrenched in their jubilant activities. Within this setting, his flute emerges as a key symbol in his relationship with the *gopis*. Not only did he use it to call them, but music was central to their activities together. The flute represents the inherent playfulness in their actions, while showing that Krishna maintained control of the relationship.

In his adolescence, Krishna's erotic play with the *gopis* took place in the forests. Both the setting and the activities are thought of as being outside normal societal bounds. The forest is on the edges of the village rather than within its boundaries, and Krishna's play with the *gopis* is spontaneous and uninhibited. He is not bound by any of the laws of duty, his *dharma*. Instead, outside of society, in the forest, he does not confine himself to *dharma* but rather gives himself over to a playfulness that is not guided by any laws or duty and that has no other purpose than to embrace the play that is the universe. In one story, he came across several *gopis* bathing in a stream. Sneaking up on them, he stole their clothes and took them up into a nearby tree. Calling to the girls, he showed them what he had done. Embarrassed, the girls begged for their clothes, but Krishna would not give in until all the girls had come out of the stream naked.

Krishna's antics in the forests of Braj, especially in Vrindaban (a forest within Braj), reflect the playful, erotic, and chaotic nature of the forest setting. His activities not only highlight the forest setting but the importance of specific places and the idea that one is transformed within this setting and in the play of Krishna. In addition, in the forest setting other gods and goddesses become secondary to Krishna; in fact, they become devotees to Krishna and are transformed into *gopis* to show their love for him. Siva (the destroyer god) is one example. Siva is present in Braj, but as a devotee to Krishna. Siva first entered Braj while Krishna was a baby. He came down from his home in the

Himalayas to visit Braj and see Krishna. When Yasoda saw Siva at the door, disheveled and wild, she slammed it in his face, screaming at him to leave. The baby Krishna recognized Siva and manifested himself as an adult, and as a boon to Siva he erected a temple in his honor. When Siva was again on his mountain top, he heard the alluring call of Krishna's flute. Enticed by the beautiful music, Siva left the mountain for Braj. This time he was overwhelmed by Krishna's presence and attempted to show his love and devotion by entering the circle dance with Krishna and the *gopis*. First, however, he had to be transformed into a *gopi*, for only as a *gopi* can one truly experience the love play of Krishna. Siva entered the Yamuna River and emerged as a *gopi* to enter the dance with Krishna.

A large part of Krishna's history is reflected in the annual pilgrimage to Braj made by thousands of Indians. In Braj pilgrims express their devotion to Krishna through physical contact with the land and by entering into his play. Throughout the pilgrimage there are *ras-lilas* (plays) performed to enact events of Krishna's life. The *ras-lilas*, which have a loose narrative style, are performed throughout Braj. Though they follow an outline they are flexible, and no two performances are ever the same. The spontaneity of the actors is meant to reflect Krishna's actions.

In addition to the *ras-lilas* performed by touring companies, pilgrims themselves enter into Krishna's *lila* (playfulness) by dancing, singing, swimming in the ponds, and climbing the hills of Braj. In the mythology of Krishna we see an emphasis on his activities in Braj. Almost all places within Braj were affected by Krishna, but especially the streams, ponds, and forests. These were the places where he and the *gopis* danced and made love. To embrace the spontaneity and play of Krishna, pilgrims jump in the streams, dance in the forest, and sing along the roads. They are not restricted to certain itineraries in their expressions of joy. Nor is performance limited to the staged *ras-lilas*; pilgrims can express their devotion and selfless love to Krishna whenever and wherever they choose.

Inherent in devotion to Krishna is the ideal of desire. Throughout his adventures in Braj it is evident that Krishna embodies desire, and his devotees must desire him and show their passion for him in order to enter his *lila*. However, it is crucial for pilgrims to understand the distinction between ordinary love and desire and the highest love. In the forest of Kamaban, "the forest of desire," this point is stressed in the myth surrounding Krishna's revival of Kamadev. Siva had killed Kamadev, the god of desire, for tempting him away from his ascetic vows into marriage with Parvati, showing Siva's susceptibility to desire. Krishna restored Kamadev because in Braj desire is essential. Simple desire is not enough to allow one to enter Krishna's *lila*; rather, in fulfillment of one's desires one should be in pursuit of the highest form of love, *prem*. *Prem* is understood as egoless love, entered into solely for the purpose of pleasing Krishna. There is no goal to *prem*; there are no children produced as in the fulfillment of ordinary desire, *kam*. *Prem* is ongoing and purposeless whereas *kam* is purposeful; it has an end, like Siva and Parvati's love, which produced children. *Prem*, then, is the ultimate form of a pilgrim's love for Krishna. The embrace of desires, of the materiality of the world must not be for oneself but for Krishna. The love must be egoless, selfless, and purposeless, all the attributes of the *lila* of Krishna. (Archer 1957; Haberman 1994; Hawley 1980; Hawley 1981; Hawley 1983; Kinsley 1975; Miller 1977; Siegel 1987)

Kumarxúo
Chamacoco, *Paraguay*

Kumarxúo, known as the Master of the Jaguars, and his human wife are the ancestors of present day jaguars. Kumarxúo was once a human being as well, but after an incestuous affair with his mother he was left in the woods by his father and turned into a jaguar by some powerful birds. Boastful, greedy, and stupid, Kumarxúo engages others in pranks for fun but usually ends up being the fool. He is injured and even killed in many of his escapades although he continuously comes back for more. Although he is described as a jaguar, he also has human qualities. He is portrayed by storytellers as slow-witted, yet he has the ability to change shape and even take on human form. But despite his powers, he does not use his intellect and is easily caught off guard by those he is trying to trick.

Kumarxúo never learns a lesson from his misguided adventures; he tries to outwit others using their methods, but because of his naiveté he is almost always the loser. His excrement is one of his few powerful tools of deception. He uses it to throw people off his track or to get himself out of bad situations. The excrement takes on a life of its own in stories about Kumarxúo, warning him of danger, helping him out of touchy situations, and leading him away from his enemies.

The butterfly, rabbit, and monkey are all known for their ability to turn Kumarxúo's pranks around on him. The butterfly, for example, saw Kumarxúo trick some unsuspecting victims out of their meat, but as he was about to devour it the butterfly flew close to his ear and told him the animals were on their way back. Believing the butterfly, Kumarxúo ran the other direction and left his meat for her. Similarly, the toad was caught in Kumarxúo's clutches but escaped by convincing Kumarxúo that he could not swim. Kumarxúo, thinking he was going to drown, let go of the toad and swam to safety while the toad laughed at his gullible neighbor.

Although Kumarxúo's antics seem relatively harmless to others, his pride gets in the way at times and he is led to violence. In one story, Kumarxúo's jealousy led him to kill the black fox. The two were out hunting together and Kumarxúo became envious of the fox's fine hunting skills. He tried to imitate him but could not. Jealous, Kumarxúo lured the fox into the water to gather potatoes. Once in the water, Kumarxúo drowned the fox. Discovering that Kumarxúo had killed their father, the fox's sons set out to avenge his death. The boys went to see Kumarxúo and told him what an excellent hunter he was and begged him to teach them his skills. Not suspecting their plot and overwhelmed with confidence, Kumarxúo followed them into the forest. Once in the forest, the foxes turned on Kumarxúo and burned him to death. For their final revenge, they cooked his flesh with another mixture and gave it to Kumarxúo's sons to eat.

Another of Kumarxúo's principal antagonists is the hunter Doxóra, who is human but can change shape into animals and material items in a matter of seconds to throw Kumarxúo off his trail or to sidestep his enemies. In one story Kumarxúo challenged Doxóra to a hunting contest. During the contest, the two came upon two tapirs, a male and a female. Kumarxúo said he would take the female and Doxóra should try his hand at the male. The two pulled back their arrows, aimed, and fired. Kumarxúo's arrow wounded the female. Going to see if she had died, Doxóra left Kumarxúo to follow the male. When Kumarxúo came upon the male, he replaced Doxóra's arrow with his own and dragged it back to camp as his catch. In camp Kumarxúo cooked the meat and ate it himself. When Doxóra arrived back to gloat as the winner, Kumarxúo had already finished eating. Doxóra was angry and asked Kumarxúo why he had eaten his catch. But Kumarxúo claimed that he had shot the male and that Doxóra was mistaken. Doxóra left the camp, but he did not forget

Kumarxúo's trick. Later that day when he saw Kumarxúo hunting again he turned himself into a poisoned rhea. When Kumarxúo ate the fat of the rhea, he died in agony, and Doxóra sat by laughing. (Métraux 1943; Wilbert and Simoneau 1987)

Kúwei
Sikuani, *Eastern Colombia*
See **Furna.**

Kwatyat
Nootka, *Northwest Coast of the United States*
Kwatyat, the mink, is a creator and manipulative shape-shifter who changes himself into any shape he wishes to satisfy his desires. The Nootka call him "the one of many tricks." He transforms himself and the physical world to his benefit, usually using trickery and deceit to outwit others, but he is also known for creating and bringing many necessities to the Nootka people. Kwatyat is both selfish and giving, helpful and disruptive. His actions are often contradictory. Kwatyat's home is not known to the Nootka, so he can disappear any time he wishes without fear that anyone could find him.

Kwatyat's adventures are related in stories that are passed down from generation to generation among the Nootka, where storytelling is a well-developed skill. Storytellers are prized because they maintain the Nootka oral heritage, and the Nootka accord higher status within the community to those who can tell a story well. There are several forms of oral narratives in Nootka culture. Stories are told in public to validate people's hereditary rights, to pass on knowledge and tradition, and to entertain. Stories about the Nootka serve both to educate and to entertain and are usually shorter than stories that tell about the origins of Nootka society and tradition. All of those story types follow a fixed pattern dictated by tradition. In contrast, Kwatyat's adventures are told in various forms depending on the storyteller and the situation. Often a storyteller will choose Kwatyat as a character to emphasize the importance of proper behavior or to reiterate the necessity of reciprocation within the community.

The Nootka live along the coast and therefore rely on fishing by small family units within the community for their sustenance. The social structure of the Nootka is stratified, so each member of the community knows his or her role and responsibilities to the group. Within each small community hereditary chiefs lead specific groups of people. Familial ties are important to the overall structure of the community in terms of responsibilities, land ownership, and political power. One of the most common ways in which the chief both maintains his authority and status and also redistributes wealth to the community is through the ceremonial distribution of wealth called a potlatch. (See also **Nankilslas** for an account of the potlatch among the Haida.) Feasts and ceremonies such as the potlatch bring the community together, demonstrating that although the communities are stratified in terms of their members' status, the society is nevertheless sustained through the reciprocal actions of community members.

Kwatyat represents the antithesis of what is expected in Nootka culture, with its focus on community, responsibility, and reciprocation. Kwatyat steals from people, including the chief, within the community; he lies to people to get what he wants; and he transforms himself into various forms to trick people out of food and lodging. Once Kwatyat turned a pool of grease into a lake so that he would be able to eat more fish, and another time he carried a river off with him to the south and the people went hungry.

Kwatyat uses whatever means possible to take advantage of others. His power to transform himself as well as the world around him is one of his most useful skills. But he also uses powerful spells, potions, and songs to manipulate people and objects. Once during a hoop-throwing game Kwatyat beat the Thunderbirds by cheating with his powers. As he threw his hoop he said to it "get small, get small," and the hoop became small enough to dodge the spears of the Thunderbirds. In another story Kwatyat saved his mother, who had been swallowed by a monster, by sneaking into the monster's mouth and then stabbing him from the inside to release both himself and his mother.

In spite of all his power, Kwatyat is also known to hold one of the lowest social positions within the society, that of the slave to the woodpecker chief. Despite his power, stories about Kwatyat often place him in this low social position to demonstrate that he is not always what he seems to be and also that power and intellect are not reserved for chiefs. Stories about Kwatyat remind people that power can be harmful as well as beneficial, that one person's actions can affect the community, and that even those who do not hold distinguished social roles are important to the community. (Arima 1983; Clutesi 1967; Curtis 1907; Drucker 1951; Sapir and Swadesh 1939)

Kwirena

Tewa, *Southwestern United States: Arizona; New Mexico*

The kwirena (winter entertainers) and the koshare (summer entertainers) are united as kossa, the winter and summer team of ritual entertainers. The kwirena are associated with the Winter People and thus the cold in Tewa society. (See **Koshare** for the Tewa creation story and explanation of the divisions within Tewa society.) The kwirena were created to bring laughter to the first people who made the long, hard journey from the underworld to the upper world. It

was the job of the kwirena to make the journey seem less arduous with their humor. During this journey to the upper world, where the Tewa live today, the kwirena established their role as the comedic performers of the Winter People. But their role was not solely defined by humor. It was through their humor that the kwirena allowed the Winter People to emerge into the upper world and begin their lives as Made People. The kwirena, like the koshare of the Summer People, used their humor as a tool to aid in the creation of the Made People, the Tewa of today. Without the kwirena, the journey to the upper world and the life of the Tewa would have been lost. They encouraged the people when they were tired and raised their spirits when they were discouraged. In ritual performances, the kwirena remind the Tewa that hard work and sacrifice are part of their responsibility to maintain their community and traditions. Although they are best known by outsiders as childlike, humorous, and obnoxious ritual performers, the kwirena make ritual activity possible through their continued performance and prodding of others.

The kwirena perform in the winter ceremonies of the Tewa, but today the kwirena play less of a role than their summer counterparts the koshare. (See **Koshare** for explanation.) When the kwirena do perform, they use their disruptive and obnoxious behavior to underscore the proper actions of the Tewa. They pull chairs out from under people, grab at people's genitals, parade around wearing almost nothing, and mock the other ritual performers by exaggerating their actions and words. The kwirena especially like to engage in mock sexual exploits and perform common activities, such as speaking, walking, and eating, backwards. They shock crowds by engaging in crude sexual exploits, pretending to copulate with animals and exposing their oversized genitals to the crowd. The kwirena are notorious for dressing like women and mocking women's roles. The night before several ceremonial dances, the kwirena will appear on the rooftops above the dance plaza dressed like women. They run around, fall into each other, squat down pretending to urinate, and make sexual gestures at men. Through their humor, the kwirena remind the Tewa of their responsibility to the members of their community and of their role in the cosmos. (Fox 1972; Handelman 1981; Laski 1959; Ortiz 1969)

L

Legba

Fon, *West Africa: Benin*

Legba is known to the Fon as the cosmic "linguist," a transformer, mediator, and comic figure. Legba's designation as the cosmic linguist comes from his relationship to Mawu, the female half of the androgynous creator being of the Fon universe known as Mawu-Lisa. Mawu, the female side, remains on earth, and Lisa, the male side, remains in the sky. Although Mawu-Lisa is seen as one being, he/she is composed of two parts. Lisa rules during the day when it is hot, the work is hard, and there is little time for pleasure. Mawu, on the other hand, rules at night after the work of the day has been done when people can relax, dance, and make love. As the youngest of Mawu's sons, Legba is associated with the pleasures in life.

As the youngest son, Legba was spoiled and undisciplined. Mawu decided to give him the job of reporting on each of his brothers, who were assigned to rule over each kingdom of the world. Thus Legba needed to be able to understand all the dialects spoken in the world. As the only one in the universe who could communicate with everyone, Legba became known as the ultimate mediator, communicating with gods, kings, diviners, and humans. Legba is also recognized as the chief among the gods. Mawu had a contest to see who could simultaneously play a gong, a bell, a drum, and a flute while dancing to his own music. The winner would be chief. One by one, the most powerful beings in the universe tried, but only Legba succeed.

Legba is also connected with the divination system, Fa. The term *fa* does not refer just to the divination system; it is also the name of the being who represents the divination system, and it refers to the destiny or fate that is particular to each individual. The first part of a person's fate is revealed at adolescence through divination. A person's complete destiny, or *sekpoli*, is revealed once he or she has reached adulthood. People are not necessarily destined to meet the fate shown to them. To the contrary, people consult diviners throughout their life to seek advice on how to change their *fa* to overcome obstacles. Legba represents the freedom people have to change the course of their lives, while Fa represents the untouched path of one's life. It is not until people have reached adulthood and have had their *sekpoli* revealed to them that they may erect a full Legba statue in front of their home, thus showing that they are in a position to properly use the divination system.

Legba's and Fa's relationship is based on their places in society: Legba's is mobile and Fa's is stationary (Legba helps people move from the path that Fa lays down for them). A story tells how this came to be. While Legba was away from home one day, Fa came to his house and had intercourse with Legba's wife. A few days later when Legba returned, he asked his wife why she behaved so badly all the time. She replied that his penis was not large enough for her so she had to look elsewhere for satisfaction. Enraged by this, Legba called the people of the community to his house. He called his wife from the house and announced to the crowd that his "penis was strong" and that he and his wife would have sex in front of them to prove it. Legba said he would have intercourse with her until she was exhausted. The people beat drums and danced while Legba and his wife had sex. All the attention embarrassed his wife. She did not want the villagers to see her and her husband having sex. When she asked him to stop, Legba turned to the crowd and announced his wife's infidelities with Fa. He decreed that because of these actions Fa would forever remain in the house and that he, Legba, would preside at the entrance to all homes and would be able to have sex with any woman he chose.

Shrines to Legba are placed at the entrance of Fon homes, marketplaces, and villages, and he is given offerings at all celebrations, even those for others. (See also **Eshu-Elegba** for similar accounts.) Legba is the voice of Fa, embodying the possibilities of Fa. People consult Legba in conjunction with divination processes. The Fon make offerings to shrines and consult diviners at important times in their lives. Legba is always a part of this process. The Fon say that Fa brought all the stories of the world to earth and that Legba embodies them in his dances. Fa is the stationary, unchangeable aspect of human life, and Legba is the ever-changing, mobile aspect of human life.

In ritual settings, dancers capture Legba's ecstatic spirit by moving about wildly, demonstrating the possibility of movement in one's life. Legba can be portrayed by either a male or female dancer. Legba's androgyny comes from his connection to Mawu. Although Mawu is seen as the female part of Mawu-Lisa, Mawu-Lisa is one being, and as the son of Mawu, Legba takes on the attributes of the united Mawu-Lisa as well. Thus Legba carries with him both male and female attributes. In the initiation into the Mawu-Lisa cult, a young girl represents Legba on the last day of the festival. She leads the initiates, dancing and carrying a large phallus under her skirt. As Legba she dances ecstatically, exaggerating sexual positions and teasing the audience. A popular Fon saying captures Legba's characteristics: "Legba everywhere dances in the manner of a man copulating."

Similarly, household shrines to Legba consist of a clay figure of a large penis or of Legba with an exaggerated penis. Legba's sexual image comes from his unwillingness to conform to social limitations placed on sexuality. In one story, Legba defied the king and publicly announced that he would have sex with the king's daughter in front of the palace. In another story, Legba made men impotent by giving them a magical powder, thus leaving all the women for himself. Legba's enormous sexual appetite is matched by his promiscuity with all women, including young girls and married women. One story tells of Legba having sexual intercourse with both his sister and his niece. When his sister, Gbadu, found out of his deception with her own daughter, she confronted Legba and they fought. Mawu stepped in and ordered Legba to undress. As he stood naked in front of her she saw his erect penis and knew he was guilty. She decreed that his penis would always be erect and that he would never be satisfied sexually.

Stories of Legba are told as part of the *hwenho* narrative genre of the Fon. *Hwenho* literally means "time-old-story." The *hwenho* genre includes stories and events seen to be "true," unlike the *heho* genre, which is comprised of stories that "never happened" or were "made up." (See **Yo** for an example of *heho* stories.) Tales of Legba's exploits and his creations are considered part of the *hwenho* genre. As such, they are told by elders of the community and are most commonly told during the daylight hours at family councils or other community gatherings. The *hwenho* are seen as living documents of the Fon's history and culture; they are important not only in ritual settings but in day-to-day life as well.

Hwenho are recounted in daily transactions, in teaching children, and in agricultural life. Legba's tales are told both as stories to individuals and as part of ritual celebrations. In both forms, Legba demonstrates the inherent possibilities in life and the comic side of human existence.

One of Legba's most common nicknames is Aflakete, meaning "I have tricked you." Legba loves to cause trouble, both for humans and for gods. Because of his position as mediator and his ability to transform himself, he has many opportunities to take advantage of people. Legba was not always so deceptive. In the beginning he was always with Mawu on earth. He was faithful to all her wishes and whatever she told him to do, he did; but people always thanked Mawu for Legba's good deeds. Whenever there was wrongdoing, Mawu pointed to Legba as the perpetrator. Soon all the people began to hate Legba. When he found out about Mawu's deception, Legba decided to get even with her. He told her that someone was planning to steal all the yams from her garden. She assembled all the people and told them she would kill anyone who entered the garden. That night Legba wore Mawu's sandals when he stole the yams from her garden. In the morning, discovering the theft, Mawu assembled all the villagers. She measured their feet one by one, but none matched the prints in the garden. Finally Legba suggested she check her own feet. Mawu was humiliated, and all the people shouted at her in dismay. In her shame Mawu left earth for the sky, but she had Legba give her a report every night. Legba soon grew tired of reporting to her, so he had an old women throw dirty water at her and had others toss their garbage on Mawu. With all this commotion, Mawu was forced to move further up into the sky, and Legba was free to roam the earth. With Mawu further away, Legba was able to play more tricks on people and fulfill his selfish desires for food and sex whenever he pleased. (Argyle 1966; Courlander 1957; Herskovits and Herskovits 1958; Pelton 1980)

Lelegurulik
Melanesia, Nissan Atoll, Papua New Guinea

Lelegurulik, whom the Melanesians know as the "little orphan," is notorious for putting himself in near-death situations and then escaping unharmed. Meanwhile, those around him are usually made to be the fool. Lelegurulik's tricks propel him into situations in which he must use his *barang* (power) to overcome others. (See also **Tansa** for more on *barang* and other aspects of Melanesian culture on Nissan Atoll.) His *barang* allows him to manipulate others and defy his enemies.

Lelegurulik is an orphan and was raised by a woman who found him in a garbage can. The woman had been a social outcast her entire life and passed on her jaundiced attitude to Lelegurulik. The old woman was bitter toward a society that had rejected her, so she taught Lelegurulik at an early age to cynically hate others and to use his power to manipulate and maim. He also learned that because of his *barang* he could outsmart almost anyone.

Lelegurulik is known to the Melanesians as an "eater of men," a result of his many deadly encounters with villagers. Tales of Lelegurulik tell of him luring people into his direction and then killing them. Lelegurulik is most often found on the fringes of society, in the bush. His existence on the periphery of the village emphasizes his ambiguous status. He is not a proper member of society who follows the village rules and cooperates with others, yet because the villagers have to contend with him on a regular basis, he is more than a stranger. His unique status focuses attention on those actions that are not acceptable within Nissan society but that nevertheless persist.

Stories of Lelegurulik present his outrageous antics in order to focus attention on people's negative acts. In stories Lelegurulik prompts people to fight him by hurling insults at them and forcing them into potentially deadly situations. Using his power, Lelegurulik disguises himself in any number of costumes to hide his identity and win others' trust. Once he has gained their affection, Lelegurulik retreats to his crude behavior and most often ends up harming innocent people.

Islanders refer to Lelegurulik using the term *sa*. *Sa* has many meanings but is most often used to refer to someone, something, or someplace that is bad, worthless, or terrible. This designation can be made in reference to someone's actions as well as his or her moral character. In the case of Lelegurulik the term applies to his reprehensible actions as well as his comical behavior. Lelegurulik's comedic activity borders on the grotesque and crude. He is known for his vulgar sexual displays and his cunning verbal skills. He is most often compared to the **tansa,** or grand sorcerers, who ruled the ritual realm of society and were feared by all. Although the tansa are no longer part of Melanesian society on Nissan Atoll, characters such as Lelegurulik carry on their legacy through their actions. (Nachman 1981; Nachman 1982)

Loki

Scandinavia

Loki, perhaps the most popular character in Norse mythology, is notorious for wreaking havoc, challenging powerful deities, and spinning the wheels of creation and destruction. His wild adventures, endless contradictions, absolute buffoonery, and deceptive antics challenge mortals and gods alike. Inheriting attributes of both his father, Farbauti, "cruel striker," and his mother, Laufey, "leafy isle," Loki is a mixture of thunderous actions and cool wit that allows him to safely navigate multiple realities and ultimately to participate in the destruction of one of many Norse mythological worlds.

Like other pre-Christian literature, pre-Christian Norse mythology did not make a sharp distinction between good and evil. Thus although Loki appears to be the epitome of contradiction, he is actually a common character type. He walks the line between good and evil by ever-so-cleverly aiding the people and gods of Asgard, while at the same time keeping them in check with his deceptions, pranks, and tongue-twisting lies. Loki brings together the ideas of good and evil, showing that gods and humans possess both traits.

Loki's first challenge was his greatest victory. After his birth as a member of the Jotuns (a race of giants), Loki convinced Odin, the most powerful god of the Aesir (the principal race of Norse gods), to allow him to become a member of their society. Prior to Loki's inclusion, the Aesir and Jotuns were sworn enemies. Loki, however, using his clever wit and charming presence along with his physical stature, convinced Odin to become his blood brother. After the exchange of blood, Loki held all the powers and rights that came with his association with Odin. The connection of the wild, ambiguous, and often crude Loki with the powerful, strong, and clever Odin meant the bringing together of chaos and order in the universe. Together the two controlled Asgard and the universe.

Loki was known throughout Asgard as a fanciful liar who could seldom be trusted. But both Odin and the people of Asgard knew that it was better to have Loki on their side than to compete against him in the cosmic game of life. Loki was powerful because he could be anywhere without being seen. He was a master of disguise, able to change himself into a female, into an animal, or into a natural phenomenon to outsmart others. His sheer physical size and strength, however,

A nineteenth-century painting of Sigyn and Loki, the Norse deity who contrives evil and mischief for his fellow gods.
(North Wind Picture Archives)

were also beneficial. Loki could beat competing gods with deadly force, and he always came out on top.

Tales about Loki focus on his love of mischief. Many of his adventures were harmless pranks meant simply to entertain himself or his traveling companions. For example, Loki delighted in teasing the goddesses. Once he cut off the hair of Thor's wife, Sif. After Thor threatened Loki, however, he went to the home of the Dark Elves and convinced the dwarfs to make Sif new hair out of spun gold. In another tale Loki kidnapped the goddess of youth, Idunna, simply for fun. When he was challenged by the gods to return her, he did so. His pranks show his strength and intellect and remind the people that even when they think they can get even with him, he has a way out. Loki is thus seen in Norse mythology as one who forces change within the world. Whether through his pranks, deceptions, or violence, Loki can and does bring about change in the universe.

Norse mythology highlights the changing nature of the universe through its description of battles between gods such as Loki, Thor, and Odin and of their ultimate demise in the reoccurring cataclysm known as Ragnarok. Ragnarok is the demise of the universe, but it is also the beginning of a new era. The new era is not guaranteed to be better or worse; it will simply be new. Loki is an active part of bringing about the new era because his escapades incite others to fight. Loki disrupts the lives of people and gods alike, pushing them to their limits and often dodging the aftermath of his antics. He delights in traveling with other gods, especially Thor, for it is in their company that he can reach his full potential as a troublemaker.

When Loki travels with Thor, who is known to be trustworthy, kind, and intelligent, people and gods forget about Loki's deceptive habits. Just when people have forgotten, Loki springs to action. In one story the Aesir were plagued by a monster who was threatening their homeland. The monster had cleverly disguised himself as a common laborer and offered to erect a wall around Asgard in exchange for the sun, the moon, and one of the goddesses. He asked to use a horse to finish the wall on time, but when he tried to mount the horse, it kicked him off. The intruder tried and tried but finally it was revealed that the horse was Loki. Although the intruder should have been allowed to leave peacefully, according to the laws of safe conduct, Thor declared that he was not bound by any such human laws and killed the outsider.

In Norse mythology Loki is a prime example of the connection between chaos and order in the universe. He is a helpful deity, yet he has three offspring who are monsters. He helps people by protecting Asgard from evil, yet he brings chaos to the world with his unpredictable escapades. (Karlsdottir 1991; Roothe 1961; Williams 1979)

Ma'ii

Navajo, *Southwestern United States: Arizona; New Mexico; Utah*

Ma'ii is a multifaceted coyote character in the Navajo world. He embodies many different characteristics and personalities that run the gamut from a selfish liar to a healer and hero. Ma'ii appears in Navajo myths as a master of pranks and shape-shifting and in rituals as a healer. His stories are told only during winter, from the first frost in autumn to the first thunderstorm of spring. His power is so great that even the mention of his name can evoke danger, fear, laughter, harmony, or chaos, depending on the situation.

Ma'ii is not the only name, word, or phrase that evokes or embodies Navajo values and social mores. For the Navajo, speech is a powerful act, akin to other physical acts that bring forth or highlight Navajo life-ways. Singing, telling tales, everyday speech, and ritual prayer are all powerful actions that not only evoke power but also have consequences, either positive or negative. Speaking of Ma'ii, or any other member of the Navajo world, does not simply refer to that being; rather, it actually brings that being into existence. Ma'ii demonstrated the power of speech in one story in which he and a badger sang for snow. The badger did not believe Ma'ii when he told him he could sing for snow. Ma'ii sang "Snow, snow, snow as high as the grass" while the badger sat and watched in disbelief. But as the snow began to fall, the badger joined Ma'ii's song. Similarly, in Navajo healing ceremonies known as Coyote Way, singers sing over patients invoking Ma'ii's power to heal others. The words are not simple representations of Ma'ii and his power; they are powerful in and of themselves. It is through speech that people can bring forth the power of several beings in the cosmos, as well as natural phenomena such as rain and snow.

The Navajo linguistic structure focuses on activity and movement. There are over 356,000 different conjugations for the verb *to go*. Ma'ii's movement, like that of all members of the Navajo world, is chronicled by the way he moves and interacts with others. *Ma'ii* designates both the coyote specifically and the canine family in general. What characterizes this group as being different from other animal groups is their movement. That is, each group of animals is classified by the way they move. Ma'ii is set apart from other animals by the feature of random movement. He is classified as *joldlooshi*, which refers to randomness, danger, and endless possibilities. Ma'ii's movement in the world reflects his characteristics and the ways in which he interacts with others.

The Navajo language does not distinguish concretely between the past and present in its verb tenses. For example, when speaking about Ma'ii in a story one may say "*Ma'ii joldlooshi lá eeyá*," which translates loosely to "Coyote is trotting aimlessly having always done so." The distinction between past and present is not as important to Navajo speakers as to speakers of English, for whom time orders thoughts. For the Navajo, movement and the interaction between members of the world is the primary concern.

Ma'ii is simultaneously a humorous character, whose awkward and disruptive behavior demonstrates the proper way to act within the Navajo world, and a sagacious adviser, who warns people of danger, assists in healing the ill, and establishes human ideals. For example, when the Navajo first emerged from the underworld, Ma'ii explained to them that death was necessary in order to maintain the population. On the other hand, Ma'ii is known for his selfish and greedy behavior. Once Ma'ii saw four beavers playing a game with hoops. After running through the hoops, they would throw their spears at a target. Wanting to join in the fun, Ma'ii begged and begged the beavers to allow him to play. They told him that it was a beaver game, not one for coyotes, but Ma'ii continued his begging. Finally the beavers let him play, but they told him he had to bet his skin just as they had. The beavers' skin grew back after they took it off, so they had little to worry about. Ma'ii, however, didn't heed the beavers' warning, and he entered the contest and bet his skin. After Ma'ii made four unsuccessful attempts at the target, the beavers skinned him. He was red and his body was burning. He was weak without his skin. The beavers tried to help him by burying him in the dirt and singing over him. But after a whole winter, Ma'ii's skin and fur coat had only grown back in a mangy pattern. This is why all coyotes have mangy fur.

Ma'ii's adventures range from his unsuccessful and greedy attempt to be like the beavers and win their skins to his power to enable others to heal. The story above focuses on both of Ma'ii's roles. Although he acts in haste and out of concern for only himself, his actions bring about others' power to heal. In fact, when people have skin ailments, songs about Ma'ii are sung and his power is invoked to aid in their healing.

Although the story of Ma'ii and the beavers, like others, has an ending that explains some aspect of the world, these are not the sole "morals" of the tales, which are rich with messages and meanings. The adventures of Ma'ii do not have one meaning, just as his actions do not have only one consequence. In fact, some tales end with conflicting explanations of attributes of the human world or natural phenomena. These stories do not seek to explain exactly how the world is but, rather, to show the world's possibilities. Ma'ii's tales do not carry one simple message. To the contrary, Ma'ii's adventures and misadventures are the catalyst for philosophical discussions within the Navajo community. Ma'ii does not tell how the world is or should be, but through his actions and interactions, through his great power to heal and his equally strong tendency to fool people, Ma'ii demonstrates the range of human actions or movements in the world.

Adults do not simply tell stories of Ma'ii to their children; they perform the tales and act out Ma'ii's behavior to impress upon them the importance of sharing, reciprocity, and harmony and the actuality of danger, chaos, and greed. In the performance of stories about Ma'ii's misadventures the adults exaggerate his foolishness and emphasize his improper behavior with humor. Yet he is also revered as one of the chief protectors of the Navajo people. Navajo singers call on him to cure the ill, and the Navajo pray to Ma'ii to bring forth his power. Ma'ii is at once a restorer of harmony and an instigator of chaos.

The duality of Ma'ii is based in the Navajo belief that the world is not determined by others but by one's own actions. The Navajo linguistic structure focuses on one's own responsibility for one's actions. In Navajo one does not say "The lightning struck me" but "I allowed myself to be stuck by the lightning." In their performance of tales about Ma'ii's antics, adults teach children that it is their actions that affect the world. It is their behavior and the way they allow themselves to act that negatively or positively affect the community.

Thus, as Ma'ii stumbles through the Navajo world causing chaos and ignoring social mores, including the prohibition of incest and murder, he teaches the Navajo that it is their own actions and interactions that disrupt the community, not those of others. It is what people allow to happen that is significant. Through Ma'ii, the Navajo demonstrate the importance of one's actions to the community and the power of action in the world. Ma'ii shows the Navajo that boundaries are not always clear, that structures are not concrete, and that one's survival is directly linked to one's actions. (Gill 1987; Haile 1984; Hill and Hill 1945; Luckert 1979; Matthews 1897; Reichard 1950; Toelken 1987; Toelken 1990; Witherspoon 1977)

Manabozho

Algonquian, including Ojibwa, Menominee, Micmac, Cree, *Northeastern United States; Southeastern Canada*
See **Nanabozhoo.**

Matsuludani

Sikuani, *Eastern Colombia*
See **Furna.**

Maui

New Zealand; Hawaii; Samoa; Tahiti; Other Pacific Islands
Maui is a well-known character who outwits others with his superior intellect and his ability to transform himself into anything he wishes. Throughout the South Pacific he is known for playing pranks on people, animals, and deities. His actions are humorous, but they are also harmful on many occasions. He changes his shape to steal food and get out of dangerous situations. He is known as a boy, but he has extensive extraordinary powers, including the ability to redirect the wind, pull up sunken islands, challenge volcanoes and human enemies, and change the course of the most powerful beings.

Maui spent his childhood in the sky with several powerful deities, from whom he learned his skills. After learning of his heritage on earth as well, Maui decided to live on earth. Coming from a human family of vast lineage, Maui was able to take advantage of human pleasures. During his short life, he used his powers to trick the very deities who had helped raise him. He was a proud boy and always wanted to prove himself, both to the islanders and to the deities.

Maui is known both as an artful master of deceit and as a gracious hero. Stories focus on his multiplicity of skills, never portraying him as a single character. The stories about Maui are found across the islands of the South Pacific, and they pick up pieces of each distinct culture in which we find him. Although the stories are similar, each culture and each storyteller brings his or her own style to the tale. Cultural and moral themes are present in stories about Maui, which focus on his humorous and powerful sides. The stories reflect the chaotic lifestyle of small fishing communities and their encounters with outsiders as well as the turbulent ocean.

In Maui the people of the South Pacific have a character who can battle the raging ocean, trick an unknowing fisherman, and save a village from disaster. As both a humorous character and a hero he plays a large role in the oral literature of these societies. Some stories portray him as a human with eight heads, each one representing a different personality. The eight-headed Maui symbolizes his many different character traits and his ability to play each part well. The eight-headed character unifies his seemingly disparate personalities. Although he is both a creator and hero, he is also a destroyer and deceiver. By depicting him with eight heads, the islanders have

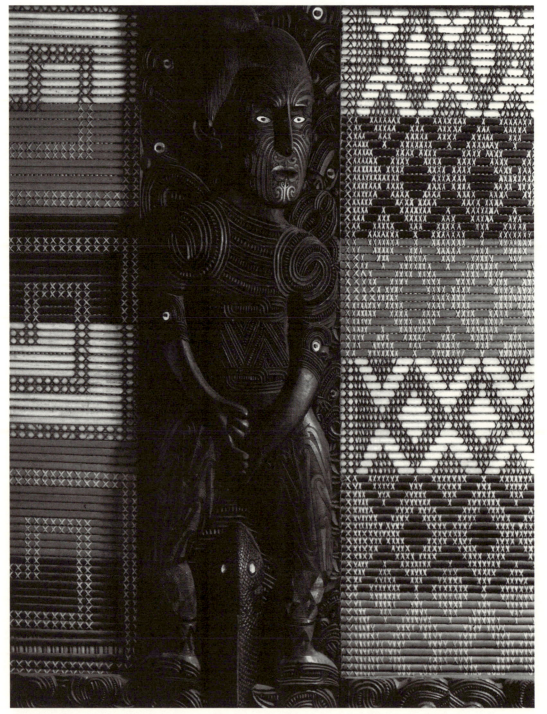

An elaborate carving of Maui, the trickster/creator character popular in many of the South Pacific islands. (Hamburgisches Museum für Völkerkunde, Hamburg, Germany)

found a way to incorporate all his traits into one character.

In Hawaii islanders tell stories of Maui and his human brothers. Maui was the youngest of four brothers from a prominent family. Although only a boy, he had superior strength and an intellect to match. In one story, his older brothers left him out of a fishing expedition because they believed he was not yet competent in fishing. The three older brothers left in their canoe, leaving Maui on the shore. Determined to show them his power, Maui changed into a sea bird and flew over their canoe. Knowing that the sea birds fed on the *aku* fish, the brothers followed the bird. When the bird stopped and flew in circles, the boys dropped their lines in. Maui's oldest brother was first to catch an *aku*. Just as he grabbed it out of the water, Maui swooped down and took the fish from him. Landing in the canoe, Maui turned himself back into his human form and laughed at his brothers for their ignorance.

In another Hawaiian tale Maui brought the islands into their current formation. One day when he was fishing he met Mr. One-Tooth, the being who held the islands together under the ocean. Maui knew he must challenge him in order to move the islands. When he went home to his brothers, he told them he would be going fishing the next day, but he did not tell them of his plans to move the islands closer together. That night, however, his mother came to him and told him that he should go far out in the ocean to find something that would help in his adventure. Taking her advice, Maui paddled his canoe far out into the ocean and found a bailing dish. As Maui and his brothers canoed back to find One-Tooth, the bailing dish turned into a mermaid. Before the boys could cast out their lines, though, the mermaid turned back into a dish. Maui's brothers angrily threw the dish out. Knowing that the mermaid would help him, Maui cast his line and felt

her tug on it and pull it deep into the ocean where One-Tooth lived. The mermaid seduced One-Tooth with her beauty and got him to open his mouth wide enough for her to slip Maui's hook in it. As she did so, Maui pulled tight and caught One-Tooth. Paddling quickly, Maui and his brothers dragged One-Tooth and the islands to their present spots. One of the Hawaiian islands is named Maui after the hero.

In a similar story from New Zealand, Maui captured the sun and tricked him into lengthening the day for the islanders. After Maui had released the people from the control of the most powerful sky-beings, he saw that he had opened up a hole for the sun to come through. Hearing of the sun's plans to move quickly across the sky, Maui's mother and others were worried. How could they cook their food in so little time? And how could the women finish their laundry and make their mats without the hot sun all day? After listening to his mother and others, Maui climbed the highest mountain and waited for the sun. As the sun ran by, Maui jumped out and grabbed him. Maui cut the sun's strong legs off, only leaving the weak ones. Just as he was about to cut those too, the sun pleaded with him not to. When the sun promised that he would follow a longer path and go much slower to allow the people to survive, Maui let him go with his two weak legs.

Maui's escapades capture his multifaceted personality. Although he uses deception to gain the respect from his brothers, deities, and islanders, he also uses his powers to help people. In New Zealand people refer to Maui as Maui-atamai, or "Maui the wise." Maui's wisdom is demonstrated in his aid to the islanders. He brought the sun to them, he helped them attain fire, and he showed them how to make fishing hooks so they could survive. For New Zealanders Maui's tricks and pranks are outweighed by his willingness to help. As do the people of other islands, the people of New Zealand

and Hawaii have many stories about Maui. Their common thread is their focus on the good that comes out of even his deceitful acts. (Alpers 1964; Cowan 1930; Gifford 1924; Green 1926; Luomala 1940; Luomala 1949; Stimson 1934; Stimson 1937; Thompson 1990; Westervelt 1979)

Mbudti

Ge, *Brazil*

In Ge oral literature, the sun, variably known as Mbudti, Mebapame, Mut, or Pud, depending on the village, has the characteristics of a human male. Mbudti is understood to be clever, strong, and superior to his companion **Mbuduvrire,** the moon. Mbudti and Mbuduvrire compete against each other in several stories that demonstrate their strengths and weaknesses as well as their creative powers. Together, the pair brought animals, plants, hunting customs, and other things important to Ge society. On the other hand, the pair's duels and continuous contests of strength also brought destruction to the Ge. As both creators and destroyers, the two demonstrate the many possibilities within the Ge world.

Ge stories deal with many of the prevalent issues surrounding the several villages of people in eastern Brazil. Spread out over a large area, people of different villages may only come together a few times a year for ceremonial purposes or for trade. However, the people share a common link through their oral history and the characters who provide the impetus for many stories. Stories are generally told at night by men. Storytellers are known individually for their abilities to entertain and bring a story to life. Although the characters are familiar, the storyteller's job is to make each story come alive for the people. Storytellers are judged by their ability to use different voices, hand gestures, and body motions in their orations. The Ge use storytelling not only to entertain but also to pass their traditions to younger generations and to maintain a sense of community throughout their many villages. Familiar characters such as Mbudti and Mbuduvrire provide a backdrop not only for educating the young about how the Ge cosmos was constructed but also for moral lessons about proper behavior. Mbudti and Mbuduvrire, although creators, show their shortcomings through their unwillingness to work together and cooperate.

In story after story Mbudti comes out on top in his adventures with Mbuduvrire. Although the two work together on occasion and Mbudti is often portrayed sharing his food and shelter with Mbuduvrire, Mbudti delights in tricking his companion and even terrorizing him for his faults. In one story, the two came to earth together and decided to build a home together. After building their home, they set out to find food and other necessities. Mbudti was successful in his hunt and returned to the designated meeting place. Mbuduvrire, not so successful, got lost and could not find his way back to their meeting place. After waiting for Mbuduvrire for some time, Mbudti set out to find him. Soon Mbudti came across the humiliated Mbuduvrire sitting on a rock waiting for Mbudti to rescue him. Mbuduvrire admitted that he had found no food or supplies and that he had become disoriented and lost after only a short while. Mbudti pretended to be sympathetic and took Mbuduvrire to a wasp's nest he had found to get honey. Because Mbuduvrire was so gullible and afraid, he believed Mbudti when he told him to stick his hand in the hive for honey. Of course, as soon as his hand was in the hive he was stung by hundreds of angry wasps, which left him blind and even more humiliated than before.

Continuing his campaign against Mbuduvrire, Mbudti then pretended to carry his sightless friend across a blocked path on their way home. As they passed under some low-hanging brush, Mbudti turned Mbuduvrire on his back, causing his testicles to be slashed in the process. After they crossed the path Mbudti dropped his companion on a thorny bush and left him there as a final testament to his lack of compassion.

In addition to his cunning wit and sharp hunting skills, Mbudti also had the power to make things disappear and to change his surroundings to suit him. In several stories Mbudti dries rivers up, moves rocks out of his path, and changes fruit to poison to trick unsuspecting hunters or Mbuduvrire. In one story Mbuduvrire begged Mbudti for a portion of the meat he had caught. Tired of Mbuduvrire's complaints that the meat was not fatty enough, Mbudti hurled a hot coal at him, burning his stomach. As Mbuduvrire ran to the stream to relieve his pain, however, Mbudti caused the stream to go dry, and Mbuduvrire was forever scarred from the ordeal.

When they do cooperate, Mbudti and Mbuduvrire are almost unstoppable in their pranks against unsuspecting people. The two team up to steal meat and arrows from hunters by distracting them from their prey, and they are never above stealing food from women and children after the men of a village have gone hunting. In one story, the two were out hunting when they came upon some men fishing with arrows. The two headed downstream, turned themselves into fish, and jumped into the stream. As they came upon the fisherman they swam close to the surface, allowing the arrows to hit them, while at the same time turning back into humans and making off with the hunters' best arrows. (Lowie 1946; Mayberry-Lewis 1971; Wilbert and Simoneau 1978; Wilbert and Simoneau 1984)

Mbuduvrire

Ge, *Brazil*

Known in various Ge villages as Mbuduvrire, Bruburé, Muturure, or Puduvrí, the moon is given the characteristics of a human male. In contrast to his counterpart Mbudti, the sun, Mbuduvrire is known to be timid, slow-witted, and antagonistic. However, the two of them are responsible for bringing to the Ge many of the things necessary for their survival. In addition, their escapades and many battles also brought destruction and chaos at times. (See **Mbudti** for more details.)

In Ge stories Mbuduvrire rarely outsmarts his companion Mbudti. In fact, he relies on Mbudti for most of his food and other necessities. Stories relate the foolishness of Mbuduvrire by showing him as dependent and unwilling to think on his own. By constantly relying on Mbudti, Mbuduvrire represents the negative aspects of a cooperative society. Although the Ge villagers work together in hunting and gardening groups, Mbuduvrire demonstrates the dangers of being too reliant on others.

Most of the stories concerning Mbuduvrire focus on his gullibility and ineptness. Instead of thinking for himself, he relies on Mbudti and is duped time and time again. In one story, Mbuduvrire was awestruck by the beautiful red color of Mbudti's feces. Wanting to have the same, he asked Mbudti how to get them. Not realizing that Mbudti's answer would probably lead him astray, Mbuduvrire listened intently as Mbudti told him to eat the *buriti* fruit. Mbuduvrire hunted for the fruit, finally found some, and sat down to his feast. But just as Mbuduvrire began to eat the fresh fruit, Mbudti changed the soft, ripe fruit to a hard, rotten one. Instead of turning his feces a beautiful red, the rotten fruit made them black and uncomfortable.

Occasionally Mbuduvrire gets the best of Mbudti, and in doing so he forces the world to change. One story relates how Mbuduvrire is responsible for bringing death to the world. When Mbudti and Mbuduvrire first arrived on earth there were no people. Together the two thought of ways to create children for themselves, competing against one another to see who would have the most beautiful and intelligent children. While they were swimming in a stream one day, Mbuduvrire reminded Mbudti of their plan to create children. Mbuduvrire dove down deep into the water and emerged with his children following him. Next Mbudti dove down and surfaced with his children, who were beautiful. Not wanting to be outdone, Mbuduvrire asked Mbudti how they would feed their children if they kept multiplying. Mbudti did not see a problem with allowing the children to revive themselves after death. But Mbuduvrire took a rock and threw it in the water, watching it sink quickly, never to return. Turning to Mbudti, Mbuduvrire told him that like the rock, when people died they would not revive themselves; instead, they would forever be dead. With the powerful stone Mbuduvrire had shown Mbudti how the children should live and die and had beaten him at his own game; in doing so he brought death to the world. (Lowie 1946; Mayberry-Lewis 1971; Wilbert and Simoneau 1978; Wilbert and Simoneau 1984)

Méri
Bororo, *Brazil*

Méri, the cunning, strong, and witty sun, delights in fooling his weaker brother Ari, the moon, who is laughably clumsy and weak. Together the brothers are responsible for creating the seasonal changes, and eventually, because of Méri's outlandish behavior, the two were permanently expelled from earth to their homes in the sky. Even in the sky, however, Méri maintains a relationship with the Bororo through their offerings. At times of harvest, selected men make offerings of food to Méri to ensure his help with seasonal changes and good weather. Prior to their offerings, Méri was known to keep earth dark all day.

Before their expulsion from earth Méri and Ari traveled together wreaking havoc on people. One story explains how Méri came to have control over the night. Méri had been stealing food from some villagers, and as he left the camp he saw two small birds in a nest. Wondering who they belonged to, Méri stuck his fingers deep in their mouths and killed the weak birds. When the birds' father, who was the owner of night, came back he was so angered by the death of his children that he ordered night to fall immediately. The darkness frightened Méri, so he went to the birds' father and offered to use his power to revive the children if he could have control of night. Not knowing that Méri was the killer, the father agreed; and from then on Méri was the owner of night.

Although Méri was normally the instigator of harmful pranks, Ari was always being caught up in his games. For example, Méri thought it was hilarious to put out people's campfires with his urine. In one story Méri first urinated on a hunting party's food and ruined it, then he urinated on their fire. The people became distressed because if the fire were to be extinguished, so would the last ember of fire on earth at the time. Luckily, however, a clever toad watched Méri from a distance and grabbed a hot coal before the fire was totally extinguished. (See also **Júko** for a Bororo character similar to Méri.)

In his days on earth Méri was known to be assertive in his dealings with others, especially his brother. Méri bullied Ari into acts he did not approve of, such as stealing and killing at random. Méri's strength, however, was his ability to revive both himself and his brother if they were ever killed during one of his pranks. For example, while Méri was urinating on the hunters' fire, Ari was caught with one of the flying embers and burned to death. But Méri's power allowed him to breathe new life into Ari and leave the hunters behind.

In another story a revengeful group of hunters started a fire near Méri and Ari to kill them. Méri escaped up a tree, but the slower Ari was caught in the fire and died. Before Méri could get back to him a hungry wolf cub, Okwa, ate Ari. Knowing that Okwa was conceited, Méri challenged him to a race to see who was faster. Okwa boasted that no one had ever beaten him in a race. Before they started Méri conceded that he really wanted Okwa to win the race, so he offered to tie his belt around Okwa's stomach to give him more strength. Caught up in his pride Okwa allowed Méri to tie the belt around his stomach. While he was tightening it, Méri told Okwa that the tighter it was the more endurance he would have. When the race began, Méri stayed close behind Okwa, letting him think he was winning. Then as they rounded a turn he tripped Okwa, who landed on his stomach, which exploded immediately. Digging out the bones of his brother, Méri used powerful potions and chants to revive him, and they were off again. (Cook 1908; Hopper 1967; Kietzman 1967; Wilbert and Simoneau 1983)

Mica

Lakota, *Plains Region of the United States*

Mica, a mischievous, deceitful coyote, is responsible for bringing cowardice, thievery, and deceit to the Lakota. He has an unending sexual appetite, he steals, he is greedy, and he is generally disrespectful. Mica disregards all Lakota social mores by being selfish and rude. For example, Mica takes advantage of his friends' wives, he steals food from his neighbors, and he lies to get whatever he wants, never working at all. Mica outwits people with lies, tricks, and any means possible. He challenges people, animals, and other powerful beings to contests that he is sure to win, or he cheats to make sure that he will be victorious.

Mica's power is so great that he can persuade people to act disrespectfully and to take part in dishonorable activities, convincing them by changing his voice and his appearance to make it seem as if he is in a position of power. Mica does not even need to be present to inflict his mischief upon others; wherever he roams, he leaves behind his spirit, or power, which allows him to stay active in Lakota communities even after he has departed physically. People are never sure where he is or, if he is gone, what might bring him back. (See **Iktomi** for more on Lakota society.)

In one story Mica heard that there was an outside trader in the village who was so cunning that he always got the best of people in trades. One day another man told the outsider that there was someone even he could not outwit. "That is impossible," the man said. "I've had a trading post here for some time and have cheated everyone in the village." But the man told him about Mica, who could beat anyone at any game. The trader went looking for Mica, and when he found him he dared him to outsmart him in any deal. Mica thought for a moment and then told the man that he could not cheat him right then because he did not have his cheating medicine with him. "Go get it," the man said. But Mica told him that he lived too far away and had no horse to get back to his home. In disgust the man told Mica he could borrow his horse so that they could get their contest under way. Just as he was about to leave Mica turned and said that he could not ride the man's horse, for the horse would know that Mica was not its master. "I will need your clothes to fool your horse," Mica said. So the trader took off his clothes and gave them to Mica. "Now go get that medicine; I know I can beat it," the trader said as Mica rode off with his horse, leaving him naked in the middle of the village.

Stories about Mica demonstrate his cunning, his wit, and his huge ego. Mica prides himself on being the most intelligent and powerful being in Lakota society. He disregards others' power, believing that he is the best. In one story Mica and Iktomi (the spider) were out hunting when Mica saw Iya, disguised as a rock. The rock was covered with streaks of green moss, and even Mica knew that Iya was very powerful. Mica decided to give Iya his blanket as a gift to show that he could be generous.

After Mica and Iktomi left Iya it started to rain, and they ducked into a cave to keep warm. Iktomi had his blanket and would not share with Mica, telling him he should not have given away his own. The rain and hail continued until Mica could not stand it anymore. He told Iktomi to go get his blanket back from Iya. Iktomi went to get the blanket, but Iya would not give it back. Upon hearing that, Mica was furious; "that greedy Iya," he thought as he ran through the rain. When Mica found Iya he assailed him with a barrage of insults, telling him he was ungrateful, greedy, and selfish, and then he pulled his blanket off Iya and went back to the cave. Soon the rain stopped and the sun came out. Iktomi and Mica were leaving the cave when the heard a great noise. They thought it was thunder at first, but then they saw Iya rolling toward them with great speed. The two ran through the forest, climbed trees, and swam across a river, but still Iya followed them. Iktomi finally left Mica, telling him that this was not his quarrel. He made himself into a ball and sneaked down a mouse hole. As soon as Iktomi left, Iya caught up with Mica, ran over him, and flattened him where he stood with his great size and speed. Later that day a hunter found Mica and took him home to use as a rug. That night, before he went to bed, the hunter laid Mica down in front of his fire. When he awoke Mica was gone, and the hunter's wife told him that she had seen his rug run away that morning. Perhaps Mica's greatest power is his ability to bring himself back to life. (Beckwith 1930; Buechel 1978; Walker 1980; Walker 1982; Wissler 1907)

Mullah Nasruddin
Iran; Afghanistan

The character of Mullah Nasruddin, the wise fool, appears in folktales throughout Afghanistan and Iran. He is linked to local communities by the problems he tackles with his comedic actions. (El-Shamy 1980; Magnarella and Webster 1990)

N

Naar
Kammu, *Northern Laos*

Naar is the lovable, innocent, yet very gullible fool in Kammu stories. He tries to outwit people and to get the best of situations, but he almost always ends up losing. Unlike his counterpart **Plaan Thoóy,** who uses his wit and tricks to deceive and outmaneuver others, Naar is forever finishing second. Although Naar is the ultimate dupe, he is treated with compassion and respect by his loving wife, even when others around him are not so kind. In fact, his wife is the only person who does not make fun of and trick Naar. His misplaced confidence and trust in people allows him to be tricked time and time again.

Humorous stories about Naar are told in all the Kammu villages for entertainment. Using common themes of village life, storytellers poke fun at the naive Naar. In some stories, Naar is asked to do chores that are normally reserved for women. Without thinking, he performs the tasks and becomes the butt of the joke. In other instances, Naar is tricked by small animals and even children, showing his gullible side. In one story, Naar failed to recognize his wife because she had new clothes on. Convinced she was another woman, he hid, waiting for her to leave his house.

Naar is always trying to fit in with others. He joins in with the other men in their hunting activities, but he almost always falls short of his goals. He lags behind when out hunting, he cannot string a proper trap, and he is always forgetting his tasks. Perhaps the most insulting characteristic attributed to Naar is his lack of confidence with women. In stories his father-in-law chides him for not having any children, telling him he is incompetent as a man. Although his wife sticks up for Naar, he remains a laughable character.

In story after story, Naar's wife has to bail him out of embarrassing situations or perform work that is normally done by men because Naar is incompetent. In one story, Naar's wife told him to burn the field so they could plant their crops. After a series of bumbles, Naar ended up burning himself, and his wife was left with the task. In another story, Naar attempted to build a hut for his family, but he mistook the proper branches for kindling and burned their hut. Naar's antics make him an entertaining character in Kammu stories; his bumbling and gullibility make him a favorite. Although the stories are humorous, like other Kammu tales they are accompanied by a lesson. Naar is the perfect example of the dangers of incompetence and naiveté. Although trust is an important virtue to the Kammu, stories of Naar show that not everyone is trustworthy and that one must be able to spot a prankster. Similarly, the character of Naar highlights the need for young men to take their responsibilities seriously so as not to play the fool themselves. (Lindell, Swahn, and Tayanin 1977a; Lindell, Swahn, and Tayanin 1977b)

Nafigi
Kalapalo, *Central Brazil*

Nafigi, a female *ifau* (cousin) of **Taugi,** is best known for her ability to change shape to outwit others and fulfill her desires. She

147

can also travel through any terrain; she can fly through the sky, burrow underground, scale mountains, and flow through rivers in both directions. She is stronger than any man and uses her strength in horrific ways, pointlessly maiming and killing people. Unlike Taugi, she is known mainly as a destructive being. Her actions are rarely helpful or creative, and they are always unpredictable.

In most stories Nafigi is juxtaposed with Taugi, representing the negative side of humanity. In addition, she and Taugi together represent opposed male and female roles in Kalapalo society. Public pranks, jokes, and trickery are part of male Kalapalo society. Men maintain sanctioned joking relationships, and their public indecencies and buffoonery are expected. Women, on the other hand, are expected to keep their playful actions to themselves, and their speech, for instance, is never characterized as in any way joking or satirical. Thus their speech is more matter of fact than men's, which includes anything from subtle innuendoes to outright jokes. Taugi and Nafigi complement each other by displaying actions that are both expected and unexpected in Kalapalo society. Nafigi is seen as destructive and crude precisely because her actions are the opposite of standard female roles.

One of Nafigi's best-known traits is her unusual ability to adopt the physical characteristics of any person, male or female, young or old, that she wishes. She is characterized by her heightened sexual drive and her dreadful actions. If she desires a man she becomes a women; if she desires a woman she becomes a man. One story illuminates Nafigi's powerful sexual drive and her destructive behavior. Nafigi appeared in the village square acting lewdly and disruptively. Screaming and drawing attention to herself, she forced herself on unwitting men by grabbing their genitals. One by one, she lured the single men out of the village and destroyed their seminal fluid by

poisoning their genitals while she raped them. Nafigi's genitals are *pingegi* (poisonous). If she is not disguised, men are repulsed by her, but because of her clever disguises and her ability to change shape, many men are seduced by her and then left sterile. A Kalapalo women's song captures Nafigi's reckless sexual behavior:

Look, look, my husband stands
    motionless,
Nafigi's doing,
Our husband is dead, once and for all,
Nafigi's doing.

It is not just her sexual passion that sets Nafigi apart. She also intrudes on other compassionate relationships. Nafigi is notorious for interfering with *funita*, compassionate longing relationships between family members. If a mother longs for her daughter, Nafigi becomes her daughter and receives all the love the mother sends the daughter's way. Nafigi takes advantage of those in emotionally vulnerable states, taking their love and compassion for herself. (Basso 1987; Basso 1988)

Nanabozhoo
Algonquian, including Ojibwa,
Menominee, Micmac, Cree, *Northeastern United States; Southeastern Canada*
Nanabozhoo is known within various Algonquian communities both for his power to create and to educate and for his masterful ability to deceive and carry out pranks. Nanabozhoo is one among many *manitos* (powerful nonhuman beings) in the Algonquian world. *Manitos* interact with humans and aid them in maintaining their communities. For example, Nanabozhoo is credited with creating animals and with forming rivers and mountains, as well as with making human beings mortal. Stories about Nanabozhoo demonstrate the complex nature of the relationships between

people, animals, and other nonhuman members of Algonquian communities.

In the escapades of Nanabozhoo, the Algonquians show the far-reaching consequences, both positive and negative, of people's actions and interactions. Nanabozhoo both creates (fire, people, lodges, birds, and animals) and destroys (homes, humans, animals, and trees) and in doing so represents the scheme of possibilities in the world. Although Nanabozhoo is known by several different names in the Algonquian communities (for example, Manabozho, Nanabush, Nenaposh, and Winabojo), he is identified by the same physical and personal characteristics. He is normally depicted as a giant with large eyes and strong facial features. He is always represented as fast, strong, intelligent, and agile.

Algonquian communities represent their interrelationships with the natural and physical world both linguistically and socially. For example, the Ojibwa may use the noun *anissinape* to refer to either human or nonhuman beings depending on the Ojibwa's relationship to those beings. Communities and families are related to the natural world through their interactions with specific beings. That is, people share with, give gifts to, and pray to those beings who not only help them but also act with them in maintaining their communities.

Stories about Nanabozhoo capture the interconnection of the Algonquian world by showing the importance of maintaining proper relationships with all members of their community. One story tells of Nanabozhoo bringing fire to the Algonquian people. One day Nanabozhoo met with his grandmother and saw that the cold was making her ill. Nanabozhoo knew that a jealous warrior had been given a spark of fire but kept it to himself. Changing into a white rabbit, Nanabozhoo ran through a stream near the warrior's house and waited for the warrior's daughters to notice him. Shivering, Nanabozhoo caught the attention of the girls, who felt sorry for him. They picked him up and carried him inside by the fire to warm him up. Waiting for the girls to go outside, Nanabozhoo sat shivering by the fire. The old warrior had awakened, but he paid no attention to the small, feeble rabbit. As soon as he had gone back asleep, Nanabozhoo turned himself into a strong man, seized the fire stick, and ran toward his canoe. As he left he threw a piece of the stick into the trees and watched them as they burned. He saw that the leaves became a beautiful red and gold when they burned, and he decreed that they would have that color from then on.

By bringing the people fire, and thus a means by which to sustain themselves, Nanabozhoo initiated a reciprocal relationship with the people, who were expected to respond to Nanabozhoo's help through gifts and ceremony. Like other *manitos*, Nanabozhoo is offered tobacco and other gifts by individuals in times of need and during hunting trips and ceremonies. Yet Nanabozhoo, unlike other *manitos*, may disregard offerings or act selfishly, wanting more than his share. Through Nanabozhoo the Algonquian communities are reminded of the possibility of chaos and disruptive behavior.

Stories about Nanabozhoo focus on all aspects of Algonquian life: the humorous and dangerous, the harmful and beneficial, the respectful and disrespectful, and the creative and destructive. Nanabozhoo represents the range of possibilities in all of life's activities in the Algonquian world. For example, in one story, Nanabozhoo was walking in the forest when he noticed the chipmunks running quickly past him with their mouths full of nuts and seeds. As he walked on, thinking of the chipmunks, he realized he was hungry. Nanabozhoo looked around at the small animals scurrying about, but they were all too small to fill his appetite. However, further on he saw a fat black bear walking his way. He hid behind a tree as the bear approached. Just as he came within reach, Nanabozhoo began to sing a song of apology to the bear, explaining that he was hungry and that the bear should not be angered; then he clubbed the bear with a large tree branch. After the bear was skinned, Nanabozhoo sat down to a large feast.

As he was about to eat, he heard something in the birch tree above him singing. It sounded as though it was saying "greedy fellow, greedy fellow." Nanabozhoo shouted to the tree to be quiet. But the wind blew through the trees, and Nanabozhoo continued to hear the tune. Enraged, Nanabozhoo leapt up from his feast, climbed up the tree, and tried to pull the great birch tree from its neighbor. As he tried to separate the two trees, his hand got stuck. Below him he heard a great commotion. When he looked down he saw a pack of wolves devouring his catch. He yelled at the wolves to stop eating their "brother's" food, but they ignored him, pleased that they could take advantage of Nanabozhoo without fear of retribution. After they finished eating they ran off, mocking Nanabozhoo and thanking him for the feast. Finally Nanabozhoo freed himself, but it was too late; all that was left was bones. In his anger, Nanabozhoo tore the branches from the birch and began whipping all the trees. He was so strong that he scarred the trees, and today all birch trees wear the reminder of Nanabozhoo's wrath.

Nanabozhoo has the power to transform himself into anything or anyone he desires. This distinctive ability affords Nanabozhoo the luxury of finding out many different things about the communities in which he lives. By transforming himself, Nanabozhoo listens to private conversations, sneaks into restricted meetings, and generally does whatever he pleases. In addition, Nanabozhoo has the power to breathe life into anything, and he created many of the first animals and people. However, he is also able to imitate his creations. Thus Nanabozhoo is best known as a multifaceted character who can be anywhere at anytime.

Among the Ojibwa Nanabozhoo is notorious for changing his appearance to get what he wants. In one story, Nanabozhoo was widowed and lonely. He tried to trick women into having intercourse with him, but the women recognized Nanabozhoo. Desperate, Nanabozhoo changed himself into a young man and married one of his own daughters to satisfy his sexual appetite. Nanabozhoo is well known for his sexual drive. Time after time he takes advantage of women and deceives them for his own satisfaction. To the Sandy Lake Ojibwa, his sexual prowess is so great that he is referred to as the "sex maniac of the north." (Brown and Brightman 1988; Coleman 1971; Fisher 1946; Landes 1968; Leekley 1965; Makarius 1973; Morriseau 1965; Reid 1963; Stevens 1971)

Nanabush

Algonquian, including Ojibwa, Menominee, Micmac, Cree, *Northeastern United States; Southeastern Canada*
See **Nanabozhoo.**

Nanawitcu

O'odam, *Southwestern United States*
The nanawitcu, ridiculous-looking comedic performers, play a role in the O'odam harvest festival, which is normally performed every four years, if crops have flourished, and lasts many days. It is up to the elders from each community to decide on the time for the performance. Each day of the festival the community gathers for various dances, prayers, and ritual performances that maintain the O'odam community. The harvest festival is necessary to ensure harmonious relationships throughout the community as well as fruitful crops.

Dressed in canvas smocks, the nana-witcu performers have spiral designs painted on their arms and spots painted on their legs. Each nawitcu (the singular form of the word) wears a large canvas mask whose small eye-holes are adorned further with feathers. Horns made out of turkey plumes are attached to the side of the mask, and down from a hawk is fastened to the top. Clouds are painted around the face of the mask. Each performer wears a tobacco pouch around his waist and carries part of a saguaro cactus as a weapon.

As part of their humorous play, the clowns mimic warriors. Along with their other paraphernalia, the nanawitcu carry crooked bows without strings and arrows made from various cacti and turkey feathers. Rushing back and forth between the warriors and other ritual performers, the nanawitcu exaggerate the others' actions by playacting battle scenes and rudely dancing and playing around the others. Prior to and after their ritual activities, the nanawitcu run into homes in the village and steal food, dump over pots, and rummage through people's things.

The nanawitcu also act seriously in parts of the harvest festival. On certain days, some nanawitcu are chosen to speak in front of the community, to offer thanks, and to offer food to select families. The nanawitcu are also credited with healing people by breathing on them. The power of the nanawitcu lies in their ability to blur the distinction between chaos and order. As part of the O'odam community, they are an integral part of both everyday and ritual activities. Without their seemingly disruptive activities, the harvest festival would not be complete, and the community's balance might be disturbed. See also **Koshare** and **Newekwe** for similar characters. (Lumholtz 1912; Mason 1920; Russell 1908; Steward 1991)

Nankilslas

Haida, *Northwest Coast of North America*

Nankilslas, whose name means "he whose voice is obeyed," is a raven who is often portrayed in stories as selfish and disrespectful of Haida social mores. Nankilslas, however, is also credited with creating many of the foundations of the Haida culture. Haida society is based on small family units who work together for their economic sustenance. In addition, the larger community, which is divided into two halves, each known as a moiety, is bound together by overarching social relationships that result in an extended kinship system between the two moieties. Each member of the Haida society belongs to either the Raven or the Eagle moiety. The clans within each of these moieties comprise the families who work as groups to maintain the community. Each clan has a responsibility not only to the people within that clan but also to their moiety. Clans represent their place within the overall social fabric with clan crests, usually carvings of the raven or eagle. These crests trace a family's lineage and place people within the larger community.

The Haida, like most of their coastal neighbors, rely on fishing as their main source of sustenance and economy (see also **Yetl,** a raven character of the Tlingit). Because the Haida culture is based so intimately on the interworkings of several

A 102-year-old Haida headdress representing the raven Nankilslas lies on a beach near Skidegate in Queen Charlotte Islands. (Dewit Jones/Corbis)

groups, one person's selfish actions can easily disrupt the balance. In the character of Nankilslas, the Haida demonstrate the problems for the community that result from the negative behavior of one member. Nankilslas is best known for his selfish behavior, which prompts him to steal from his family, neighbors, and friends. This type of behavior runs contrary to the Haida social system, which uses a communal potlatch (a large community event in which people give away their wealth to others in the community) as one of its main sources of wealth distribution. Traditionally people gave away sea otter skins, fish, blankets, and other goods that were necessary for survival. People who hold a potlatch gain status within the community, and people who have not been as prosperous obtain the items they need to survive. Thus Haida society is bound together through reciprocal interactions in which each person in the community takes part, and selfish antics like Nankilslas's disrupt community life.

Nankilslas takes what he wants by disguising himself as someone else or by using his wit to outsmart others. Often he disguises himself as an elder or uncle to take advantage of their status and thus fool his friends. In one story Nankilslas pretended to be dead in order to receive the gifts that people brought to his funeral. He also likes to prey on people when they are mourning or celebrating. In either case, Nankilslas waits until people least expect him to show up and then plays his tricks. In one story Nankilslas stole berries from his own sister by pretending to hear the call of warriors and sending his sister off for her protection. Once his sister was gone, Nankilslas ate all the berries she had collected. In another story, Nankilslas convinced the people of one village to put him in the canoe with the salmon eggs they were sending to sell to their neighbors. Nankilslas told the people he was sick and that he must have care from another healer. Once in the canoe, he ate all the salmon eggs and left the people with nothing to trade.

Nankilslas's pranks are not always successful. Often his foolish and disruptive behavior is discovered, and he is punished. Nankilslas cannot resist the temptation of sexual liaisons with young girls or married women and often ignores Haida social restrictions on these types of sexual exploits, using his ability to change form and his charm to convince women to have sex with him. Once, for example, Nankilslas desired a married woman. He brought the beautiful skin of a robin from a nearby island and walked with it by the woman's house when he knew her husband would be outside. When her husband saw the beautiful feathers of the robin he asked where Nankilslas had gotten the bird. Nankilslas told him that they could only be found on his island nearby but that he would take him there. The next day Nankilslas and the man went to the island. Nankilslas told the man to wait in the boat while he went and looked for the birds. Once inland Nankilslas changed some branches into robins; he then returned to the man and told him to go deep inland to find the birds. The man left, and Nankilslas climbed into the boat and headed back for the woman.

When Nankilslas arrived back at the man's house, he changed himself into the man and told the woman how badly he had been treated by the raven. He asked her for some fish and oil because he was hungry. After they ate, Nankilslas convinced the woman to lay down and sleep with him before they ate again. While Nankilslas slept, the woman awoke to find her husband hiding in the trees outside their home. He told his wife what Nankilslas had been up to, and he waited outside for Nankilslas. When Nankilslas awoke, he scampered outside to look for the woman. As he walked down the path, the man jumped out, beat him severely, and threw him into the water.

Not all of Nankilslas's actions are disruptive or viewed by the Haida as negative. Nankilslas is responsible for bringing the Haida people to earth and for creating such things as the moon, sun, and stars. Before the Haida lived on earth, Nankilslas roamed the earth by himself. One day in his travels, Nankilslas found a large cockleshell that had been tossed about by the waves for some time. When Nankilslas found the shell it was cracked in several spots. Nankilslas listened inside and heard some noise. He opened the shell and out came the first Haida people.

Many of Nankilslas's gifts, however, are the result of his misbehavior. For example, in one story Nankilslas transformed himself into a needle that was swallowed by the chief's daughter while she was pregnant. Once the child was born, Nankilslas was inside the child, controlling it. The child cried and cried for days until he was given the moon to play with; once the child had the moon, Nankilslas turned back into a raven and flew away with it. He flew over some people who were fishing and asked for a fish to eat, promising in return to give them light. They were reluctant because they recognized him as Nankilslas, "the one who always plays tricks." But the fisherman indulged him with a fish, and Nankilslas cracked the moon in half, creating the sun out of the other half and the stars from the fragments that were left, making the sun and stars as they are today. Thus, Nankilslas gave the moon, sun, and stars to the people, but only as a result of stealing the moon and breaking it in half.

Nankilslas has several ways of getting what he desires or of retaliating against people. One of his most useful powers is his ability to change shape. Nankilslas can take on the form of humans and other animals. If he is not recognized as Nankilslas, he can easily trick people. Once, when the chief's wife had just given birth, Nankilslas skinned the newborn child and took the skin for his own disguise in order to obtain all the gifts the child would soon be getting. Disguised as the child, Nankilslas was able to hoard all the gifts, and once he had them piled away, he tore the skin off and left the chief's lodge with them. The next morning, the chief's wife awoke to find nothing but her baby's skin.

Nankilslas is not only a deceptive prankster; he is also a source of life-sustaining gifts for the Haida community. Holding such an ambiguous position gives Nankilslas the power to obtain most of the things he seeks because people are never sure what will result from his actions. Nankilslas is selfish, greedy, independent, and disruptive to the Haida, but he is also an important part of the Haida culture. Nankilslas appears not only in Haida oral culture but in their art, religious ceremonies, and everyday life. Representations of Nankilslas are carved into canoes, family posts, clan emblems, dance rattles, and containers and carvings of Nankilslas are found throughout Haida society. These carvings serve as representations of the importance of Nankilslas to the Haida as well as a reminder of the many roles he takes. Rattles shaped in the form of Nankilslas are used during the dances at community potlatches as a symbol both of what Nankilslas brought to the people and of what he could potentially take away through his selfishness. For the Haida, Nankilslas brings together the many aspects of their lives and culture by representing the many possibilities in the world. (Boas 1970; Chowning 1962; Drew 1982; Durlach 1928; Goodchild 1991; Reid and Bringhurst 1984; Rooth 1962; Swanton 1905; Van Den Brink 1974)

Nasreddin Khoja
Turkey

Nasreddin Khoja is a gullible but wise mythological character known for his comical adventures, riddles, and anecdotes.

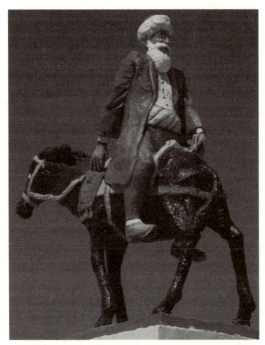

A statue of the Turkish folkloric figure Nasreddin Khoja riding backward on an ass. (Chris Hellier/Corbis)

Although mythological, some speculate that he may be based on a real person who lived during the thirteenth or fourteenth century. His existence has never been substantiated, but stories about him still flourish.

Khoja means "religious teacher," and it is in this role that Nasreddin receives much of his acclaim. He uses paradoxical statements, rhymes, and odd behavior to teach moral and cultural lessons. Sometimes his actions are ridiculous, but his ability to teach through humor and play make him one of the most popular characters in Turkish mythology.

In tales he is most commonly depicted riding his favorite donkey through the countryside and stopping along the way to share his knowledge with others. Although his adventures are used for education, they also show the humor in life. For example, in one story Nasreddin Khoja was walking along the road when he saw a mirror lying in his path. He picked up the mirror, looked at it closely, and then threw it aside.

As he walked away he exclaimed what an ugly thing it was and that it was no wonder someone had thrown it out. Nasreddin Khoja is never afraid of poking fun at himself along with others. His humor shows the simpler, less serious side of life that people often forget. Stories about Nasreddin Khoja emphasize his role as a wise fool. His entertaining advice highlights the humor in all aspects of life.

In one story, Nasreddin Khoja was working by the side of the road preparing his pack when a man walked by and asked him how long it would take to reach the next town. Although he heard the man's question, Nasreddin Khoja said nothing. The man asked twice more but then gave up, believing Nasreddin Khoja to be either deaf or dumb. Once the man had walked a few yards, however, Nasreddin Khoja called to him that it would take him half an hour to reach the next town. The man stopped in his tracks and asked why he had not answered him before. Nasreddin Khoja replied that he had to see how fast the man walked before he could properly answer the question.

Nasreddin Khoja always chooses his words carefully, using them to catch people off guard. In one anecdote, Nasreddin Khoja was at home when his neighbor asked to borrow his donkey. Nasreddin Khoja lied and said the donkey was not there, but as his neighbor walked away he heard the donkey in the back yard. The neighbor went back and told Nasreddin Khoja that he had heard the donkey in the back yard. Nasreddin Khoja looked straight at the man and asked sharply why he would believe an ass over a teacher such as he. (El-Shamy 1980; Magnarella and Webster 1990; Webster-Jain 1988)

Nasruddin Hodja
Turkey
See **Nasreddin Khoja.**

Nenaposh

Algonquian, *Northeastern United States;
Southeastern Canada*
See **Nanabozhoo.**

Newekwe

Zuni, *Southwestern United States: Arizona;
New Mexico*

Newekwe is a general term for a society of men who are known for both their healing powers and their abrasive behavior. The Zuni have several different men's societies that perform various ritual functions throughout the year. Although each society has its own roles and responsibilities, each also interacts with its "younger brother" *kiva* (a *kiva* is an indoor ceremonial room, but the word also refers to the group who run the ceremonies conducted within), linking the members in the common goal of sustaining the Zuni cosmos. The ritual dances and performers are chosen from the various societies at the beginning of each ceremonial year by the dance chiefs of the kachina society.

Newekwe members engage in ritual activity throughout the year. They take part in *Shalako* (a performance of the Zuni creation; see **Koyemshi** for further explanation), celebrations of the summer and winter solstices, and initiations. In addition, Newekwe society members use their curing powers to heal people, using medicines that only they can handle. Among the Zuni, medicines are classified as either "hot" or "cold." The Newekwe have the power and knowledge to use both types of medicines in healing illnesses. The Newekwe dance and sing over the sick person, rubbing one or more of the several different medicines available to them onto the painful area or spitting the medicine into their patient's mouth in order to heal him or her. The medicine and the Newekwe's power then merge within the patient. The Newekwe are so powerful that they (and only they) can handle the extreme hot and cold medicines. Their power to heal combined with their humor illustrate the balance of life, the range of activities that are possible for people.

The Newekwe came into existence through the efforts of the first healers, a woman and two men. These three, who were relatives, wanted some companionship. With the help of the War Chiefs, they took parts of their own skin, placed them under a blanket, and sang over them, and the first Newekwe, known as Paiyatemu, emerged. Paiyatemu is known as a jester and musician to the sun. He is constantly talking, singing, and making fun of everyone. He always says the opposite of what he means. He lives near the Zuni village in a place known as Ashes Springs. The members of the Newekwe society identify with Paiyatemu by rubbing ashes over their bodies and acting ridiculously during ceremonial events.

During ceremonies Newekwe members run around wildly, talk backwards, and perform many activities in reverse. For example, when a medicine man wants the Newekwe to come to the village he must call for them to leave; otherwise they will not come. Sometimes Newekwe members dress up with a bear's paw on one hand and a wolf's snout on their nose and lampoon the *kokko* (masked performers who represent and even become Zuni ancestors during ritual performances; they are also called kachinas) and other performers with sticks. They are notorious for running around eating bits of refuse, small insects, and rodents and drinking dirty water. This behavior presents the Newekwe as the opposite of medicine men, of ritual specialists, and even of the lay people. In fact, the performers epitomize behavior opposite to that acceptable to the Zuni people. They act outrageously, without regard for people or social mores; they are unpredictable and powerful, and this is what makes them frightening and entertaining.

During initiation ceremonies the Newekwe members perform for short periods when the main performers rest. They run wildly into the main plaza area and shout at the audience. They toss bean bags around the plaza and into the crowd, they soak one another with buckets of dirty water or urine, and they mock the other performers. Upon the completion of the initiation ceremonies, when the other Zuni ritual performers have left, the Newekwe members' antics reach their climax. They exaggerate all their normal antics to bring the initiates' experience to a close.

Similarly, during *Shalako* the Newekwe feed the *kokko* ashes instead of cornmeal, which is the proper food to offer. They ridicule the audience by throwing urine and excrement on them. They drench themselves in urine as well and throw excrement at each other, rubbing it into their skin and eating it. The excrement is said to help them maintain their healing powers and guard against "hot" medicines, which might burn them. Their roles as healers and entertainers merge to represent the many different types of power within the Zuni cosmos. (Bunzel 1933; Cazeneuve 1955; Cazeneuve 1956; Cushing 1891–1892; Handelman 1981; Makarius 1970; Stevenson 1904; Tedlock 1975; Wright 1985)

Niyel Carnival
Wape, *Papua New Guinea*

The Niyel carnival, a curing festival, is performed every few years in Wape villages at the discretion of village leaders. The festival lasts several months and culminates in a two-day carnival, so considered because of the large numbers of people who attend, the playful atmosphere, and the many activities that go on. The carnival atmosphere is heightened by reversals of gender and kinship roles, transvestitism, and crude joking. Both men and women exaggerate the actions of the opposite sex and mimic their normal roles. Although curing is the focus of the Niyel carnival, the comedic inversions and role reversals highlight the disruptive nature of the festival and the distinctive way it presents social commentary and reinforces values.

The Wape Niyel festival focuses on several community concerns, the most prevalent of which is healing. The Wape live in villages in the Torricelli Mountains of Papua New Guinea, which are situated between the northwest coast and the Sepik river. The Wape practice some agriculture but rely mainly on hunting for their sustenance. The Wape have one of the highest infant mortality rates in the world, and their poor nutrition is a source of constant concern, a concern reflected in their many curing ceremonies. The Niyel festival is the largest of their curing ceremonies. It is timed to occur during the full moon so that the villages' dancing grounds will be lit at night. One Wape village sponsors the event, which is attended by people from all the surrounding villages. The festival is a time not only for curing but for the exchange of goods between kin members of different villages. Wape society is based on the division of people into patriarchal clans who support each other and engage in reciprocal gift-giving relationships. The Niyel festival reinforces these relationships between villages.

After months of preparation, gift exchange, and small-scale rituals, the festival culminates in the weekend carnival in the sponsoring village. Friday and Saturday nights are marked by dancing, role reversals, comedic performances, and general foolishness. Sunday is greeted by small groups involved in the actual healing of the afflicted people. The contrast between the activities on Friday and Saturday and those on Sunday provides a framework for understanding the many societal issues dealt with during the Niyel. That is, the contrast between the jovial and the serious activities allow us to glimpse the many ways in which the Wape deal with internal social and physical problems.

Hundreds of costumed people and masked performers dance and perform throughout the day and night. People decorate themselves with shells, paint their bodies, and adorn their skin with feathers. Men and women, boys and girls dance together in the village center along with performers masked in powerful Niyel masks. The masks represent the powerful negative forces in the Wape community, forces that bring sickness, death, and disease to people. There is no single word for these forces; instead, they are named according to the ceremony in which they are involved. In Olo, the Wape language, *niyel* means "fish," and in a ceremonial context it refers to the fish spirits who cause sickness and death. Similarly, other ceremonies are named after other spirits according to the occasion or illness.

Members of the Niyel society don the Niyel body masks and are commissioned to perform at the ceremony. Family members of those who are sick honor the masked performers by dancing with them. It is against the serious backdrop of the masked performers that comedic performances arise. Dancing and moving around the serious performers, men dress like women and women like men, mimicking the actions of the opposite sex. Women carry hunting sticks and men prance around in skirts. In addition, the family members of the sick break avoidance and kinship rules by dancing with initiates of the Niyel festival who carry the powerful masks. By breaking taboos and making themselves the center of laughter, the family members publicly shame themselves and thus call attention to the plight of the ill member. In addition, they call attention to the kinship system, which normally underlies every activity in Wape life. By ignoring the kinship rules, which stipulate who one may or may not

talk to, interact with, or honor, family members reverse their roles and give that power to the Niyel members.

One way in which the inversion of roles is highlighted is through mock sexual intercourse as well as the public exposure of one's genitals before the crowd. In Wape society a man's wife's parents are owed respect by their son-in-law. But if that son-in-law is being initiated into the Niyel ceremony, his in-laws must publicly shame themselves during the Niyel in order that he may gain his power to heal. By them bringing shame to themselves, they transfer power to their son-in-law. Ultimately the in-laws' actions help themselves, for with a powerful son-in-law they can be assured of aid when they are in need. One way in which the in-laws shame themselves is through lewd sexual dancing and genital exposure. A father may expose his penis and dance wildly around his son-in-law using his own shame as a catalyst for his son-in-law's initiation and power to heal.

Along with the central performances of the masked dancers and their family members, small skits are performed that mock the status quo and serve as avenues for the young to air their grievances and frustrations. In Wape society the young have almost no way of voicing their frustration with their parents and other senior members. Because kinship rules hinge on respect the youngsters have only the comedic performances to highlight their problems. Young males especially delight in mocking their mother's protectiveness by acting out skits dressed as women. The young Wape men and women also poke fun at the Europeans, whom they portray as greedy and lazy. Anything and everything that bothers people is brought to the fore in the comedic dancing, skits, and songs of the Wape during the Niyel festival. The festival is a time when people from all the villages take notice of the concerns of others through their masquerades, satires, and foolishness. (McGregor 1982; Mitchell 1987; Mitchell 1990; Mitchell 1992a)

Nowarera
Mocovi, *Argentina*

Nowarera, the fox, steals, cheats, commits adultery, and deceives others for his own benefit. (See **Tatú Bolita** for more on animal characters in Mocovi mythology.) Nowarera is clever in all his undertakings. He is able to deceive people, who do not find out it until it is too late. Like his animal counterpart, Nowarera is stealthy, quick, and sly. His one weak point, however, is his incredible ego, which leads him to boast about his success and often to forget about his surroundings so that he is the one duped in the end. Although Nowarera takes on the physical appearance of a fox, stories about him attribute human traits to animal characters in human situations. In this way the Mocovi avoid characterizing human beings as the only dangerous or deceptive characters.

In stories about Nowarera's adventures, the jaguar is the usual target of Nowarera's tricks. The jaguar is portrayed as Nowarera's opposite: He is slow-witted and gullible, and he fails to use his strength to his benefit. Time and again Nowarera takes advantage of the unsuspecting jaguar. In one story the jaguar let Nowarera into his camp after hunting. They were tired and decided to go to sleep after eating. The jaguar and his wife lay down by the fire and Nowarera lay down next to the jaguar's wife. When he thought they had been asleep awhile, Nowarera got on top of the jaguar's wife and began to have intercourse with her. When she woke, Nowarera told her she was only dreaming. Soon, however, the jaguar awoke and saw Nowarera taking advantage of his wife. Nowarera told him too that he was dreaming. At first the jaguar believed him, but soon he knew it was a trick and he leaped up to chase Nowarera. Nowarera, however, had already left, suspecting that the jaguar would soon figure out what was going on. Nowarera ran through the forest to a muddy bank, where he covered his legs in mud and lay down, pretending to be dead. The jaguar found Nowarera there and returned home believing him to be dead, but of course he was not, and he returned again and again to trick the gullible jaguar.

Nowarera, however, usually meets his match when he tries to pull his tricks on Tatú Bolita, the small armadillo. Tatú outwits Nowarera time and time again by intelligently taking advantage of Nowarera's mistakes and oversights. Although they are both clever, Nowarera falls victim to Tatú because he is rash and quick to jump to conclusions.

In one story, Tatú and Nowarera, both hungry, met in the forest to look for food. They decided they would split up and look for honey. As soon as one found a beehive he was to call back to the other. After looking a bit, Tatú decided to pull a prank on Nowarera. He climbed up a tree and changed himself into a beehive, and then he called to Nowarera. When Nowarera arrived and did not see Tatú, he thought he could take all the honey for himself. So he grabbed a stick and swung at the beehive. Tatú laughed as Nowarera swung and missed and swung again. Then Tatú began to urinate, and Nowarera held out his hand thinking it was the honey falling. He licked some out of his hand and discovered that it was not honey, and that he had been fooled by another one of Tatú's tricks. (Métraux 1946; Wilbert and Simoneau 1988a)

Nyame
Akan (includes Ashanti, Brong, Fante), *West Africa: Ghana*
See **Ananse.**

O

Odosha

Makiritare, Venezuela

The menacing, deceptive creator Odosha is
in a constant struggle with people to bring
negative forces to the world. He brings disease to earth because he wants to be the
most powerful of the primordial beings, and
he leaves people without food to show that
his rules must be followed. He changes
shape to trick people into helping him harm
others. He spies on people in their own
homes, and he kills on a whim. He conspires
against proper Makiritare customs and
channels his power toward antisocial behavior, including murder, incest, and theft. A
Makiritare creation story demonstrates both
the deceptive and creative powers of
Odosha: Before the creation of human beings, Odosha lived on earth with other primordial beings. At a celebration feast prepared for all, Odosha waited until Wanadi (a
powerful being) left to get more cassava (the
staple food), and then he took on Wanadi's
appearance. Disguised in this way, Odosha
showed the others how to perform sexual intercourse. Wanadi was disgusted by
Odosha's actions and stayed in the sky with
the cassava, and the beings began to die.

Odosha's corruption stems from his
birth. Before human beings lived on earth,
all beings lived in the sky. One day Shi, the
sun, decided that human beings should live
on earth, and he sent Wanadi to earth.
Wanadi brought knowledge, tobacco, and
the *maraca* (gourd-shaped rattle filled with
seeds) used by shamans and people. When
Wanadi was born on earth, however, he
buried the placenta, and worms ate some
of it and the rest rotted. From the rotten
placenta Odosha was born. Odosha has the
shape of a human man, but he is covered
with hair and is so ugly that the sight of
him sends people running. The opposite of

Wanadi, Odosha began his life on earth as
a master of deception and dishonesty, using
whatever means necessary to fool and outwit humans.

The Makiritare call themselves the *So'to*,
or the "true people." Unique to the *So'to* is
the Watunna, an oral history that describes
the Makiritare universe and orders their society. The Watunna has two parts, one recited at ritual occasions and another told
anytime. The Watunna as a whole is not a
static set of narratives, and the Makiritare
have incorporated the events of their modern existence in the Watunna. For example,
many stories address at great length their
contact with the Spanish conquistadors,
and beings such as Odosha show up not
only in creation stories but in stories of the
Makiritare's battles with other tribes and
invading Europeans. The section of the
Watunna that is only used in ritual celebrations is handed down through the generations in a set of rituals known as Wan-
wanna. The rituals include singing,
feasting, and dancing and culminate in the
new "owners" of the stories entering into
trancelike states of ecstatic dancing.

Stories of Odosha are integral to both
parts of the Watunna. Odosha is a central
character both in the creation and ordering
of the Makiritare cosmos and in day-to-day
life. Odosha is known for his selfish actions
and his contempt for the proper behavior
established by Wanadi on earth. Stories of
Odosha illustrate his constant battles with
other primordial beings as well as with con-

temporary humans. In one story, Odosha and Wanadi were matched in a battle of wits, each using his creative power to try and outwit the other. Each time Wanadi had a positive thought, such as "cassava for all," Odosha had a counteracting negative thought, such as "hunger everywhere." The two were locked in battle for days, each winning some battles but losing others. In the end Odosha and Wanadi were responsible for bringing both positive and negative things to the earth.

Odosha brought death and disease to earth because he did not want Wanadi to have all the power. In one story, Wanadi noticed that he had the power to revive people after they had died. He deduced that death was not final, as he had thought, but, rather, was just an illusion. Odosha watched as Wanadi practiced his power over and over. Not wanting anyone to have more control than he did, Odosha made Wanadi kill his own mother. Wanadi had planned to come back later to revive her to show all the people his great power, but in the meantime, Odosha made his way into Wanadi's camp, opened his *chakara* (pouch with powerful items), and stole his power, leaving the earth dark and forcing Wanadi to return to the sky. Without Wanadi on earth people are susceptible to disease and death and are in a constant struggle with Odosha. (Civrieux 1980; Métraux 1946; Sullivan 1988)

Ogo

Dogon, *West Africa; Western Sudan*
The pale fox Ogo, a part of the creator, Amma, is well known for the false tales he tells, his backwards speech, and his deceptive behavior. Amma created human beings from a cosmic egg that contained all possible ways of being in the world (that is, all possible personalities, physical features, etc.). Within the egg there were two sections. In each section Amma created *nommo*-beings, the ancestors of human beings. Each *nommo*-being

was created as a pair of male twins, although they were conceived of as androgynous beings. Each pair would ultimately be given one female twin, making three. All were also given the gift of proper speech and made to occupy the water as fish. Ogo, however, the last *nommo* to be created, was not given the gift of speech, and unlike the others he was created as a pale fox, not a fish.

Ogo was impatient inside the egg and did not wait for Amma to release him. Due to his impatience he was not given a twin but had the characteristics of both males and females. He schemed to get out, thus introducing chaos into the as yet incomplete world. Leaving Amma before he was completely formed, Ogo penetrated the earth and gave birth to the *andummolo*, small creatures who hide in holes and torment people. Realizing he could not create anything by himself, Ogo left earth to return to Amma. His return disrupted the final creative process, and each of the *nommo* pairs was broken apart by Ogo's reentry into Amma. Ogo also killed one of the *andummolo* on his journey back to Amma and thus introduced death into the world.

Ogo's second attempt to enter the earth was marked by his circumcision by another *nommo*-being, which indicated Ogo's defeat. Amma finished creating the other *nommo* and allowed them to penetrate the earth. Ogo also returned to earth, but he was marked by his selfish introduction of death and chaos into the world.

After Ogo was on earth, he attempted to fashion a new language for himself so that he, and not Amma, would be in control. He entered into Amma's body and tried to tear from him the parts that would allow him to make a new world. Amma detected the intruder, and when he caught Ogo he cut off his tongue, so whenever he tried to speak it would be backwards, incomplete, and false. Yet Ogo outwitted Amma because with his new reversed language he brought a divination system to the Dogon, a system of which he would be in control.

Divination is a central part of Dogon life; diviners are consulted throughout one's life for counsel, insight into one's own actions, and advice on ways of achieving one's goals (see also **Legba** for the Fon divination system and **Eshu-Elegba** for the Yoruba). Through Ogo one is able to re-create the path of one's life. It is Ogo's ability to speak through his paws that allows the Dogon to communicate with other powers in the universe. Ogo's paws are seen in the movements of the diviner's hands on the divining table. When a diviner traces the movement of a person's life on the divining table, it is Ogo who is moving his or her hands. A Dogon saying sums up Ogo's relationship to divination: "Under the movement of the fox's paw, the earth turns."

The creation of the divining table was also a result of Ogo's disruptive behavior. Once when Amma (who is both male and female) was sleeping, Ogo thought he was dead, so he put on Amma's skirt and went to the roof of Amma's house to mourn him. He danced, and as he spoke he honored his mother and made fun of Amma. As he moved, he traced the image of the world in the dust and in doing so invented the diviner's table. The iconography on the diviner's boards present images of Ogo in various forms. The tables are drawn in the sand between the village and the bush. Each panel in the six-sided table presents either Ogo, Amma, or the interaction between the two. It is Ogo who moves the diviner's hands at the request of the individual. Thus, each year the diviners gather to offer libations of beer to Ogo for his continued help.

The all-male Awa society, the Society of Masks, is connected to Ogo through a secret language, called the *sigi so*, that they trace to Ogo and that is known only to the initiated male members of the Awa society. The language allows the members to un-

derstand the speech of other powerful beings in the cosmos, like Ogo, who speak differently from humans. The Awa society takes its name from their large altar, the Great Mask. The Great Mask is an enormous, elaborately decorated wooden mask some 16 meters long. The men of the society make sacrifices and offerings to the Great Mask during their ceremonies, in which the dancers wear masks that aid them in communicating with the other powerful beings in the cosmos. The masks are also elaborately painted and carved. Each man fashions his mask, which may be made of wood or fiber, to resemble another being in the Dogon cosmos, such as an animal, a bird, a deceased relative, or a living member of the society. The masked dancers, like Ogo, demonstrate the duality of life; they are at once the image they present and themselves.

The Awa society's ritual duties tie them to Ogo. They oversee the funeral rites, the Dama and Sigui ceremonies. Ogo is connected in myth to the first death, which is represented in the Dama ceremony, and through divination to the renewal of life, which is represented in the Sigui ceremony, the main activities of the Awa society. The Awa society moves a person after death into the next stage through their masked dances of the Dama ceremony and the songs they sing in *sigi so*. The masked dancers present the images of many powerful beings in the Dogon cosmos. The Dama is only performed for deceased members of the Awa society who have participated in the Sigui ceremony. These members are honored in the Dama and are aided in their transition to the next stage in their life because they have participated in the renewal of their society by their participation in the Sigui.

The Sigui ceremony, which is performed once every six years and recounts the actions of Ogo in dance and song, is performed to renew the life of the community. The male dancers mourn the death of members of the society and rejoice in the new life that has been made possible by those relatives who have died. Like Ogo's separation from Amma, the deaths of society members ensure that the world will continually be re-created. The dance itself, with its serpentine movement, demonstrates the flexibility of the cosmos and the ever-changing pattern of one's life. The dancers are said to "cry like the pale fox" during these performances. The Awa society renews the world in the same way that Ogo helped create it, through their dancing and their singing. (DeMott 1982; Douglas 1968; Griaule 1965; Pelton 1980; Verboven 1986)

P

Paiyakyamu

Hopi, *Southwestern United States: Arizona*

The paiyakyamu, black-and-whited-striped, horned clowns, are Hopi performers known for their pranks, jokes, wild behavior, and indecent acts. After the Tewa immigration into Hopi country early in the eighteenth century led to sustained contact and shared cultural and social traditions (including the **koshare**), the Hopi began to use the Tewa term *koshare* for the paiyakyamu. The Tewa term refers to one half of a larger group of ceremonial performers known as **kossa.** Kossa include both the koshare, summer performers, and the **kwirena,** winter ceremonial performers. The term *paiyakyamu,* however, is used by the Hopi to refer to both winter and summer ceremonial performers. The paiyakyamu's name shows their connection to the underworld: The word *kyamu* refers to the speech spoken in the underworld. Like the other Hopi comedic ritual specialists, the tsukuwimkya, the paiyakyamu are known for their pranks, jokes, wild behavior and indecent acts.

The paiyakyamu's activities amuse audiences, but their origin in the underworld and their power to direct social attention and action through their wrongdoings places them in the position of keepers of Hopi tradition. Through their reversed behavior and speech they show the Hopi the need to maintain a balanced lifestyle. They engage in ritual activity alongside the kachinas (relatives of the Hopi who live in the clouds and protect the people), aiding them in their ritual performances and demonstrating the opposite and improper activities of Hopi life. Together the paiyakyamu and the kachinas demonstrate the balance of Hopi life, the proper and the improper, and the choices people have be-

Kachina doll of Paiyakyamu, the Hopi comedic performers who are similar to, but not the same, as the koshare of the Tewa people. (Lowie Museum)

163

tween the two. In addition the paiyakyamu interact with and make fun of the kachinas to show that behavior such as theirs has negative repercussions for the community. (See **Tsukuwimkya** for further explanation of kachinas.)

In their ceremonial antics the paiyakyamu make fun of, imitate, and parody the problems of the Hopi and their contact with outsiders. The paiyakyamu's actions change depending on who they are making fun of and in what setting. No one is off limits to the paiyakyamu. Their humor is directed at those people, things, events, and actions that are outside the accepted Hopi way of life. During the mid-1960s, facing changing reservation lifestyles and the whims of the government, the paiyakyamu poked fun at government officials and missionaries by dressing like them and mocking their speech and behavior. The U.S. space program was the butt of one paiyakyamu performance. The paiyakyamu in the village of Hotevilla fired a home-made rocket with a mouse in the hull into the air, heading for the moon. They danced around and smiled, pleased with their launch. When the rocket eventually fell back to the ground, they rushed to it, shrieking and yelling with excitement. When they opened the rocket there was no mouse inside, only a hunk of green cheese. Their parody of the government's space program mocked the attention given to the program with a modern-day satire based on the tale that the moon is made of cheese.

The paiyakyamu also have a repertoire of antics they use over and over to amuse audiences. They always enter the plaza from the rooftops and come down the ladders headfirst. One of their favorite attention getters is to arrange themselves in two facing lines and tie their penises together, engaging in a tug of war. Or, in lines facing the crowd, each one grabs the foot of the man in front of him and hops around the plaza. The paiyakyamu also enjoy playing

games with the children, chasing them around, throwing things at them, playing tug of war with them, and generally being loud and disruptive.

Like the tsukuwimkya, the paiyakyamu mock the kachinas during their dances and erect an ash house as the paiyakyamu's home in the dance plaza. Unlike the tsukuwimkya, however, anyone crossing the line of the ash house is initiated as a member of the paiyakyamu. The female relatives of the paiyakyamu bring them food during their performances, and they display their gluttonous behavior by throwing food, eating wildly, and never sharing. Their behavior emphasizes the ridiculous, and although it is entertaining, it is meant as a display of how not to act.

The paiyakyamu always paint their bodies with black-and-white stripes and wear old sacks of ripped cloths around their waists. Their headdresses are horns made of sheepskin stuffed with heavy grass and tasseled at the top with corn husks, held on by a bit of string or cloth. Each performer keeps his headdress for several years; only when they cannot be reused are they ripped apart and made anew. The performers wear old moccasins or shoes, and each carries a sack of cornmeal around his neck and wears rattles made of animal hooves around his ankles.

The paiyakyamu are also represented as carved objects, or "dolls." The term *dolls* does not capture the importance of these objects to the community. Although they are carved for sale, they were traditionally and are still today carved as reminders of the power of other beings in the Hopi cosmos and of people's responsibility to interact with and respect those beings. In carved representations, the paiyakyamu usually have blue faces and a yellow body striped in black. However, there are numerous carvings and representations depending on the artist. Each depicts the paiyakyamu at play, in their best-known activities. (Bandelier

1954; Fewkes 1985; Handelman 1981; Hieb 1972; Parsons 1939; Stephen 1936; Steward 1991; Titiev 1944; Titiev 1971; Wright 1994)

Palu
Sikuani, *Eastern Colombia*

Palu, a clever rabbit who changes back and forth from a male to female rabbit depending on the need of the moment, uses his small size, speed, and cunning to outwit and take advantage of others, especially the jaguar. Palu's adventures are humorous and entertaining; stories about his pranks are popular among Sikuani storytellers. Storytellers weave new stories, incorporating Palu's familiar character traits, about deception and fraud both to entertain and to educate. Youngsters are introduced to Palu and other such characters at a very early age and through them learn that their actions affect not only themselves but their community as well, an important lesson for a society that depends on communal horticulture for its survival in both the savannas and along several small rivers in Colombia.

Although Palu's antics are entertaining, they are also dangerous, especially for the jaguar, who typically ends up hurt or killed. Stories emphasize the unpredictable nature of the world in which the Sikuani live as well as the importance of fully using one's skills. The gullible jaguar is duped time and time again because he fails to think situations through, acting on impulse alone, and because he trusts Palu even though he has been tricked by him before. Although Palu often deceives, he also demonstrates the importance of quick wit and cunning intelligence.

The interaction between the jaguar and Palu are the center of many Sikuani stories. In one story Palu, as a female, was taking care of the jaguar's children and killed the youngest. Palu then cooked the baby jaguar over an open flame so that the jaguar would not recognize her meal, and when the jaguar returned, Palu laid out the feast she had prepared. Not suspecting that Palu was up to no good, the jaguar asked what kind of animal it was, and Palu told her it was a mouse. Believing her without question, the jaguar sat down and ate her own child.

In another story, Palu came upon a male jaguar in the forest. Although Palu had previously transformed himself to a female rabbit to dupe a female jaguar, he changed back to a male when he saw the male jaguar approaching. "Brother-in-law," he called to the unsuspecting jaguar, "listen; there is a storm approaching." The jaguar stopped next to Palu and listened. Palu told him that all the village had left and that the hurricane was fast approaching so they had to tie themselves down or they would blow away. The jaguar conceded, and although he could not see or hear the storm he allowed Palu to tie him to a tree. Once the jaguar was tied to the tree, Palu danced around and made fun of him, telling him he had tricked him and tied him up simply to whip him. The jaguar fought and kicked but could not get loose as Palu beat him and then left him. In another story of humiliation, Palu said that the food he was eating was from his own testicles, and the jaguar believed him. He told the jaguar that he must pound his testicles with a special rock to obtain the food without injuring himself. Of course, the jaguar ended up bleeding to death after he following Palu's outrageous instructions.

Unlike the jaguar, Palu uses his intellect to get the best of most situations. His size is an advantage, enabling him to hide, spy on others, and learn helpful information. In one story Palu's small size allowed him to outwit the fox. He lured the fox into chasing him by throwing stones at him. Once the fox began to run after him, Palu headed directly for a hole from which he knew the fox could not escape. Palu jumped down the hole, and the fox followed but could not escape. Palu went out the other end and back to the fox's food, while the fox remained trapped. In some cases, Palu teams up with others. For example, in one story Palu and the anteater confused the jaguar by telling him different stories and convincing him that they had taken away his ability to hunt; he thus left his prey for them. (Wilbert and Simoneau 1992)

Panakawan
Java, *Indonesia*

Panakawan is a general term for clowns in all forms of Javanese theater, including *taledek* or *ronggeng* (street performances or dances), *bedaja* (court dances), and formal plays concerning Hindu or Muslim myths. The plays, whether the performers are puppets or humans, always include panakawan. Panakawan are set apart in the theater by their personal names, failure to marry, sexual ambiguity, and stylized costumes. They are cast out from Javanese society because they break social norms relating to marriage, dress, and sexuality. Yet they are revered throughout Java for their power and knowledge. Images and carvings of panakawan are put in boxes to make traveling safe and to lighten the load on long trips. Statues of them are found on many household altars.

Traditionally panakawan were also referred to as *kijai* (teacher) highlighting their representation of knowledge. The Javanese theater and panakawan have a long tradition, dating back to 800 B.C.E. Temples throughout Java have carvings of clowns on them, and records show that theater has long been a significant part of Javanese culture. In fact, even sultans used to perform in the theater. The many forms of Javanese theater remain active today, adapting to and adding plays from the Muslims and Hindus who are now part of Javanese society.

Javanese theater and the importance of the panakawan did not diminish with the influx of Hindus and Muslims. On the

Painted wooden dance mask of a Panakawan, the comedic performers in Javanese theater. (Honeychurch Antiques, Ltd./Corbis)

contrary, the panakawan have demonstrated their cultural importance by withstanding pressure from foreign religious ideals as well as by being a source of Javanese pride. The panakawan have always represented the struggle between stratified classes in Java. The panakawan mocked, criticized, and chastised sultans, ritual specialists, and other powerful rulers. They still perform this function today: Whether in the popular puppet plays performed throughout rural Indonesia or in the formal theatrical plays, the panakawan continue to raise their voices in protest and social commentary, bringing laughter to audiences.

Street plays and less-formal plays usually have the panakawan playing the servants of a government official or bureaucrat. In such roles, the panakawan disturb the order of the government, but they also act as aids to the officials, advising them in military, business, and political matters. In more formal plays, the panakawan may play the counterpart to a Hindu or Muslim prince. The panakawan place themselves as servants to the higher-ranking officials, but their actions suggest that they are just as smart or smarter than the other characters.

For example, the panakawan in the Hindu Mahabharata myth play the roles of servants to the Hindu princes. The three panakawan known as **Semar,** Petruck, and Gareng are employed by a Hindu prince. Semar plays one of Prince Arjuna's servants in a segment from the Mahabharata. Arjuna had been tricked by the great deity Siva, one of the most powerful Hindu deities, into killing Semar. Semar, however, learns about the plan, and just before he is to be incinerated he turns into a giant, powerful monster and defeats Siva, which shows Semar's power and resourcefulness. Although only a servant and a clown, Semar's powerful role shows that even the most feared of deities can be overcome.

Likewise, in the Muslim Amir Hamzah myths, the panakawan play the servants Marmade and Umar Madi. Although their status is lower than that of the prince, they give the prince advice in matters of love and war and are said to be blood kin to Muslim royalty. The panakawan, no matter what role they take on, are fat, grotesque, and sexually ambivalent, and they speak in an informal, slangy language. The panakawan perform great feats in their roles as servants: They defeat gods, advise sultans, and save people. Yet they are always inclined to antics and unpredictable behavior. (Buurman 1991; Kroef 1956; Peacock 1968; Peacock 1978; Rassers 1959)

Pascola

Yaqui, *Southwestern United States and Northwestern Mexico*

Pascola dancers are ritual dancers who both entertain and protect the community during ritual performances. They are part of a group consisting of the pascola dancers, musicians, and their manager, who trains them and accompanies them in all their duties. Pascolas wear masks made of wood adorned with goat's hair. Some masks also have the facial features of a goat painted on them. Though the faces painted on the masks may contain some animal characteristics, they are always horrible, even demonic, but also strikingly human. The pascolas are the devil's "sons." The Yaqui say that the pascolas are brought into ceremonial service as sons of the devil to "bring laughter to the community." (See **Chapayeka** for details on Christian influence in Yaqui life.) But during their ritual activities they expose themselves to attack by witches or other harmful beings, and so although their work in the community is necessary, it is very dangerous. People who are in trouble or who believe they are being affected by negative forces call the pascolas into ritual service. The pascolas put on masks that have a white cross painted on them Some masks also have flowers and lizards painted on them in white. All of these are symbols of the pueblo and of the way things ought to be. Because of their association with devil and with those activities that are the antithesis of Yaqui tradition, the pascolas are said to be mischievous, gluttonous, and even abusive.

The pascolas are called *pahkola* in Yaqui, which derives from the Yaqui words *pahko*, meaning "fiesta," and *o'ola*, meaning "old man." The pascolas are also referred to by the term *pahkoalente*, "the pascolas and everything they do." Although the pascolas do not belong to a society with a hierarchy and structure like other Yaqui societies, they are integral to the performance of fiestas. A common Yaqui way of referring to a fiesta is "We are going to make a pascola."

During small fiestas conducted in people's homes, the pascolas act as ceremonial hosts for the family. They dance throughout the night, they give cigarettes and water to people, they tell jokes, stories, and far-fetched tales to entertain the audience during breaks in the dancing, and they engage in foolery with the men who cluster around the entrance to the home. The Pascolas tease the men, jibe at them, chase them, and joke with them and each other. The Pascolas act like fools, running into things and people, eating things that should not be eaten, and telling lies. They also mimic sexual acts in their play with the deer dancer, they eat his feces, mock his power, make the sign of the cross backward, and in general reverse every social and religious guideline of the Yaqui. They are models of what the Yaqui should not be. Their actions and selfish ways provide a counterpart to the deer and other cherished aspects of Yaqui life. But without the pascolas to remind people of what they might become and without the pascolas' activities in the Easter ceremony and small fiestas, the people would also be in danger of losing their community to the destructive forces in their world.

The pascolas act within ceremonial performances as part of their commitment to their pueblo and with their hearts dedicated to Jesus. They spend days in preparation for fiestas, practicing dances and taking care of their masks. Their actions show their responsibility for and dedication to their pueblo. Within Yaqui culture, people recognize others who have been given gifts, such as the ability to dream or dance well and thus aid the community. In dreams, the Yaqui are shown their talents, the societies to which they should belong, and even the songs and dances they should perform. To be a pascola it is not necessary to have been so directed in a dream, but those who are directed in a dream are said to be better dancers and singers. Pascolas are said to get their power "from the left," that is, from the *yoania* (the Yaqui homeland). Others may learn from books, but the pascolas learn their craft directly from the desert,

from their homeland, the *yoania*. As such, their power is very great and at the same time dangerous.

Pascolas must approach their ritual work *tu'i hiapsimak* (with good heart) to avoid any danger they may incur from the negative forces in the cosmos with which they are associated. Yaqui society places great emphasis on the interaction of all members of their community; they expect that people will share and demonstrate their power and gifts. The most visible way of sharing one's gifts with others is through ritual participation, for all to see. By acting within their community, showing their respect and responsibility to the pueblo, Yaqui keep their vows, serve their communities, and remain "with good heart."

With the contact with Europeans, and especially Christian missionaries, the Yaqui have integrated many Christian aspects into their ceremonial lives, including the Easter ceremony, of which the pascolas are an integral part. According to the Yaqui, the Easter ceremony began in the very beginning, with aid from the *yo'ora*, the Yaqui elders. The Yaqui understand the world to have originated with the *Surem*, the original Yaqui people, in the *yoania*, which refers not only to their homeland but also to their way of life prior to contact. For the Yaqui, the Easter ceremony is a distinctly Yaqui tradition.

The Yaqui Easter ceremony is a large-scale performance that spans several weeks and involves most of the members of the community. The *Kohtumbre Ya'ura*, "protectors of the tradition," are in charge of the Easter ceremony. The *Kohtumbre Ya'ura* society consists of two groups, the Caballeros and the Fariseos. During the ceremonial activities, the Caballeros represent the cavalry and the Fariseos the infantry in a militaristic duel to maintain the Yaqui world. The two groups interact with each other and with other Yaqui groups in the dramatization of the Passion of Jesus. The

Easter ceremony is an enactment of the pursuit, capture, and crucifixion of Jesus in which the Fariseos represent the men who persecuted Jesus and the Caballeros the men who attempt to free him. The Easter ceremony is actually made up of a series of performances by all of the Yaqui ceremonial groups: the church group, who prepare the church; the matachins, who dance for the Virgin as her army; the deer dancer, who dances with the pascolas and marches in the lead procession on Easter Sunday; and other Yaqui people who have made vows throughout the year, who dance, carry figurines into the church, and aid in any way they can.

Pascolas play an important role in the Easter ceremony. On Holy Saturday morning they dance quickly toward the Fariseos, throwing flowers at them, threatening them, and eventually defeating them. (See **Chapayeka** for an explanation of flowers as protective objects.) They also act as ritual hosts for the all-night fiestas that take place on several nights. During the fiestas they entertain the audience by joking with them, engaging in play with the deer dancers, and chasing each other around the complex. However, despite all their playful acts and obnoxious activities, the pascolas themselves must never laugh while they are performing. It is their job to aid in the ritual work by easing the minds of others, but they "laugh inside their hearts." (Lutes 1983; Montell 1938; Painter 1986; Parsons and Beals 1934; Spicer 1984)

Pilandok
Philippines

Pilandok is a witty, cunning, young man who enjoys tricking others. He is similar to **Juan Pusong**, another Filipino prankster. Both delight in teasing, tricking, and generally wreaking havoc on anyone they can. Pilandok is a humorous character with little regard for social mores who tries as hard as he can to uproot the normal social rules, especially those that govern sexuality. Pilandok can be crude and obscene, but his pranks and jokes are never intended to be malicious.

Pilandok is greedy, overanxious, prone to grand lies, and always entertaining. Stories about Pilandok emphasize his overzealous nature: He is constantly looking for something bigger, better, and more prestigious than what he already has. He prides himself on being able to manipulate anyone he comes across in order to fulfill his unending desires. He especially loves to take advantage of the sultan and his court.

In one story the sultan sent his subjects to look for Pilandok, who had nearly killed the sultan's sons with one of his pranks. Knowing the sultan would reward handsomely anyone who returned with Pilandok, hordes of people scattered in all directions looking for him. Pilandok heard of the sultan's orders but was not worried. He just sat under a tree next to a coiled-up python waiting to be found.

The sultan had sent orders to find "Pilandok with one eye," but when the sultan's younger brother Sabandar came upon Pilandok, he was not one-eyed. Pilandok told Sabandar that there were two Pilandoks in the area. He was Pilandok from downstream, but the one-eyed Pilandok was from upstream. Sabandar asked him what he was doing hiding under the tree if he was not the prankster; Pilandok replied that he was guarding the queen's black belt. Intrigued, Sabandar asked to hold the belt. At first Pilandok refused, saying that the queen would be furious if he let anyone touch her prized black belt. Sabandar offered Pilandok everything he had to be allowed to hold the black belt. Finally Pilandok agreed, but he told Sabandar that he had to wait for Pilandok to leave so that if the queen found out she would not blame him. As Pilandok walked off, Sabandar grabbed what he thought was the black belt but was really the sleeping python. Pilandok escaped unharmed, and Sabandar was left to fend off the angry python.

Humans are not the only ones tricked by Pilandok. In one story Pilandok cleverly outwitted a mass of crocodiles. He was sitting by a river with no way to cross to the other side. He knew that the crocodiles in the river would eat him if tried to swim across, and he had no raft. He pondered awhile and came up with a plan. He stood up and yelled to the crocodiles to come out of the river so that they could be counted for the sultan. The largest crocodile arose first, asking why they were to be counted. Pilandok told him that the sultan wanted to bring them food but needed to know how much to bring. The largest crocodile called back to the others, and all the crocodiles surfaced. As they did, Pilandok jumped from one to the next, counting, until he reached the other side. Once on dry land he laughed out loud and told the crocodiles that there was no food for them but that they had made an excellent bridge for him. (Alburo 1977; Eugenio 1982; Ness 1992)

Piptuyakamu
Hopi, *Southwestern United States: Arizona*
The piptuyakamu are an assembly of male performers who join together for impromptu skits during Hopi ceremonies. Normally their faces are painted white or they wear masks, and although they may dress in any manner they wish they are usually shabbily dressed in rags. Their appearance varies, but some have come to be known by specific names and have a standard appearance, such as Tasavu, a representation of a Navajo comic performer, and Kocha Omau-u Tsuku, the white-cloud clown. Tasavu paints long black stripes on his body, red arcs under his eyes, and black arcs over his eyebrows. He usually wears a red bandanna around his head and carries a rattle and feathers meant to show that he

represents a Navajo. Kocha Omau-u Tsuku paints his entire body white; ties black strings around his wrists, knees, and neck; and usually drapes a large necklace around his neck. His face is painted with red circles on the cheeks and black dots over the eyebrows, and he wears a white wig. The piptuyakamu take their appearance from the day-to-day events of Hopi life and their contact with outsiders. Thus, for example, piptuyakamu may appear as storekeepers, missionaries, government officials, or members of neighboring tribes. (See also **Paiyakyamu** for similar activities by ritual performers.)

The term *piptuyakamu* is derived from the word *piptuka*, meaning "one who keeps coming." Known for their grotesque behavior and their foolish antics, the piptuyakamu return to every Hopi ceremony, thus justifying their name. The piptuyakamu delight in exaggeration and distortion. They are always loud and always demand attention. Their humor plays on typical events within Hopi life, such as marital problems, disagreements between neighbors, and interactions with non-Hopi.

For example, in one instance the piptuyakamu addressed the problems of a young man who had recently wed a Navajo woman. Since the young man had brought his new wife to live with him, their fighting had increased to the point that the entire village knew of their problems. Their loud fights rang through the village at night. Basing their skits on the couple's accusations toward one another, the piptuyakamu enacted all the problems that the couple had been overheard fighting about. As the piptuyakamu ran around the dance plaza fighting, chasing each other, and engaging in mock sexual intercourse, the couple were embarrassed and the audience was amused. The piptuyakamu showed the couple that their marital problems had escalated to include the community and their satire enabled the couple to see that their problems could be handled in better ways.

Similarly, the piptuyakamu mocked the intentions and actions of early European schoolteachers. One piptuka, dressed in long pants and a dress shirt, played the teacher. He carried a cane and a briefcase and had whitened his face and put on black whiskers. He ordered the other piptuyakamu to line up in a straight line in front of the crowd. The teacher piptuka pretended to write on a blackboard and to give the others their lessons. When the other piptuyakamu started to act up, the teacher pulled off their breechcloths, had them bend over and touch their toes, and inserted a twig crosswise between their buttocks. When they stood up they cried with pain. Believing he had taught them a lesson, the teacher picked up his things to leave, but as he did, the other piptuyakamu grabbed him, pulled him down, and yanked off his pants, revealing his distorted and disfigured penis. Then they made him bend over and did to him what he had done to them. After they inserted the twig, they chased him around the plaza with his pants down around his ankles. This performance, and others like it, demonstrate the place of the piptuyakamu as ritual satirists. That is, they mock and mimic the actions and interactions of others, revealing the wrongheadedness of their behavior.

The piptuyakamu base their skits on any and all interactions. Their performances are amusing, but they are also educational, in that they demonstrate the importance of proper, respectful behavior. The skit about the schoolteacher shows the Hopi view of the government's mandatory education system and of the disrespectful actions of some of the teachers. The piptuyakamu act as cultural commentators, showing through their satires their understanding of the world and their cultural values. (Bandelier 1954; Fewkes 1985; Hieb 1972; Parsons 1939; Stephen 1936; Steward 1991; Titiev 1944; Titiev 1971; Wright 1994)

Plaan Thoóy
Kammu; *Northern Laos*

Plaan Thoóy, a popular character in Laotian stories, is a master liar. He may also be known as Kaám Páa and Púu Raankla, depending on the storyteller. In some cases these names refer to three brothers, but the names are usually used interchangeably for the same character.

Plaan Thoóy uses deceit and trickery to gain control of situations. Stories about Plaan Thoóy highlight the intimate nature of the small-village system and the problems that come with it, as well as the Laotian understanding of outsiders. His antics force people to look at their social and political circumstances by bringing to the fore issues that may not be discussed otherwise. Storytellers use Plaan Thoóy's adventures to deal with internal and external problems. The storyteller's skill lies in his or her ability to interweave social issues with entertaining plots. Plaan Thoóy offers the storytellers a perfect character with his clever antics and unrelenting wit. (See also **Naar** for another, similar Kammu character.)

The Kammu traditionally lived in small villages in northern Laos. Their lives revolved around the interworkings of the village and the day-to-day activities therein. The three-clan system, in which people married outside of their clan and villages, ensured that marriages brought together members from various clans while maintaining a continuity with other villages. Solidarity was maintained through a reciprocal marriage and trade system. For example, in a marriage each family and each clan involved entered into a relationship with the new family that included gift exchange, mutual respect, and economic responsibilities. With the migration in the early 1970s, however, these types of marriage arrangements lessened. Today young people have moved to cities and are marrying outsiders. The popularity of storytelling and of the character of Plaan Thoóy, however, has not faded. Instead, the new experiences that people are facing have been incorporated into the stories about Plaan Thoóy. Topics such as marriage to outsiders, government policies, and migration have all become part of Kammu storytelling.

Plaan Thoóy has remained an important character in Kammu storytelling because of his ability to focus on social issues and make light of them. On the one hand Plaan Thoóy shows people the error of their ways, but on the other hand he allows people to laugh at the absurdity of their actions. Traditionally young men learned stories from their male elders during their time in the common house. After a boy went through puberty, he would spend the majority of his time in the common house with other young men and their elders. There they would learn the arts of hunting and spinning traps, as well as their responsibilities as men of the village. Although traditionally a male endeavor, today storytelling is passed on by women as well, and all children grow up listening to their elders tell stories of their history, culture, and village life.

Plaan Thoóy was a common character in the stories that young men were told by their elders, who used the stories to illustrate both inappropriate and appropriate activities. That is, they showed how Plaan Thoóy's actions could be both destructive and constructive. As storytellers, the older men concocted riddles, word games, and narratives that forced the younger men to grapple with the issues of the time; the best storytellers could both tell an entertaining story and impart an important lesson. Stories were normally told in a dialogue style. The young men were encouraged to interact with the storyteller during his tale, and together they would complete the tale.

When Plaan Thoóy's antics expose corruption or abuse of power, he is an excellent role model for young men. But when his activities are purely selfish and destructive,

he becomes a character whose example is to be avoided, not imitated. Stories of Plaan Thoóy, then, were never clear-cut. Children reared on these stories are forced to think about his actions, as well as about their own, and to make moral choices based on them.

In some stories, Plaan Thoóy mocks those with authority, such as monks and clan and village leaders. For example, in one story, Plaan Thoóy accompanied a priest to buy some salt. Plaan Thoóy, as the priest's helper, was expected to carry the salt blocks while the priest rode on a horse. Not fond of the priest's authority over him, Plaan Thoóy decided to make the trip uncomfortable to teach the priest a lesson. As he prepared the priest's horse, he spread a sticky fruit on the cloth used to cover the horse's back. As the priest sat on the horse in the hot sun he began to itch, and he became very uncomfortable. Plaan Thoóy walked easily along next to him, whistling, carrying the salt from the market. The priest became angry that his servant was more comfortable than he, and he ordered Plaan Thoóy to ride the horse while he walked. Smiling in victory, Plaan Thoóy reversed the cloth on the horse and rode home in comfort.

Another popular story pits Plaan Thoóy against a tiger, one of the most common animals in Kammu stories. Tigers are feared because they are said to possess unrelenting spirits. Although some animals help the Kammu in hunting and other activities, the tiger has always been seen as an adversary, one not to be trusted. Because tigers are understood to be negative spirits, people often wish their enemies to come in contact with a tiger. In the story, Plaan Thoóy tricked his own grandmother into believing that a pile of excrement was a bird. When she attempted to catch the bird, the excrement got all over her and she yelled at Plaan Thoóy, saying that a tiger would bite him. Soon after, as Plaan Thoóy was making his way through the woods, he met a tiger. The tiger approached him, but Plaan Thoóy asked him what he was doing. The tiger replied that he was going to bite him as his grandmother had directed. But Plaan Thoóy convinced the tiger to wait until that evening, promising that he could feast on his grandmother's pig instead. That night the two went to Plaan Thoóy's grandmother's house and captured the pig. In addition to the pig Plaan Thoóy stole vegetables to eat with the pig and utensils to cook them with. As they headed into the woods to prepare their feast, Plaan Thoóy suggested to the tiger that they share the burden and both carry the pig. Thinking Plaan Thoóy was being kind, the tiger agreed. Plaan Thoóy cut some branches to spear the pig with, shaving the spikes off of his side but leaving them on the tiger's side. As they carried the pig the tiger became more and more irritated by the spikes. His paws were bleeding, and raw. The tiger complained, and the two decided to stop to cook their meal. As Plaan Thoóy began to prepare the meal he told the tiger that they needed a fire to cook the pig, and he sent the tiger off to chase the sun for fire, saying that he was much faster than Plaan Thoóy. After the tiger left, Plaan Thoóy used the matches he had stolen from his grandmother and cooked the pig for himself. (Fleeson 1899; Lindell, Swahn, and Tayanin 1977a; Lindell, Swahn, and Tayanin 1977b; Tayanin and Vang 1992; Thompson 1955)

Pulcinello
Europe

Pulcinello, a popular comedic character in the Italian traveling theater groups of the commedia dell'arte, delighted audiences with his style, acrobatics, and wit. (See **Harlequin** for another example.)

Pulcinello often gets out of dangerous and precarious positions by tricking others into freeing him or by confusing people with wordplay and cunning language. In one popular play of the time, *Pulcinello, Brigand Chief*, he successfully dodged an attempt by the king to have him hanged. Once the king's men had caught him, Pulcinello began to speak quickly and cunningly and convinced the hangman that he was incapable of hanging him. Outraged by such a suggestion, the hangman gave the noose to Pulcinello to show him that it was strong. Once he had the noose, Pulcinello slipped it around the hangman's neck and strangled him.

Pulcinello's pranks amused audiences who were no strangers to the abuses of power committed by the king's men. The character of Pulcinello allowed audience members to air their grievances and to cheer on the underdog, who always managed to outsmart the "normal" hero. As a

An N. Bonnart engraving of Pulcinello, the Harlequinhero who figures in Italian comedy. (Corbis-Bettmann)

comedic character Pulcinello was no threat to the king himself, but his role highlighted the anxieties of the time. (Billington 1984; Fuller 1991; Oreglia 1968; Towsen 1976)

Punia

Hawaii

In the character of Punia, a boy who outwits ocean prey, including the largest sharks, the Hawaiians illustrate one facet of their relationship with the creatures of the sea. On the Hawaiian islands, fishing has always been critical for survival. A large portion of traditional Hawaiian oral literature focuses on the problems and conquests in the lives of fisherman. Dealing with large sea animals, especially sharks, often requires the most cunning of schemes.

Stories about Punia focus on his uncanny ability to trick and manipulate sharks, large fish, and other sea creatures. Although only a boy and physically small, Punia possesses superior strength and an intellect to match. He is known for his ability to challenge even the fiercest shark and survive. He is able to misdirect, confuse, and trick sharks into his net using tactics even the most cunning fisherman could not imagine.

When Punia was very young, his father was attacked and killed while diving for lobsters by the shark followers of the King of the Restless Seas. Stories about Punia focus on this pivotal moment in his life as the catalyst for his focus on the sea and especially sharks. From that moment on, Punia gave all his energy to thinking of ways to avenge his father's death and outwit the strong animals.

After his father's death, Punia's mother would not allow him to dive near the cave where the king lived. One day, however, Punia convinced his mother that he had a plan to outwit the sharks and their king to get some lobsters. As he sat on a cliff above the water near the cave entrance, Punia threw a large stone into the water.

The sharks left the cave when they heard the splash, and in their absence Punia dove down, grabbed two lobsters, and surfaced without trouble. Bringing the lobsters to his mother, he shouted thank you to the king and Opunui, the biggest shark, confident that he could outwit them whenever he wanted. Hearing the boy, the king accused Opunui of aiding Punia. Before Opunui could defend himself, the other sharks surrounded and killed him, leaving only nine sharks to guard the cave.

Over the next few months Punia used the same trick to lure the sharks from the cave one by one. Soon only the King of the Restless Seas was left. Punia knew that the king was craftier and that it would certainly take a new trick to get him. He spent several weeks pondering his mission. Finally, he told his mother of his plan, collected a woven mat from her, and left for the ocean. Once on the cliffs above the cave, Punia called out, pretending to talk with his mother. Punia said that he knew how strong and fast the great shark was but that the only way the shark could kill him would be to swallow him whole. Knowing the king shark was listening, Punia waited a few minutes and then dove into the water. As he expected, the king was waiting for him with his mouth wide open, and Punia swam inside the large beast. Before the shark could close his mouth, Punia drove a stick between his teeth and propped his jaws open. Then he placed his mat over the shark's mouth to keep the water out, and there he lived for several days eating the shark's stomach. Frantic, the shark swam back and forth, dove deep, and twisted around, trying to release the stick from his mouth. Finally Punia got tired of living inside him and, pretending to be concerned for his own safety, said aloud that he hoped the shark would not take him up to the shore where the evil spirits lived. Desperate to be rid of Punia, the shark swam to shore, beached himself, and died right there on the shore.

After Punia's encounter with the King of the Restless Seas and his companions, he rarely had problems tricking other sharks out of their caves. Punia and his family lived contentedly eating lobsters and were rarely bothered by other prey. Because of Punia's success, the other ocean animals cringed when they saw him, and it was easy for him to get anything he wanted. (Beckwith 1970; Green 1926; Thompson 1990)

Purna
Sikuani, *Eastern Colombia*
See **Furna.**

Purnaminal
Sikuani, *Eastern Colombia*
See **Furna.**

Púu Raankla
Kammu, *Northern Laos*
See **Plaan Thoóy.**

R

Rabbit

Africa; South America

The rabbit, despite his small size, is a popular character in South American and African folk literature and is most commonly portrayed as a powerful trickster who fools those stronger and bigger than himself. The rabbit's ability to trick others comes from his clever wit and superior intellect. The stereotype of the wise rabbit appears in folktales throughout South America and Africa. Probably based on the actual antics of live rabbits, trickster rabbits epitomize the craftiness of these small creatures forced to use deceptive techniques to survive.

A prime example is the agile **At'pana** of the Guajiro. At'pana uses his quick wit and small stature to outrun, outmaneuver, and outthink people and animals alike. He is best known for his ability to steal food from others and then escape without being harmed. At'pana is constantly taking food from people's gardens, fields, and homes without being caught. His size allows him to sneak around undetected, and his cleverness allows him to elude his predators.

Similarly, the African **Zomo,** a mischievous and cunning hare, displays the deceptive, witty, and humorous side of Hausa life. Zomo's tricks show that even those of small stature can prevail if they use their intellect. Stories about Zomo are used both for moral and entertainment purposes. Storytellers highlight Zomo's cleverness by placing him in situations in which he seems to be the underdog but in which his quick thinking always prevails, leaving him the winner. (See also **Chibuga, Konehu, Nanabozhoo,** and **Palu** for more examples.)

Reversal

Reversal, that is, turning situations, actions, or events around or upside down to elicit a comedic response or gain control, is a part of tricksters' and clowns' arsenals. By reversing their speech, gestures, gender, or morals, clowns and tricksters call attention to the unpredictable nature of the world and the power they have in the world.

The Hopi **paiyakyamu,** for example, delight in reversing everything. During ritual performances they walk backward, wear their clothes inside out, eat excrement, and speak in a garbled language that no one can understand. Pitted against the moral example of the kachinas, the paiyakyamu highlight the necessity of chaos in the world. Whereas the kachinas symbolize order and peace, the paiyakyamu remind their audience that chaos is never far from order.

In addition to being entertaining, tricksters' and clowns' reversals are often meant as moral messages. These characters can reverse any situation, either as a warning against what not to do or as a sign of what could happen if chaos reigned. Oftentimes, role reversal is a popular form of social commentary. By mimicking the roles of those in power, characters often air their grievances and highlight inequalities.

The Yaqui **pascola** dancers are a prime example of the power of reversal, especially when it comes to morals. The pascolas act like fools, running into things and people, eating things that should not be eaten, and telling lies. They also mimic sexual acts in their play with the deer dancer, they eat his feces, mock his power, make the sign of the cross backward, and in general reverse every social and religious guideline of the Yaqui. They are models of what the Yaqui should not be. Their actions and selfish ways provide a counterpart to the deer and other cherished aspects of Yaqui life.

The **kaka** of Sierra Leone is another example of reversal in its most extreme form (the word *kaka* literally means "shit devil"). The kaka is a masked performer who is contrasted to other heroic performers. As a reminder of the possibility of negativity and an embodiment of immorality, the kaka performer has a powerful role. He is seen as a slow-witted, antisocial misfit. While other performers are neat and clean, with costumes that never show wear, the kaka purposely wears torn clothes, rolls in the dusty streets, and lets himself get dirty to entertain the audiences. By throwing himself at the audience or spouting profanities at them, the kaka reverses the acceptable, and for that performance, at least, the unacceptable is what is expected. (See also **Ananse, Bribal, Newekwe, Niyel Carnival, Ogo, Tachukti, Tsukuwimkya,** and **Yiyi** for more examples.)

Reynard
French, Flemish, *Europe*

Reynard is a crafty fox who takes on his rival the wolf in many tales. Tales of Reynard became popular in France in the late twelfth century with the publication of the *Roman de Renart*. The *Roman*, as it is known, pits the fox, Reynard, against Ysengrin, the wolf. In the adventures of Reynard and Ysengrin, the seeds of social commentary were born. Although Reynard was born in the *Roman*, he became so popular that many other authors used him as a character representing disobedience. Many other so-called branches of the Reynard

tales exist. All, however, share the common theme of Reynard's cunning ways practiced in the face of the powerful but always ludicrous government.

Using the characters as embodiments of the government, the church, and any other institutional body, the *Roman* tackles issues of the morality of a feudal system, the mistreatment of peasants, and the misuse of power by the government. With Reynard as the main character, the *Roman* highlights the revolutionary possibilities for the masses. Although the *Roman* was the first to establish the character of Reynard as bearing an antigovernment message, other authors, poets, songsters, and playwrights captured the sentiments of the time by using Reynard as a symbol of change. In fact, the French word for fox, *goupil*, was all but replaced by *reynard* by the end of the thirteenth century.

Reynard exposes the weaknesses of a society built on a collapsing feudal system and a popular revolutionary movement. The book and its characters are clearly antiestablishment, as Reynard tramples his enemies and ignores the voice of reason. He is a murderer, liar, thief, adulterer, and rogue. His crafty ways are hidden by his many disguises. As a symbol of the abuse of institutional power, King Noble, the lion, shows that government and church officials hide behind their masks of power and truth while leaving the masses in poverty. With his ability to sidestep the powers that be and to set out on his own, however, Reynard also shows that the power can be trampled.

The supremacy of the king and his misuse of power are the common themes the *Roman* addresses. In one court scene, Reynard was accused of raping Ysengrin's wife. In another he was accused of committing murder. Reynard, however, subverted the court by suggesting that he be allowed to go on a religious pilgrimage to make amends for his wrongdoing. Once the magistrates agree, Reynard was off on his own again, across the countryside to do as he pleased.

Although most of the characters in the *Roman* are animals, the humans in the *Roman* are either monks or hermits. No matter who they are, Reynard delights in taking advantage of them. He convinced one monk to leave his food behind and then stole it, and he took advantage of a kindly hermit's help by stealing his cane. Reynard, however, loves to confess his wrongdoings to anyone who will listen. He often confesses to the monks and hermits he meets. But he also confesses to the other animals, such as the badger, who absolve him of all his sins. Parodying the power that the church held over its constituents in twelfth-century France, the badger's forgiveness of Reynard showed that any sin could be washed away if the church saw fit. (Sands 1960; Terry 1983)

Ritual Performance

Ritual perfomances, found all over the world, are community activities that focus on meaningful life-changing events. Whether they are social or overtly religious, ritual performances always shed light on the ways in which societies view the world. Because of their focus on pivotal moments in the lives of individuals as well as communities, ritual performances are often events in which all aspects of life are brought to the forefront. Often clowns and tricksters find their way into rituals as the embodiment of wrongheadedness, immorality, and negativity. But they are also entertainers and so highlight the lighter side of life. As complex characters, tricksters and clowns bring both tension and relief to ritual performances.

The **komali** of India, for example, are described as grotesque, and part of their humor lies in their juxtaposition with other performers who portray the serene and beautiful. They act like "madmen," running and jumping about, mocking singers and dancers with their exaggerated mimicry, and directing the audience's attention to themselves and away from the main performers. The komali are intentionally ambiguous in their performances; they dress in the clothing of the opposite gender or in clothing appropriate to both; they purposely jumble their speech, trip over unseen objects, and confuse simple directions. The komali appear as reminders that the world is not as it is always perceived. Their association with inauspicious forces makes them feared by spectators, while their crazy antics highlight their playful side.

Unlike clowns, tricksters are not found in ritual performances themselves but are embodied by human beings through trances, dances, costumes, and songs. The Yoruba trickster **Eshu-Elegba** is often portrayed through spirited dancing and costumes that include elongated penises. Focusing on his erotic nature as well as his energetic and comedic pranks, ritual participants show their affinity for Eshu-Elegba by becoming him in performances.

Sometimes ritual performances can be the setting for mass clownlike behavior. For example, the **Niyel carnival** in Papua New Guinea has curing as its focus, but the comedic inversions and role reversals highlight the disruptive nature of the festival and its distinctive brand of social commentary and reinforcement of values. The carnival is marked by role-reversals, transvestitism, and crude joking. Men and women swap roles in the two-day feast that emphasizes the reversal of kinship and gender roles. Both men and women exaggerate the actions of the others and mimic their normal roles. (See also **Anaanu, Ananse, Ch'angbu, Chapayeka, Difisi, Gabruurian, Hagondes, Heyoka, Ikaki, Ipani, Kamdaak Waneng, Koshare, Koyemshi, Kwirena, Legba, Ma'ii, Nanawitcu, Newekwe, Ogo, Paiyakyamu, Susa-no-o,**

Tachukti, Talawasi, Tansa, Tenali Rama, To Ninilii, and **Tsukuwimkya** for more examples.)

Roadrunner
United States

The speedy Roadrunner is **Wile E. Coyote's** nemesis, always eluding capture. He seems simple-minded, yet he always eludes the Coyote's best-laid plans. The Roadrunner never hurts the coyote; he only "beep-beeps" at him and runs on. The Roadrunner, with his cool, calm demeanor, however, is the downfall of the Coyote, who cannot seem to ignore him and so is forever taunted by his speedy travels. (See **Wile E. Coyote** for more on the two.) (Jones 1989)

Saint Peter

Europe and United States

The New Testament apostle Saint Peter has been interpreted in popular Christianity as a prankster, liar, and dupe who unknowingly upends almost every situation in which he finds himself. This modern image of Saint Peter arose not only out of popular reconstruction of biblical tales but also out of their interpretation by other cultures, especially Mexican, Hispanic, and Yaqui cultures. All of these peoples had prolonged encounters with missionaries who attempted, oftentimes through violence and force, to bring Christianity to their communities. By adapting Saint Peter to their stories, these people were able to show the ambiguity even in something as seemingly concrete as the New Testament. Saint Peter, then, came to represent the necessity of chaos and the unpredictability of the world to people who encountered such situations firsthand.

Biblical accounts of Saint Peter only hint at his role as a trickster. The first hint of his ambiguity is his name change from Peter to Simon. Taking on the name of Simon, Peter testifies to his great faith in Jesus and his message. As Peter, however, he shows little faith and waivers in his acceptance of Jesus' message. He both affirms and denies Jesus as the messiah, and he tries unsuccessfully to replicate Jesus' miracles. In the New Testament, stories show Peter as impetuous, always wanting to do the right things but sometimes failing because of his spontaneous nature. Most commonly, he is seen as someone who professes great faith in Jesus but who then acts as if he does not quite believe. His wavering faith is taken as a metaphor for the common person's struggle with faith in a world that makes temptation a priority.

This statue of Saint Peter stands in Vatican City, Rome. (Fulvio Roiter/Corbis)

Although the traditional accounts of Saint Peter ignore his subversive accounts of Jesus as well as Saint Peter's misguided attempts at miracles, popular accounts expand on Saint Peter's inconsistencies and show him as an adversary to Christ as well as a prankster and troublemaker. In fact, his persona in popular accounts celebrates chaos and disorder; he loves to highlight the unknowable aspects of reality but his bumbling wit often shows his lack of confidence and inability to follow through with his pranks.

In tales, Saint Peter constantly exceeds the limits set by his contemporaries. After hearing of Jesus' death he asks to be crucified too in a show of solidarity, but he wants to be crucified upside down. He breaks pollution taboos by eating things he is not supposed to and then encourages others to do the same, thus shifting the emphasis on purity. He attempts to imitate Jesus' miracles but ends up disappointing everybody when his words do not produce.

In many Spanish-speaking cultures, Peter is known as San Pedro. A vast amount of oral and written literature exists concerning the misguided adventures of San Pedro. In a Yaqui tale (see **Chapayeka** and **Pascola** for more on Yaqui culture) about San Pedro, we see his proclivity toward deception and lies. San Pedro and Jesus were walking along when Jesus sent San Pedro to get a cooked chicken from a nearby house. On his way back with the chicken, San Pedro was overcome by hunger and ate one of the legs. Upon reaching Jesus, San Pedro told him that all the chickens in the area only have one leg. As the two continued their journey, they came upon a tree where a flock of chickens were asleep. As chickens do, they were sleeping with one leg tucked up under their bodies. "See," San Pedro exclaimed, "they only have one leg." But as he smiled, thinking that he had fooled Jesus, Jesus threw a rock at the chickens, and one of them awoke and stood up on two legs. "What a miracle," San Pedro announced. Then, thinking quickly, he threw a large stone at the rest of the chickens, and they too awoke and walked on two legs. "See," San Pedro boasted, "I, too, can perform miracles."

San Pedro is a bold character who twists one small lie into a web of lies. He never wants to seem the fool but always ends up looking like one. His attempts at humor are fleeting; he is known mostly for his deceptive

pranks and rude behavior. For example, in one story, San Pedro put some figs in a bag and told Jesus that he was enjoying a bag of burro dung. As he ate the figs in front of Jesus he embellished his delight telling him how good the dung was and that Jesus should try some. The next day when he saw Jesus again he reached into his bag, but this time the figs really were burro dung, and San Pedro's face turned green when he took a bite. Although San Pedro attempts time and again to outsmart Jesus and others, he almost always fails, and he is shown to be the fool.

Other tales show the lengths to which San Pedro will go to get the best of others. His foolery highlights his selfishness. In one tale San Pedro was supposed to be taking care of the herd of goats he and his brother Juan shared. While his brother was away, San Pedro filled the goats with air so that they looked full, and he kept the food for himself. In another story, while San Pedro was at home his mother got hungry and asked for some of his cornmeal. Angry that he had to share, he fed it to her quickly, causing her to choke and die. After he realized the enormity of his situation, he dressed his mother in fine clothes and propped her up next to her spinning wheel at the door. When Juan came in, he knocked his mother over and thought that he had killed her. (Giddings 1959; Hynes and Steele 1993; Rael 1977)

Scogan
England

Scogan was a jester in the court of Edward IV of England. See **Jester** for more information on Scogan and other jesters throughout Europe.

Sega
Lusi-Kaliai, *Papua New Guinea*

The verb *sega* means "to clown or act a fool." There is no Lusi noun that designates a clown character; instead the term *sega* denotes an action or actions that can be performed by anyone. The term *sega-nga*, "clowning," is most often used to describe people's humorous or foolish actions. People act *sega* in two main contexts: formal ceremonies or informal family or nonpublic functions.

The Lusi-Kaliai are isolated from the main centers of Papua New Guinea society in five villages on the west coast. They interact mainly with each other and have been able to avoid much of the Western influences felt by their neighbors inland. The communities sustain themselves through fishing, small-scale farming, and the harvesting of several coconut plantations. The *kambu*, or kin group, is the main community unit within each village. Everyone belongs to a specific *kambu*, and one's rights, roles, and responsibilities are determined by that kin group. The *kambu* acts together as a cooperative group. They fish and garden together; they arrange ceremonies and support one another in daily activities. Because of their ties to their *kambu*, people have structured roles within the Lusi-Kaliai society. One way of breaking that structure is by acting *sega*.

At important ceremonies such as weddings, puberty rites, and first-born ceremonies, individuals from the *kambu* of those being honored are chosen to act *sega*. For example, at a wedding, an older woman from the bride's *kambu* is asked to perform *sega* at the ceremony. (See also **Han mane 'ak su** for a similar female performer in Rotuma.) In her performance, she acts as a transvestite. In other ceremonies men dress like women in their *sega* performances. Acting out the stereotypical gestures of the opposite sex provides a comedic overtone as well as one of social commentary. Performers take this opportunity to divulge and exaggerate the shortcomings of leaders, *kambu* members as well as outsiders. No one is safe from the ridicule of a *sega* performance. Many anthropologists and missionaries report being

the butt of the jokes at a *sega* performance. The performance gives people the chance to air their grievances and frustrations without direct confrontation, which is not generally accepted in Lusi-Kaliai society.

During a wedding ceremony, the woman performing *sega* will chase, tease, and even attack the members of the groom's *kambu*. She calls out lewd comments, reports on their indiscretions, and embarrasses them with her direct comments. People who are under attack may flee from the performer, which may lead the performer to chase or physically attack them. The woman performing *sega* may take on the tone of a warrior or chief in her antics as a male, or she may mock the sexual attributes of men by mimicking sexual intercourse. Prior to sustained contact with Europeans, there had been a history of naked *sega* performances in which the performers went to great lengths to mimic or burlesque the sexual exploits of both men and women. Today this practice is less common. Those performing *sega* are normally clothed and less vivid in their sexual burlesque.

At weddings and other ceremonies, those in the audience are not passive. They aid the performers by trapping their victims and they call out comments to cheer them on and keep the comedic performances going. During puberty ceremonies, the audience, made up of *kambu* members, may taunt those performing *sega* by shouting rude comments or complaining that they are not doing enough. Those performing *sega* are chosen by the families, and if their performances are not entertaining enough they will not be chosen again. They are paid by the family members, who say that they "buy their shame." That is, during *sega* performances the performers act shamefully and contrary to the proper behavior accepted in Lusi-Kaliai society. By paying for their shame, the family members offset the actions of the performers.

In addition to performing at formal ceremonies, people may act *sega* in informal settings or on the fringes of public ceremonies. These performances are generally impromptu, unlike the requested performances at weddings and puberty ceremonies. Often during a public gathering people will voluntarily act *sega* in order to mock the actions of another and thus demonstrate the other's foolishness. That is, although the actions are humorous they are meant as a warning to the person being mimicked that his or her actions are unacceptable. For example, New Guinea officials, missionaries, and anthropologists have all been the focus of impromptu *sega* performances. In most cases the performer does not change his or her outward appearance but, instead, exaggerates the speech, stature, and movements of the individual, to the delight of those around. These performances, however, do not normally take place in front of the individual being mocked. Instead, the outbursts of *sega* normally occur after the person has left the area. Thus one only finds out one is being mocked by word of mouth, if at all.

People often perform *sega* toward powerful members of society, whom they cannot address directly with their complaints. Most recently these performances have been directed at government officials, who come into Lusi villages without permission, and at Europeans in the area. By mimicking their actions and exaggerating their shortcomings, the Lusi performers provide a social commentary on their postcolonial situation, much as the formal performances provide a commentary on the inner workings of the community itself. (Counts 1982; Counts and Counts 1992; Harding 1967)

Semar
Java, *Indonesia*
Semar, a clown character, is a popular character in Javanese mythology, making his way into puppet plays as well. Semar is cast as a comedic presence in the court of the

kings. He usually upstages the kings and princes with his humor, making them the butt of his jokes. (See **Panakawan** for a general discussion concerning Javanese clowns and Semar.) Semar is a prototypical panakawan, using his comedic power to twist and turn any situation to his favor.

Semar and other clown characters are found most often in Javanese *wayang kulit* (shadow puppet) performances. Semar is often depicted as a peasant among the ruling elite; despite his low status, he becomes the hero and the voice of common sense, making the others look like fools. Semar is an ambiguous character precisely because he embodies the characteristics of both a king and a peasant. Although he appears in physical form to be a peasant, his advice, wisdom, and power point to his role as a king or deity. In his actions, Semar reminds the nobility that their status is tenuous and that anything can happen to them.

The common *ludruk*, or street plays, highlight the role of Semar as an icon of the lower class. Normally performed in regional shantytowns, the *ludruk* plays act as vehicles for social commentary. Characters such as Semar show the absurdity of those in power and call attention to the chaotic nature of the world in general. Semar is highly effective as a source of comedic wit, but perhaps his most cherished role is that of the counterpart to the gods and rulers. It is Semar who stands up to prince Arjuna, and it is Semar who defeats Siva the mighty god. Semar is not just a comedic character but an embodiment of the power struggle within Javanese society. (Buurman 1991; Geertz 1973; Peacock 1968; Peacock 1978; Towsen 1976)

Sendeh
Kiowa, *Plains Region of the United States*
The shape-shifter Sendeh can change shape at will to get what he wants. Sendeh is most commonly seen as a coyote, but he

often takes on a human appearance. He is greedy and is best known for his constant hunger and insatiable sexual desires. (Voegelin 1933)

Seth
Egypt
Seth is a trickster god of ancient Egypt. (El-Shamy 1980)

Sex
Many myths and rituals include a focus on sex or the imitation of sexual intercourse, and sexual antics, sexual exaggeration, and intercourse are the subject of many trickster tales and clowns' escapades. This concern stems from clowns' and tricksters' association with the pleasures of life as well as from their immoral and oftentimes crude antics. Highlighting both the positive, fun aspects of life along with the obnoxious and rude, tricksters and clowns delight in playing with the accepted sexual mores of their societies.

Often sex is the only thing on the mind of the trickster. He will do anything to satisfy his unending sexual appetite, including committing rape, incest, and murder. **Ture,** the Azande spider trickster, waited until his mother-in-law was asleep and then had intercourse with her. Similarly, **Chunga,** the Toba bird trickster, tainted some honey and fed it to a young girl so that he could have sexual intercourse with her after she went to sleep. Tricksters around the world pride themselves on their large sexual appetites and their willingness to go to any lengths to satisfy that desire. As characters in the mythologies of many cultures, tricksters shed light on the necessity of sexual restrictions by their harmful, deceitful tactics.

Clowns often exaggerate and mimic sexual intercourse in their performances, attempting to be as rude as they can. A subset of the Hopi **tsukuwimkya** clowns, the

A bas-relief of a sculptured throne base features carvings of the Egyptian deities Horus and Seth. (Gianni Dagli Orti/Corbis)

paiyatam', are especially known for their sexual antics aimed at women. They sing obscene songs, make sexual gestures, and poke at the women in the audience. Sometimes they have mock penises hidden in their costumes and use them to taunt the women. The women, however, retaliate by pouring buckets of water over the heads of the paiyatam'.

Not all of the sexual antics of tricksters and clowns are negative. Some simply highlight the inherent pleasure and joy of sexuality. The Indian deity **Krishna** is a perfect example. Krishna's behavior, including his sexual behavior, is most often playful and carefree. His sexual exploits with the women of many villages is not devious; instead, the women come willingly to Krishna, anxiously waiting for the pleasure he will share with them. See also **Ananse, Arioi Society, Cufalh, Eshu-Elegba, Fai Fale Aitu, Gabruurian, Gu-e-krig, Han mane 'ak su, Ikaki, Italapas, Kaik, Kamdaak Waneng, Komali, Koshare, Koyemshi, Kwirena, Legba, Mica, Nafigi, Nanabozhoo,**

Nankilslas, Niyel Carnival, Odosha, Pascola, Pilandok, *Sega*, Sendeh, Sinkalip, Talawasi, Taugi, Tokwaj, Txamsem, Wayayqaláchiyi, Yenaldlooshi, Yiyi, and Yogovu for more examples.

Shape-Shifter

One of the most powerful weapons in the arsenal of a trickster or clown is shape-shifting, that is, the ability to change into any form or shape or to assume any disguise in order to fool others, to take control of a situation, or to flee from impending disaster. Although some shape-shifters have the power to actually change from animal to human form, others simply possess the power of disguise. That is, they are masters at changing their appearance so as not to be recognized.

The ability to change form or appearance is necessary for tricksters to escape punishment for their deceptive behavior. More often, disguises and shape-shifting allow them to catch others off guard so that they can take advantage of them. **Kitsune,** the Japanese fox, changes shape so others will not suspect he is in the area. Because people are on the watch for a fox, Kitsune changes into human form to play his pranks. **Iktomi,** the Lakota spider trickster, changes shape to elude punishment but also to satisfy his unending hunger. Once he changed into a buffalo and wandered the plains taking food from others. Similarly, the Nivakle character **Cufalh's** ability to change his appearance is his most potent attribute. Disguising himself from his unsuspecting victims, Cufalh is able to satisfy all his needs. Neither a man nor a woman, human nor animal, Cufalh is an unethical shape-shifter who will take advantage of anyone.

Nankilslas, the Haida raven, takes what he wants from others by disguising himself as a relative or friend. Often he disguises himself as an elder or uncle to fool his friends and take advantage of their status.

Because the Haida social system is based on proper etiquette from relatives, Nankilslas is able to take advantage of others' generosity when he pretends to be a relative. See also **Ananse, Dahusúi, Furna, Krishna, Kumarxúo, Kwatyat, Legba, Ma'ii, Nafigi, Odosha, Sendeh, Tatú Bolita, Taugi, Tokwaj, Ture, Txamsem, Wayayqaláchiyi, Wesucechak,** and **Windigo** for more examples.

Shodieonskon

Seneca, *Southeastern United States*

Shodieonskon is also known as "brother of death." The word *shodieonskon* means "he abuses people by craft often," and the ability to deceive, abuse, and manipulate people is exactly what characterizes Shodieonskon. He delights in his disruptive behavior and likes nothing more than to cause trouble among people and other beings. He lies, steals, and tricks people into doing what he wants simply for his amusement. Being the brother of death, Shodieonskon is associated with powerful forces in the world and people fear him. He manipulates people mainly through his lies, for he can phrase almost anything in such a manner that people will listen to him.

In one story, Shodieonskon tricked an entire village into believing that his urine was a powerful bear oil that they must drink to ward off evil and maintain harmony. As the villagers all drank his urine from a large well, Shodieonskon sat back and laughed at their stupidity, knowing that he was more powerful and clever than they would ever be. Another story tells how he once convinced people that the only way to avoid falling ill from a terrible plague that was striking the area was to have intercourse with other people's spouses. When the people followed his advice, jealous fights broke out, and the villagers were soon set against each other; Shodieonskon, of course, watched as the community fell apart under his manipulation and deception. (Curtin and Hewitt 1918)

Simpson, Bart
United States

Bart Simpson is an animated comedic troublemaker known for his rude behavior, disobedience, and love of jokes. He is the only son of Homer and Marge Simpson in the animated television series *The Simpsons.* The Simpson characters first appeared in 1987 in a series of animated shorts on the *Tracy Ullman Show.* In 1989 *The Simpsons,* propelled by Bart's hilarious antics, quickly became a hit show viewed by children as well as adults. Bart's signature sayings, "Eat my shorts" and "Don't have a cow, man," have become familiar to most Americans. The cross-generational appeal of the show is credited to the lack of a sense of boundaries that Bart and the other characters display. All the Simpsons cross the line between the acceptable and unacceptable in their humorous depiction of a dysfunctional suburban family.

Bart has a total disregard for authority. He is constantly pulling pranks at school, often at the expense of Principal Skinner. Bart is a terrible student, often misbehaving in class in order to get the other students' attention. In one episode, Bart showed his complete disregard for both school authority and the presidency by putting a fake nose and eyes on his butt, making it look like President Richard Nixon, and saying "I am not a crook."

At the beginning of every episode Bart is shown writing a sentence repeatedly on a classroom chalkboard, presumably as punishment for some wrongdoing. Bart's famous chalkboard sayings include "I will not instigate revolution," "I will not carve gods," "Beans are neither fruit nor musical," and "I will not hang donuts on my person." Not only are Bart's deeds hilarious, even shocking, but the punishment for them is just as ludicrous.

Perhaps one of the best-known tricksters in the United States is the character Bart Simpson from the animated television series The Simpsons. *(© Twentieth Century Fox Film Corp./1994)*

One of Bart's favorite pranks is to call Moe's tavern, asking for fictional people, playing on Moe the bartender's ignorance. On different occasions, Bart asks for Al Koholic, Oliver Klozoff, Hugh Jass, Amanda Huggenkiss, Mike Rotch, and Ivana Tinkle. Moe invariably embarrasses himself by calling out the name ("Is there Amanda Huggenkiss here? Why can't I find Amanda Huggenkiss?"). When asked if he expects to ever catch the prank caller, Moe responds, "I don't know. He's tough to catch. He keeps changing his name."

Bart's own hero is Krusty the Clown, the host of a children's comedy variety show. Bart shows his love for Krusty by buying all the merchandise Krusty promotes, including Krusty Dolls, Krusty Walkie-Talkies, Krusty Trading Cards, Krusty Bedspread, and Krusty Brand Mayonnaise. Bart even attends Camp Krusty, where they serve Krusty Brand Imitation Gruel. Anything is all right to Bart, as long as it has the Krusty Brand seal of approval. Bart's affinity for all things "Krusty" highlights his comedic tendencies and his love of jokes.

Sometimes Bart's pranks backfire on him. In a classic episode Bart switched IQ tests with Martin, a model student, and was labeled a genius. He was sent to a school for gifted children, but the other students soon realized he was far from gifted. Bart returned to his old school, but the kids who had once considered him "cool" now called him "Poindexter." To make matters worse, Marge took him to the opera in order to stimulate her little genius's mind. Finally, after his science project almost blew up his new school, Bart was forced to admit that he was no genius. Even in defeat, however, Bart is a classic class clown and juvenile prankster. (Groening 1997)

Sinkalip
Salish, *Northwest Coast of North America*

Sinkalip, a coyote character, is best known for his ability to outwit and deceive both friends and enemies. Although the Salish refer to coyote as Sinkalip, when he speaks of himself he calls himself *Smyaw*, derived from the root word meaning "important." Sinkalip's designation of himself defines his most notable characteristic: his ego. Sinkalip is self-important, greedy, overconfident, and cocky.

Everything Sinkalip does is motivated by his ego. Even when his actions seem to be motivated by goodness, he is always looking out for himself first. This is an outlook that is contrary to the Salish values of the social system, which promotes the principles of reciprocity and sharing. The small Salish fishing communities support themselves by distributing their wealth throughout the community. This focus on reci-

procity is reflected in the creation story in which the salmon and the bear offered their flesh to human beings in return for careful treatment and respect. Many other animals and nonhuman beings have earned respect and power within the community in similar ways. Sinkalip not only ignores reciprocity, but he does so without any sign of regret. Even when Sinkalip's actions result in benefits for the community, these are seen as accidental by-products of his selfishness rather than intentional support of the community.

Stories about Sinkalip are most commonly told at night in the winter when fishing and other activities are in a lull. People come together at night to hear tales of their favorites characters. Although the educational value of these stories can not be denied, they are primarily intended as entertainment. If they have a "moral" or an explanation, it is usually "tacked on" at the end without specific reference to the story line itself. Storytellers are both male and female, young and old; however, older storytellers generally outnumber younger ones, for the younger people are still learning the subtleties of the various characters and their personalities. During storytelling events, the audience interacts with the storyteller by giving their approval and encouragement with a low tone signaling the affirmative. Families and clans have stories unique to themselves, and the larger community shares common characters, scenes, and plots.

One story about Sinkalip demonstrates not only his overzealous pride, greed, and egotism but also his importance to the shape and makeup of the Salish community. When the Council of Elders was meeting to finish making the world and human beings, Sinkalip decided he wanted to have the most powerful position. The leader had set up a pole with a stack of rings in front of it, each one representing a position to be handed out to various species. Sinkalip decided to stay up all night so that he would be the first one at the meeting in the morning. As night wore on, however, Sinkalip fell asleep, and he did not awake until late in the morning. He ran to the meeting to find the leader just about to pass out names and assignments. Sinkalip rushed in to the meeting and straight up to the leader, demanding that he be given the greatest name. The leader was so impressed by Sinkalip's speech, reasoning, and wit that he reversed the pole and gave him the most important position, which was to finish up the creation of the world.

As the leader continued handing out names and positions, he also gave each being a set of powers. As he handed out the powers, he pointed to the heart, where the beings were to keep the power, which they were to use to help all members of the world. With his unending hunger, Sinkalip misunderstood the leader's gesture and thought he was pointing to his stomach. Sinkalip's power, then, was set in his stomach and not his heart as the others' powers were. Whenever Sinkalip calls on his powers, then, they come out in the form of five feces. Sinkalip's power resides in his excrement.

When Sinkalip receives proper advice from his powers, he mimics them and calls them his younger siblings, saying he never needed their help. He gloats that he is the most brilliant and that they are simply mouthpieces for his wisdom. If the powers dare to deny him their advice, Sinkalip bullies and threatens them with rainstorms that would wash them away. Although the excrement tries to manipulate Sinkalip into doing the right things, he normally refuses to listen to their advice, doing whatever gives him pleasure instead. Although he is very powerful and intelligent, he uses his gifts only for himself and his own gratification.

In one story, Sinkalip's selfishness and greed end up aiding the community. Sin-kalip heard that there were five sisters living down by the river breeding fish and keeping them for themselves. Gloating that he would stop this selfishness, Sinkalip headed for the women, longing to assuage his unending hunger. When he came near the women's camp, he turned himself into a baby and began crying for help. The women heard the cry and immediately went to rescue the infant. The youngest sister was leery of the baby, suspecting a trick, but all the other sisters became fond of it, feeding and caring for it. Each day, after the women left to do their chores, Sinkalip changed himself back into a coyote and headed for the fishing traps. Slowly, day by day, Sinkalip loosened the traps.

One day, after the women went off to work and Sinkalip headed for the traps, the youngest sister decided to check her suspicions. She went back to the house, only to find the baby missing, and she spotted Sinkalip chewing through the traps. Just as she and the other women got to the traps, Sinkalip finished chewing through them, and the fish were released. Sinkalip led the salmon upstream, stopping at each village along the way trading fish for a wife. The more attractive the wife the more fish he would leave at the village. Satisfying both his sexual appetite as well as his love of food, Sinkalip made his way to all the villages along the river. (Ashwell 1978; Boas 1895; Hilbert 1985; Hill-Trout 1978; Mourning Dove 1990)

Spider

The small spider, a popular character in African and Native American folk literature, is a trickster par excellence. He is greedy, mischievous, selfish, and cunning. Most spider tricksters' power lies in their ability to change shape and manipulate any situation in which they find themselves. Although only an insect, the spider is seen as crafty and potentially dangerous.

Spider Rock in Canyon de Chelly, Arizona, the sacred home of the Navajo deity Na'ashju'I Asdzau (Spider Woman). (North Wind Picture Archives)

A spider design on a gorget from prehistoric manuals in Missouri and Illinois, illustrating the ancient heritage of this trickster character in Native American mythologies. (Dover Books)

The apparent paradox of such a small creature being deadly is what fuels the stories of spiders throughout Africa. Although the spiders are pranksters, often they also have creative abilities and are known for bringing things to human beings. But like his North American counterpart the coyote, the spider is best known for his foolish, deceptive antics.

The spider, like other tricksters, is greedy for food and sex. The Ewe spider **Yiyi** is no exception. He delights in chasing women and flaunting his penis. He breaks social restrictions by having intercourse with his daughter, and he rapes village women. Yiyi is also characterized by his huge round belly, which is a testament to his unending appetite for food.

Another spider, Gizo, is also portrayed as a malicious trickster who uses his mischievous ways to trick others. Although his actions are humorous, they also result in destruction for the people and animals involved. In one story, Gizo was single-handedly responsible for the deaths of all his animal neighbors. One by one, he tricked each of his neighbors into killing

another. (See **Gizo.**) His greed and unending appetite drove him to murder all those around him.

The spider, like other trickster characters, highlights the chaos that negative, destructive, and antisocial behavior might bring to a community. The spider is widespread in African folktales as an antisocial character because the life-threatening diseases carried by his insect counterpart really can bring chaos to a community. As a trickster, the spider highlights the inherent unpredictability of the world. See also **Anaanu, Ananse, Iktomi, To, Ture, Wanto, Wosi,** and **Yo** for more examples.

Sri Thanoncha
Thailand

Sri Thanoncha is a deceptive, witty prankster who challenges social norms and ignores laws to get the best of people. Stories about Sri Thanoncha abound throughout Thailand. In some parts of Thailand he is also known by the name Siengmieng, or at times Phra Sri, an honorific title. But the stories remain the same. They catalog Sri Thanoncha's life from birth to death through his continuous pranks, deceptions, and challenges.

Stories about Sri Thanoncha were first told orally during the Ayudhya period between 1350 and 1767. This period was marked by a feudal system in which many officials used their positions of power in abusive ways, either stealing money or handing down harsh physical punishments to those who did not obey. Sri Thanoncha emerges from this era as a voice of opposition.

Since then the stories have been written in many different formats and continue to be told orally to generation after generation. Sri Thanoncha's life is celebrated in paintings, murals on temple walls, books, movies, and theater. Although stories concerning his adventures may vary from village to village, the central themes of his life and actions remain the same. Sri Thanoncha is notorious for his cunning wit and devilish wordplay, with which he fooled kings, monks, and sages alike. He showed a total lack of respect for social mores by taking advantage of young girls, conning elders out of money, and even deceiving his own parents. Stories about Sri Thanoncha are entertaining because they play on the scandalous and bizarre. They exaggerate common stereotypes, such as the gullible stranger and the devious merchant, to show how easy it is for Sri Thanoncha to trick anyone. Sri Thanoncha, with his powerful wit, highlights the vulnerability of all types of people, from the most powerful to the most benign.

Sri Thanoncha can always be found engaged in deception. Yet he is also seen as hero because although he was born a peasant, his intelligence and wit have enabled him to rise above many of the powerful officials who normally would not be challenged. In Sri Thanoncha, then, the Thai have a character who outwits the upper class, kings, and monks, thus gaining some control over his own life. He displays the power of one individual to overcome the restrictions of a society built on structured hierarchies and strict rules of respect. Thai parents tell his stories to teach their children the power of agile thinking. He rarely resorts to physical violence; he outwits others by using their own words against them. He is notorious for doing exactly, word-for-word, what people tell him to, usually to their dismay. Yet with his quick tongue, he is able to talk himself out of even the most dangerous of situations. He is a model of the independent, self-reliant individual who can overcome oppressive and threatening situations simply by saying the right thing.

From the beginning of his life, Sri Thanoncha was destined to be powerful. Stories of his childhood stress a monk's prophesy prior to his birth. His parents,

Nantha and Rao, had tried to have children for years. Unsuccessful, they resorted to fertility herbs, incantations, and blessings by monks. Finally, Rao became pregnant after dreaming that a spirit invaded her. Curious about the child and her dream, Rao went to the temple to ask a monk for his interpretation. The monk, only a novice, told Rao that she was carrying a boy who would be powerful and unscrupulous. Sri Thanoncha's actions even in the first years of his life showed that the monk had been right.

A few years after Sri Thanoncha was born Rao had another son. Being the eldest, Sri Thanoncha was expected to help with his younger brother as well as do chores around the house. One day a woman selling candy came to the door, and Rao bought some candy for the boys. The woman selling the sweets took an instant liking to Sri Thanoncha's brother and ignored Sri Thanoncha, even going so far as to give his brother extra candy. This outraged Sri Thanoncha, who became jealous of his brother. The next day when his parents left to work in the fields they told him to clean his brother thoroughly and to make sure the house was spotless when they returned. Taking their mandate literally, Sri Thanoncha took a knife and slit his brother's stomach open, cleaning him thoroughly, inside and out. Next, he took everything thing in the house and threw it out, making sure the house was "spotless." When his parents came back from the fields they were so horrified by his actions that they threw him out, banishing him from their house and the village.

This was neither the first nor the last time Sri Thanoncha would use people's mandates against them to take advantage of them or to get revenge. In a story from his later life, Sri Thanoncha was the servant of a prestigious man in government. One of his jobs was to carry the man's bag of nuts as he walked to town or to a meeting. Every important official had such a servant, showing his high status and wealth. One day as Sri Thanoncha followed the man, the nuts fell from the bag one by one. When his master asked for a nut, there were none left in the bag. Furious, the man yelled at Sri Thanoncha, but before he could beat him Sri Thanoncha explained what had happened and calmed the man, who told Sri Thanoncha that if the nuts fell out again he should pick up everything. The next time the master was on his way to an important meeting, he packed a bag full of nuts to give to his colleagues. Sri Thanoncha followed dutifully behind him. As they walked, the nuts again began to spill out, but this time Sri Thanoncha picked up everything in the path. When the man reached the town court and threw open the bag to his peers, it was full of garbage, weeds, dust, and rocks. The others laughed at him, and in his rage he grabbed Sri Thanoncha. But Sri Thanoncha smiled and told him he was following his orders; he had collected everything in his path, leaving out nothing. Furious at how easily Sri Thanoncha could twist the facts, the man let him go and told him to leave the village at once; he was no longer welcome.

Although Sri Thanoncha normally comes out on top, even he can be defeated. In one story Sri Thanoncha borrowed some money from an elderly woman in his village and told her that he would repay her when there had been two full moons. Sri Thanoncha spent her money frivolously on sweets and alcohol. Soon two months had passed and the woman waited for Sri Thanoncha to repay her. She waited and waited but he never came. Finally she went to his house and confronted him. But looking at her calmly he told her that she was mistaken, that there had not been two full moons. Not sure of herself, the woman left and came back again in another two months, and Sri Thanoncha told her the same thing. After a year of attempts to collect her money and of Sri Thanoncha's insistence that there had not been two moons, she went to a monk for help. The monk sought out Sri Thanoncha for an explanation. Confidently, Sri Thanoncha told the monk to look in the sky. Were there two full moons? Had there ever been in the last year? Seeing through his word games, the monk told Sri Thanoncha to meet him and the woman that night outside the temple gates. When they met, the monk took Sri Thanoncha to a pond nearby. He pointed to the full moon in the sky and the one in the reflection of the pond. Indeed, there were two full moons on that night, and Sri Thanoncha was forced to pay the woman.

Sri Thanoncha's superior intellect and his ability to twist words and situations are his trademark characteristics, which are still today celebrated in stories by the people of Thailand. Although he can be vengeful and even inflict pain on others, his ability to get the best of almost any situation places him among the favorite characters in Thai literature. (Davies 1971; Tipaya 1991; Vathanaprida 1994)

Sug
Thailand
Sug, a clever prankster who enjoys fooling others for his own pleasure, is known in popular and entertaining stories in villages throughout northern Thailand as a devious character who uses his wit to get the best of people, even monks and other authority figures. Sug can always be found stirring up chaos or causing trouble between people. His actions are motivated by his love of joking and are not intended to be malicious, although he does get carried away at times. Sug is a popular literary character in northern Thailand because he confronts authority figures and is never cowed by people of higher status. In a culture marked by status positions, Sug shows that one can rise

above the system and do whatever one wants.

In northern Thailand there are two types of oral literature, *So* and *Cia*. The *So* tradition is a formalized oral tradition that is passed on directly from teacher to student. The *So* tradition is marked by its formality; it is performed on stage by men and for men only and deals with a range of social and religious issues including love, Buddhist laws, and politics. *Cia*, on the other hand, is marked by its informality. The *Cia* prose tradition focuses on family life, moral tales, and community issues. The stories are performed by men of all ages, with women and children as audience members. The women and children, however, often leave when the stories become too bawdy or lewd.

In addition to its oral literary traditions, Thailand has many written forms. One of the things Buddhism brought to Thailand was a written canon of ideas, stories, and rules. Buddhist doctrine is well preserved in written form, and its stories are widely known by villagers throughout Thailand. Although the stories have been written down, they are passed on through oral storytelling, normally from parent to child. Boys, however, are expected to join the monastery for at least three months at some point in their lives for a more formal indoctrination.

Some stories about Sug play on the tension between monks and the Thai population. Monks are honored in Thai society, and it would be considered rude and disrespectful to play tricks on any monk. Further, because Buddhist doctrine focuses on gaining merit in this life in order to gain a higher status in the next, people shy away from any negative action toward monks.

Sug, however, ignores these social and religious rules and is disrespectful to monks. He often dupes them into doing things they would normally never do. In one story, Sug lured a monk into eating excrement by cleverly disguising it. The monk had told Sug to look after his belongings and not to let anything happen to them. While the monk was away, Sug formed some sesame seeds and sugar water into a pile of excrement. When the monk returned and found the excrement on his mattress he chided Sug and forced him to eat it. As Sug ate the pile he smiled and remarked on how delicious it was. The monk watched him until finally he had a bite and agreed that it was delicious. The monk told Sug to watch his mattress again, and to call him when the dogs left their mark. Following his directions, Sug waited until a dog relieved himself on the monk's mattress and called the monk to eat it. Smiling at his feast, the monk grabbed the pile and took a big bite; this time, however, his face turned red with anger, and Sug ran away laughing.

The humor in Sug's dealings with monks comes from their status. Normally monks are revered and respected as wise and clever. Around Sug, however, they become fools, easily tricked by Sug's boyish pranks. Sug's pleasure in tricking monks does not come from any desire to hold such a position; he simply delights in the fact that he can make fun of those in honored positions. In one story he disguises himself as a monk and makes the rounds in the village to collect alms from the people. Because he is not a monk, his collection is thievery, but by stealing from the village people in this way he shows his complete disrespect both for authority and for community. (Brun 1976; Davies 1971; Vathanaprida 1994)

Sulwe

Ila, *Central Africa: Zimbabwe*

Sulwe is a popular hare character in Ila stories. In Ila the characteristics of animals are used to highlight similar traits in humans. Hares are known to be quick and clever; they use their speed to steal food from gardens and elude human punishment. Although Sulwe is called a hare in stories, he is also given human characteristics such as speech. Combining the characteristics of hares and humans, Sulwe takes on a personality of his own, demonstrating both the presence of deception in the world and also the need for social institutions that deal with antisocial behavior. Folktales, such as those about Sulwe, are usually told at night to large groups of people who have gathered after the day's work has been done. The stories are told mainly for entertainment and amusement, although it is clear that they have social and educational purpose. Some are told to warn people against improper actions, and some are historical.

Sulwe is notorious for his skill in outwitting people; he is a clever practical joker, he is cunning, he lies and cheats, and he is cruel. Not only is he a jokester, but his jokes often end in their victim's death. He is known to have eaten little children and to have killed entire packs of lions. Even with his negative characteristics, Sulwe is a source of entertainment for the Ila people.

Sulwe is small, quick, and clever. Despite his size, he is able to get the best of even the largest and strongest animals. Once he convinced the lion's wife to let him nurse her children, and he ate them one by one. Another time he fooled all the horned animals into thinking he was horned too by gluing horns to his head. Once he had horns, he was admitted to their party and was able to drink all the beer he wanted. As the evening wore on, the glue on Sulwe's head weakened and the horns fell off, exposing his deceit. Sulwe's quickness allowed him to run from the party before any of the other animals could catch him. In another story, Sulwe called out to his uncle the lion, asking for his help in retrieving some ants. Sulwe asked the lion to start a fire around the anthill. The lion started the fire and then retreated so as not to get burned. After the fire burned out, Sulwe rolled in the ashes and then went back to his uncle, claiming to have been in

the fire and not gotten burned. The lion asked how he managed such a feat and Sulwe told him that he had taken a special medicine that kept him from being burned. The lion asked his nephew for the same medicine so he too could repel fire. Sulwe gave the lion some leaves, telling him that they were the medicine. After rubbing himself with the leaves, the lion lay atop an anthill and asked Sulwe to set it on fire. As he lit the fire, Sulwe reminded the lion not to yell out or he would be burned for sure. Sulwe knew the lion, engulfed in fire, would soon be dead, and he ran off gloating that he had played a trick on his uncle, the fierce lion. Sulwe always enjoys gloating after his victories.

In one story, Sulwe used his cunning to deceive the jackal three times. The two left to visit their friends. On the way, Sulwe told the jackal to pick some grass so they could use it to build a fire for dinner that night. When they reached their destination, their friends gave them some nuts for dinner. Sulwe told the jackal to go start a fire so they could eat. As soon as he left, Sulwe ate all the nuts himself. When the jackal returned, he told him that the owners of the house had come and eaten all the nuts. They departed the next day for the cattle post. Along the way they found some pieces of a calabash. Sulwe told the jackal to pick them up so they would have something to carry the milk from the cattle post. When they arrived at the cattle post Sulwe went inside, telling the jackal to wait outside. Once inside Sulwe drank all the milk himself. Sulwe told the jackal that the owners would not give them any milk. When they left, Sulwe promised the jackal that they would surely find some food to eat at their next stop. Soon they came upon a cornfield. Sulwe told the jackal to be quiet so the owners would not catch them. They ate and ate until they both fell asleep in the field. At daybreak Sulwe awoke, dug a hole, and buried the jackal's tail in it. After he was finished he yelled to the jackal to wake up because the owners were coming to get them. Sulwe ran off, but the jackal was stuck, and the owner killed him for his theft.

Fulwe, the tortoise, is the only character who seems to be able to get the best of Sulwe. Although Fulwe is slow and not as clever as Sulwe, he manages to use his steadfast shrewdness to lead Sulwe from his path of trickery. Fulwe retreats into his tough outer shell when necessary, and his built-in camouflage often enables him to catch Sulwe off guard. Though Fulwe is not always successful, whenever he can overturn one of Sulwe's pranks he is adored by all the villagers. Once Fulwe won a race with Sulwe by placing his relatives along the path of their race. Each time Sulwe thought he was ahead he saw Fulwe around the next corner. For days Sulwe ran and ran trying to beat Fulwe, but in the end he was exhausted, dehydrated, and close to death, whereas Fulwe was well rested and victorious. Sulwe let his greediness for victory get in the way of his intelligence. Once he got tired, he did not think of the possibility that Fulwe might have tricked him. Believing he was the cleverest of all, Sulwe allowed himself to be outwitted. Sulwe demonstrates that cleverness does not always guarantee that one will come out on top. In the character of Sulwe, the Ila have a figure who reinforces proper behavior through his failure and illustrates the impact of negative behavior for the individual and the community. (Finnegan 1970; Smith and Dale 1920; Werner 1968)

Sungula
Kaguru, *East Africa: Tanzania*
See **Chibuga.**

Susa-no-o
Japan
Susa-no-o, a swift, impetuous male, is one of three offspring of the mythical parents of Japan, Izanami and Izanagi. The *Kojiki*, the oldest mythical text in Japan, recounts the escapades of the formation of Japan and Japanese culture. The *Kojiki* was completed in 712 C.E., and it codifies many of the explanations of the order in the world and Japanese society. Susa-no-o is a powerful male character in the tales of the *Kojiki*. Further, his popularity can be seen in rituals, shrines, and popular folktales concerning his adventures and accomplishments.

Susa-no-o is an ambiguous character in Japanese mythology. He is both a creator and destroyer. He wreaks havoc on people and then returns to aid them in their times of need. He knows no boundaries, social, physical, or moral. He challenges all established rules and breaks those he does not agree with. Because Susa-no-o is the son of the creators Izanami and Izanagi he

An Evelyn Paul illustration after a painting depicting the Japanese deity Susa-no-o. (Werner Forman/Art Resource)

has divine powers, but he uses his power to corrupt others, including his sister. He ignores social mores that prohibit incest, and he mocks the social hierarchy of the gods by ignoring all their rules and established ways.

The story of Susa-no-o's birth highlights his disruptive behavior. Izanami and Izanagi came to earth and produced the land, the people, and the other gods. Susa-no-o's mother, Izanami, died giving birth to the fire god. She left earth for the underworld and Izanagi followed her, but he was chased by hideous beings and was forced to leave Izanami. When Izanagi cleansed himself in the ocean waters before returning to the heavens, he produced three offspring, Amaterasu from his left eye, Tsukiyomi from his right eye, and Susa-no-o from his nose. His three children immediately wielded all the powers of their parents. Izanagi then mandated that his daughter Amaterasu rule the high plains of heaven, Tsukiyomi the night, and Susa-no-o the oceans. Amaterasu and Tsukiyomi quickly left for their rightful posts, but Susa-no-o sat down and cried. He told Izanagi that he wanted to join his mother in the underworld. Enraged that he would defy him, Izanagi banished Susa-no-o from the earth.

On his way to the underworld, Susa-no-o went to his sister in the high plains of heaven. In disregarding Izanagi's wishes Susa-no-o committed his first act of deception, and when he came upon his sister he committed an even greater transgression, persuading her to have intercourse with him to produce divine offspring. Although Amaterasu tried to outwit him by portraying herself as a warrior, the more cunning Susa-no-o saw through her and used his charm to seduce her. After they had had intercourse, Susa-no-o boasted of his feat and

roared with his victory over his sister, his father, and the established rules. His victory celebration quickly turned into a tirade as he uprooted trees, churned up rice paddies, and threw excrement all over the area that was designated for the upcoming Harvest Festival. Frantically looking for Amaterasu, he dropped a skinned horse in the room where she and her maids were weaving garments for the festival. One of the maids was hit by the horse, pierced her genitals with the needle, and died. In his rage, Susa-no-o demonstrated his chaotic nature and his willingness to break the rules just to demonstrate that he can.

On the other hand Susa-no-o is also known for his creative activities that help people. In another story, after Susa-no-o returned to earth he met Ogetsuhime, the goddess of food. Repulsed by the way she produced food from her own body, Susa-no-o killed her. But after her death many plants grew from her body and spread throughout the Japanese countryside to feed the people. In another tale, Susa-no-o heard a couple wailing, devastated at the death of their daughter. A terrible eight-headed monster had terrified the village so much that they were forced to sacrifice a virgin every year, and that year the couple's daughter had been sacrificed. Listening to their plight, Susa-no-o vowed to stop the monster. He tracked the monster down and, pretending to befriend him, gave him gallons of wine. Once the beast was subdued, Susa-no-o struck him dead with his sword, pulled the young girl from his stomach, and returned her to her parents. Even today, rituals in rural villages celebrate Susa-no-o's actions by slaying fictitious straw serpents and throwing their parts into the water. (Ellwood 1993; Kenji 1960; Miller 1984; Ouwehand 1958–1959)

T

Tachukti

Hopi, *Southwestern United States: Arizona*

Literally meaning "ball-on-head," the term *tachukti* refers to a group of humorous and obscene masked ritual performers among the Hopi. The name stems from their masks, which are studded with large round objects. There are usually three "balls" on each mask, one on the top and one on each side. The tachukti are commonly referred to as "mudheads" or by the Zuni term *koyemshi.* The term *mudheads* comes from the mud and clay with which the performers adorn their bodies, and the Zuni name *koyemshi* was adopted between 1860 and 1880 when the Hopi and Zuni came in close contact with one another. The term *koyemshi* means husband in Zuni and refers to the function of these performers as caring for the kachinas (Hopi ancestors who live in the clouds and protect the people; see also **Tsukuwimkya** for an explanation of kachinas). The indigenous Hopi tachukti are similar to the Zuni koyemshi; they act ridiculously, wear similar masks, cover their bodies in clay or mud, and generally wreak havoc on the audience members at ceremonies. One explanation for the Hopi's adoption of the Zuni term and some of the characteristics of the koyemshi is that with the Christian missionary presence, the tachukti's almost naked bodies and rude acts came to be seen as offensive. Although the actions of the koyemshi were also obscene, they were toned down from those of the tachukti of the early 1880s.

The tachukti are best known for their backward behavior. In fact, their names are a reversal of their actual traits; so that "the speaker" only babbles. All tachukti say the opposite of what they are doing and do the opposite of what they say. While they are running wildly about they speak calmly of walking; while they are shouting they say they are whispering; while they eat quickly they say they are in need of food. They enjoy teasing people by claiming to have something of theirs and asking for a description that is never complete. They scamper around the plaza asking for people who are right next to them, and they exaggerate fear and sorrow when they hear of any misbehavior. The tachukti are also powerful and dangerous; people never refuse them anything they ask, for fear of retribution. Although they have no formal society, the tachukti take their ceremonial activities seriously. They are selected for duty by each *kiva* (a *kiva* is an indoor ceremonial room, but the word also refers to the group who run the ceremonies conducted within) depending on the *kiva*'s needs. Each *kiva* within the village is responsible for certain ceremonies and duties, and it is up to the *kiva* leader to pick the tachukti for their performances.

Unlike the tsukuwimkya or the **paiyakyamu,** the tachukti enter the village on the ground, alongside the kachinas. They are always masked, and they may appear with the kachinas as their chorus or as a single drummer. The tachukti also perform their own dances in the plaza as well as entertaining the audience with their games. They are well known for their games, especially their guessing games. They interact with the audience in direct games as well as in parody. In one such game, an audience member is chosen to name the colors of the directions by choosing associated colors of corn. When people successfully complete such a task, the tachukti go wild with delight, picking them up, carrying them about, and making a spectacle of them.

The tachukti are not only pranksters or vehicles for amusement; they are also healers, messengers, dance directors, and warriors. The tachukti act as intermediaries between the kachinas and humans. The tachukti live near the kachinas and announce the entrance of the kachinas at the beginning of ceremonies. They are also sprinkled with cornmeal by the *kiva* leaders and given prayer sticks by the tsukuwimkya as they leave the plaza, and they deliver solemn prayers after their antics. The tachukti, whether they are called mudheads or koyemshi, represent an aspect of Hopi life dedicated to showing the power of all types of characteristics in the world. The tachukti show that although their behavior is odd, obnoxious, and entertaining, they can also be serious, respectful, and proper. Their duality demonstrates the balance within the world while emphasizing the necessity of proper, respectful, and beneficial behavior by all community members. (Bandelier 1954; Fewkes 1985; Hieb 1972; Parsons 1939; Stephen 1936; Steward 1991; Titiev 1944; Titiev 1971; Wright 1994)

Talawasi
Tubetube, *Papua New Guinea*

A talawasi is a jest or a joke. The people who live on the island of Tubetube are part of a larger chain of eight islands known as Bwanabwana. The people of Tubetube speak a distinct language known either as Kaina Wali or Kaina Tubetube. The term *tala* is often used in conjunction with the suffix *wasi*, denoting social interaction. The suffix literally means "sharing" and when used with *tala* the word connotes an active

form of joking and clowning, including that in ritual celebrations. In addition, *talawasi* can be used as an adjective to describe the humorous actions of a person or event.

On Tubetube women are the most prolific comic performers and jokesters. Although men may joke with each other in all-male groups, it is only elder women who perform talawasi at public events, including funeral rites. (See also **Ipani** for an example of similar funeral rites among the Mekeo.) Talawasi performances are normally social events, although women also joke among themselves, especially when they are working in their gardens or in other community activities. Talawasi activities, whether in ritual settings or in more informal settings, are humorous; the intent of the person delivering the jokes is to entertain rather than to humiliate. Talawasi performances, then, are the opposite of *kiyo*, or shaming ceremonies, in which the intent is to humiliate, shame, and punish someone for moral indiscretions. People who ignore social restrictions after funerals, who owe money, or who are sexually promiscuous are normally the focus of a *kiyo*.

Talawasi performances focus on humor either to entertain or to bring the community together after a death or some other loss or tragedy. The most common talawasi public performances are during funeral rites. After a person has died, a central mourner from the family and their kin are expected to mourn the loss for three days and nights. During this time, the body of the deceased is watched over by the mourners, who weep, wail, and sing over the body. In contrast to the deceased, whose body has been washed and painted for burial, the mourners do not groom themselves; nor do they eat or engage in any activities outside of mourning their loss.

After the three-day mourning period the body is buried, and the mourners become the focus of the community and the talawasi performance that follows the burial.

Just after sunset the community comes together for a feast. Before the food is served, an elder woman, who has already been chosen, steps forward to begin the talawasi. She first summons the people to join her in the central village clearing. Her tone is harsh, yet her demeanor suggests that she is jovial. Once a crowd has gathered the woman begins by telling simple stories and anecdotes directed at people in the audience. The woman exaggerates the escapades of actual people without ever directly referring to them. Part of the humor lies in the fact that in such a small community everyone knows whom she is making fun of. The woman drops hints and mimes the ridiculous actions of those who have been boastful, sneaky, or too self-important. The joking provides a way to let them know of their arrogance without direct confrontation.

As the night progresses, the talawasi become more animated. The woman jibes at those who are pompous; outsiders, especially Europeans, are a favorite target. The woman makes fun of outsiders' inability to do even the simplest task, such as gardening. At this point the woman may mock the outsiders by exaggerating their movements, imitating their speech, or otherwise burlesquing them. The harder the audience laughs the more ridiculously the woman acts. Women performing talawasi at funeral rites even mimic sexual practices. They use bawdy pantomime and satire to bring the crowd and specifically the mourners to laughter. The focus of their performance is always on integrating the mourners back into the community by taking them out of their mourning duties and making them laugh. As the performance goes on, each mourner is taken quietly from the audience to be bathed and given clean clothes, the final step in their reintegration into society. Once the talawasi performance is over, the mourners shift to their role as hosts, one of the most respected positions in the society. As hosts they now bring food to their guests and pay the performers for their work. As the feast comes to an end, the community is restored, and the deceased has been properly acknowledged.

Part of the humor in talawasi performances lies in the fact that mature women are normally quiet, dignified, and respected as elders who carry on the traditions of the people. In these public performances, however, they are bawdy, lewd, and obnoxious. The inversion of their roles makes their jokes even funnier.

Women on Tubetube, however, do not only joke at public performances. On the contrary, when in female groups women are known for their impromptu talawasi performances. In fact, on Tubetube it is considered antisocial for a woman not to get a joke or to ignore another who is joking. When women work together in their gardens, for example, they banter with one another, especially through mime and riddles. Women are known for their cunning wit in deciphering riddles and mimicking the shortcomings of their peers. Their joking, although funny, never crosses the lines of *yakasrsi* (respect). Instead, the impromptu talawasi performances are entertainment among peers as well as ways to direct someone's attention to her behavior. That is, women jest and joke about actual situations. In doing so they comment on the activities of others without making direct complaints. In addition, they simply poke fun at others for daydreaming, eating too much, or other benign activities that are simply humorous. Taken as a whole, talawasi performances on Tubetube are entertaining and fun for all. (Macintyre 1989; Macintyre 1992)

Tansa
Melanesia, *Nissan Atoll, Papua New Guinea*
Although the tansa, the "masters of terrible powers," are no longer active on Nissan

Atoll, their previous actions and their brand of sorcery and comedy are still celebrated through stories, masked dances, and traditional initiation rights.

The tansa were feared by the islanders because of their ability to kill and inflict pain and strife on individuals. Ironically, that fear came from the tansa's ability to use comedy to invoke fear. The tansa was said to have *barang*, a force that allowed him to practice his sorcery against people. The Tansa's *barang*, along with his skillful use of comedy, placed him in a powerful place in the island society. The tansa presided over the initiation of young boys into adulthood. In addition, he would give public performances periodically to demonstrate his power and to instill fear in people.

The islanders were concentrated in several villages connected through intermarriage and trade. People are still connected to one another by kinship as well as by their mutual reliance on subsistence crops and hunting. The tansa added to the anxiety of hunting because of their presence in the forest and power to wreak havoc on people. Living outside the villages, the Tansa were associated with many of the feared spirits of the forest as well as of the *san* (bad) places, which they were known to visit. The tansa were further perceived as "wild" because they did not wash themselves or cut their hair.

The power of the tansa was most readily seen in initiation ceremonies. The tansa of a particular village, wearing banana leaves covering his head, would lead a group of young boys out of the village. The boys never knew where they were going, but their destination was always a *san* place. The term *san* refers to whatever the people consider morally reprehensible and can apply to people, places, and situations. In this case, the tansa would take the boys to a place inhabited by nonhuman bush spirits that were known for harming people. Once there, the tansa exposed his penis, which was painted yellow, white, and red. The tansa would run around with his penis exposed, calling out unknown words. Any boy who smiled or laughed at the ludicrous sight would be clubbed. The tansa used comedy to show his power over the boys and over the world outside the village. Some tansa were even known as "eaters of men" because of their ambiguous positions.

The harsh treatment of the boys highlights the ideas of *matol* (shame) and comedy among the islanders. The tansa played on the belief that the ability to feel *matol* is what separates people from animals. Within the islander culture, *matol* can be brought about by boasting about oneself; by calling attention to oneself, especially through nudity or sexual exploits; or by doing something that results in injury to others. The tansa, then, embody the very concept of *matol*, yet they used it to show their power rather than their vulnerability. It is the connection between the comedy of their actions and their known power to cause harm that gave them status among islanders.

Islanders try to avoid *matol* at all costs. In initiation ceremonies, the boys learned that although the tansa was purposely acting shamefully, his disgrace was fueled by his power outside the village and his *barang*. The boys knew that if they acted in similarly disgraceful ways they would pay the price. Although there are no more tansa, male masked dancing societies use the same tactics to teach the importance of avoiding *matol* in one's life. In addition, children are told stories about the tansa, and almost all of the stages of life marked by ritual activities include some understanding of *matol* through comedic performances. (Lawrence and Meggitt 1965; Nachman 1981; Nachman 1982)

Tatú Bolita

Mocovi, *Argentina*

Tatú Bolita, a small, clever, sharp-witted armadillo who is in control of every situation he comes across, is one of the most popular characters in Mocovi oral tradition. The Mocovi both fear and respect him. Stories about Tatú, which the Mocovi tell for entertainment as well as for education, demonstrate that although strength and intelligence are beneficial, if used solely for selfish ends they can be harmful to the community.

Tatú can change his size, shape, and gender in any situation to outwit people as well as other animals. Mocovi stories are full of animal characters with both human and animal attributes. Such characters are the actors in the majority of Mocovi stories that deal with social and cultural laws; that is, these characters are used to demonstrate the proper way to act in Mocovi society.

Since Tatú's actions are usually the opposite of proper behavior, his antics are used as examples of how not to act. For example, Tatú is notorious for his unending appetite. He tricks people out of their food by lying to them or changing shape so they do not recognize him. Tatú is ruthless in his hunt for food. He will do anything to satisfy his large appetite, even maim or kill. In one story, Tatú Bolita killed his own children to get honey. He could not get the honey out of a tree on his own, so he hit his children against the tree one by one to shake the honey free. Always inconsiderate, Tatú invariably places his needs above those of others.

Tatú is often pitted against his rival and sometimes companion **Nowarera,** the fox. Tatú is portrayed as the clever, more sophisticated hunter and intelligent character, whereas Nowarera, although a sly character himself, is often the butt of Tatú's jokes and pranks. The two sometimes travel together in their quest for food, but Tatú almost always takes advantage of Nowarera. In one story, Nowarera saw Tatú eating biscuits by the side of the road and wanted some for himself. He asked Tatú how he had obtained so many biscuits for himself. Tatú

told him that delivery trucks had been driving by all morning full of biscuits. He told Nowarera that as the trucks got close to him he would lay down in a soft spot in the road with one of his shoulders aimed toward the truck. As the truck rolled over him the bump would shake the biscuits loose. Nowarera decided to try the trick for himself. What Tatú had not said and what Nowarera in his haste did not realize was that Tatú's protective shell kept him from being hurt by the trucks. Nowarera, of course, did not fare so well. He was thrown from under the passing truck and up against a tree, injured and still hungry. (Wilbert and Simoneau 1988a; Métraux 1946a)

Taugi
Kalapalo, *Central Brazil*

Taugi's name, which means "lies about himself," suggests his most notorious characteristic: his willingness to lie to get what he wants. He is also referred to as *tikambingifingi,* meaning "a secretive person" and *enggugukigine,* "the baffler." Taugi is known for his destructive tendencies, which bring with them the label of *itseke,* "powerful being." Taugi's power lies in his unpredictable nature, which is both dangerous and powerful. He is, however, also known by the Kalapalo as the "father" of humanity. In addition to creating human beings, Taugi also created light, fire, and water for human beings so they could live and flourish in their surroundings.

Taugi is a complex being, and stories centered on him and his activities are a focal part of Kalapalo oral tradition. Kalapalo narratives can be heard almost anyplace and anytime throughout the village. Kalapalo narratives are unique for their dialogic format. Storytellers choose a *tiitsofo* (a "whatsayer") to whom the story is given. The job of the *tiitsofo* is to interact with the storyteller by responding to parts of the story and affirming the storyteller's narrative. The *tiitsofo* also asks questions of the storyteller and contributes to the overall narrative performance. Although stories range from short, ten-minute dialogues to epics told over weeks, months, and even years, the structure generally remains interactive. Storytellers are evaluated on their ability to convey the message of their narrative as well as on the effectiveness of their particular presentation. Because the Kalapalo have many familiar characters, each storyteller has to work to provide a new and entertaining way of telling his or her story.

Taugi offers storytellers a range of possibilities. He is both a creator and a destructive force; he is uncontrollable and yet often works for the benefit of the community. He is dangerous, angry, and capricious, and he is the source of all human problems and negative emotions such as jealousy, envy, and greed. Taugi is a shapeshifter and an incorrigible liar. He can change shape, gender, and age to get what he wants. Taugi usually takes on the appearance of a father, uncle, grandfather, or some other male relative, but he is also known to appear as a woman or as a *kw ifi oto*, or "witch." In these various roles Taugi is best known for his intelligence and imaginative pranks. The Kalapalo value imagination and creativity, and although Taugi uses his power negatively at times, stories of his adventures are among the most popular.

Despite his cleverness, even Taugi gets duped when he acts without thinking or out of greed or lust. In fact, his sexual jealousy and promiscuity are oftentimes his own worst enemy. In Kalapalo stories, characters who proceed with their actions even after they have failed or after their actions are shown to be misplaced are characterized as "foolish." Although Taugi is both feared and revered, he is also considered foolish when his stubbornness gets in the way and he fails miserably in his attempts to outwit others.

In one story Taugi's rivalry with his cousin Kafanifani highlights his tendency to become distracted, jealous, and careless in his efforts to help people. Taugi invited the dead to return to the village because people were being "used up." The dead agreed, but they expected to be given gifts upon their arrival. Knowing this was proper procedure, Taugi's wives went to the river to prepare special drinks for their honored guests. Once they were at the water's edge, Kafanifani captured the women and carried them away underwater. Forgetting his powerful guests, Taugi was overcome by anger and jealousy, thinking that Kafanifani was taking advantage of his wives. Leaving the dead at the edge of the village without a proper escort, Taugi rushed off to find his wives. In the meantime the dead left the village and vowed never to return.

Searching for his wives, Taugi went to Kafanifani's house. When he arrived, he thought he saw his wives outside the door laughing at the way they had deceived him. When he got close, however, all he saw were pots. Dismayed, Taugi left for home. On the way he came across Agouti, who reminded him to "use his powers" to see through deception. He then returned to Kafanifani's house and realized that the pots were his wives disguised. He kicked and hit the pots until they changed back to his wives, and he avenged himself by throwing Kafanifani to the sky. The dead, however, had already vowed not to return to the village. Because of Taugi's jealousy he allowed himself to be tricked, and he put the community in jeopardy.

Many stories involving Taugi end with a particular effect on society and on the way people live today. Usually Taugi declares that things will remain as they are as the result of his actions. In the case of the story above, Taugi declares that the dead will remain "as they are" and will not be able to aid the living. In his jealousy and anger, Taugi severed humanity's ties with their deceased ancestors and thus left the living to protect themselves from many ill effects that the dead had once controlled. In other stories Taugi brings benefits to the community, such as when he brought erections to men. Once men could only have intercourse with their fingers. The men's wives began to complain that the *ufiti* lizard had all the erections. Soon even Taugi's wives complained and made fun of him because, for all his powers, he had no erections. But with Taugi's cleverness (and some prodding from his wives), he was able to get erections from the *ufiti* lizard, who kept them in his house. Taugi sweet-talked the lizard, calling him grandfather and sharing his plight with him; nevertheless, his greediness showed when he picked the largest erection in the building and fastened it to his penis. (Basso 1987; Basso 1988)

Tawkxwax

Mataco, *Argentina*
See **Tokwaj.**

Tenali Rama

Tamil Nadu, *India*

Tenali Rama is a *vikatakavi*, that is, a ridiculous jester, associated with King Krsnadevaraya of the Tamil and Telgu traditions. The king reigned from 1509 to 1529 when jesters such as Tenali Rama were popular figures in Indian courts. (See also **Bribal** for a similar figure in northern India.) In southern India, particularly, Tenali Rama has become a figure of legendary proportions. Throughout Indian villages one finds both oral and written stories of his antics. In fact, Tenali Rama is so popular that he has been written about in popular comic books and prose and his character occurs in Indian plays.

Tenali Rama appeared at a time in Indian history when peasants began to comment on their own situation. Most of the stories of Tenali Rama are told from the viewpoint of local villagers—who saw Tenali Rama as a hero—rather than from the viewpoint of the king's court. He was the one who brought the king back to "reality" by shocking him, tricking him, and being generally outrageous. Tenali Rama reminded all that although the king might be a ruler for the time being, nothing was permanent and chaos was always lurking around the corner. Part of Tenali Rama's appeal was that he was of the Brahman class before his conversion to a *vikatakavi*. Within traditional Indian society, the Brahmans are the priestly ruling elite. One must be born into the Brahman class, and to give up one's status as a Brahman is almost unthinkable. Yet this is exactly what Tenali Rama did.

The story of Tenali Rama's shift from Brahman to *vikatakavi* highlights his role as both a witty character and an able, intelligent young man who chose the path of a *vikatakavi* in order to demonstrate the absurdity of the hierarchy. As a young boy Tenali Rama enjoyed all the pleasures of life. He was given an education befitting his status and was expected to use his position of power to further his family name. However, he was always defiant. He tested the boundaries set by his family and his position by constantly questioning his teachers and priests. One day when he was out for a walk, he met a *sannyasin* (a person who leaves his community to search for enlightenment). The wise *sannyasin* taught the young Rama a mantra that would, if recited 30 million times in one night in the temple of Kali, bring the fierce goddess to him. Knowing that Kali was feared by all who worshipped her because of her raging temper and grotesque appearance, Tenali Rama decided to test the wise man's mantra.

That night at the temple of Kali, Tenali Rama recited the mantra 30 million times, and Kali appeared before him in all her rage. She had a thousand grotesque heads, blood dripped from her body, and a dark cloud surrounded her. In two of her four hands she held two different potions: the elixir of wisdom and the elixir of wealth. Kali told the young Rama to pick one, but, defiant as usual, Tenali Ram grabbed both potions and drank them down without hesitation. Kali was furious, and she began a tirade before the boy, but he just laughed at her enraged outburst. No one had ever dared to laugh at the powerful Kali. Stunned, she confronted the boy: "How dare you laugh at me?" Tenali Rama just stared at her and told her he thought it funny that she had so many heads and how hard it must be for her to wipe all her runny noses. Outraged, Kali shouted at him that he would forever be a *vikatakavi*. Happy at the prospect of such a title, Tenali Rama smiled and thanked her for the boon. Taken by the boy's wit and charm, Kali calmed down and told him that although he would always be a *vikatakavi*, he would be praised by kings and peasants alike for his jests at the royal court.

Kali's decree was fulfilled, and in story after story Tenali Rama is praised for his wit and boldness. He is able to turn the tables on anyone with whom he comes in contact. His most praised attribute is his ability to laugh in the face of terror, a trait he displayed in his first contact with Kali. Nor is Tenali Rama afraid of anyone—god, goddess, or human. He uses verbal play and subtle attacks to triumph. In one story, Tenali Rama offended a powerful king with his antics and was sentenced to death. Standing before the king, he was asked how he chose to die and he answered, smiling, "old age." Amused by his wit, the king laughed and let him go.

Tenali Rama is always doing and saying the unthinkable. One of his best-known character traits is his affinity with excrement. Tenali Rama always relieves himself wherever and whenever he feels the need. He sees defecation as one of life's greatest pleasures, and he tells people so. In one

story, Tenali Rama told a company of kings and sages that it was neither sex nor food that was the greatest pleasure of life but, rather, defecation. Disgusted by his pronouncement, the men kicked Tenali Rama out while they feasted. Tenali Rama sneaked by the chamber and locked the door with the men inside. When they attempted to get out to relieve themselves after their large meal, Tenali Rama asked them what they now thought was life's greatest pleasure. In an agony of aching bellies, the men finally admitted that Tenali Rama was correct.

In another story, Tenali Rama was taken to the execution chamber to be killed. Once there he asked the executioners if he could have one last purifying bath before his death; they consented and allowed him to bathe. The two swordsmen agreed that they would swing their axes at the moment Tenali Rama emerged from the bath, and as he bathed they positioned themselves on either side of the bath and awaited his signal. Just as he appeared to be coming out of the water, he turned and dove back in; the two men swung their axes, killing each other. Tenali Rama escaped unharmed.

Tenali Rama's power lies in his ability to outwit death, even when it appears he has no chance. In another story, Tenali Rama had again offended a king and was taken to be put to death. This time the royal elephant was to trample him to ensure his demise. Two of the king's men took him into the royal courtyard and buried him in the mud so that only his head was showing. Leaving him there, the executioners went to prepare the elephant. While Tenali Rama was waiting he saw a hunchback in the distance and called to him, telling the man that this new mud bath had cured Tenali Rama's hunchback and could do the same for his. Believing the crafty Tenali Rama, the hunchback dug him out and allowed him to bury him. Before the hunchback could tell the king he was not Tenali Rama, the elephant trampled him.

Tenali Rama is well known for his clever wit, but he is even better known for his ability to humiliate the king and his court. In one story, the king's mother was gravely ill and asked her son to bring her golden mangoes before she died. The king sent his best men to get the mangoes, but they did not return before she died. Scared that his mother would haunt him, forever unfulfilled, he asked the advice of his Brahmans, who told him that if he gave a golden mango to each of 100 Brahmans his mother's soul would be provided for and she could make her way to the next stage. Agreeing, the king prepared a feast and invited 100 Brahmans from the area. As they arrived they were greeted at the gates by Tenali Rama, who held a fiery branding iron. Tenali Rama told the Brahmans that whoever was branded would receive two or even three of the golden mangoes. Many of the Brahmans agreed, but when they asked the king for their additional mangoes he was furious. The king confronted Tenali Rama and demanded an explanation. Tenali Rama calmly explained that his mother had died of rheumatism and the doctors' had advised him to place hot irons on her joints, but he had been unable to do so before she died. Tenali Rama explained that he was simply following the example of the king so that his mother too could rest peacefully. Seeing the foolishness of his decree, the king praised Tenali Rama for his candor.

Part of Tenali Rama's appeal is due to the social commentary his actions provide. Not only does he trick, fool, and humiliate kings and Brahmans, but he does so without suffering any repercussions. He mocks Brahmanical power, ritual efficacy, and the traditional notions of hierarchy with his antics, always keeping the upper hand. Tenali Rama reminds the Indian masses that they too can have the upper hand and that the order they perceive is always balanced by chaos. (Kunjunni Raja 1969; Pope 1973; Robinson 1885; Shulman 1985; Siegel 1987)

To

Ngbaka, Central Africa: Congo

To, a spider character who is notorious for his misfortune, fails at almost all of his undertakings because he never prepares for his adventures and he almost always underestimates his opponents. To's jealous nature leads him to attempt to outdo others. He is inevitably unsuccessful because, acting alone, he is unable to overcome the majority of his opponents. To's unwillingness to ask for assistance is his biggest weakness. He tries to imitate others but rarely succeeds because he neglects to consider the entire situation and his own physical limitations. In many Ngbaka stories To is pitted against a wise character, usually initiated beings (that is, those who have been through the necessary rituals and therefore have the knowledge to perform powerful deeds). To, on the other hand, attempts to practice rituals and powerful rites to serve his own ends even though not initiated. His actions portray him as an ignorant imitator, always attempting to gain wealth, food, and positive attributes.

To's activities are those that would be considered uncouth if performed within Ngbaka society. For example, To refuses gifts from nonrelatives, a sign of disrespect. He engages in ritual activities that are dangerous for the uninitiated. He is forever trying to improve his reputation by imitating the more successful Gbaso, an initiated character who can perform feats that To can only imitate poorly.

Usually Gbaso tells To that not everyone can perform every feat and that one should not be afraid to ask for assistance. To's greediness and self-indulgence, however, keep him from heeding Gbaso's advice. In one story To left home to see if he could swindle Gbaso. When he arrived at Gbaso's house, he found him building a henhouse. To watched as Gbaso took a piece of wood, covered it with white mushrooms, and threw it quickly into the henhouse. As the wood flew through the air Gbaso, with his powers and knowledge of secret spells, transformed it into white chickens. When Gbaso saw To he offered his friend some of the chickens he had just produced, but To refused, saying that he could make his own. Gbaso tried to explain that not everybody could do as he had, but To refused to listen and left for his mother's house. He asked his mother for a piece of wood covered with mushrooms, telling her that he would soon supply her with all the chickens she could want. He took the piece of wood and threw it into the henhouse as he had seen Gbaso do. But when he threw the wood his shirt caught on the edge, and he too was carried into the henhouse and got his neck stuck in the wall. To's mother went to find Gbaso to help free To. As he pulled To from the wood, Gbaso told him that he should have let him explain the process before he tried it with no supervision.

In another story To's refusal to accept his status as one of the uninitiated not only gets him into trouble but ends up hurting others. One day To and Gbaso went hunting with a large group. After hunting for quite some time they became very thirsty, but there was no water in sight. Gbaso stamped his feet and announced, "My father stamped his feet; in turn I stamp my feet," and suddenly water began to gush up from the ground. Later To went hunting with a different group of friends, telling them that he knew how to get water in the forest. When the others asked To for the water, he stamped his feet and announced, "My father stamped his feet; in turn I stamp my feet." But no water appeared, and his foot got stuck in the ground. To's friends were so thirsty and tired that they died there in the forest. Once again To's egotism got the best of him, but

this time others lost their lives. (Burssens 1958; Paulme 1977; Thomas 1970)

To Ninilii

Navajo, *Southwestern United States: Arizona*

To Ninilii, also known as Water Sprinkler, is one of many Navajo *ye'ii*, or powerful beings, who performs at ceremonial functions throughout the year. In contrast to many of the more serious *ye'ii*, To Ninilii is best known for his humorous behavior at ritual performances. To Ninilii's humorous behavior is told in stories of the Navajo creation. When some of the other *ye'ii* were preparing for a ceremony, getting logs for a fire and collecting corn meal, To Ninilii ran alongside them making fun of their appearance, mimicking their actions, and playing tricks on them. To Ninilii's actions showed the other *ye'ii* that he was happy with what they were doing.

The *ye'ii* are central to Navajo life in many ways. Not only did the *ye'ii* help create Navajo life-ways, they continue to interact with the community through their representations in ceremonies. After the Navajo emerged from the underworld the *ye'ii* were created by First Man, who blew his own breath into their lifeless bodies to give them life. With this life force the *ye'ii* were able to begin the process of creating Navajo culture. The Navajo recognize several *ye'ii*, including Hashcheltii, usually translated as "Talking God," or "Calling God"; Naachee neezghani, "Monster Slayer," or "Born for Water"; and Ghaa askidii, "Humpback."

Each of the *ye'ii* has specific functions within Navajo ceremonies and may also be represented in sand painting used at curing ceremonies. The *ye'ii* are masked performers who never speak to the audience or each other. Their silence stems from the time of creation when the Corn Beetle called them and they failed to respond. Since then the *ye'ii* have been silent, and they are often referred to as *hashche*, which means "he failed to speak."

To Ninilii is named after his ability to control the rain and water supply for the Navajo. To Ninilli appears as a comical, antisocial being in the Nightway *yebichai* dance. As the other performers dance respectfully and in step, To Ninilii dances out of step, bumps into others, falls down, and disrupts the other performers. During the dancing he engages in amusing games with the audience. To Ninilii tries to call attention to himself by rolling on the ground, running around the dance plaza, and generally acting disrespectfully. He usually wears an animal skin on his head, which invariably falls off during his antics. As he searches for the skin he trips, stumbles, and incites the audience to laughter. To Ninilii is so self-involved that he never notices when the other dancers have left the plaza. He remains alone, striving for the audience's attention. (Curtis 1907; Matthews 1897; Matthews 1902; Reichard 1939; Reichard 1944)

Tokhuah
Mataco, *Argentina*
See **Tokwaj.**

Tokwaj
Mataco, *Argentina*
The creator and humorous deceiver Tokwaj is both selfish and helpful, practical and unpredictable, intelligent and foolish. His antics and his imaginative adventures brought the Mataco such things as rain, painless sexual intercourse, food restrictions, disease, and death. He helps people by creating things they need, but he also fails when he attempts to push the limits of nature too far. For instance, when he attempted to soar like a bird he fell from a cliff, hit his head, and remained unconscious for days. Tokwaj is portrayed as an artful deceiver as well as a skillful, creative force in the universe; like human beings, he is restricted by physical limits.

Tokwaj's adventures are often selfish but have positive repercussions for members of society. For example, before men and women lived together, women were wild and destroyed the men's crops; they terrorized men and injured their penises with the teeth in their vaginas, sometimes even mutilating them beyond repair. Tokwaj did not believe that the women could do him any harm, so he had intercourse with one. During intercourse, his penis was sliced off, but he replaced it with a bone. When he found the woman again she was squatting by a fire; he threw a stone between her legs and broke the teeth on her vagina. From then on, men could have sexual intercourse with women without being mutilated, and men and women learned to live together in one society.

The Mataco call their oral tradition *onkey*, "our way," and the stories reflect their history both prior to and after contact with Europeans and their foreign lifestyle, customs, and beliefs. In fact, the Mataco have included modern themes in their oral history by interweaving the modern themes with common characters such as Tokwaj. Stories are told mainly at night after the day's work has been completed. During the day male and female activities are relatively segregated, but at night the people come together to share meals as well as stories. *Onkey* brings together the myriad of activities and aspects of Mataco life and culture. Almost all the stories reflect the tension in the world between order and chaos, between what people do for themselves and what they do for their communities. These themes, although present in most stories, are brought to the fore in those concerning Tokwaj.

In Mataco oral tradition Tokwaj is pitted against Sipilah, the creator of the world and human life, in stories of creation and destruction. Sipilah appears as the powerful but not indestructible creator; Tokwaj deceives him time and time again, challenging his established ways. Although the two go head-to-head in many stories, they also complement each other and Mataco society. The pair demonstrate both the secure and the ambivalent aspects of human life. Although Sipilah appears to win some battles, Tokwaj usually comes back fighting and outwits him in the end.

In one story, Sipilah is credited with coming to humanity, disguised as a young boy, and teaching them how to catch and cook fish. The people praised Sipilah and lived off the fish for some time until Tokwaj appeared to the people as a skinny dog. Suspecting the dog was Tokwaj up to no good, Sipilah warned the people, and they beat him until he left the village. But this did not stop Tokwaj. Unscathed, he reentered the village as a young man and settled down with the people. Sipilah had warned the people against killing the *dorado* fish, but Tokwaj of course ignored the sanction and speared one anyway. After Tokwaj speared the fish, the water burst from underneath the tree and took the fish with it. Angry at his insolence, Sipilah ordered Tokwaj to lead the water to another suitable spot. Once he found a site he was to plunge his staff into the ground and the water would flow into it. Tokwaj walked and walked, but the water was rushing so fast that it swept him up and he drowned. When Sipilah heard the news, he gloated that the deceitful Tokwaj was dead. He went to the site of Tokwaj's death and pulled his intestines from the water to display his victory. But when Sipilah threw Tokwaj's intestines into the sky they landed in a tree, where they turned into climbing plants. The plants are still called the intestines of Tokwaj, and although Sipilah seemed to defeat him, Tokwaj came back again and again to challenge Sipilah's order. (Métraux 1939; Métraux 1946; Sullivan 1988; Wilbert and Simoneau 1982a)

Tsukuwimkya

Hopi, *Southwestern United States: Arizona*

The tsukuwimkya are a group of ritual performers who are best known for their loud exclamations, obscene behavior, mockery of other performers, and disruptive dancing. Individual performers are known as *tsuku*, and as a group they are referred to as *tsutskutu*. The tsukuwimkya perform only during spring and summer ceremonies, and

A kachina doll of the Native American clown trickster Tsukuwimkya. (Lowie Museum)

they perform mainly in the afternoon. The group enters the dance plaza over the rooftops and fumbles their way into the center of the plaza. Sometimes they fall down the ladders leading to the plaza, and other times they come down head first, just one example of their backward behavior.

The tsukuwimkya are said to belong to the underworld, where conditions are the opposite of what they are in the world in which the Hopi live today. In the underworld it is summer when it is winter for the Hopi; when it is light here it is dark there; whoever is powerful here is weak there; every trait is reversed in the underworld. Coming from such a place, the tsukuwimkya do everything the opposite of the accepted Hopi way. They mock the social mores and traditions of the Hopi through their crude behavior and disclose the transgressions of the audience members in their ritual play. The tsukuwimkya realize their disruptive behavior and generally confess their wrongdoings to the audience, but as they apologize, they mock and ridicule audience members. Yet being from the underworld, the tsukuwimkya are seen as the "fathers" of the kachinas (Hopi ancestors who live in the clouds and protect the people; the word *kachinas* can also refer to the masked performers who represent the ancestors of the Hopi) and the keepers of tradition. Their antics and disruptive behavior demonstrate what life would be like if people did not behave properly and act responsibly. Thus, in their backward and inappropriate behavior, the tsukuwimkya maintain Hopi culture.

During spring and summer ceremonies, the tsukuwimkya enter the Hopi dance plaza with great vigor. Their long journey from the underworld gives them the strength to perform for long periods of time. They fall down the ladders to the dance plaza and usually end up in a heap at the edge of the main dance circle. Seeming to ignore the kachinas' dancing, the tsukuwimkya dance alongside them, crash into each other, and finally realize they are not alone. When they discover they are not alone, they poke and prod the kachinas in an attempt to discover who they are and what they are doing.

The kachinas' work in ceremonial settings is necessary to maintain the balance of the Hopi world. Without them the Hopi would lose their connection to their ancestors. The kachinas are the opposite of the tsukuwimkya. They act quietly and respectfully and thus show the Hopi the proper and accepted ways of living. The tsukuwimkya, on the other hand, indulge in pranks and antics that disrupt and disturb the ritual process of the kachinas. Yet both are needed to demonstrate all the possible ways of being in the world. The actions of the tsukuwimkya are just as important as those of the kachinas.

Once they discover they are not alone in the center plaza, the tsukuwimkya question the kachinas, yelling at them and pushing them around in the plaza. Because the kachinas are under a vow of silence, they never speak to the tsukuwimkya during all of their antics. The kachinas act with great dignity as representatives of the ancestors. Going from one kachina to the next attempting to get some answers, the tsukuwimkya finally come to the kachina father, the village representative who leads the kachinas in and out of the plaza. It is the kachina father who explains to the tsukuwimkya and to the audience that the kachinas bring blessings and the gift of good crops, rain, fertility, and health to the Hopi. Hearing about these rewards, the tsukuwimkya quickly scheme to get some for themselves. They rush around, running into each other and causing a great commotion in their attempts to claim all the kachinas for themselves. After they have them they realize that they do not know how to get any of these gifts from them, so they return to the kachina father for advice.

He explains that the Hopi send their prayers with the kachinas throughout the year. Thinking they can receive the benefits of the kachinas' power, the tsukuwimkya shout out their wants, greedily demanding that the kachinas respond. They ask for good-looking girls, bushels of corn, cars, and money. The tsukuwimkya's wants are purely selfish. They ask the kachinas for things that will benefit themselves alone, never thinking of the community.

After the kachinas listen to the tsukuwimkya and finish their dances they exit the plaza, leaving the tsukuwimkya behind. Once they are gone, the tsukuwimkya discover a spruce tree planted at one end of the dance plaza. They rush to the tree and declare it their home. Their paternal aunts then emerge from the audience with gifts of food and water for them. Squatting by the tree, they eat gluttonously, devouring all the food they have been given. Once again the kachinas return and the tsukuwimkya mimic their actions, making fools of themselves trying to imitate the graceful moves of the kachinas. After their performance is complete the kachinas leave again without the tsukuwimkya. Alone in the dance plaza, the tsukuwimkya decide to build a house for themselves and have their "sister" take care of them. Their "sister" is usually a ragged, stuffed doll. They debate over the style of the house, and they envision a grand mansion full of everything they could want. Running to each corner of the plaza in search of components for their house, each *tsuku* returns with a handful of ashes. With the ashes they make an outline on the plaza ground representing their house. They wittily entertain the crowd by pretending to have locked themselves in the house, pushing and shoving and clamoring until they finally break free.

After more antics, the tsukuwimkya are met by the warrior kachinas. These kachinas are known for their great strength and power. Watching the antics of the tsukuwimkya, the warrior kachinas tell them to improve their behavior. The tsukuwimkya do not listen and continue playing games, running around wildly, and mimicking the power of all the kachinas. Finally the warrior kachinas attack the tsukuwimkya, throwing them in a pile, whipping them, and finally drenching them with water. Each *tsuku* then confesses his wrongdoings to the crowd, and as a group the tsukuwimkya sprinkle cornmeal on the kachinas in the proper manner. (People normally make offerings of cornmeal to the kachinas during ceremonies as an acknowledgment of their help throughout the year.) By offering cornmeal to the kachinas the tsukuwimkya show that they understand the importance of the kachinas and the wrongheadedness of their own actions, although the tsukuwimkya always return to their antics.

Within the tsukuwimkya group there are several subdivisions: the *sikya* (yellow), *paiyatam'* (red-striped), and *kocha* (white) *tsutskutu*. Although they do not always perform together, they dress and act similarly. They all wear an old kerchief or piece of cloth around their necks, black yarn at the wrists and knees, and a pair of shorts. Each carries a small bag of cornmeal around his neck and has a bandolier looped around his shoulders and draping to his waist that contains a small amount of food for his long journey from the underworld.

The *sikya tsutskutu* dab thick yellow paint over their entire bodies and heads and dab black paint underneath their mouth and each eye. In addition, a black dot is placed over each eyebrow and the nose. The black dots divert the *tsuku's* attention, making them look upward and causing them to stumble and fall into things. The *paiyatam' tsutskutu* also cover themselves with yellow paint. In addition, they paint red stripes over the yellow background. Their heads are covered with black sheepskin wigs, and red-stained tufts of rabbit fur dangle from their ears. Each *tsuku* also wears a red necklace and a small bag of cornmeal around his neck. The *paiyatam'* are especially known for their antics toward women. They sing obscene songs, make sexual gestures, and poke at the women in the audience. The women, however, retaliate by pouring buckets of water over their heads.

Their are two variations of the *kocha tsutskutu*, the *na'somta* (hair-knot) *tsuku* and the white *tsuku*. The hair-knot *tsuku* differ from the white *tsuku* in their headdress. Both varieties cover their bodies in the white clay that is found on the cliffs around the Hopi village. The white clay dries on the body to a spotted and speckled rather than evenly white coat. The hair-knot *tsuku* divide their hair into two rows on their heads and tie them upright with a string that drapes across the back of their heads. Both types of the *kocha tsutskutu* paint black dots over their eyebrows and a black arc underneath each eye and wrap blankets around their waists. All of the separate subdivisions of the tsukuwimkya participate in ceremonial antics and play with the kachinas, audience members, and each other. They use their disruptive behavior and interactions with the kachinas to show the opposite of the Hopi way of life. Through their disruptions and obscenities, they demonstrate what it is like to act in a non-Hopi manner. Yet their actions are a necessary and integral part of the Hopi life. (Bandelier 1954; Fewkes 1985; Hieb 1972; Parsons 1939; Stephen 1936; Steward 1991; Titiev 1944; Titiev 1971; Wright 1994)

Ture

Azande, Central Africa: Sudan

Ture, whose name literally means "spider," is characterized by his readiness to use any means necessary to get what he wants, especially food and sex. However, Ture is also credited with bringing water and fire to the Azande people, both of which they need to survive. Although Ture is a spider, he is referred to in Sangba Ture (Ture tales) by the personal, masculine pronoun *ko*, showing his ambivalent nature as both human and nonhuman, deceptive and helpful. Ture's dual nature demonstrates the Zande emphasis on the interactive nature of all beings in the cosmos. The Zande recognize several helpful and malicious beings. In Ture the Zande represent the combination of those forces. Ture presents an ambiguous case for the Zande in that he both constructs life and destroys it; he brings order to the world and then disrupts it; he gives people food and shelter and then he takes them away. Ture's dual character demonstrates the ambiguity of the Zande social and moral system, showing that the categories of these systems can be blurred, that what is helpful in some instances is destructive in others.

In the stories told about Ture, as well as in the dramatic performances of these tales, he frequently takes advantage of proper kinship relations by claiming to be someone's *ando* (maternal uncle) or *bakure* (a "blood brother" or close friend) and thus persuading that person to help him with his tricks and jokes. In Zande culture both the *ando* and *bakure* relationships are important; those are the people one can turn to in times of crisis. Ture shows his disrespect for these relationships by continually making false claims on them. (See also **Difisi** for an example of similar social relations by the Kaguru.)

The story of how Ture got food from the sky emphasizes his dual role. Ture lied to his neighbor, saying that he wanted to be his "blood brother," an honored position in Zande culture. The partners in this relationship are expected to help one another with food, shelter, and protection when needed. Ture's neighbor agreed, and Ture asked for food for himself and his wives. The man took him to the sky to get the food. Once they were back on earth, the man overheard

Ture speaking badly of him, saying that the man was stupid. The next time Ture went to his neighbor for food the man took him to the sky, but this time he left him there. Ture carried an enormous amount of food back to earth without any help; he brought every kind of food imaginable to the earth and spread it around to everyone, and so he is credited with bringing food to human beings for all time. Although Ture was disrespectful and used his blood-brother relationship deceitfully, he brought food to the world and allowed people to continue living.

Ture lies and cheats and he is greedy, but the Zande say that his intentions are never malicious. In one story, Ture was able to scare a bee into releasing him after the bee had captured him by transforming himself into an animal the bee had never seen before. Many of Ture's tricks are harmless, yet others result in death and tragedy. In one story Ture set fire to the entire village when he fell asleep after cooking some meat he had stolen from his neighbors. In another tale an entire hunting party was swallowed by a giant bird because Ture fell asleep when he was supposed to be keeping watch and singing protective songs for the hunters.

Ture introduces himself by saying, "I am Ture, the son of Ture's father, who tricks people all the time." Ture always does what he pleases, disregarding all restrictions. One story involving Ture and his mother-in-law exemplifies his disrespect for Zande social mores. Ture desired his mother-in-law, which is strictly forbidden. Telling her he needed her help to collect food for her daughter, Ture fooled his mother-in-law into staying out in the bush with him. He told her that the fire was low and persuaded her to sleep near him, but he also told her that her clothes might catch on fire and so persuaded her to remove them. As she slept, Ture began to ravish her. When she woke, she did not stop Ture because she enjoyed it. The next day they returned home and Ture's wife prepared them dinner. As they ate, Ture's penis said, "Oh! So you're eating termites, you who were just sleeping with your mother-in-law!" After this revelation, Ture and his mother-in-law were banished from the village for violating a sexual taboo. Ture's lack of respect for social restrictions constantly forces him out of the village, yet he always returns. (Evans-Pritchard 1967; Paulme 1977; Street 1972)

Txamsem
Tsimshian, *Northwest Coast of North America*

Txamsem is a giant being within Tsimshian society who uses his ability to change shape and identity to manipulate and trick people. He wears a raven cloak that gives him the appearance of a raven, but he does not have the stature and birdlike characteristics of a raven. Although Txamsem is usually portrayed as taking on the appearance of a raven, he also dons the skins of other animals to get what he wants. In various stories he wears a woodpecker's skin to fly into the sky, he covers himself in a duck's skin to seduce the chief's daughter, and he dons a deer's skin to steal food from unsuspecting hunters. Whatever his form, Txamsem is always hungry, greedy, and selfish, and he is always the instigator of trouble.

Txamsem plays tricks on everyone. He changes his shape to get everything he wants, from food to sex. Although Txamsem's tricks benefit himself, they are often harmful to others. He maims and kills people to satisfy his hunger. He ruins villages, destroys homes, and breaks weapons—all to fulfill his needs. In Txamsem the Tsimshian have a character who epitomizes the opposite of proper behavior. Although he is credited with aiding the Tsimshian in the creation of their society, Txamsem is best known for his upheaval of that same society through his selfish behavior.

Tsimshian society is based on small family units with an intricate system of crests relating families to each other. A crest is not only a physical representations of a group but also a symbol of the group's cohesion and interconnection with other groups within the community. In their physical manifestation crests portray the lineage and history of the group in relation to their clan (Raven, Grizzly Bear, Eagle, and Wolf). Thus the crests denote not only what clan one belongs to but also the history and status of the group. The Tsimshian further divide their society into four subsections (divisions), giving each division a distinct role and status within the society. (See also **Yetl,** a Tlingit raven character, and **Nankilslas,** a Haida raven character, for similar systems.)

Txamsem is credited with stealing the sun and fire from the monsters who kept them from the world before the Tsimshian lived on the earth. By stealing the sun and fire, Txamsem provided the first human beings with basic necessities for sustaining themselves. The irony in the character of Txamsem is that his seemingly unselfish actions, such as bringing the sun and fire to the world, result in his ability to disrupt that same world. For example, Txamsem brought sunlight to the world because he could not find enough food in the darkness. Although Txamsem's action allowed people to find food as well, his motivations were selfish and the result was that he could steal food from people or trick them out of it instead of having to hunt for it himself.

Stories about Txamsem relate not only his tricks and negative behavior but also the inappropriateness of such actions for the community. Txamsem is seen as a humorous character, but he also represents the negative aspects of people's behavior. Stories about Txamsem show children and adults alike the negative repercussions of greedy, self-indulgent activities. In one story Txamsem stole from his relatives after they refused to give him a portion of their food. Txamsem claimed that he was enti-

tled to a share of the fish they had caught, but his kinsman denied him their food because of his laziness. Txamsem waited until they had gone to sleep and took what he believed was rightfully his. When his relatives woke they found their fish gone; many starved to death before they could get more. Txamsem justifies his actions by claiming to have the same rights as those who contribute to the group's welfare. Stories about Txamsem, however, show that his actions are purely self-motivated.

Txamsem will take advantage of anyone to satisfy his unending hunger and greed. His only companion is his own excrement. In story after story Txamsem seeks advice from his excrement on how to finish a prank or how to get the most of what he wants. In one story Txamsem tried to catch a steelhead salmon. He kicked over a rock in the mud and called belligerently to the salmon, "Ha, salmon come up to the beach." The salmon jumped out of the water and knocked Txamsem down. But this was all part of Txamsem's plan. Twice more Txamsem called to the salmon, overturning another rock each time. The third time he called to the salmon and the salmon jumped out of the water, he was trapped in the holes Txamsem had left from the rocks. Because Txamsem was lazy and depended on others for his food, however, once he had the salmon he did not know how to cook it. He sat down on the beach and asked his excrement what to do with the fish. His excrement told him how to smoke the fish in a hole. The story of Txamsem and the steelhead salmon, however, has another twist. The story ends with Txamsem changing crows from black to white after they steal his fish and leave only their excrement behind, and it thus shows Txamsem's power to change the course of the world. Although Txamsem is portrayed as a humorous character, his power is never underestimated. (Boas 1970; Durlach 1928; Goodchild 1991; Miller and Eastman 1984)

U

Utuum-khriin min

Bimin-Kuskusim, *Papua New Guinea*

Utuum-khriin min is the general term for Bimin-Kuskusim comedic prankster figures. This term is used to designate characters in *utuum-khriin sang*, that is, oral literature. These tales are part of a larger category of *agetnaam sang*, wisdom tales. These stories pose or reveal moral dilemmas through the actions of the utuum-khriin min. The stories are spoken, sung, performed, and accompanied by instruments, especially drums. The plots of the stories contrast social norms and proper relations by casting the characters in situations in which they violate normal social order, specifically sexual and ritual restrictions. This genre of stories is part of the Bimin-Kuskusim's oral tradition and is used especially in rites of passage. The stories are often concerned with the trickster character's lack of *finiik* (socially proper aspects of personhood), which is represented in the stories by the lack of fire. In Bimin-Kuskusim society a character who does not have fire is an undeveloped *kunum* (human, person).

A special group of *utuum-khriin sang* stories are used to show boys the *diab kunum* (man's path). In male initiations elders relate the tales to the initiates, and then the children interpret the stories and the morals revealed in them. The boys and the elders interpret the stories anew each time they are told. After the elders tell the stories, the boys are left to discuss and discover the moral for themselves. At this stage in their lives they are familiar with the proper ways to act and with the antics of characters such as **Gabruurian** and **Kamdaak Waneng**. Through their interpretation, the boys are set on the "man's path" of life in Bimin-Kuskusim society.

The stories are constantly changing, depending on the storyteller and the setting, but they are always concerned with *weeng keeman* (moral instruction).

Utuum-khriin min characters appear in many forms. They generally live outside the community in the high forests and are set apart by their morally inverted behavior, including sexual liaisons with their family as well as improper ritual behavior such as using ritual objects incorrectly or ignoring sanctions during rituals. The characters are sexually ambiguous and often they are physically deformed; they violate all social boundaries with their pranks. For instance they eat the food of the opposite gender, ignore ritual sanctions by appearing in places they are not allowed (male in female ritual or vice versa), and misuse ritual objects such as the *tiinba* leaf.

In one story Gabruurian wrapped *tiinba* leaves around his penis, showing the utmost disrespect for the sacred nature of the leaf. The sexual exploits of these characters further violate proper *naa-kunum* (kin, literally "same person") relationships by being incestuous or by involving one who is not yet initiated into a male or female role. Gabruurian, for example, is constantly seducing young, uninitiated girls into having intercourse with him. These types of actions offend the spirits and ancestors; the possibility that they might take retribution puts the entire group in danger. (Beidelman 1980; Poole 1983; Poole 1987)

V

Vidusaka
India

The vidusaka, a clown character, is one of the standard characters in traditional Sanskrit dramas. Classical Indian literature includes a cannon of plays, stories, and epics that deal with moral, ethical, religious, and social issues. Sanskrit literature is brought to life in books and in oral traditions as well as in plays, performed throughout India today.

In these dramas the vidusaka is juxtaposed against a king or other *nayaka* (hero) character. The vidusaka is portrayed as a dwarf, deformed, ugly, clumsy, and totally without any social graces. He is the opposite of the handsome, elite *nayaka* in all ways, physically, socially and morally. Physically the vidusaka illustrates the ugly and the grotesque; socially he is inept at even the most basic skills; morally he is confused at best. The vidusaka lacks any self-awareness, either of his reprehensible appearance or his ludicrous actions. He chases after young girls, although his ultimate desire is food. His lust for food prompts his most foolish and comedic actions.

In one Sanskrit drama, aptly titled *Mahodara*, the great stomach, the vidusaka enters the play holding his enlarged stomach and crying out in pain because he has indigestion from stuffing himself. The audience delights in the vidusaka's pain, which is self-induced. During this and other dramas, the vidusaka directs any conversation toward food. Once the conversation is on the topic of food, the vidusaka bumbles about, trying to find any morsel or crumb on the stage. He salivates and directs the audience's attention away from the main drama at hand to his self-proclaimed plight.

The vidusaka craves all food, but he especially loves *modakas*, sweetmeats. He sees food in all situations; he will stare up into the sky and see the moon as two *modakas*. The vidusaka thus simplifies the Sanskrit understanding of pleasure to eating. Unlike the *nayaka*, who is normally engaged in some type of romantic struggle, the vidusaka's only worry is getting food. His actions contrast with the serious and all-encompassing focus of the main characters. In this way he relates any drama to the most common and basic of human needs. His lust for food overshadows the main characters' struggles in love and pokes fun at their worrying about such things as love, companionship, and proper actions.

The vidusaka is easily frightened, insecure, and lazy. He runs from the *nayaka* when he has pushed his vulgarity too far. Clamoring to get away from the *nayaka*, he shows his physical ineptness. The vidusaka, however, tempts other characters and can even outwit sages and kings. He uses his innocence to get others to believe his far-fetched stories, which usually leads to his getting something for nothing. He is terribly lazy. He mocks the idea of education, saying that he learns all he needs from others. In all that he does the vidusaka reverses the norms of Indian society, in which education, intelligence, morality and courage are rewarded.

The vidusaka, however, also highlights the ambiguous, unknowable, and essential parts of life. Sanskrit dramas focus on the unity of the *nayaka* and the vidusaka, seemingly opposite characters. The vidusaka shows the absurdity of taken-for-granted social mores and illustrates the necessity of basic human qualities. In Sanskrit dramas, the vidusaka shatters illusions of a perfect world or a perfect life. (Bhat 1959; Jefferds 1981; Shulman 1985; Wells 1963)

Vishnu
India

Vishnu, the Hindu deity of preservation, is known for his comedic triumphs over other deities and monsters. Part of Vishnu's power is his ability to triumph through his wit. Although his physical appearance can be whatever he wishes it to be, Vishnu uses his intellect and trickery to outwit others.

Vishnu is one of the three main deities in the Hindu pantheon, and numerous tales are told of his escapades. In addition, as a powerful deity, Vishnu has many avatars (physical incarnations of himself) on earth (see **Krishna**). As a deity and a artful prankster, Vishnu reminds people of the ambiguity in life. Far from being a one-sided deity, Vishnu highlights the many varied aspects of life, not only in his own dealings with other deities, monsters, and humans but through his avatars as well.

One famous story about Vishnu shows his cleverness and his ability to alter the course of the world with his wit. Vishnu and the other deities had been fighting for some time to claim dominion over the monsters and other malicious forces in the cosmos. The battle between the gods and demons had turned into a contest of wits. Each side scored some victories, but neither could win ultimate control. After the demon Hiranyakasipu had won a round in the cosmic battle, he was assured by Brahma (the creator) that he could not be killed during the day or night, neither indoors nor out, and neither by man nor beast. Hiranyakasipu gloated that he now ruled the cosmos. Hiranyakasipu was ignorant of the fact that the ultimate battle could never be won or lost,

that the existence of the cosmos was always to be in flux.

Knowing that Hiranyakasipu's arrogance would cloud his judgment, Vishnu devised a scheme to turn the tables on him. Part of Hiranyakasipu's victory tirade was his warning that all gods, beasts, and men were to worship him as the new ruler of the cosmos. But Hiranyakasipu's own son refused. Instead, he pledged allegiance to Vishnu, who he said was everywhere. Hiranyakasipu was enraged by his son's disobedience and began to beat him, asking him where Vishnu was now that he needed to be saved. His son replied again that Vishnu was everywhere. In his anger Hiranyakasipu grabbed a bat and swung it at a large pillar, shouting that if Vishnu was everywhere he would be in the pillar and soon would be dead. Just as Hiranyakasipu took aim to swing, Vishnu appeared, neither as man nor beast but as a man with a lion's head, neither indoors nor out but in the doorway, neither during the day nor at night but at dusk, and he slew Hiranyakasipu.

In a similar story of cleverness and wit, Vishnu confronted another demon. The malicious Bali had conquered the cosmos and was tormenting both humans and gods. Changing himself into a dwarf, Vishnu appeared in Bali's court and asked if he might have all the land he could cover in three steps. Laughing at the audacity of such a wish by a dwarf, Bali agreed. Before the smirk had left Bali's face, Vishnu had transformed himself into a giant and covered the earth in his first step, the sky in his second, and the waters in his third, reclaiming the cosmos for the gods.

The many faces of Vishnu are honored by Hindus throughout India. His is an ever-changing image, but the most popular is his image as a cosmic prankster. In both oral and written traditions a myriad of stories are recounted as a testament to his cleverness and power. Temples, statues, and paintings attest to his popularity, and many festivals

A high-relief architectural sculpture of the Hindu deity Vishnu at the Keshava Temple in Somnathpur, India. (Sheldan Collins/Corbis)

demonstrate his emphasis on humor and playfulness. For example, the Onam festival in Kerala celebrates Vishnu in song, dance, and comedic plays. People focus on the playfulness of life by putting aside their daily routines and sharing in games and performances attributed to Vishnu. Highlighting the lighter side of life, the people of Kerala mock characters such as Bali and Hiranyakasipu by exaggerating their foolishness in the performances of their demise at the hands of Vishnu. Ultimately, however, the aim of this festival, as with others throughout India, is fun. (Siegel 1987)

Wakalulu

Lamba, *Central Africa: Zimbabwe; Congo*

Kalulu refers to a small hare, but in folktales *Wakalulu* refers to the character Mr. Little Hare, an artful prankster. He is best known for his cunning ability to make the most of any situation, even if it seems he will surely lose. He challenges lions, elephants, and hyenas and outwits them all. Wakalulu bridges the gap between wit and wisdom. He demonstrates that these two character traits are neither mutually exclusive nor incompatible but complementary. In Wakalulu the Lamba present a character who proves that power does not belong only to the strong and that actions may have more than one outcome. Time and time again, Wakalulu challenges dominant power structures by forcing those in power to admit that they are susceptible to pranks.

Stories about Wakalulu are enacted in a storytelling performance. The performance is just as important as the actual story. The audience and the storyteller interact throughout by call and response. There is no formalized procedure. (See also **Anaanu, Wanto, Wosi,** and **Yiyi** for examples of this type of storytelling.) Storytellers pick from a variety of characters and themes, but it is always their goal to invent new scenes and adventures for the familiar characters. For example, stories now include airplanes, cars, and money, all the result of European contact. The flexibility of the stories and the performances, as well as Wakalulu's character, speak to the inherently ambiguous nature of the cosmos.

The Lamba distinguish two different types of oral narratives: the *ulusimi, icisimi,* or *akasimi* and the *icisimicisyo*. The *ulusimi, icisimi,* and *akasimi* have been referred to by scholars as "choric stories" because songs are interspersed within the stories.

The second type, the *icisimicisyo,* is a larger category that includes folktales and stories that range in topic from hunting and gardening to moral tales showing the proper ways to act. Both types of stories deal with several topics of Lamba life. *Icisimicisyo* stories are told by both male and female storytellers. The characters in the stories are both human and animal, although animal stories tend to be the most popular. Within these tales animals are given human traits and characteristics; many are referred to with the respectful prefix *wa,* which means "Mister." Adding the prefix denotes the status of the characters in the stories; they are not only animals but are representative of humans as well.

Wakalulu is one of the most familiar characters in *icisimicisyo* tales. The tales demonstrate his cunning ability to get what he wants without penalty. Once Wakalulu tricked the lion out of his food by impersonating one of the lion's servants. Wakalulu went to the lion and told him his cubs were hungry. The lion ordered Wakalulu to feed them. Wakalulu walked into the lion's kitchen and took all the food he wanted; no one suspected him because they believed him to be a servant. Wakalulu left the lion's house with plenty of food for himself, and the cubs went hungry. In another story, Wakalulu told the lioness that he was pinching the baby cubs to make them cry so she would chase him into a trap he had set. Trapped, Wakalulu and his friends drank from her nipples.

223

Only the tortoise, Wafulwe, is able to catch Wakalulu in his pranks. For example, once all the animals got together to dig a well for the village, but Wakalulu never showed up to help. After they were finished the lion asked where Wakalulu was, but nobody knew. The lion thus decreed that if Wakalulu was found trying to drink the water from the well he should be killed. Wakalulu heard of the decree. The next morning the rhinoceros waited at the well to see if Wakalulu would come for water. Soon Wakalulu came from behind the bushes with his calabash and a jar of honey. The rhinoceros caught him and tried to take him to the lion, but Wakalulu told him he had a special food called "tightly bound" that any cunning person should eat. He asked the rhinoceros to try it and said that if he did not like it he could take him to the chief. The rhinoceros tried it and liked it, but Wakalulu said he could only eat more if he was tied up, as that was the proper way to eat the special food. Wakalulu tied the rhinoceros up and then took all the water he needed. The next day the elephant tried to catch Wakalulu, but the same thing happened. Finally Wafulwe, the tortoise, said he would catch Wakalulu. Knowing that Wakalulu would try the same trick, Wafulwe was prepared. When Wakalulu came to the well, Wafulwe was waiting with rope to tie him up. Wakalulu was not able to fool the tortoise, who knew Wakalulu's prank. Instead, Wafulwe turned the trick around on him; he told Wakalulu he would taste the food, but as Wakalulu approached, the tortoise caught him and tied him up. Even Wafulwe, however, was only partially successful. After he took Wakalulu to the lion, Wakalulu was able to convince the king to put him to death in the sand. Once they reached the sand Wakalulu burrowed down and ran quickly to safety.

Wakalulu is selfish and greedy, and he steals from his friends, neighbors, and family. Once he made friends with a pack of guinea fowl. For days the guinea fowl and Wakalulu played and ate together. One day Wakalulu told them he had a new game. He built a crate and asked the guinea fowl to get in. Trusting him, they all leaped into the crate. Once they were in the crate, Wakalulu tied it up and carried it over his head into the bush. After a while the guinea fowl asked Wakalulu to let them out, but he would not. He said he had another friend who wanted to meet them. When they reached the outskirts of the village, he hung up the crate and along came a leopard. He told the leopard he wanted to be his friend and to show his friendship he would give him the guinea fowl. That night Wakalulu and the leopard feasted on the guinea fowl.

In another tale Wakalulu tricked the big hare out of his food. Wakalulu told him that he should pick not the ripe berries but only the green ones. Wakalulu told the hare that his mother had told him not to eat the ripe berries because they were dangerous. Believing him, the big hare picked only the green ones, and Wakalulu picked all the ripe ones for himself. Wakalulu ate well, but the big hare was sick from eating the green berries. In another story Wakalulu and a monkey went hunting. When they got back Wakalulu told the monkey to go down to the river behind the house and wash up for dinner. Once the monkey left, Wakalulu followed him and burned the grass behind him all the way, and then he ran back to the house. Each time the monkey walked back to the house his hands got dirtier than they had been when he left because of the ash on the ground. For hours the monkey went back and forth. When he finally gave up and went into the house, he found that all the food had already been eaten.

Wakalulu is lazy as well; he does not like to participate in the activities of the rest of the village, and he often outwits the group to gain food, water, and shelter from their hard work. Through all of this, however,

Wakalulu is looked upon as a wise and intelligent being. Sometimes he is even consulted when things go wrong for others or when the people need advice on how to deal with a more malicious thief. Wakalulu shows both that antisocial behavior harms the community and also that, at times, pranks are able to baffle those who are misusing their power. (Doke 1927; Doke 1934; Finnegan 1970; Werner 1968)

Wanto

Gbaya, *Central Africa: Cameroon; Congo*

Wanto is a popular spider character of the Gbaya. He is rarely characterized as actually being a spider, being more commonly viewed as an ambiguous human character with the physical manifestation of a spider. Six categories describe the different types of oral narratives within the Gbaya's rich oral history and literature, which they continue to create. One of the largest categories is called *to*, meaning "tale." Over one-third of all the stories told within this genre have Wanto as the central character. In addition, the word *wanto* can be separated into *wan*, meaning "chief," or "master," and *to*, which gives Wanto the title of "master of the tale."

Stories about Wanto are told in relaxed social settings. Oral performances among the Gbaya are a community activity. Although there is clearly one storyteller, the audience participates by commenting throughout the event, both on the storyteller's performance and on the actions of the characters in the stories. The performer enacts his or her version of the tale, adding or leaving out parts and creating the characters in his or her own way to make the story unique. For example, Wanto is known for confusing words, pronouncing them incorrectly and speaking with a strange lisp that makes him hard to understand. In stories about Wanto, performers create Wanto's speech patterns differently to get across the same point about Wanto's ineptness. Thus the *to* genre is always expanding. Although the characters are well known and their actions sometimes predictable, Gbaya storytellers make the story and the moral relevant to their contemporaries and their current situations by incorporating modern events and objects into their stories. Stories in this genre are entertaining, but they also contain morals and pass on to children the ideals and social mores of the Gbaya culture. (See **Anaanu, Wakalulu, Wosi,** and **Yiyi** for further examples of interactive storytelling.)

Part of Wanto's appeal is that he is both a hero and a prankster. Wanto never maliciously tries to hurt or deceive others, but in his selfish and greedy attempts to satisfy his unending hunger and passion for dancing he winds up tricking people, stealing, and even hurting members of his own family. Wanto's lustful appetite for food is shown not only by his taking food from his own wife and children but in the names he chose for his children. Each of Wanto's children is named after a cooking utensil; one is named "stirring stick"; another, "cooking pot"; and still another, "food scoop." In addition Wanto continually shows disrespect for social mores such as proper hunting etiquette (by distracting others with his dancing while they are hunting) and responsibilities to one's family (by not sharing his food). Still, Wanto is the favorite character within the *to* genre; storytellers and audiences alike delight in hearing about his adventures and misadventures.

Wanto's insatiable appetite and his love of dancing continually get him into trouble. Although dancing is an important part of Gbaya culture, Wanto's love of dancing usually exceeds the bounds of acceptable behavior. The Gbaya recognize dancing as part of ritual and social settings. Dancing, therefore, has a specific place in Gbaya culture. Wanto, however, ignores these social boundaries and offends people with his dancing. For instance, in one story, Wanto and a hunting party left town for the bush. On the way, Wanto took every opportunity to stop and dance. He stopped and danced under a mahogany tree, he stopped and danced when the birds were overhead, and he stopped and danced when he met others along the path. Finally the others left Wanto behind. When the hunters returned along the path, Wanto was waiting for them. He knew that it was the custom to give one's scraps to those along the path, and so he was able to get food without having to work for it. When Wanto returned home, he carried the basket of meat scraps over his head into his house. Once inside he told his wife to be very careful not to knock over the basket because if she did all the meat would turn to scraps. When he put the basket down, he pretended to trip over his wife and spilled the meat, thus turning it into scraps. He blamed the fact that they had only scraps to eat on his wife.

In another story Wanto and his family set out to make a camp in the bush, where Wanto said there would be good hunting. As his wife prepared their camp, Wanto left to set some snares around the area. After setting snares at the base of the hill and near the lake, Wanto came back to camp for two days. On the third day, he checked his snares. His family was hungry, and they were counting on Wanto to catch some animals for them. When Wanto came to his first snare he saw that he had caught a bush buck. Pleased with himself, Wanto tied up the buck and carried it to the top of the hill overlooking his camp. From the top of the hill, Wanto disguised his voice and threw down the animal, saying that no one was to eat it except Wanto. When Wanto arrived back at camp his wife told him of the voice and the bush buck that had fallen from the top of the hill. That night Wanto had a feast for himself while his family went hun-

gry. The next day Wanto did the same thing. Wanto sat eating by himself, and his wife, Laiso, went to get some water. On the way she stubbed her toe on a tree. The tree told her about Wanto's trick and how to get back at Wanto without his knowing. Laiso went back to camp angry but determined to teach Wanto a lesson. When she arrived back at the camp, she rubbed some tree sap on Wanto's head without him knowing. The next day Wanto left to check his snare and again found a large animal. Again he dragged it up the hill, raised it up over his head, and called out that no one but he was to eat it. This time, however, as he tossed the animal, he went tumbling with it because his head stuck to the animal's hair. Wanto was hurt badly, but that night Laiso and the children ate well.

In most tales about Wanto his tricks backfire. Although Wanto is clever, his attempts to get those things that are not rightfully his usually end in his defeat. (Finnegan 1970; Noss 1971; Paulme 1977; Samarin 1966)

Wayayqalachiyi
Toba, *Argentina*

Wayayqalachiyi, an insatiably hungry fox with the power to change shape to deceive others, is notorious for using his power of transformation to get the best of others. He disregards all social mores and laws by hurting, killing, stealing, lying, and cheating to get what he thinks he deserves. Like his animal counterpart, Wayayqalachiyi is crafty, quick, and always around when he is not wanted. Like all foxes, Wayayqalachiyi steals food from people's gardens and kills their livestock.

Although Wayayqalachiyi is characterized as a fox, in stories he is portrayed with human features and flaws. He talks people into doing things they do not want to do and outsmarts even the most cunning animals. In one story he appeared as a missionary and persuaded the people to move their camp; he then gorged on all their food. In another he sent an old woman to get water and ate her grandchildren. Wayayqaláchiyi's ruthless actions are perhaps his most notable characteristic, making him both a feared character and a respected adviser.

Toba oral narratives focus on Wayayqaláchiyi as the preeminent deceiver in society. Stories about him and his adventures demonstrate the negative effects of antisocial behavior as well as the Toba's recognition of multiple types of beings in the universe. Toba oral literature is full of characters like Wayayqaláchiyi, characters who are not human but who have human characteristics and personalities. For example, thunder speaks through the giant anteater, a giant dog saved people from a cataclysmic flood, and the jaguar taught people how to cure certain diseases.

Wayayqaláchiyi is known not only for manipulating and tricking people but also for bringing important things, especially fire, to the Toba. Before people had fire, Wadíñi (rabbit) was the owner of fire, and he did not allow people to use it. People ate their meat raw, and they could not warm themselves during the cold season. Finally the hummingbird decided to steal the fire from Wadíñi. This was no easy task, so he enlisted the help of Wayayqaláchiyi and others. Distracting Wadíñi with his charm, the hummingbird was able to steal the fire. Once the animals had it, no one could decide what to name it, until Wayayqaláchiyi told everyone that it was *dolé* ("fire"). After their success, the animals had fire, but people did not. Wayayqaláchiyi broke off a piece of wood from the smoldering fire and distributed it to the people.

In another story, Wayayqaláchiyi brought painless sexual intercourse to men. Before Wayayqaláchiyi intervened, women's vaginas were full of teeth that would cut or tear off men's penises. One day, Wayayqaláchiyi gloated that he would break the teeth of the women's vaginas. Ignoring the eagle's warning that he would not survive in one piece, Wayayqaláchiyi had intercourse with one of the women, and his penis was chewed off. Pretending it did not hurt, Wayayqaláchiyi went to the woods and fashioned a new penis for himself out of bone. The next day he went back and had intercourse with a woman and his new penis broke all her vaginal teeth. Following Wayayqaláchiyi's example, all men broke the vaginal teeth of the women and married them.

Wayayqaláchiyi's antics affect the world in terms of the form or shape of animals or natural features. In one story, Wayayqaláchiyi roamed through the forest for days eating everything in sight. He could not get enough food to satisfy himself. After gorging himself for days he was so bloated and constipated that he could hardly move. Lying down on a path he cried for help from his friend the woodpecker. He promised the woodpecker all the food he had if he would peck a hole in his anus to relieve him. The woodpecker agreed and pecked away until finally a pile of excrement blew out of Wayayqaláchiyi's anus and covered the woodpecker's head. Ever since, all woodpeckers have a reddish-brown crown on their heads. Wayayqaláchiyi is also responsible for human beings' acquisition of watermelons and chickens and for the striped color of some small birds. His actions, although sometimes beneficial, are usually burdensome to people.

More often than not, Wayayqaláchiyi's adventures lead to trouble for others. In one story, Wayayqaláchiyi was drinking *chicha* (alcohol) and singing. His friend **Keyók** (the jaguar) heard him and wanted to join in the fun. Wayayqaláchiyi saw Keyók coming and offered him some of the *chicha*. After they had been drinking awhile Keyók wanted to sing with Wayayqaláchiyi, but Wayayqaláchiyi told him he could not sing without a rattle like his. Wayayqaláchiyi's rattle was actually his heart. Not sure if he should believe Wayayqaláchiyi, but too drunk to argue, Keyók allowed Wayayqaláchiyi to stick his arm up Keyók's anus to get to his own heart. Several times Keyók cried out in pain, but Wayayqaláchiyi assured him that he would be fine. Finally, as Wayayqaláchiyi grabbed Keyók's heart, he passed out and died immediately.

One of Wayayqaláchiyi's greatest strengths is his ability to revive himself after he dies. Time and again he is killed because of his clumsiness, eagerness, or egotistical antics, but he is always able to revive himself. Using either water or wind to bring himself back to life, Wayayqaláchiyi always exclaims that he has had "a great sleep." Once Wayayqaláchiyi wanted to fly like the eagles. He tried and tried to change into an eagle but he could not, so he decided to make his own wings and fly. He glued some feathers to his torso, climbed to the top of a tree, and jumped out, flapping his wings. He flew higher and higher, approaching the sun. As he got closer to the sun the heat intensified and the glue melted. His feathers fell off, and he tumbled to his death below. As he lay dead on the ground a storm began, and the wind picked up speed. As the wind blew overhead, Wayayqaláchiyi's mouth opened; when he breathed in the wind, his eyes opened, he sprang to life, and he announced to all "what a good sleep" he had had. (Karsten 1923; Métraux 1946b; Miller 1980; Wilbert and Simoneau 1982b; Wilbert and Simoneau 1989; Wright 1986)

Wesucechak

Cree, *Subarctic Region of North America*
Wesucechak, a humorous being known for his multiple disguises, unending hunger, and quick wit, is notorious for using his intellect to manipulate and trick people. He is usually depicted as a moose or wolf, but he also takes human form in many of his adventures. Wesucechak's ability to change his outside appearance is one of his most effective tools for fooling people. Stories of Wesucechak's shape-shifting ability also reflect the Cree understanding that some beings have the ability to manipulate their form. Wesucechak is deceitful and malicious, but his intelligence and power command the respect of his community. People both fear and respect Wesucechak, for they know that he can both help and harm them.

Stories about Wesucechak reflect and represent the wide range of possible relationships in Cree society. For the Cree the world is not neatly divided into animate and inanimate, human and nonhuman beings. Instead, many beings take on attributes that might not be expected of them by non-Cree people. For example, a rock, an animal, or the wind may have the power to speak, act, and interact with others in certain situations. In Wesucechak the Cree demonstrate the possibility that nonhuman beings might take on human characteristics and vice versa. In the Cree cosmos all beings interact to maintain the world and their community. Thus Wesucechak's positive actions demonstrate the power of cooperation and respect, and his negative actions highlight the possibility of chaos, disruption, and danger. In stories about Wesucechak the Cree shed light on their complex kinship system by referring to nonhuman beings as "grandfather," "son," or "younger brother." By using various kin titles normally used for humans the Cree show that their community is peopled with many types of beings who share the same responsibilities.

Wesucechak is a familiar character to the Cree, and storytellers use his antics to demonstrate many aspects of community life. The Cree have two types of oral narratives: *acaoohkiwin*, those stories set in the past, and *acimowin*, contemporary stories. Both types of stories share their emphasis on animal, human, and nonhuman interaction and reciprocation. Unlike Europeans, the Cree do not categorizes their stories along the lines of "supernatural" versus "natural" phenomena. That is, both Cree categories contain stories about creation, powerful beings, extrahuman activities, and destruction.

Wesucechak is credited with aiding in the creation of human beings and the world in which they live. He gave shape and form to many of the physical aspects of the world while at the same time creating the Cree and their society. (See also **Nanabozhoo** for a similar Algonquian character.) One story tells how Wesucechak fearlessly fought off Michi-Pichoux (the water lynx) after a great flood that threatened the community. Overpowering Michi-Pichoux, Wesucechak saved the people from inevitable destruction. However, Wesucechak is also accused of chasing people from their homes, stealing goods from his community, and manipulating women. Wesucechak's unending hunger drives him to deceive people in any way possible to receive food. Cree storytellers use stories about Wesucechak both to entertain and to demonstrate the wrongheadedness of selfish actions. The character of Wesucechak is also found in the stories of other nearby Algonquian communities. (Bloomfield 1930)

Wile E. Coyote
United States

Wile E. Coyote (*Carnivorous vulgaris*), a crafty but foolish coyote who is doomed to failure because of his overzealous nature, first appeared with the **Roadrunner** in the 1949 cartoon "Fast and Furry-ous." According to Chuck Jones, their creator, initially Wile E. Coyote tries to capture the Roadrunner in order to eat him, but after a number of failures it is his loss of dignity that forces him to continue. In fact the only enemy of the Coyote is the Coyote himself. He is obsessed with catching the Roadrunner, to the point that he will employ what-

ever means necessary, even if it means hurting himself repeatedly. But the Coyote never catches the Roadrunner, and each cartoon ends in failure for the Coyote.

The basic problem facing the Coyote is that he cannot catch the Roadrunner by chasing him on foot because the Roadrunner is much faster. In order to catch his prey, the Coyote hatches elaborate plans that employ various devices from a company called Acme, Inc. Alas technology is the Coyote's enemy as well, and even with its help the Coyote is still no match for the speedy Roadrunner. No matter how precise the Coyote's plan, something always goes wrong, ending in another failure.

"Guided Muscle" is a typical Coyote-Roadrunner cartoon. It opened with the Coyote reduced to eating his supper from a tin can. The Coyote saw the Roadrunner and sped off after him, only to be outpaced by the bird's road-burning speed. Realizing he cannot outrun his prey, the Coyote bought a giant bow and placed himself in it like an arrow. As the Roadrunner ran past him, the Coyote launched himself toward his quarry, only to impale himself on a cactus, which promptly fell off into a vast canyon. Unwilling to give up, the Coyote resorted to shooting himself at the Roadrunner from a massive slingshot. But the slingshot merely hurled him onto the road at great velocity. Undaunted, the Coyote then tried a half-dozen other half-baked plots, using a cannon, a giant steel ball, and finally dynamite in attempts to slow down the evasive Roadrunner. However, all of the Coyote's tricks backfired, ending in great harm to him. At the end of the cartoon, the Coyote gave up and put out a sign reading "Wanted: One Gullible Coyote. Apply to manager of this theater."

The Coyote teaches us a lesson. When he cannot catch the Roadrunner by simply chasing him, he does not try to improve himself; instead, he employs mechanical means to outwit his prey. As the stories progress, the Coyote, getting more and more desperate, employs more and more desperate measures. A bow and arrow is replaced by a slingshot, which is replaced by a cannon, which is replaced by dynamite, which ultimately blows up in his face. The lesson of the Coyote is that the relentless pursuit of a simple dinner eventually leads to the relentless buildup of ever more destructive devices, which simply lead to a bigger failure and ultimately to one's own destruction.

Indeed, sometimes the Coyote finds himself almost unaware of his own obsessiveness until it is too late. In a classic episode, the Coyote had suspended tons of rocks between two cliffs above the road, held up by a trap door. As the Roadrunner sped toward his presumed doom the Coyote released the trap door, but, amazingly, the rocks remained suspended between the cliffs. Frustrated, the Coyote grabbed a stick and, standing directly under the tons of rocks, started angrily poking at them with it. As a few pebbles started to fall on his head the Coyote's eyes widened and he held up a sign reading "In heaven's name. What am I doing?" A moment later, the rocks came crashing down on the bewildered Coyote. (Jones 1989)

Winabojo
Algonquian, including Ojibwa, Menominee, Micmac, Cree, *Northeastern United States; Southeastern Canada*
See **Nanabozhoo.**

Windigo
Algonquian, *Canada; Northeastern United States*
A windigo is a giant, physically distorted, havoc-wreaking being who inhabits the forest and is known for its ability to terrify people and to invade their bodies, causing them to go crazy. A person is said to be cap-tured by a windigo creature, or is said to "turn windigo," if they become crazed in any of several variations. Someone who does not recognize his or her kin after a long journey or someone who will not share his or her food from a kill may be classified as windigo. In Algonquian society self-indulgent behavior or concern only for oneself is considered antisocial. Traditionally Algonquian peoples, including the Ojibwa, Cree, and Micmac of the woodlands area, were tied together into tight communities by their common economic, social, and religious bonds. Communities supported one another during the harsh winters by joining group hunting parties and dispersing food among the entire group. Because Algonquian communities are fundamentally based on intimate group interconnections, selfish and disruptive actions by a windigo or by people who are taken over by windigolike qualities are seen as antisocial and unnatural. The word *windigo* thus names both a type of being in the world as well as a way of being in Algonquian society.

As a character the windigo is notorious for striking fear into people in its home, the woods. It is known as a bloodthirsty monster just waiting for an unsuspecting person who is traveling alone or who is not cautious of his or her path. Windigo are huge beings, over ten feet tall; their limbs are powerful, and they can move as fast as the wind. Windigo have unusually large heads with twisted mouths and irregular features. Their bodies are disfigured, and they are said to have hearts of ice, not respecting at all the people with whom they share the forest. They are always hungry, and they constantly search the forest for human beings. If they cannot kill and eat human flesh, they take away a person's individuality by invading that person's soul and claiming it as their own. One story tells of a young woman whose body was invaded by a windigo after a journey to another village.

The young woman was treated by the medicine man at her own village when she returned, but after her bout with the windigo she never strayed far from home and rarely came out of her lodge. The windigo had made her so scared that she feared another attack. Windigo beings instill fear in people through their unprovoked attacks. There is no logic to their conquests; they will attack on a whim and without warning. All of the windigo's activities are selfish, disrespectful, and disruptive.

Windigo beings lack all respect for cultural practices. They demand food at all times, even when the supply is low. They kill people for their own pleasure and appetite, and the community considers their cannibalism disrespectful and unwarranted. Windigo beings chase people through the forest, claiming it as their own instead of sharing it with the community. They are notorious for preying on people who are fasting because they are weak from lack of food and can be more easily defeated. Once a windigo came to a young man who had been fasting in the hills for several days. The windigo came in a dream disguised as another, more benevolent being and promised the young man that he would always have food and wealth. The young man believed the being and continued to fast. After he finished his fast he returned to the village but forgot his dream. Years later, after he married, he felt a terrible hunger inside him and could not satisfy it. He tried and tried, but no matter what or how much he ate he was still hungry. He ran around looking for food until he passed out, and he was then transformed into a windigo being, so tall he could reach the clouds. As a windigo he went from village to village eating all he could. Then he returned home to sleep, and when he woke he was a man again. This continued for several weeks before he realized that he was turning into the windigo and that it had been a windigo

that had visited him in his dream all those years ago, tricking him into believing him and following his ways.

Windigo beings, however, can be defeated. Once a young hunter decided to forge a path through the thickest part of the forest. He consulted his sister first, telling her of his plan. She warned him not to go into the forest alone, for others had done so and never returned. Wanting to prove his bravery and hunting ability and hopeful that he would find a wife at another village, however, the young man left for the forest. Before he left on his journey, his sister packed him plenty of dried meat and several pairs of shoes that she had made. After several weeks of travel through the forest, the young man came upon a village and went directly to the chief's lodge. The chief told the young man that it was not safe in the village. Every day a giant, called a windigo, would come to the village and take two men to eat. The young man had never heard of such a thing. He told the chief that he would stay and see this giant for himself.

In the morning, the windigo came into the village, scaring the children and running about demanding that he have the stranger who was in the village. The chief begged the windigo not to take the stranger, for he should be treated with hospitality, but the windigo did not care about respect or tradition. Inside the lodge the young man heard the commotion and came out to confront the giant. As he emerged from the tent he was singing and praying, which only enraged the windigo more. "Why do you come out here making that noise? I am going to eat you," exclaimed the windigo. The young man approached the windigo, still singing. Once he was standing toe to toe with the windigo, he grabbed his bow and arrow and shot at it; then, disarming the giant, he took his tomahawk and cut its head off. The young man used the power of his songs and prayers to defeat the windigo. But the windigo beings have a tool more powerful than any human being: They can continue to multiply by invading others. Thus, although the young man defeated one windigo, there are always more.

Windigo beings are disruptive in any shape they take in a community. The windigo beings who inhabit the forest not only wreak havoc on travelers, they also perpetuate their disruptive behavior by making people windigo. Becoming windigo is a malady unique to the Algonquian culture. People who have been lost or who have relatives who have been lost are especially susceptible. Once a person has become windigo they have unnatural desires and indulge in antisocial behavior; they often are confused by their surroundings and do not recognize their families and other familiar things. In the early twentieth century anthropologists and missionaries classified this specific phenomenon as the "windigo psychosis." Anthropologists claimed that when people "became windigo," they lusted after human flesh and became crazed. However, the Algonquian community has not adopted this line of characterization, and there is little evidence to support any claims of cannibalism. The stories of a windigo character and the actual state of being windigo may be the source of confusion. Confusing stories with accounts of people's actual behaviors may have resulted in the inaccurate conception of a "windigo psychosis." To the contrary, people who suffer from any sort of trauma connected with being lost, or with terrifying storms, can recover fully with the aid of their families and religious leaders. To become windigo is not to become forever crazed or cannibalistic but, rather, to lose one's sense of reality, however temporarily. (Brightman 1988; Colombo 1982; Cooper 1933; Marano 1985; Morrison 1979; Morrisseau 1982; Preston 1980; Stevens 1982; Teicher 1960)

Wosi

Limba, *West Africa: Northern Sierra Leone*

Wosi (whose name literally means "spider") is a well-loved character in Limba stories. His behavior, though far from admirable, nevertheless leads to humorous adventures, and although some stories about him do have a moral, their main purpose is entertainment.

The tales told about Wosi fall within a large category known in Limba as *mboro*. This general category includes tales, tribal history, parables, riddles, and metaphors. Most of the tales about Wosi are told during the evening in an informal setting. Stories are often accompanied by songs, since Limba singing and dancing are closely related to storytelling as artistic and ritualistic forms of expression. People are set apart within Limba society as singers, dancers, storytellers, or artists, but the performers in the various media interact during performances and rituals. The Limba live mainly in small towns that have an open, circular space in the center, where much of Limba life is conducted. This space is used as a market and for dance performances, rituals, and funeral rites. The Limba gather as a community in this central part of town when they are not working, and at night it is full of activity. Once a crowd has gathered, the center part of town is used as a forum for storytelling.

Tales about Wosi are very fluid, having no fixed pattern or sequencing. Each storyteller is known for his or her own style and form. Young children are encouraged to tell stories and to begin to develop the skills needed to become a respected storyteller. Storytellers begin to tell their tales at night when a small crowd has gathered, usually beginning with short stories. As more people arrive the stories become longer and more involved. There is usually more than one storyteller each night, and they take turns performing different stories. If there are songs within the tales, the audience echoes the storyteller's verse; they also participate by calling out suggestions and criticisms. Sometimes one person is chosen to be the designated "answerer" for a story. This person's job is to reply to the storyteller at appropriate times and to lead the audience in clapping, singing, and murmuring agreement. (See also **Anaanu, Wakalulu, Wanto,** and **Yiyi** for examples of audience interaction.)

A storyteller usually begins by telling the audience that he or she has a story for them. Storytellers use mimicry, rhymes, repetition, and song in their performances. A good storyteller is judged by the entertainment value of the performance. Routinely the storytellers end the story with the announcement "It is finished." An element common to all storytellers' repertoires is the use of interjections of time to indicate a change of scenery or character in a story. For example, a storyteller might use the phrases "in the morning," "after some time," or "when the sun rose" to indicate a switch in tempo or character.

In *mboro* Wosi takes on human characteristics. Wosi is known to be stupid, gluttonous, selfish, greedy, and irresponsible; he has a large appetite and an equally large ego. Wosi tells everyone that he is the best, the strongest, the fastest, the most handsome, or whatever he feels will impress them most. He is forever getting himself into trouble, often dragging his family along with him. He steals, insults his mother-in-law, and abuses his wife. He calls his wife lazy even though she does the majority of the work, and he ignores his economic and social duties. If he has food, he does not share it with his family, and if he wins a prize or cheats the chief out of money, he never buys anything for his children. He cheats his neighbors and ignores his responsibilities to the community. Whenever the village is called on to help the chief with his crops, Wosi finds an excuse to avoid the work, but he usually ends up getting food from his family. In the character of Wosi the Limba show how one may use one's social status to one's own advantage.

The Limba social system comprises several societies, some for men, some for women, and some for both. In addition, in the Limba kinship system one looks to one's closest relatives for primary care. But because the Limba depend mainly on rice farming for their sustenance and economy, each small town within the larger village works as a unit. Wosi demonstrates the negative repercussions that may befall the community if one person acts selfishly.

Wosi is well loved because of his humorous adventures and the trouble he gets into along the way. He tries and tries to avoid working, planting crops, or sharing in community responsibilities, but he almost always fails in his pranks. He hides tools from others and steals their food by pretending to befriend them. He always celebrates his victories before he even comes close to winning. Everyone knows that Wosi is the biggest meat lover in the world and that he will go out of his way to get all he can. Once the chief announced that whoever could carry a large metal pot to his field, which needed hoeing, would receive the head of an ox. Jumping at the chance to win the prized ox head, Wosi went to the chief and told him he would win the contest. Wosi also told his wife and neighbors that he would be victorious, that he was the wisest and strongest of all the villagers. The chief asked Wosi what would happen if he failed, and Wosi, being confident in himself, answered that the chief could thrash him if he failed; the chief agreed. Wosi set out with the pot on his head, and two of the chief's servants followed to make sure he did not cheat. As Wosi walked the pot sank further and further into his head. He came upon a rock and tried to step over it, but because of the weight of the pot he slipped and fell, breaking the pot. Before he could get away, the servants grabbed him and thrashed him right there. As they beat him, Wosi dwindled in size to escape the pain, and this is why spiders are small. Even though Wosi failed in his attempt to gain the ox head, he escaped his punishment, but he forever changed the shape of spiders.

One of Wosi's main antagonists is his own wife, Kayi. Relationships between husbands and wives are a common theme in stories of the Limba. Men and women share the chores of cultivating rice crops and raising children, the two main activities in Limba society. A woman is independent of her husband's control, and although a man may believe that taking a wife is his main goal, the roles of married women are not easily defined. Women, with their sometimes-ambiguous positions, find their way into Limba storytelling, which is almost exclusively a male activity. Wives tricking their husbands is a common story line in all types of Limba narratives. In tales about Wosi, his wife tricks him and usually wins, but she does so because Wosi has taken advantage of her.

Kayi is notorious for overturning or foiling Wosi's pranks. Wosi continually attempts to get the best of his wife; he steals from her, embarrasses her, abuses her, and neglects to treat her with the respect a wife deserves. Kayi is able to turn Wosi's tricks back on him. Wosi's behavior toward his wife and family displays his antisocial nature. He does not respect the customs and laws of the Limba. Wosi is in every way an outsider within his own community.

Once Kayi and Wosi went to work in the chief's fields, knowing that the chief would have breakfast for all the workers. Upon seeing the smoke from the chief's fire, Wosi and Kayi split up; Wosi went for the yams and Kayi went for the rice. Wosi returned with a basket full of cooked yams and Kayi returned with a basket full of rice, and the two sat down and ate. Kayi saved some of the rice for their children and for the future, but Wosi ate all the yams himself. When Kayi discovered that Wosi had eaten all the yams she was furious. That night she placed white cowries on her eyes to make it look as if she were awake. The whole night Wosi tried to sneak into the kitchen to eat the rice, but each time he tried to pass Kayi he thought she was awake. In the morning Wosi was tired and hungry and angry at Kayi. He did not understand why Kayi seemed so well rested. Kayi and the children ate their rice, but she did not give any to Wosi, and Wosi abused her. It is not clear what kind of "abuse" Kayi suffered at the hands of Wosi. Wosi is known for calling her names and ridiculing her.

As an outsider, Wosi is likened to Kanu, the creator of the Limba. In sacrifices and prayers Kanu is spoken of as distant from the Limba but as having ultimate control over their lives. In tales about Kanu, however, he is an active member of the society, often appearing as a father, a chief, and even a seeker of palm wine. Although Kanu often appears as an intimate member of Limba society, it is only in tales that he is seen as part of the community. On all other occasions, Kanu, like Wosi, is an outsider in his own community.

Wosi also resembles "spirits" in Limba culture. Spirits live in the bush away from the Limba. However, like Wosi, they come into town either to help people or to cause them trouble. In stories the spirits are mainly spoken of as animals, if they are given a specific form at all. A Limba person can enter the bush and "take" one of the spirits if he or she has the power to do so. This is always risky, however, because the spirit is just as likely to cause harm as to be helpful. Although Wosi is not conceived of as a spirit or as a manifestation of Kanu, the stories about his escapades portray him as an outsider as well. (Bockarie and Hinzen 1986; Clarke 1971; Finnegan 1967; Finnegan 1970; Werner 1968)

Wuaiagalachiguí
Toba, *Argentina*
See **Wayayqaláchiyi.**

Wu'sata
China

Wu'sata, a monkey, is both a humorous prankster and a vehicle for enlightenment. Within the Buddhist tradition in China there are many ways that one may gain eternal enlightenment. Although Wu'sata's jokes and tricks often seem to be merely entertaining, he highlights the many pathways to enlightenment by showing the illusive nature of reality. That is, he shows people that even through humor and the seemingly absurd things in life one can gain freedom.

Wu'sata changes form, redirects people's attention through deception, and loves to mask the seriousness of situations with his light-hearted comedy. All of his actions demonstrate that reality is not always what it seems. In popular tales he changes easily from a monkey into water to put out fires, he tricks demons into leaving the world, and he directs people down the proper pathways by diverting their attention from negative forces. When Wu'sata's stories are appreciated for their entertainment as well as their philosophical message, they are complete. (Yu 1980)

A wine ewer from the Tang dynasty in the form of the monkey Wu'sata holding a wineskin. (Werner Forman/Art Resource)

Y

Yaut

Umeda, *Papua New Guinea*

Yaut are ogres or fiends. There are several yaut, both male and female, whose comedic performances during the Ida fertility ritual serve as entertainment.

The performers who embody the yaut during Ida performances cover their bodies in mud from a local river. They add to their costume by covering their heads with branches from a fern and carrying clubs and gourds. During a break in the Ida the yaut appear at the center of the village brandishing their clubs. After they enter the ritual plaza area, they dance in a burlesque style mimicking the ritual performers who have already danced. Their disruptive actions make them even more frightening. They chase people, especially women and children, and drive them from the plaza with their shouts, jeers, and insults.

Although the yaut seem to have the upper hand, after the initial shock of their performance wears off, the audience gathers together and turns the tables on them. Using the same kind of disruptive behavior as the yaut do, men, women, and children chase the yaut, throw trash at them, and shout out obscenities. The yaut's performance ends with the audience laughing at them as they turn in embarrassment and return to their home in the bush. (Gell 1975)

Yenaldlooshi

Navajo, *Southwestern United States: Arizona; New Mexico*

Yenaldlooshi (whose name means "he who trots around here and there on all fours") are antisocial human beings who move through the world naked with only a coyote skin on their backs and a mask to cover their faces. Yenaldlooshi are normally more the subjects of anecdotes than of formal stories; they are brought to life as examples of negative behavior.

In anecdotes yenaldlooshi are characterized by their complete lack of respect for Navajo social and religious mores. As a group or alone, they travel throughout the community causing problems for and between people, they act disrespectfully toward elders, and they disrupt ceremonies with their destructive behavior. Yenaldlooshi travel at night to hide their appearance from others and to add to their elusiveness. Often they gather as a group to plan their malevolent deeds. They are best known for meeting in dark caves where they cannot be detected.

Through anecdotes of the yenaldlooshi the Navajo people demonstrate the ill will of others within their community. The actions of the yenaldlooshi are portrayed as antisocial and antithetical to the accepted Navajo ways of living. They offend and reject proper Navajo life-ways in every possible way. The yenaldlooshi always appear on the last night of a Night Chant ceremony to interfere with the dancers. They mimic the male dancers and disrupt the ceremony with their obscene play. They create sandpaintings, which are the most powerful of Navajo curing agents, only to urinate and defecate on them. They mock Navajo singers, powerful humans who aid in curing the ill and maintaining balance in the world. They have sexual intercourse with the deceased and practice cannibalism.

237

Decorating the walls of their caves are the heads of the deceased and baskets full of human flesh, which they feast upon in their own rituals. In all of their activities, the yenaldlooshi characters do the opposite of what is acceptable in Navajo society. (See also **Ma'ii** for Navajo coyote stories.) (Brady 1984; Matthews 1897)

Yetl

Tlingit, *Southern Alaska to Northern British Columbia*

Yetl, who takes the physical traits of a raven, acts both as a helpful, creator character and a disruptive, selfish thief. Tlingit stories tell how Yetl brought fire and sunlight to the world and helped the people learn how to fish to sustain themselves. Yet he is also notorious for his selfish adventures that result in some of his victims losing their food, their shelter, and even their lives. Yetl transforms himself into different people, animals, and objects for his own benefit.

Representations of Yetl are found within Tlingit oral literature, art, and community life. Designs of the raven are carved into wood, especially onto house posts, which represent each group's distinct history. These posts are commonly called "totem poles" by people outside the community. This designation, however, does not recognize the place of the poles in the Tlingit community. Tlingit house posts represent a community system and culture that relies on human beings, animals, and other beings within the cosmos for their continuation. The Tlingit have a kinship system based on moieties (a classification system in which everyone belongs to one or the other of two groups, each called a moiety); people are born into either the Raven or the Wolf moiety and are further related to people through extended clan affiliations. The economy of the Tlingit has always relied on fishing and fur trade based on multifamily plank houses that band together in their economic activities. The Tlingit community relies on people working together and acting responsibly for their well-being. Anyone who acts selfishly or whose behavior disrupts the group activities is seen as irresponsible and antisocial. Therefore many of Yetl's activities run contrary to the most important values of the Tlingit community.

Yetl uses his deceptive powers to convince people that he is their friend, and then he takes advantage of them. He preys on the innocent and powerless, but he also takes on the most powerful, such as the grizzly bear. Once Yetl invited the grizzly bear and his wife to accompany him on a fishing expedition. Yetl caught many fish, but the grizzly bear had no luck. Noticing how well his companion was doing, the grizzly bear asked Yetl what he was using for bait. Yetl told the bear that he was using his testicles for bait. The grizzly bear was surprised, but since he could not catch any fish he decided to try it. The grizzly bear reached into his sack, pulled out a sharp knife, cut off his testicles, and hung them on his fishing pole. He was in so much pain that he did not notice that Yetl had fed his wife halibut filled with stones. The grizzly bear and his wife laid on the ground in pain as Yetl collected his fish and left them to die. Yetl had no reason to be angry with the grizzly bear, but his selfishness and egotism drove him to demonstrate his power by demeaning the most powerful of creatures. Yetl is well known for attacking without warning or cause. Stories about Yetl highlight the unpredictable nature of the world and of people. In Yetl's actions the Tlingit have at once examples of the most beneficial and the most destructive behaviors for their community and the world.

Entertaining stories about Yetl demonstrate his disruptive behavior. Many of the stories tell of Yetl wielding his power by convincing people to give him food even though he has not worked. Often he takes advantage of his friends by promising them great wealth or much food if they give him what he needs at that moment. Yetl will trick anyone to get what he wants, no matter the cost. Once Yetl convinced a group of fishermen to take him with them on their fishing trip. He promised that he knew the best spots to catch halibut. Once they were there, the men hung their lines out and waited. Hours went by, and they had not caught any fish. Yetl told them he would dive into the water and see if their bait was still on the hooks. Once Yetl was underwater, he ate all the bait from the hooks; then he returned to the fisherman and told them that their bait had been stolen. Then men replaced their bait and waited again. Again, Yetl pulled the same prank and ate all their bait. The third time Yetl tried the trick some of the fishermen got suspicious. While Yetl was under water the men tugged on their lines. One caught him, but Yetl braced himself against the bottom of the canoe and held on until the man pulled off his beak. The men left and when they got home they hung Yetl's beak on the wall of their lodge. Yetl, however, was not to be outdone. He made a beak out of spruce gum, entered the lodge, and stole his own beak back.

Yetl uses his cunning to convince people to do things they know are wrong, and he takes advantage of kinship relationships for his own benefit. Tlingit society is matrilineal—that is, ancestry is traced through the mother's side—and therefore the maternal uncle–nephew relationship is central to the family unit. Uncles teach their nephews how to fish and trap, and nephews rely on their maternal uncles for guidance throughout their lives. Yetl uses his position as an uncle to the crows to get the crows to do what he wants. Once Yetl and some crows were fishing. When the crows had caught some salmon, Yetl told his nephews to go get some skunk cabbage to wrap the fish in. After his nephews left, Yetl ate all the salmon for himself and went to sleep. When he woke up, his nephews were sitting beside him and the fish bones were scattered about. His nephews said they did not know what had happened to the fish. To keep up the charade, Yetl accused them of stealing the fish and eating them while he slept. Yetl threw ashes on their white feathers, branding them forever as thieves, to punish them for their disobedience. (Boas 1970; Chowning 1962; Durlach 1928; Goodchild 1991; Krause 1956; Martin 1978; Miller and Eastman 1984; Pelton and Di-Gennaro 1992; Rooth 1962; Swanton 1909)

Yiyi

Ewe, West Africa: Southern Togo; Ghana

The tenacious spider Yiyi is a common character in Ewe *gliwo* stories. He is characterized by his use of deception, illusion, reversal, and disguises to trick people.

Gliwo stories, oral narratives characterized by their impromptu form, are just one type of oral narratives found among the Ewe. Other genres include *nutinya*, history and genealogies; *lododowo*, proverbs; *adzowo*, riddles; and *alobalowo*, dilemma tales. Each of these genres flourishes in the newly introduced written language. Since European contact the Ewe have been influenced by print media, but stories and storytelling, one of their many types of performing arts, remain central to their lifestyle. The Ewe possess a wide range of expressive performances. Each week, people gather to see "concert parties" and humorous plays performed. Storytelling brings together many types of performances. For example, audience members will interrupt the storyteller to sing or dance to express their interpretation of the story or to show the way they believe the story should unfold.

Gliwo stories are dynamic narratives whose plot and scene change each time they are told. The storyteller indulges the audience by making the stories as lively and outrageous as possible. The performance aspect of the storytelling is crucial, and storytelling styles vary from storyteller to storyteller. They are judged on their overall performance, not simply the verbal telling of the story. The performer chooses his or her performance from a wide range of cultural images. Because the images and characters are familiar, the performers must bring the characters to life through action. Each particular storyteller uses several different instruments, movements, and props to convey his or her story (See **Anaanu, Wakalulu, Wanto,** and **Wosi** for other examples of interactive performances.)

Gliwo narratives are performed by both men and women, although men perfom more often. Drumming precedes the storytelling. As the crowd gathers they listen to the drumming and settle in for the performance. Throughout the telling, songs are sung to recap important parts of the narrative. Each storyteller decides on the songs, usually adding a line such as "I was there" or "This surely happened" in order to demonstrate the truth of the narrative. The audience keeps the storyteller in check by shouting their approval or disapproval throughout the performance.

Some of the most prominent types of stories in the *gliwo* genre are those centered on ambiguous, humorous characters. These stories are characterized by their emphasis on "the trick" and on the absurd and uncharacteristic actions of characters. Yiyi is among the most common characters found in *gliwo* stories. However, animals of all types, including the rabbit, lizard, bird, frog, and mouse, are portrayed as foolish pranksters. The stories typically begin with the introduction "*Mise gli loo* [Listen to a story]" and the audience response, "*Gli ne va* [Let the story come]." The stories end with morals, although some storytellers simply add moral endings without linking them directly to the story.

Stories about Yiyi catalogue his disrespectful behavior. Yiyi is known for his round belly, rapid speech, small size, and nasal voice. He is married to Funo and has three children, but he does not behave as one who is married ought. He delights in chasing women and flaunting his penis. His behavior typifies that of one who does not respect his wife or the other members of the community. In stories Yiyi constantly tricks people, usually for food and sex. Yiyi's large sexual appetite is a recurring theme.

In one story Yiyi committed incest with his only daughter. His daughter cooked and cleaned for him daily. As she grew, the girl became beautiful, and Yiyi began to lust after her large breasts. One day he took an egg and put it in his mouth, telling his child he was sick. He told his daughter to go behind the house to a diviner and ask him what to do for his illness. As soon as she left the house Yiyi took the egg out of his mouth, painted his face white, hung a sack around his neck, and went to the back of the house. Believing he was the diviner, the child asked his advice. Yiyi told the girl that her father's fate was linked to hers and that she should make love to him seven times and the sickness would be cured. When she returned home, Yiyi was waiting for her, groaning as if he was dying. The child told her father what the diviner had said and Yiyi pretended to be shocked. Still he acted as if he might die, and this frightened his daughter. That night the child made the bed for Yiyi, and they began to have sex. As they continued, the girl became ill and died.

Yiyi deceives people for the sheer pleasure of the trick, never fearing any retribution. For example, once Yiyi was helping the crocodile paint the eggs he had gathered. He convinced the crocodile he was done painting and left for the evening, promising to come back the next day to help some more. After a while the crocodile's wife went in to the room and found that Yiyi had eaten all the eggs and had defecated in the room, filling it full of excrement. Not only did Yiyi leave their house in a state of disarray, he also deprived the crocodile and his wife of their food.

Yiyi is said to be everywhere in the world causing trouble and playing tricks. Through Yiyi's character, the Ewe account for the recurring wrongdoings in their society. Yiyi represents the ways in which people take advantage of others and work for their own benefit. One story tells how Yiyi, and thus trouble as well, came to be everywhere in the world. During a famine Yiyi was running out of food. He convinced Detsuevi (a member of his family) to help him get food by hanging some rope on a tree and planting spears in the ground just far enough away that no one would see them but close enough that anyone swinging from the rope would land on them. When the squirrel walked by, Yiyi stopped him. "Brother," he asked, "where are you going?" The squirrel told Yiyi he was on his way to his father-in-law's house. Yiyi told him that if he swung from the rope he would get there quicker. The squirrel agreed. Yiyi flung the rope with the squirrel on it, and when the squirrel landed he was killed by the spears. Yiyi was also able to trick the cow and the partridge in a similar fashion. When he tried to trick the pigeon, however, his luck changed. When the pigeon walked by, Yiyi asked him to try the swing, but the pigeon was clever. He went under the tree and took the rope in his hand, asking "How will this propel me?" Yiyi took the rope and showed him how to hold it, but the pigeon continued to say he did not understand, until finally Yiyi grabbed the rope and flung himself into the spears. When Yiyi landed on the spears, he broke apart and was spread throughout the world. Yiyi's deception not only got the best of him, but it also brought deceit into the world for everyone. (Ellis 1966; Konrad 1994)

Yo

Fon, *West Africa: Benin*

Yo, the protagonist in many Fon humorous tales, is known especially for his unusually large and gross appetite. He eats large amounts of food and bones and has canni-

balistic tendencies. Each of Yo's attributes sets him up to break the rules within Fon society. The Fon society was traditionally based in small community groups, each of which acted as a unit in the production and collection of crops. Yo's unusually large appetite and greediness put him at odds with Fon social mores, which promote cooperation. Yo's character flaws are highlighted in tales for their comedic value. Yo, unlike other Fon characters, is only told of in stories; he is not depicted in art or other symbolic forms.

The stories about Yo belong to the *heho* category of Fon oral literature. *Heho* stories are comical and are told mainly for entertainment. They allow for greater interpretation by the storyteller than do those of the *hwenho* genre (historical stories). Storytellers take common settings and characters to their extremes to entertain the audience. They begin by saying, "This is another story about Yo." Audiences interact with storytellers by calling out to interject their ideas, to let the storyteller know they do not believe the story, or to cheer the narrator for telling a lively story.

Yo was assigned the position of comedic protagonist by Dada Segbo, the king who ruled at the beginning of time. (See **Legba** for the Fon creation story.) Yo and the vulture were good friends, and in a time of drought Yo went to the vulture in search of food. The vulture told Yo that he would take him to a place where there was plenty of food. But Yo had no wings to fly there. So the vulture made Yo some wings out of clay and placed them in the sun until they dried properly. After the wings were dry Yo and the vulture set off for a small palm tree in the middle of the sea. Once there Yo began to fill up his bag with nuts. Shortly after, it began to rain. The vulture told Yo they must leave. Yo did not listen and continued to collect nuts. Finally the vulture left without Yo. Yo was still filling his bag with nuts as it rained harder and harder. Soon Yo's wings softened and he could not

fly. Trapped, Yo decided to see if a boatsman would pick him up. He made careful
marks on a stick and dropped it in the sea.
Soon a boatsman saw the stick and the
wonderful marks, and he sailed around
until he found Yo. The boatsman asked
why he had made the sticks. Yo answered
that he made them to help girls grow to
maturity. The boatsman then invited him
back to his village to do the same for his
girls. Yo told the people they must build
him a house and give him food and eight
girls before he could make the marks again.
The people gave him all that he asked for,
and he told them not to bother him for a
month.

Once Yo had the girls in the house he
began to eat them, one by one. On the fif-
teenth day, after the eight girls were eaten,
Yo called for the people to get him a boat so
he could go to the other shore for some
medicine. Not knowing of his crime, they
let him go. Shortly after he left, the people
found the girls' bones and were outraged.
But Yo had escaped. On the other shore, Yo
bumped into Dada Segbo's son. He asked
the boy if he wanted to see the beautiful
marks he could make. The boy was afraid
of Yo, so he gave him a bird as a gift and
pretended to leave. Thinking the boy had
left, Yo killed the bird and began to roast it.
The boy watched and then went to Yo, asking him where the bird was. Yo tried to escape, but the boy captured him and took
him back to his father, Dada Segbo, who
beat Yo until he could not talk or walk. Yo
dragged himself out of the village.

Because of his greediness, disrespect, and
cannibalism, Yo is forced to live outside of
human society. Dada Segbo did not want
Yo ever to feel accepted in society again, so
he decreed that Yo would forever be the
butt of people's jokes. Yo instigates trouble
between people. Because he cannot live
comfortably within society he causes others
to feel uncomfortable as well. Yo is known
not only for his ability to dupe others but
also for the ease with which he can be
duped in return.

The Fon say that Yo is an animal, although they do not specify which one, and
that he is capable of becoming invisible,
which adds to his elusiveness. In some stories Yo uses a powerful powder to change
himself into insect or animal form. During
a time of great famine, Yo made a bargain
with Death: If he could have two yams a
day from Death's field, he would allow
Death to strike him twice after each collection. Death agreed, but warned Yo that this
would certainly result in Yo's demise. Yo did
not worry. On the way home, Yo saw the
pig and told him if he and his family did not
want to be hungry anymore, they should
come to his house. After they ate, Yo invited them to sleep at his house. The next
morning when Death arrived with the
yams, Yo placed the pig at the front door so
that Death's blows would strike the pig instead of Yo. The next day Yo tried the same
thing with the antelope. The rabbit, however, came to visit the antelope. Not finding
the antelope at home, the rabbit went to
look for her. When she arrived at Yo's, the
rabbit saw the antelope lying on the floor.
The rabbit knew Yo was plotting against
Death and immediately went to Death's
house to tell him of Yo's plans.

The rabbit told Death that Yo was planning to eat all his yams that night while he
slept. At once Death collected all his yams
and took them to the rabbit's house. The
rabbit told Death to sleep near the yams.
Once he fell asleep, the rabbit went to Yo's
house and told him that Death was planning to burn down his house that night and
that he should come sleep at the rabbit's
house. Once they were both there, the rabbit loudly asked Yo how he had survived
Death's blows. Yo said that Death was stupid, that he had tricked him with the pig
and the antelope. Death heard every word
that Yo spoke and stood up to kill him, but
Yo used a special powder to turn himself

into a spider so that Death could not find him anywhere. Death was angry, thinking that the rabbit had tricked him into believing that Yo was there. They went to Dada Segbo to settle the argument. Dada Segbo said they must fight that night.

The rabbit had the moles help him prepare for his challenger by digging deep holes in the ground and covering them with grass. As Death made his way to the rabbit's house he fell into the holes. Ashamed, he would not come out. This is why when people die they are buried in the ground. This story not only shows Yo's trickery but the rabbit's as well. Although Yo's deception and greed fooled Death, it also put others into danger. The rabbit, on the other hand, used his cunning to help the people. This is a common theme in Fon narratives. Yo is seen as bumbling and no good, whereas others use their skills for the benefit of the community.

Yo is renowned for his greed and gluttony, and the telling of his antics are always comical events. Storytellers recite Yo stories frequently, knowing that the audience will enjoy his humorous adventures. In fact, Yo is the most famous character in *heho* tales. (Berry 1991; Courlander 1975; Herskovits and Herskovits 1958)

Yogovu

Ute, *Southwestern United States: Utah; Colorado*

The term *yogovu* is used to designate both coyotes and the coyotelike character found within Ute oral narratives. Normally, the term *yogovu* has the suffix *ci* added to it to indicate an animate noun. The character Yogovu is crafty, like his animal counterpart, and is best known for his pranks and deceitful behavior. In the character of Yogovu the Ute demonstrate their blunt, unsparing humor. Ute humor is dry and often offensive to outsiders because of the focus on sex, human excrement, and urine. Often oral narratives center on graphic sexual exploits, on Yogovu or his enemies being soiled with the excrement of others, and on generally obscene behavior.

Ute narratives focus on those things that seem offensive or improper within their own society. But humor, especially in the form of tales about Yogovu, is meant to show that the unmentionable or unsavory does exist and is part of everyone's life. Ute oral narratives do not usually provide the audience with one straightforward ending or reason for the story. Some tales do end with phrases such as "and that is why dogs go around sniffing assholes," but these endings are tagged on, almost as an afterthought by the storyteller. To an outsider these endings may not seem to mesh with the stories, but the Ute humor and narrative style is known for its loose boundaries and free style. Narratives generally focus on a specific character's actions in a certain place, but there is usually not a clear plot. Thus a clear-cut ending, such as one would expect in a European narrative, is not part of Ute storytelling.

Stories about Yogovu focus on humor through general events and actions. The stories are meant to entertain through their graphic telling. Ute storytellers are masters in the art of narrative performance. Without any props or stages, they convey the actions of Yogovu and his band to the audience, eliciting laughter and praise. Because Yogovu is a well-known character Ute audiences need little introduction to his whimsical pranks. Even the mention of his name brings audiences to laughter. Yogovu ignores all social mores, and his adventures provide a representation of the negative effects of antisocial behavior through a highly comedic genre.

Stories about Yogovu are notorious for their pervasive sexual and anal references. Yogovu is always manipulating his way into sexual liaisons with married women, young girls, and his relatives. One story tells of

Yogovu dressing up like a woman with a baby on his back to go picking berries with a group of women. After a long day the women made a camp and went to sleep. When all the women were asleep, Yogovu went to each, one by one, and had intercourse with her as she slept. To leave his mark Yogovu left the women's dresses up over their heads. In the morning when they awoke the women knew that Yogovu had taken advantage of them and they ran to find Yogovu. When they found him, he mocked them, dancing and singing, yelling that he had copulated with all of them. They threw stones at him and hit him, but he continued until the women went away ashamed.

Yogovu delights in mocking people by mimicking their actions, and stories about him abound with references to his leaving behind piles of excrement or traces of urine to mark his spot. In one story, Yogovu heard a group of children talking, and he approached them and asked where their mother was. The children told Yogovu that she had gone down the path for food. After hearing that the children were alone, Yogovu urinated on all of them and then left. Further along the path, after he had picked some berries, Yogovu came upon his brother the bear. The bear asked him where he got the wonderful berries. Yogovu told him, and the bear set off to get the berries, leaving Yogovu alone with his children. Yogovu slit the baby bear's throat and then placed the head back on the cradle board as if the baby were still alive. Then he boiled and ate his nephew. When his brother and his sister-in-law returned, Yogovu gave them some of the freshly cooked meat. They ate and ate while they thought their baby was asleep. After dinner, Yogovu got up to leave. A little way down the path Yogovu yelled back to the bear, "You ate your baby, you ate your baby." Incensed, the bears ran after Yogovu, but he slid down a hole and they never found him. Later that night, while they mourned the loss of their baby, they could hear Yogovu singing, "You ate your baby." (Krober 1901; Lowie 1924; Sapir 1930; Smith 1974; Smith 1992)

Z

Zomo

Hausa, *West and Central Africa*

Zomo is a mischievously cunning hare who, like **Dila** and **Gizo,** portrays the deceptive, witty, and humorous side of Hausa life. The characters each have distinctive styles of mischief making. Gizo is known for his malice, Dila for his wisdom, and Zomo for his ability to be deceitfully cunning. He uses his wisdom to get what he wants, in any way possible and without regard for other people's well-being. Zomo triumphs over those more powerful than he by turning their strength against them. (See **Dila** and **Gizo** for an explanation of the Hausa social and economic conditions that lead to power struggles.) Even though he is small Zomo is quick and agile, and he uses these traits to manipulate even the strongest animals like the elephant and hippopotamus.

In one tale, Zomo tricked both the elephant and the giraffe and ended up with all the food he needed without lifting a hand. Zomo suggested to the elephant that they become partners in their farming practices. Zomo told the elephant to clear the trees and said that he would burn them after the land was cleared. While the elephant began his work clearing the area, Zomo went to see the giraffe. Again, he suggested they become partners. Zomo told the giraffe that he would push over the trees if the giraffe would burn them afterward. The giraffe agreed and burned all the trees that the elephant had pushed over. Zomo did nothing except take care that neither the giraffe nor the elephant knew about his scheme.

After the first rain, Zomo went to the elephant and told him that if he would do the sowing, Zomo would do the hoeing. The elephant sowed the field, and Zomo returned to the giraffe, claimed to have already done the sowing, and told the giraffe

that he should do the hoeing. Likewise, he tricked the two into doing both the reaping and the gathering. When all the work had been done, Zomo told the elephant they should collect their crops. He warned the elephant to be careful because he had heard that the giraffe wanted to steal their crops.

Zomo told the giraffe the same story about the elephant. The next day the giraffe met Zomo at the cornfield. Before they could begin collecting their corn, they saw the elephant coming. The giraffe became frightened at the size of the elephant. Zomo told him to lie down. When the elephant arrived, he asked Zomo if he had seen the giraffe sneaking around. Zomo told him that the giraffe had been there but that he had gone home, leaving his guitar behind. Zomo pointed to the giraffe's long neck, telling the elephant that it was his guitar. The elephant became frightened, thinking that any animal with a guitar that large would be too much for him to handle. Zomo told the elephant to go and he would take care of the giraffe. Zomo went to the giraffe and told him he should leave quickly before the elephant returned. After the giraffe and elephant had both left, Zomo collected all the corn and went back to his home to rest for the remainder of the year, as he had all the food he would need.

Zomo's cunning helps him in many situations, even those that seem impossible. For example, once Zomo became ill. When he was able to get out of bed, he went to look for food. He went to the hyena's den, and the cubs were the only ones at home. He yelled to them saying his name was "All-of-Us" and asked if he might enter. The cubs allowed him to come in, and Zomo told them that their mother was also his mother. When their mother came back with the food, she yelled to them that she had brought food. They asked her if it was for All-of-Us. She replied, "Of course it is." So Zomo collected all the food from the cubs, saying it was rightfully his because their mother had said so.

This continued for several days until the cubs became thin. Their mother asked them why they were so thin. They told her that she had brought all the food for All-of-Us and that they had gotten none. "Who is All-of-Us?" she asked. She yelled inside the cave for whoever was in there to come out. Zomo came out with his long ears dragging behind him. The mother hyena grabbed him and threw him into the woods, warning him to stay away. As Zomo was walking away he ran into the dog. The dog asked how he had gotten so fat, and Zomo told him of the cave and the secret name. The dog left, but as he approached the cave he forgot the name and said he was "Hamizga," but the cubs let him in anyway. When their mother arrived they asked if they could give some food to "Hamizga." "Who is this?" she asked, and the cubs showed her the dog. The mother hyena leapt on the dog immediately and told the cubs to hold him down while she went to get a stick to kill him. As soon as she left, the dog pushed the cubs off and ran away. As the dog ran, he met up with Zomo. Angry, the dog began to chase Zomo. As they ran through the forest, Zomo came upon the hyena and told her that the dog was quickly approaching. Zomo ducked off to the side, and the hyena caught and killed the dog, leaving Zomo behind unscathed. (Johnston 1966; Rattray 1969a; Sigel 1982; Skinner 1969)

References and Further Reading

Abrahams, Roger. 1968. "Trickster, the Outrageous Hero." In *Our Living Traditions: An Introduction to American Folklore*, ed. Tristram Coffin, 170–178. New York: Basic Books.

Adams, Kathleen. 1988. *Carving a New Identity: Ethnic and Artistic Change in Tana Toraja, Indonesia*. Seattle: University of Washington Press.

Adamson, Joe. 1990. *Bugs Bunny: Fifty Years and Only One Grey Hare*. New York: Henry Holt.

Addae, T. 1970. "Some Aspects of Ashanti Religious Beliefs." *Africa* 25: 162–165.

Addiss, Stephen. 1985. *Japanese Ghosts and Demons: Art of the Supernatural*. New York: George Braziller.

Akesson, S. K. 1950. "The Secret of Akom." *African Affairs* 49: 237–240.

Alburo, Erlinda. 1979. *Bibliography of Cebuano Folklore*. Cebu City, Philippines: Cebuano Studies Center, University of San Carlos.

Alburo, Erlinda, ed. 1977. *Cebuano Folktales*. Cebu City, Philippines: San Carlos Publications.

Alford, Finnegan, and Richard Alford. 1981. "A Holo-Cultural Study of Humor." *Ethos* 9, no. 2: 149–163.

Alpers, Antony. 1964. *Maori Myths and Tribal Legends*. London: John Murray.

Andersen, Johannes. 1969. *Myths and Legends of the Polynesians*. Rutland, VT: Charles E. Tuttle.

Anstey, F. 1933. *Three Moliere Plays*. London: Oxford University Press.

Appiah, Peggy. 1966. *Ananse the Spider: Tales from an Ashanti Village*. New York: Pantheon.

Apte, Mahadev. 1985. *Humor and Laughter: An Anthropological Approach*. Ithaca, NY: Cornell University Press.

Arabi, Ibn. 1989. *Sufis of Andalusia*. London: Allen and Unwin.

Archer, William. 1957. *The Loves of Krishna in Indian Painting and Poetry*. New York: Macmillan.

Ardener, Edwin. 1956. *Coastal Bantu of the Cameroons*. London: International African Institute.

Arewa, Ojo, and G. M. Shreve. 1975. *The Genesis of Structures in African Narrative*. Vol. 1: *Zande Trickster Tales*. New Paltz, NY: Conch.

Argyle, W. J. 1966. *The Fon of Dahomey: A History and Ethnography of the Old Kingdom*. Oxford: Clarendon Press.

Arima, E. Y. 1983. *The West Coast People: The Nootka of Vancouver Island and Cape Flattery*. Victoria: British Columbia Provincial Museum.

Armstrong, Robert Plant. 1977. "Tragedy—Greek and Yoruba: A Cross-Cultural Perspective." In *Forms of Folklore in Africa: Narrative, Poetic, Gnomic, Dramatic*, ed. Bernth Lindfors, 235–256. Austin: University of Texas Press.

Arnold, James, ed. 1996. *Monsters, Tricksters, and Sacred Cows: Animal Tales and American Identities*. Charlottesville: University Press of Virginia.

Arnott, Kathleen. 1963. *African Myths and Legends*. New York: Henry Z. Walck.

Ashwell, Reg. 1978. *Coast Salish: Their Art, Culture, and Legends*. Seattle, WA: Hancock House.

Athanassakis, Apostolos N. 1976. *The Homeric Hymns*. Baltimore: Johns Hopkins University Press.

Babcock-Abrahams, Barbara. 1975. "A Tolerated Margin of Mess: The Trickster and His Tales Reconsidered." *Journal of the Folklore Institute* 11: 147–186.

———. 1984. "Arrange Me into Disorder: Fragments and Reflections on Ritual Clowning." In *Rite, Drama, Festival, Spectacle: Rehearsals toward a Theory of Cultural Performance*, ed. John MacAloon, 102–128. Philadelphia: Institute for the Study of Human Issues.

Babcock-Abrahams, Barbara, ed. 1978. *The Reversible World: Symbolic Inversion in Art and Society*. Ithaca, NY: Cornell University Press.

Baker, Margaret. 1994. "The Rabbit as Trickster." *Journal of Popular Culture* 28, no. 2: 149–158.

Bame, Kwabena. 1985. *Come to Laugh: African Traditional Theatre in Ghana*. New York: Lilian Barber Press.

Bandelier, Adolf. 1954. *The Delight Makers*. 1890. Reprint, New York: Dodd.

Barker, W. H. 1919. "Nyamkopon and Ananse in Gold Coast Folklore." *Folklore* 30.

Barker, W. H., and Cecilia Sinclair. 1928. *West African Folk-Tales*. 1917. Reprint, London: Sheldon Press.

Barnaby, Karin, and Pellegrino d'Acierno, eds. 1990. *Jung and the Humanities: Toward a Hermeneutics of Culture*. Princeton, NJ: Princeton University Press.

Bascom, William. 1969a. *If a Divination: Communication between Gods and Men in West Africa*. Bloomington: Indiana University Press, 1969.

———. 1969b. *The Yoruba of Southwestern Nigeria*. New York: Holt, Rinehart and Winston.

———. 1978. "African Folktales in America: Trickster Seeks Endowment." *Research in African Literature* 9, no. 2.

Basso, Ellen. 1973. *The Kalapalo Indians of Central Brazil*. New York: Holt, Rinehart and Winston.

———. 1987. *In Favor of Deceit: A Study of Tricksters in an Amazonian Society*. Tucson: University of Arizona Press.

———. 1988. "The Trickster's Scattered Self." *Anthropological Linguistics* 30, no. 3/4: 292–318.

Beck, Horace P. 1966. *Gluskap the Liar and Other Indian Tales*. Freeport, ME: Bond Wheelwright.

Beckwith, Martha Warren. 1930. "Mythology of the Oglala Dakota." *Journal of American Folklore* 43: 339–442.

———. 1970. *Hawaiian Mythology*. 1940. Reprint, Honolulu: University of Hawaii Press.

Beidelman, T. O. 1961. "Hyena and Rabbit: A Kaguru Representation of Matrilineal Relations." *Africa* 31: 61–74.

———. 1963. "Further Adventures of Hyena and Rabbit: The Folktale as a Sociological Model." *Africa* 33: 54–69.

———. 1975a. "Ambiguous Animals: Two Theriomorphic Metaphors in Kaguru Folklore." *Africa* 45: 183–200.

———. 1975b. "Kaguru Oral Literature: Texts (Tanzania) Part I." *Anthropos* 70: 537–574.

———. 1976. "Kaguru Oral Literature: Texts (Tanzania) Part II." *Anthropos* 71: 46–89.

———. 1980. "The Moral Imagination of the Kaguru: Some Thoughts on Tricksters, Translation, and Comparative Analysis." *American Ethnologist* 7: 27–42.

Beik, Janet. 1987. *Hausa Theatre in Niger: A Contemporary Oral Art*. New York: Garland Publishing.

Belmonte, Thomas. 1990. "The Trickster and the Sacred Clown: Revealing the Logic of the Unspeakable." In *Jung and the Humanities: Toward a Hermeneutics of Culture*, ed. Karin Barnaby and Pellegrino d'Acierno, 45–66. Princeton, NJ: Princeton University Press.

Benedict, Ruth. 1935. *Zuni Mythology*. Columbia, NY: Columbia University Press.

Berry, Jack. 1991. *West African Folktales*. Edited by Richard Spears. Translated by Richard Spears. Evanston, IL: Northwestern University Press.

Best, Thomas. 1983. *Reynard the Fox*. Boston: Twayne Publishers.

Bhat, Govind. 1959. *The Vidusaka*. Ahmadabad, India: New Order Book Co.

Bierhorst, John. 1985. *The Mythology of North America*. New York: William Morrow.

———. 1988. *The Mythology of South America*. New York: William Morrow.

Billington, Sandra. 1984. *A Social History of the Fool*. New York: St. Martin's Press.

Black Elk, Charlotte, and Tim Giago. 1980. "The Ancient Legend of Iktomi the Trickster and Modern Tribal Leadership." *Wassaja, the Indian Historian* 3, no. 1: 34–36.

Blanc, Mel, and Philip Bashe. 1988. *That's Not All Folks*. New York: Warner Books.

Bloomfield, L. 1930. *Sacred Stories of the Sweet Grass Cree*. Toronto: National Museum of Canada, bulletin 60.

Boas, Franz. 1894. *Chinook Texts*. Report no. 20. Washington, DC: Bureau of American Ethnology.

———. 1895. "Salishan Texts." *Proceedings of the American Philosophical Society* 34: 31–48.

———. 1896. "The Growth of Indian Mythologies." *Journal of American Folklore* 9: 1–11.

———. 1970. *Tsimshian Mythology*. Washington, DC: Smithsonian Institution, Bureau of American Ethnology, 1916. Reprint, New York: Johnson Reprint.

Bockarie, Samura, and Heribert Hinzen. 1986. *Limba Stories and Songs*. Freetown: People's Educational Association of Sierra Leone.

Bórmida, Marcelo. 1978. "Ayoreo Myths." *Latin American Indian Literatures* 2, no. 1: 1–13.

Bowers, Faubion. 1952. *Japanese Theatre*. New York: Hermitage House.

Brady, M. K. 1984. *Some Kind of Power: Navajo Children's Skinwalker Narratives*. Salt Lake City: University of Utah Press.

Bricker, Victoria. 1973. *Ritual Humor in Highland Chiapas*. Austin: University of Texas Press.

Briggs, Janet. 1973. "Ayore Narrative Analysis." *International Journal of American Linguistics* 39, no. 3: 155–163.

Bright, William, ed. 1978. *Coyote Stories*. The Native American Text Series. Chicago: University of Chicago Press.

Brightman, R. A. 1988. "The Windigo in the Material World." *Ethnohistory* 35: 337–379.

Brinton, Daniel. 1868. *The Myths of the New World*. Philadelphia: David McKay.

———. 1882. *American Hero Myths*. Philadelphia: David McKay.

Brown, Jennifer, and Robert Brightman. 1988. *The Orders of the Dreamed*. St. Paul: Minnesota Historical Society Press.

Brown, Mary Wise. 1941. *Brer Rabbit*. New York: Harper and Brothers.

Brown, Norman. 1947. *Hermes the Thief: The Evolution of a Myth*. New York: Random House.

Browne, Ray, and Michael Mardsen, eds. 1994. *The Cultures of Celebrations*. Bowling Green, OH: Bowling Green State University Popular Press.

Bruchac, Joseph. 1988. *The Faithful Hunter: Abenaki Stories*. Greenfield Center, NY: Greenfield Review Press.

Brun, Victor. 1976. *Sug: The Trickster Who Fooled the Monk. A Northern Thai Tale with Vocabulary*. London: Curzon.

Buechel, Eugene. 1978. *Lakota Tales and Texts*. Edited by S. J. Paul Manhart. Pine Ridge, SD: Red Cloud Indian School.

Bunzel, Ruth L. 1932a. *Introduction to Zuni Ceremonialism*. Report no. 47. Washington, DC: Smithsonian Institution, Bureau of American Ethnology.

———. 1932b. *Zuni Katcinas*. Report no. 47. Washington, DC: Smithsonian Institution, Bureau of American Ethnology.

———. 1932c. *Zuni Origin Myths*. Report no. 47. Washington, DC: Smithsonian Institution, Bureau of American Ethnology.

———. 1933. *Zuni Texts*. New York: G. E. Stechert.

Burssens, H. 1958. *Les Puuplades de l'entre Congo-Ubangi*. London: International African Institute.

Busia, K. A. 1954. "The Ashanti of the Gold Coast." In *African Worlds: Studies in the Cosmological Ideas and Social Values of African Peoples*, ed. Daryll Forde, 190–209. London: Oxford University Press.

Buurman, Peter. 1991. *Wayang Golek: The Entertaining World of Classical West Javanese Puppet Theatre*. Oxford: Oxford University Press.

Canda, Edward. 1981. "The Korean Tiger: Trickster and Servant of the Sacred." *Korea Journal* 21, no. 11: 22–38.

Cannizzo, Jeanne. 1983. "The Shit Devil: Pretense and Politics among West African Youth." In *Culture and Performance*, ed. Frank Manning, 125–144. Bowling Green, OH: Bowling Green University Popular Press.

Cardinall, A. W. 1970. *Tales Told in Togoland*. 1931. Reprint, Oxford: Oxford University Press.

Carroll, Michael. 1981. "Lévi-Strauss, Freud, and the Trickster: A New Perspective upon an Old Problem." *American Ethnologist* 8, no. 2: 301–313.

———. 1984. "The Trickster as Selfish-Buffoon and Culture Hero." *Ethos* 12, no. 2 (Summer): 105–131.

Cazeneuve, Jean. 1955. "Some Observations on the Zuni Shalako." *El Palacio* 62, no. 12 (December): 346–356.

———. 1956. "Sacred Clowning in New Mexico." *United States Lines Paris Review*.

Champe, Flavia. 1980–1981. "Origins of the Magical Matachines Dance." *El Palacio* 86, no. 4 (Winter): 35–39.

Charles, Lucile Hoerr. 1945. "The Clown's Function." *Journal of American Folklore* 58: 25–34.

Chatelian, Heli. 1894. *Folk-Tales of Angola*. Boston and New York: American Folklore Society.

Chauvenet, Beatrice. 1929. "A Zuni Shalako." *El Palacio* 27, no. 23 (December): 299–306.

Chindahl, George. 1959. *History of the Circus in America*. Caldwell, ID: Caxton.

Chowning, Ann. 1962. "Raven Myths in Northwestern North America and Northeastern Asia." *Arctic Anthropology* 1, no. 1: 1–5.

Civrieux, Marc De . 1980. *Watunna: An Orinoco Creation Cycle*. San Francisco: North Point Press.

Clark, Ella. 1960. *Indian Legends of the Pacific Northwest*. 1953. Reprint, Berkeley: University of California Press.

Clarke, Mary Lane. 1971. *A Limba-English Dictionary*. 1922. Reprint, Heppenheim, Germany: Gregg International Publishers.

Clutesi, George. 1967. *Son of Raven, Son of Deer*. British Columbia: Gray's Publishing.

Coleman, Sister Bernard. 1971. *Ojibwa Myths and Legends*. Minneapolis, MN: Ross and Haines.

Collins, Jim. 1991. "Batman: The Movie, Narrative: The Hyperconscious." In *The Many Lives of Batman*, ed. Roberta Pearson and William Uricchio, 164–181. New York: Routledge.

Colombo, John Robert. 1982. *Windigo: An Anthology of Fact and Fantastic Fiction*. Saskatoon, Saskatchewan: Western Producer Prairie Books.

Cook, W. A. 1908. *The Bororo Indians of Mato Grosso, Brazil*, vol. 50, no. 1789, 48–62. Washington, DC: Smithsonian Institution, miscellaneous collections.

Cooper, J. M. 1933. "The Cree Witiko Psychosis." *Primitive Man* 6: 20–24.

Counts, David, and Dorothy Counts. 1992. "Exaggeration and Reversal: Clowning among the Lusi-Kaliai." In *Clowning as Critical Practice: Performance Humor in the South Pacific*, ed. William Mitchell, 88–103. Pittsburgh, PA: University of Pittsburgh Press.

Counts, Dorothy. 1982. *Tales of Laupa*. Papua New Guinea: Institute of Papua New Guinea Studies.

Courlander, Harold. 1957. *The Hat-Shaking Dance and Other Tales from the Gold Coast*. New York: Harcourt Brace Jovanovich.

———. 1975. *A Treasury of African Folklore*. New York: Crown Publishers.

Courtney, Richard. 1974. *Play, Drama, and Thought*. New York: Macmillan.

Cowan, James. 1930. *Legends of the Maori*. Wellington, New Zealand: Harry H. Tombs.

Coze, Paul. 1952. "Of Clowns and Mudheads." *Arizona Highways* 26, no. 8 (August): 18–29.

Crump, J. I. 1990. *Chinese Theater in the Days of Kublai Khan*. Ann Arbor: University of Michigan.

Crumrine, N. Ross. 1969. "Japakoba, the Mayo Easter Ceremonial Impersonator: Explanations of Ritual Clowning." *Journal for the Scientific Study of Religion* 8, no. 1: 1–22.

Curtin, J., and J. N. B Hewitt. 1918. *Seneca Fiction, Legends, and Myths*. Report no. 32. Washington, DC: Smithsonian Institution, Bureau of American Ethnology.

Curtis, Edward. 1907. *The North American Indian*. Cambridge, MA: University Press.

Cushing, Frank. 1891–1892. "Outline of Zuni Creation Myths." Thirteenth annual report of the Bureau of American Ethnology, Washington, DC: Smithsonian Institution.

———. 1920. *Zuni Breadstuff*. Indian Notes and Monograph no. 7. Washington, DC: Smithsonian Institution.

Cushing, Frank Hamilton. 1979. *Zuni*. Edited by Jesse Green. Lincoln: University of Nebraska Press.

Davidson, Clifford, ed. 1996. *Fools and Folly*. Kalamazoo, MI: Medieval Institute Publications, Western Michigan University.

Davies, Christie. 1990. *Ethnic Humor around the World*. Bloomington: Indiana University Press.

Davies, Marian. 1971. *Tales from Thailand*. Rutland, VT: Charles E. Tuttle.

Davis, Erik. 1991. "Trickster at the Crossroads: Eshu-Elegba, the West African God of Messages, Sex, and Deceit." *Gnosis* 19: 37–43.

Davis, Hadland. 1913. *Myths and Legends of Japan*. London: George G. Harrap.

DeAngulo, Jamie, and L. S. Freeland. 1948. "Miwok and Pomo Myths." *Journal of American Folk-Lore:* 41: 232–252.

Deloria, Ella C. 1932. *Dakota Texts.* Vol. 14 of Publications of the American Ethnological Society. New York: American Ethnological Society.

DeMott, Barbara. 1982. *Dogon Masks: A Structural Study of Form and Meaning.* Ann Arbor, MI: UMI Research Press.

Disher, Willson M. 1968. *Clowns and Pantomimes.* 1925. Reprint, New York: B. Blom.

Dixon, R. B. 1916. *The Mythology of All Races: Oceanic.* London: Cambridge University Press.

Doke, C. M. 1927. *Lamba Folklore.* New York: American Folklore Society.

———. 1934. "Lamba Literature." *Africa* 7, no. 1: 351–370.

Doran, John. 1966. *The History of Court Fools.* 2nd ed. 1858. Reprint, New York: Haskell House.

Dorje, Rinjing. 1975. *Tales of Uncle Tompa.* San Rafael, CA: Dorje Ling.

Dorson, Richard. 1962. *Folk Legends of Japan.* Rutland, VT: Charles E. Tuttle.

Doty, William. 1978. "Hermes, Guide of Souls." *Journal of Analytical Psychology* 23, no. 4: 358–364.

———. 1991. "The Trickster." In *Mirrors of the Self: Archetypal Images That Shape Your Life,* ed. C. Downing, 237–240. Los Angeles: Tarcher.

———. 1993. "A Lifetime of Trouble-Making: Hermes as Trickster." In *Mythical Trickster Figures,* ed. William Hynes and William Doty, 46–65. Tuscaloosa: University of Alabama Press.

———. 1995. "Everything You Never Wanted to Know about the Dark, Lunar Side of the Trickster." *Spring* 57: 19–38.

Doueihi, Anne. 1984. "Trickster: On Inhabiting the Space between Discourse and Story." *Soundings* 67, no. 3: 283–311.

Douglas, A. B. 1931. "The Anansesem in Gold Coast Schools." *Gold Coast Review* 5.

Douglas, Mary. 1968. "The Social Control of Cognition: Some Factors in Joke Perception." *Man* 3: 361–376.

Drew, Leslie. 1982. *Haida: Their Art and Culture.* British Columbia: Hancock House.

Drewal, Margret Thompson. 1992. *Yoruba Ritual: Performers, Play, Agency.* Bloomington: Indiana University Press.

Drucker, Phillip. 1951. *The Northern and Central Nootkan Tribes.* Bulletin 114. Washington, DC: Smithsonian Institution, Bureau of American Ethnology.

Dumezil, Georges. 1948. *Loki.* Paris: Maisonneuve.

———. 1968. *Mythe et épopée.* Vol. 1. Paris: Gallimard.

Durang, John. 1966. *The Memoir of John Durang.* Pittsburgh, PA: University of Pittsburgh Press.

Durlach, Theresa Mayer. 1928. *The Relationship Systems of the Tlingit, Haida, and Tsimshian.* New York: American Ethnological Society.

Dykstra, Gerald. 1966. *Ananse Tales: A Course in Controlled Composition.* New York: Teachers College Press.

Edwards, Jay. 1978. *The Afro-American Trickster Tale.* Bloomington: Indiana University Press Folklore Publications no. 4.

Ellis, A. B. 1966. *The Ewe-Speaking People of the Slave Coast of West Africa.* Oosterhout, Netherlands: Anthropological Publications.

Ellwood, Robert. 1993. "A Japanese Mythic Trickster Figure." In *Mythical Trickster Figures,* ed. William Hynes and William Doty, 141–158. Tuscaloosa: University of Alabama Press.

El-Shamy, Hasan. 1980. *Folktales of Egypt.* Chicago: University of Chicago Press.

Ennis, Merlin. 1962. *Umbundu: Folktales from Angola.* Boston: Beacon Press.

Eugenio, Damiana. 1982. *Philippine Folk Literature: An Anthology.* Diliman, Quezon City: Folklore Studies Program, University of the Philippines.

———. 1993. *Philippine Folk Literature.* Diliman, Quezon City: University of the Philippines Press.

Evans, E. E. 1957. *Irish Folk-Ways.* London: Routledge and Paul.

Evans-Pritchard, E. E. 1967. *The Zande Trickster.* Oxford: Clarendon Press.

Falassi, Alessandro, ed. 1987. *Time out of Time.* Albuquerque: University of New Mexico Press.

Feldman, Susan. 1963. *African Myths and Tales.* New York: Dell Publishing.

Fenton, William. 1936. *An Outline of Seneca Ceremonies at Coldsprings Longhouse*. Publications in Anthropology no. 9. New Haven, CT: Yale University Press.

———. 1941a. *Masked Medicine Societies of the Iroquois*. Washington, DC: Smithsonian Institution Annual Reports.

———. 1941b. "Museum and Field Studies of Iroquois Masks and Ritualism." In *Explorations and Fieldwork of the Smithsonian in 1940*, 95–100. Washington, DC: Smithsonian Institution.

———. 1987. *The False Faces of the Iroquois*. Norman: University of Oklahoma Press.

Feraca, Stephen E. 1963. *Wakinyan: Contemporary Teton Dakota Religion*. Browning, MT: Museum of the Plains Indian.

Fewkes, Jesse Walter. 1900. "The New Fire Ceremony at Walpi." *American Anthropologist* 2: 80–138.

———. 1902. "Minor Hopi Festivals." *American Anthropologist* 4: 482–511.

———. 1985. *Hopi Katchinas*. 1903. New York: Dover Publications.

Fienup-Riordan, Ann. 1996. *The Living Tradition of Yup'ik Masks*. Seattle: University of Washington Press.

Finnegan, Ruth. 1967. *Limba Stories and Story-Telling*. Oxford: Clarendon Press.

———. 1970. *Oral Literature in Africa*. London: Oxford University Press.

Fisher, Margaret. 1946. "The Mythology of the Northern and Northeastern Algonkians in Reference to Algonkian Mythology as a Whole." In *Man in Northeastern North America*, ed. Fredrick Johnson, 226–262. Mensha, WI: George Banta Publishing.

Fleeson, Kathrine Neville. 1899. *Laos Folklore of Father India*. New York: Fleming Revell.

Fox, Charles, and Tom Parkinson. 1969. *The Circus in America*. Waukesha, WI: Country Beautiful.

Frey, Rodney. 1987. *The World of the Crow Indians*. Norman: University of Oklahoma Press.

Fuller, Fred. 1991. "The Fool, the Clown, the Jester." *Gnosis*, no. 19: 16–21.

Gantz, J. 1981. *Early Irish Myths and Sagas*. New York: Penguin.

Gargi, Balwant. 1991. *Folk Theater of India*. Calcutta, India: Rupa.

Geertz, Clifford. 1973. *The Interpretation of Cultures*. New York: Basic Books.

Gell, Alfred. 1975. *Metamorphosis of the Cassowaries*. London: University of London, Athlone Press.

Giddings, Ruth. 1959. *Yaqui Myths and Legends*. Tucson: University of Arizona Press.

Gifford, Edward W. 1924. *Tongan Myths and Tales*. Bulletin no. 8. Honolulu, HI: Bernice P. Bishop Museum.

Gill, Sam. 1979. *Songs of Life: An Introduction to Navajo Religious Culture*. Leiden, Netherlands: E. J. Brill.

———. 1987. *Native American Religious Action*. Columbia: University of South Carolina.

Godolphin, F. R. B. 1964. *Great Classical Myths*. New York: Modern Library.

Goldfrank, Esther. 1923. "Notes on Two Pueblo Feasts." *American Anthropologist* 25, no. 2: 188–196.

Gonzales, Clara. 1966. "The Shalakos Are Coming." *El Palacio* 73, no. 3: 5–17.

Goodchild, Peter, ed. 1991. *Raven Tales*. Chicago: Chicago Review Press.

Goody, Jack. 1957. "Anomie in Ashanti?" *Africa* 27: 356–363.

Gray, Muriel. 1995. *The Trickster*. New York: Doubleday.

Green, Laura S. 1926. *Folk-Tales from Hawaii*. Poughkeepsie, NY: Vassar College Press.

Greenwood, Isaac J. 1898. *The Circus*. New York: Dunlap Society.

Griaule, Marcel. 1965. *Conversations with Ogotemmeli*. London: Oxford University Press.

Grindal, Bruce. 1972a. *Growing Up in Two Worlds*. New York: Holt, Rinehart and Winston.

———. 1972b. "The Sisla Trickster Tale." *Journal of the Folklore Institute* 9: 173–175.

Groening, Matt. 1997. *The Simpsons*. New York: Harper Perennial.

Grottanelli, Cristiano. 1983. "Tricksters, Scapegoats, Champions, Saviors." *History of Religions* 23, no. 2: 117–139.

Haberman, David. 1994. *Journey through Twelve Forests: An Encounter with Krishna*. New York: Oxford University Press.

Haile, Berard. 1982. *The Upward Moving and Emergence Way*. American Tribal Religions, ed. Karl Luckert, no. 7. Lincoln: University of Nebraska Press.

———. 1984. *Navajo Coyote Tales: The Curly Tó Aheedliinii.* American Tribal Religions, ed. Karl Luckert, no. 8. Lincoln: University of Nebraska Press.

Hallowell, A. Iriving. 1926. "Bear Ceremonialism." *American Anthropologist* 28.

Hampton, Bill. 1967. "On Identification and Negro Tricksters." *Southern Folklore Quarterly* 31, no. 1: 55–65.

Handelman, Don. 1981. "The Ritual-Clown: Attributes and Affinities." *Anthropos* 76: 321–370.

Harding, Thomas. 1967. *Voyagers of the Vitiaz Strait.* American Ethnological Society Monograph no. 44. Seattle: University of Washington.

Harris, Joel Chandler. 1972. *Told by Uncle Remus.* Freeport, NY: Books for Libraries Press.

Harrison, Alan. 1989. *The Irish Trickster.* Sheffield, England: Sheffield Academic Press.

Hart, Donn V. 1964. *Riddles in Filipino Folklore: An Anthropological Analysis.* Syracuse, NY: Syracuse University Press.

Harvey, Youngsook Kim. 1979. *Six Korean Women.* St. Paul, MN: West Publishing.

Hathaway, Flora. 1970. *Old Man Coyote: Crow Legends of Creation.* Billings: Montana Reading Publications.

Hau'ofa, Epeli. 1981. *Mekeo: Inequality and Ambiguity in a Village Society.* Canberra: Australian National University.

Hawley, John S. 1980. "Pilgrims Progress through Krishna's Playground." *Asia* 3, no. 3: 9–12, 45.

———. 1981. *At Play with Krishna: Pilgrimage Dramas from Brindavan.* Princeton, NJ: Princeton University Press.

———. 1983. *Krishna the Butter Thief.* Princeton, NJ: Princeton University Press.

Hazlitt, William. 1864. *Old English Jest Books.* 3 vols. London: Willis and Sotheran.

Heilbig, A. K., ed. 1987. *Nanabozhoo: Giver of Life.* Brighton, MI: Green Oak Press.

Helm, J., ed. 1981. *Handbook of North American Indians.* Vol. 6: *Subarctic.* Washington, DC: Smithsonian Institution Press.

Hendry, Jean. 1964. *Iroquois Masks and Mask Making at Onodaga.* Bulletin 191. Washington, DC: Smithsonian Institution, Bureau of American Ethnology.

Hereniko, Vilsoni. 1992. "When She Reigns Supreme: Clowning and Culture in Rotuman Weddings." In *Clowning as Critical Practice: Performance Humor in the South Pacific,* ed. William Mitchell, 167–191. Pittsburgh, PA: University of Pittsburgh Press.

———. 1995. *Woven Gods: Female Clowns and Power in Rotuma.* Honolulu: University of Hawaii Press.

Herskovits, Frances, and Melville J. Herskovits. 1937. "Tales in Pidgin English from Ashanti." *Journal of American Folklore* 50:60–62.

Herskovits, Melville J., and Frances S. Herskovits. 1958. *Dahomean Narrative: A Cross-Cultural Analysis.* Evanston, IL: Northwestern University Press.

Hieb, Louis. 1972. "Meaning and Mismeaning: Toward an Understanding of the Ritual Clown." In *New Perspectives on the Pueblos,* ed. Alfonso Ortiz, 163–195. Albuquerque: University of New Mexico Press.

Hilbert, Vi. 1985. *Haboo: Native American Stories from Puget Sound.* Seattle: University of Washington Press.

Hill, K. 1963. *Glooscap and His Magic.* London: Gollancz.

Hill, W. W., and Dorothy Hill. 1945. "Navaho Coyote Tales and Their Position in the Southern Athanaskin Group." *Journal of American Folklore* 58, no. 227: 317–343.

Hill-Trout, Charles. 1978. *The Salish People.* Edited by Ralph Maud. Vancouver: British Columbia Cultural Fund.

Hiltebeitel, Alf. 1980. "Siva, the Goddess, and the Disguises of the Pandavas and Draupadi." *History of Religions* 20: 147–174.

Hobart, Angela. 1985. *Balinese Shadow Play Figures.* London: British Museum.

———. 1987. *Dancing Shadows of Bali.* New York: KPI.

Holien, Elaine Baran. 1970. "Kachinas." *El Palacio* 76, no. 4: 1–15.

Hollis, A. C. 1969. *The Nandi.* 2nd ed. 1909. Reprint, Oxford: Clarendon Press.

Honigmann, John H. 1942. "An Interpretation of the Social-Psychological Functions of the Ritual Clown." *Character and Personality* 10, no. 3: 220–226.

Hopper, Janice H. 1967. *Indians of Brazil in the Twentieth Century.* Washington, DC: ICR Studies.

Horton, Robin. 1962. "Kalabari World View: An Outline and Interpretation." *Africa* 32: 197–220.

———. 1963. "The Kalabari Ekine Society: A Borderland of Religion and Art." *Africa* 33, no. 2: 94–114.

———. 1967. "Ikaki: The Tortoise Masquerade." *Nigeria Magazine* 94: 226–239.

Hughes, K. 1966. *The Church in Early Irish Society.* Ithaca, NY: Cornell University Press.

Huntingford, G. W. B. 1953. *The Southern Nilo-Hamites.* London: International African Institute.

Hymes, Dell. 1981. *"In Vain I Tried to Tell You": Essays in Native American Ethnopoetics.* Philadelphia: University of Pennsylvania Press.

Hynes, William. 1980. "Beyond Sacred and Profane: Tricksters as Cosmic Dissembling Others." Paper presented at American Academy of Religion conference, Dallas, TX.

Hynes, William, and William G. Doty, eds. 1993. *Mythical Trickster Figures: Contours, Contexts, and Criticisms.* Tuscaloosa: University of Alabama Press.

Hynes, William, and Thomas Steele. 1993. "Saint Peter: Apostle Transfigured into Trickster." In *Mythical Trickster Figures: Contours, Contexts, and Criticisms,* ed. William Hynes and William Doty, 159–173. Tuscaloosa: University of Alabama Press.

Irizarry, Estelle. 1987. "The Ubiquitous Trickster Archetype in the Narrative of Francisco Ayala." *Hispana* 70, no. 2: 222–230.

Isaacs, H. L., and B. Lex. 1980. "Handling Fire." In *Studies in Iroquois Culture,* ed. Nancy Bonvillian, 5–13. Rindge, NH: Occasional Papers in Northeastern Anthropology.

Jablow, Alta. 1962. *An Anthology of West African Folklore.* London: Thames and Hudson.

Jacobs, Melville. 1959. *The Content and Style of an Oral Literature.* New York: Wenner-Gren Foundation.

———. 1960. *The People Are Coming Soon: Analyses of Clakamas Chinook Myths and Tales.* Seattle: University of Washington Press.

Jahner, Elaine. 1977. "The Spiritual Landscape." *Parabola* 2: 32–48.

Janelli, Roger. 1975. "Anthropology, Folklore, and Korean Ancestor Worship." *Korea Journal* 15: 34–43.

Jefferds, Keith. 1981. "Vidusaka Versus Fool: A Functional Analysis." *Journal of South Asian Literature* 16: 61–73.

Johansen, Ruthann Knechel. 1994. *The Narrative Secret of Flannery O'Connor.* Tuscaloosa: University of Alabama Press.

Johnson, Thomas. 1974. "Far Eastern Fox Lore." *Asian Folklore Studies* 33.

———. 1990. "The Shape Changer Kitsune." *The World and I* 5, no. 4: 637–644.

Johnston, Basil. 1995. *The Manitous: The Spiritual World of the Ojibway.* New York: HarperCollins.

Johnston, H. A. S. 1966. *A Selection of Hausa Stories.* Oxford: Oxford University Press.

Jones, Chuck. 1989. *Chuck Amuck.* New York: Avon Books.

Jurich, Marilyn. 1986. "She Shall Overcome: Overtures to the Trickster Heroine." *Women's Studies International Forum* 9, no. 3: 273–279.

Kanya-Forstner, A. N. 1969. *The Conquest of the Western Soudan.* London: Cambridge University Press.

Karlsdottir, Alice. 1991. "Loki, Father of Strife." *Gnosis,* no. 19: 32–36.

Karsten, Rafael. 1923. "The Toba Indians of the Bolivian Gran Chaco." *Acta Academia Aboensis, Humaniora* 4, no. 4: 1–26.

Keene, Donald. 1973. *Bunraku: The Art of the Japanese Puppet Theatre.* Tokyo: Kodansha International.

Kendall, Laurel. 1985. *Shamans, Housewives, and Other Restless Spirits.* Honolulu: University of Hawaii Press.

Kenji, Kurano. 1960. *Kojiki Hyokai.* Tokyo: Yseido.

Kesey, Ken. 1990. *The Further Inquiry.* New York: Viking.

Kietzman, Dale. 1967. "Indians and Culture Areas of Twentieth Century Brazil." In *Indians of Brazil in the Twentieth Century,* ed. Janice Hopper, 3–68. Washington, DC: Institute for Cross Cultural Research.

Kinsley, David R. 1975. *The Sword and the Flute.* Los Angeles: University of California Press.

Knappert, Jan. 1971. *Myths and Legends of the Congo.* London: Heinemann Educational Books.

Koelle, Wilhelm Sigismund. 1970. *African Native Literature*. 1854. Reprint, Freeport, NY: Librarian Press.

Koepping, Klaus-Peter. 1985. "Absurdity and Hidden Truth: Cunning Intelligence and Grotesque Body Images as Manifestations of the Trickster." *History of Religions* 24: 191–214.

Konrad, Zinta. 1994. *Ewe Comic Heroes: Trickster Tales in Togo*. New York: Garland Publishing.

Krause, Aurel. 1956. *The Tlingit Indians: Results of a Trip to the Northwest Coast of America and the Bering Straits*. 1885. Translated by Erna Gunther. Reprint, Vancouver: Douglas and McIntyre.

Krober, A. L. 1901. "Ute Tales." *Journal of American Folklore* 14: 252–285.

Kroef, J. M. 1956. "Transvestitism and the Religious Hermaphrodite." In *Indonesia and the Modern World*. Bandung: Masa Baru.

Kunjunni Raja, K. 1969. *Indian Theories of Meaning*. Madras: Adyar Library and Research Center.

Laidaw, G. M. 1906. "A Pelondok (Kantjil) Tale." *Journal of the Malayan Straits Branch of the Royal Asiatic Society* 25: 73–102.

Lamadrid, Enrique, and Michael Thomas. 1990. "The Masks of Judas: Folk and Elite Holy Week Tricksters in Michoacan, Mexico." *Studies in Latin American Popular Culture* 9: 191–208.

Landes, Ruth. 1968. *Ojibwa Religion*. Madison: University of Wisconsin Press.

Laski, Vera. 1959. *Seeking Life*. Memoirs of the American Folklore Society, vol. 50. Philadelphia: American Folklore Society.

Lawrence, P., and M. J. Meggitt. 1965. *Gods, Ghosts, and Men in Melanesia*. London: Oxford University Press.

Lawuyi, O. B. 1990. "Is Tortoise a Trickster?" *African Languages and Cultures* 3, no. 1: 71–86.

Leekley, Thomas. 1965. *The World of Manabozho*. New York: Vanguard Press.

Lester, Julius. 1990. *Further Tales of Uncle Remus*. New York: Dial Books.

Levine, Lawrence W. 1974. "Some Go Up and Some Go Down: The Meaning of the Slave Trickster." In *The Hofstadter Aegis: A Memorial*, ed. Stanley Elkins and Eric McKitrick, 94–124. New York: Knopf.

Lindblom, Gerhard. 1969. *The Akamba in British East Africa*. 2nd ed. 1920. Reprint, New York: Negro Universities Press.

Lindell, Kristina, Jan-Ojvind Swahn, and Damrong Tayanin. 1977a. *Folktales from Kammu*. Vol. 4. London: Curzon.

———. 1977b. *Folktales from Kammu*. Vol. 5. London: Curzon.

Linderman, Frank. 1932. *Old Man Coyote*. New York: Junior Literary Guild.

Lockett, Hattie Greene. 1933. *The Unwritten Literature of the Hopi*. Tucson: University of Arizona Press.

Lowie, Robert. 1913. "Dance Associations of the Eastern Dakota." *Anthropological Papers of the American Museum of Natural History* 11, no. 3: 103–142.

———. 1916. "Plains Indian Age-Societies: Historical and Comparative Summary." *Anthropological Papers of the American Museum of Natural History* 11, no. 8: 876–1031.

———. 1918. "Myths and Traditions of the Crow Indians." *Anthropological Papers of the American Museum of Natural History* 25, no. 1: 1–308.

———. 1924. "Shoshonean Tales." *Journal of American Folklore* 37: 1–242.

———. 1935. *The Crow Indians*. New York: Holt, Rinehart and Winston.

———. 1946. "The Northwestern and Central Ge." In *The Handbook of South American Indians*, vol. 1, 477–517. New York: Cooper Square Publishers.

———. 1993. *Myths and Traditions of the Crow Indians*. 1918. Reprint, Lincoln: University of Nebraska Press.

Luckert, Karl. 1979. *Coyoteway: A Navajo Holyway Healing Ceremonial*. Tucson: University of Arizona Press.

Lumholtz, Carl. 1912. *New Trails in Mexico*. New York: Scribner's Sons.

Lundquist, Suzanne Evertsen. 1991. *The Trickster: A Transformation Archetype*. San Francisco: Mellen Research University Press.

Luomala, Katherine. 1940. *Oceanic, American Indian, and African Myths of Snaring the Sun*. Bulletin 168. Honolulu, Hawaii: Bernice P. Bishop Museum.

———. 1949. *Maui-of-a-Thousand-Tricks*. Bulletin 198. Honolulu, HI: Bernice P. Bishop Museum.

Lutes, Steven. 1983. "The Mask and Magic of the Yaqui Paskola Clowns." In *The Power of Symbols*, ed. N. Ross Crumrine and Marjorie Halpin, 81–92. Vancouver: University of British Columbia.

Lutkehaus, Nancy, and Paul Roscoe, eds. 1995. *Gender Rituals: Female Initiation in Melanesia*. New York: Routledge.

Macintyre, Martha. 1989. *Family and Gender in the Pacific*. New York: Cambridge University Press.

———. 1992. "Reflections of an Anthropologist Who Mistook Her Husband for a Yam: Female Comedy on Tubetube." In *Clowning as Critical Practice: Performance Humor in the South Pacific*, ed. William Mitchell, 130–144. Pittsburgh, PA: University of Pittsburgh Press.

Mackenzie, Donald. 1923. *Myths of China and Japan*. London: Greham.

Magnarella, Paul, and Sheila Webster. 1990. "The Paradox: The Wise Fool in Turkish Oral Tradition." *The World and I* 5, no. 4: 633–636.

Makarius, Laura. 1970. "Ritual Clowns and Symbolical Behavior." *Diogenes* 69: 44–73.

———. 1973. "The Crime of Manabozo." *American Anthropologist* 75: 663–665.

Malo, Tiu. 1975. *Rotuman Marriage*. Suva, Fiji: South Pacific Social Sciences Association.

Malotki, Ekkehart. 1978. *Hopitutuwutsi: Hopi Tales, A Bilingual Collection of Hopi Indian Stories*. Flagstaff: Museum of Northern Arizona Press.

———. 1985. *Gullible Coyote: Una'ihu, A Bilingual Collection of Hopi Coyote Stories*. Tucson: University of Arizona Press.

Malotki, Ekkehart, and Michael Lomatuway'ma. 1984. *Hopi Coyote Tales: Istutuwutsi*. Lincoln: University of Nebraska Press.

Manning, Frank E. 1983. *The Celebration of Society: Perspectives on Contemporary Cultural Performance*. Bowling Green, OH: Bowling Green University Popular Press.

Marano, L. 1985. "Windigo Psychosis: The Anatomy of an Emic-Edic Confusion." *Current Anthropology* 23: 385–397.

Marriott, John. 1989. *Batman: The Official Book of the Movie*. New York: Bantam Books.

Martin, Calvin. 1978. *Keepers of the Game: Indian-Animal Relationships and the Fur Trade*. Berkeley: University of California Press.

Mason, Alden J. 1920. "The Papago Harvest Festival." *American Anthropologist* 22: 13–25.

Matthews, Washington. 1897. *Navaho Legends*. London: Houghton, Mifflin.

———. 1902. *The Night Chant: A Navaho Ceremony*. New York: Knickerbocker Press.

Mattielli, S. 1977. *Virtues in Conflict: Tradition and the Korean Woman Today*. Seoul, Korea: Royal Asiatic Society.

Maxfield, Berton, and W. H. Millington. 1906. "Visayan Folktales." *Journal of American Folklore* 14 (April-June): 97–112.

———. 1907. "Visayan Folktales." *Journal of American Folklore* 20 (April-June): 89–103.

Mayberry-Lewis, David. 1971. "Symposium: Recent Research in Central Brazil." *Proceedings of the 38th International Congress of Americanists* (1968) 3: 333–391. Munich.

Mayer, David. 1969. *Harlequin in His Element: The English Pantomime 1806–1836*. Cambridge, MA: Harvard University Press.

Mbiti, John S. 1966. *Akamba Stories*. Oxford: Clarendon Press.

McGregor, Donald. 1982. *The Fish and the Cross*. 2nd ed. Goroka, Papua New Guinea: Melanesian Institute for Pastoral and Socio-Economic Service.

McKean, Philip Frick. 1970. "The Mouse-Deer (Kantjil) in Malayo-Indonesian Folklore: Alternative Analyses and the Significance of a Trickster Figure in South-East Asia." *Asian Folklore Studies* 30: 71–84.

McLaughlin, Marie L. 1916. *Myths and Legends of the Sioux*. Bismarck, ND: Bismarck Tribune Co.

Mercier, P. 1954. "The Fon of Dahomey." In *African Worlds: Studies in the Cosmological Ideas and Social Values of African Peoples*, ed. Daryll Forde, 210–234. London: Oxford University Press.

Metman, Philip. 1958. "The Trickster Figure in Schizophrenia." *Journal of Analytical Psychology* 3: 5–20.

Métraux, Alfred. 1939. "Myths and Tales of the Matako Indians." *Etnologiska Studier* 9: 1–127.

———. 1943. "A Myth of the Chamacoco Indians and Its Social Significance." *Journal of American Folklore* 56: 113–119.

———. 1946a. "Ethnography of the Chaco." In *Handbook of South American Indians*, ed. Julian

Steward, vol. 1, 197–370. Washington, DC: Smithsonian Institution, Bureau of American Ethnology.

———. 1946b. *Myths of the Toba-Pilaga Indians of the Gran Chaco*. Philadelphia: Memoirs of the American Folklore Society, vol. 40.

Métraux, Alfred, and John Armstrong. 1948. "The Goajiro." In *The Handbook of South American Indians*, vol. 4, part 4: 369–383. Washington, DC: Smithsonian Institution, Bureau of American Ethnology.

Meyerowitz, Eva Lewin-Richter. 1958. *The Akan of Ghana*. London: Faber and Faber.

Miller, Alan. 1984. "Ame No Miso-Ori Me: The Cosmic Weaver in Early Shinto Myth and Ritual." *History of Religions* 24, no. 1: 27–48.

Miller, Barbara S. 1977. *Love Songs of the Dark Lord*. New York: Columbia University Press.

Miller, Elmer S. 1980. *A Critical Annotated Bibliography of the Gran Chaco Toba*. New Haven, CT: ARAFlex Books.

Miller, Jay, and Carol Eastman. 1984. *The Tsimshian and Their Neighbors of the North Pacific Coast*. Seattle: University of Washington Press.

Mitchell, William. 1987. *The Bamboo Fire: Fieldwork with the New Guinea Wape*. Prospect Heights, IL: Waveland Press.

———. 1990. "Therapeutic Systems of the Taute Wape." In *Sepik Heritage: Tradition and Change in Papua New Guinea*, ed. N. Lutkehaus, 423–438. Durham, NC: Carolina Academic Press.

———. 1992a. "Horrific Humor and Festal Farce: Carnival Clowning in Wape Society." In *Clowning as Critical Practice: Performance Humor in the South Pacific*, ed. William Mitchell, 145–166. Pittsburgh, PA: University of Pittsburgh Press.

Mitchell, William, ed. 1992b. *Clowning as Critical Practice: Performance Humor in the South Pacific*. Pittsburgh, PA: University of Pittsburgh Press.

Montclair Art Museum. 1987. *The Eagle and the Raven Speak: Highlights from the Native American Collections of the Montclair Art Museum*. Montclair, NJ: Montclair Art Museum.

Montell, G. 1938. "Yaqui Dances." *Ethnos* 3, no. 6 (December): 144–166.

Morrison, Grant. 1989. *Arkham Asylum*. New York: DC Comics.

Morrison, Kenneth. 1979. "Towards a History of Intimate Encounters: Algonkian Folklore, Jesuit Missionaries, and Kiwake, the Cannibal Giant." *American Indian Culture and Research Journal* 3, no. 4: 51–80.

———. 1984. *The Embattled Northeast: The Elusive Ideal of Alliance in Abenaki-Euramerican Relations*. Berkeley: University of California Press.

Morrisseau, Norval. 1965. *Legends of My People: The Great Ojibway*. Toronto: Ryerson Press.

———. 1982. "The Death of Windigo." In *Windigo: An Anthology of Fact and Fantastic Fiction*, ed. by J. R. Colombo, 204–205. Saskatoon, Saskatchewan: Western Producer Prairie Books.

Mosko, Mark S. 1992. "Clowning with Food: Mortuary Humor and Social Reproduction among the North Mekeo." In *Clowning as Critical Practice: Performance Humor in the South Pacific*, ed. William Mitchell, 104–129. Pittsburgh, PA: University of Pittsburgh Press.

Mourning Dove. 1990. *Coyote Stories*. Edited by Heister Dean Guie. Caldwell, ID: Caxton, 1933. Reprint, Lincoln: University of Nebraska Press.

Nachman, Steven. 1981. "Social Play on Nissan: The Magical Contest." In *Play as Context*, ed. Alyce Taylor Cheska, 61–83. New York: Leisure Press.

———. 1982. "Anti-Humor: Why the Grand Sorcerer Wags His Penis." *Ethos* 10, no. 2: 117–135.

Nagy, Joseph Falaky. 1981. "The Deceptive Gift in Greek Mythology." *Arethusa* 14, no. 2: 191–204.

Nelson, Richard. 1983. *Make Prayers to the Raven*. Chicago: University of Chicago Press.

Ness, Sally Ann. 1992. *Body, Movement, and Culture: Kinesthetic and Visual Symbolism in a Philippine Community*. Philadelphia: University of Pennsylvania Press.

Newton, Douglas. 1958. *Clowns*. London: Harrap.

Nimmo, Arlo. 1970. "Posong, Trickster of Sulu." *Western Folklore* 24: 186ff.

Noss, Philip. 1971. "Wanto: The Hero of Gbaya Tradition." *Journal of the Folklore Institute* 8, no. 1: 3–16.

Nozaki, Kiyoshi. 1961. *Kitsune: Japan's Fox of Mystery, Romance, and Humor*. Tokyo: Hokuseido Press.

Nunley, John, and Judith Bettelheim. 1988. *Caribbean Festival Arts*. Seattle: University of Washington Press.

Oberg, Kalervo. 1949. *The Terena and the Caduveo of Southern Mato Grosso*. Washington, DC: Smithsonian Institution for Social Anthropology no. 9.

Okediji, Moyo. 1994. "Eshu: The Yoruba Trickster God." *Faces* 10, no. 6: 35–43.

Oliver, Douglas. 1981. *Two Tahitian Villages*. Provo, UT: Institute for Polynesian Studies.

———. 1989. *Oceania: The Native Cultures of Australia and the Pacific Islands*. Honolulu: University of Hawaii Press.

Opler, Morris Edward. 1994. *Myths and Tales of the Chiricahua Apache Indians*. New York: American Folk-Lore Society. 1942. Reprint, Lincoln: University of Nebraska Press.

———. 1994. *Myths and Tales of the Jicarilla Apache Indians*. New York: American Folk-Lore Society. 1938. Reprint, Lincoln: University of Nebraska Press.

Oreglia, Giacomo. 1968. *The Commedia Dell'Arte*. New York: Hill and Wang.

Ortiz, Alfonso. 1969. *The Tewa World: Space, Time, Being, and Becoming in a Pueblo Society*. Chicago: University of Chicago Press.

Ortiz, Alfonso, ed. 1972. *New Perspectives on the Pueblos*. Albuquerque: University of New Mexico Press.

Ortolani, Benito. 1995. *The Japanese Theatre*. Princeton, NJ: Princeton University Press.

Osborn, Henry. 1960. "Textos Folkloricos Guarao." *Anthropologica* 9: 21–38.

Osgood, Cornelius. 1937. *The Ethnography of the Tanaina*. New Haven, CT: Yale University Press.

O'Suilleabhain, S. 1973. *Storytelling in Irish Tradition*. Dublin: Mercier Press.

Ouwehand, Cornelius. 1958–1959. "Some Notes on the God Susa-No-O." *Monumenta Nipponica* 14, no. 3: 138–161.

Owomoyela, Oyekan. 1977. "Folklore and Yoruba Theater." In *Forms of Folklore in Africa: Narrative, Poetic, Gnomic, Dramatic*, ed. Bernth Lindfors, 258–270. Austin: University of Texas Press.

———. 1990. "No Problem Can Fail to Crash on His Head: The Trickster in Contemporary African Folklore." *The World and I* 5, no. 4: 625–632.

Painter, Muriel Thayer. 1986. *With Good Heart: Yaqui Beliefs and Ceremonies in a Pascua Village*. Tucson: University of Arizona Press.

Parker, Arthur C. 1909. "Secret Medicine Societies of the Seneca." *American Anthropologist* 2, no. 11: 161–185.

———. 1923. *Seneca Myths and Folk Tales*. Buffalo, NY: Buffalo Historical Society.

Parsons, Elsie Clews. 1922. "Winter and Summer Dance Series in Zuni in 1918." *University of California Publications* 17, no. 3 (August): 171–216.

———. 1923. "The Hopi Wowochim Ceremony in 1920." *American Anthropologist* 25: 156–187.

———. 1926. *Tewa Tales*. New York: American Folk-Lore Society.

———. 1929. *The Social Organization of the Tewa of New Mexico*. Menasha, WI: Collegiate Press for the American Anthropological Association.

———. 1939. *Pueblo Indian Religion*. Chicago: University of Chicago Press.

Parsons, Elsie Clews, and Ralph Beals. 1934. "The Sacred Clowns of the Pueblo and Mayo-Yaqui Indians." *American Anthropologist* 36, no. 4: 491–514.

Paulme, Denise. 1977. "The Impossible Imitation in African Trickster Tales." In *Forms of Folklore in Africa: Narrative, Poetic, Gnomic, Dramatic*, ed. Bernth Lindfors, 64–103. Austin: University of Texas Press.

Peacock, James L. 1968. *Rites of Modernization: Symbolic and Social Aspects of Indonesian Proletarian Drama*. Chicago: University of Chicago Press.

———. 1978. "Symbolic Behavior and Social History: Transvestites and Clowns in Java." In *The Reversible World: Symbolic Inversion in Art and Society*, ed. Barbara Babcock-Abrahams. Ithaca, NY: Cornell University Press.

Pearson, Roberta, and William Uricchio. 1991a. "I'm Not Fooled by That Cheap Disguise." In *The Many Lives of Batman*, ed. Roberta Pearson and William Uricchio, 182–213. New York: Routledge.

Pearson, Roberta, and William Uricchio, eds. 1991b. *The Many Lives of the Batman*. New York: Routledge.

Pelton, Mary Helen, and Jacqueline DiGennaro. 1992. *Images of a People: Tlingit Myths and Legends*. Englewood, CO: Libraries Unlimited.

Pelton, Robert D. 1980. *The Trickster in West Africa: A Study of Mythic Irony and Sacred Delight*. Berkeley: University of California Press.

Pemberton, John. 1975. "Eshu-Elegba: The Yoruba Trickster God." *African Arts* 9: 20–27.

———. 1977. "A Cluster of Sacred Symbols: Orisa Worship among the Igbomina Yoruba of Ila-Orangun." *History of Religions* 17, no. 1: 1–28.

Poole, John Porter. 1983. "Cannibals, Tricksters, and Witches: Anthropophagic Images among Bimin-Kuskusmin." In *The Ethnography of Cannibalism*, ed. P. Brown and D. Tuzin, 6–32. Washington, DC: Society for Psychological Anthropology.

———. 1987. "Morality, Personhood, Tricksters, and Youths: Some Narrative Images of Ethics among Bimin-Kuskusmin." In *Anthropology in the High Valleys*, ed. L. L. Langness and Terence Hays. Novato, CA: Chandler and Sharp Publishers.

Pope, G. U. 1973. *Tamil Heroic Poems*. Madras: South Indian Saiva Siddharta Works Pub. Society.

Powers, William. 1975. *Oglala Religion*. Lincoln: University of Nebraska Press.

———. 1982. *Yuwipi, Vision and Experience in Oglala Ritual*. Lincoln: University of Nebraska Press.

Preston, R. J. 1980. "The Witiko: Algonkian Knowledge and Whiteman Knowledge." In *Manlike Monsters on Trial: Early Records and Modern Evidence*, ed. M. Halpin and M. Ames, 111–131. Vancouver: University of British Columbia Press.

Pyun, Y. T. 1946. *Tales from Korea*. Seoul, Korea: International Cultural Association of Korea.

Radin, Paul. 1956. *The Trickster: A Study in American Indian Mythology*. New York: Philosophical Library.

Rael, Juan. 1977. *Cuentos Espanoles de Colorado y Nuevo Mexico*. Sante Fe: Museum of New Mexico.

Raman, Parvathi. 1979. *Kalulu the Hare and Other Zambian Folk-Tales*. London: Arthur H. Stockwell.

Rassers, W. H. 1959. *Panji, the Culture Hero: A Structural Study of Religion in Java*. The Hague: Martinus Nijhoff.

Rattray, R. S. 1930. *Akan-Ashanti Tales*. Oxford: Clarendon Press.

———. 1969a. *Hausa Folk-Lore, Customs, Proverbs, Etc.* 2 vol. 1913. Reprint, Oxford: Oxford University Press.

———. 1969b. *Some Folk-Lore, Stories, and Songs in Chinyanja*. 1907. Reprint, New York: Negro Universities Press.

Ray, Dorothy Jean. 1967. *Eskimo Masks, Art, and Ceremony*. Seattle: University of Washington Press.

Ray, Verne F. 1938. *Lower Chinook Ethnographic Notes*. Seattle: University of Washington Press.

Reed, A. W. 1973. *Myths and Legends of Australia*. New York: Taplinger.

Reichard, Gladys. 1939. *Navajo Medicine Man*. New York: J. J. Augustin.

———. 1944. *The Story of a Navajo Hail Chant*. New York: G. A. Reichard.

———. 1950. *Navajo Religion: A Study of Symbolism*. Princeton, NJ: Princeton University Press.

Reid, Bill, and Robert Bringhurst. 1984. *The Raven Steals the Light*. Seattle: University of Washington Press.

Reid, Dorothy. 1963. *Tales of Nanabozho*. New York: Henry Z. Walck.

Rensel, Janet. 1991. "Housing and Social Relationships on Rotuma." In *Rotuma: Hanua Pumue, Precious Land*, ed. Chris Plant, 185–203. Suva, Fiji: Institute of Pacific Studies.

Ricard, Alain. 1975. "The Concert Play as a Genre: The Happy Stars of Lome." *Research in African Literature* 2: 165–179.

Richards, Audrey. 1982. *Chisungu: A Girl's Initiation Ceremony among the Bemba of Zambia*. London: Tavistock Publications.

Ricketts, Mac Linscott. 1966. "The North American Indian Trickster." *History of Religions* 5, no. 2: 327–350.

Roberts, Andrew. 1973. *A History of the Bemba*. Madison: University of Wisconsin Press.

Robinson, Edward. 1885. *Tales and Poems of South India*. London: T. Wolmer..

Rooth, Anna Birgitta. 1961. *Loki in Scandinavian Mythology*. Lund, Sweden: C. W. K. Gleerup.

———. 1962. *The Raven and the Carcass: An Investigation of a Motif in the Deluge Myth in Eu-*

rope, *Asia, and North America*. Helsinki, Finland: Suomalainen Tiedeakatemia.

Roszak, Theodore. 1969. *The Making of a Counter Culture*. Garden City, NY: Doubleday.

Roth, Walter. 1915. "An Inquiry into the Animism and Folklore of the Guiana Indians." Thirtieth Annual Report of the Bureau of American Ethnology: 103–386.

Rubin, Neville. 1971. *Cameroun: An African Federation*. New York: Praeger.

Russell, F. 1908. *The Pima Indians*. Washington, DC: Smithsonian Institution, Bureau of American Ethnology, no. 26.

Samarin, William. 1966. *The Gbeya Language*. Berkeley: University of California Publications in Linguistics.

Sands, Donald. 1960. *The History of Reynard the Fox*. Cambridge, MA: Harvard University Press.

Sapir, Edward. 1930. "Tales of the Ute Indians." *PAAA* 65: 297–535.

Sapir, Edward, and M. Swadesh. 1939. *Nootka Texts: Tales and Ethnological Narratives*. Philadelphia: University of Pennsylvania, Linguistic Society.

Schechner, Richard. 1985. *Between Theater and Anthropology*. Philadelphia: University of Pennsylvania Press.

———. 1993. *The Future of Ritual*. London: Routledge.

Schechner, Richard, and Willa Appel, eds. 1990. *By Means of Performance: Intercultural Studies of Theatre and Ritual*. New York: Cambridge University Press.

Schwartz, Herbert. 1969. *Windigo and Other Tales of the Ojibways*. Toronto: McClelland and Stewart.

Shelton, Austin J. 1971. *The Igbo-Igala Borderland: Religion and Social Control in Indigenous African Colonialism*. Albany: State University of New York Press.

Sherman, Ernest. 1993. "Merleau-Ponty and the Trickster: Philosophy as the Mytho-Logos of Ambiguity." *Dialectical Anthropology* 18, no. 1: 103–120.

Sherman, Josepha. 1990. "Child of Chaos, Coyote: A Folkloric Triad." *The World and I* 5, no. 4: 645–650.

Shore, Bradd. 1977. "A Samoan Theory of Action: Social Control and Social Order in a Polynesian Paradox." Ph.D. diss., University of Chicago.

———. 1978. "Ghosts and Government." *Man* 13: 175–199.

Shulman, David Dean. 1985. *The King and the Clown in South Indian Myth and Poetry*. Princeton, NJ: Princeton University Press.

Siegel, Lee. 1987. *Laughing Matters: Comic Tradition in India*. Chicago: University of Chicago Press.

Sigel, John. 1982. *Wasan Bahaushe Gaskiyarsa* (What the Hausa says in play, he really means). Madison: African Studies Program, University of Wisconsin.

Simmons, D. C. 1955. "Specimens of Efik Folklore." *Folklore* 66: 417–424.

Sinavaiana, Caroline. 1992. "Where the Spirits Laugh Last: Comic Theatre in Samoa." In *Clowning as Critical Practice: Performance Humor in the South Pacific*, ed. William Mitchell, 192–219. Pittsburgh, PA: University of Pittsburgh Press.

Skinner, Alanson. 1914. "Political Organizations, Cults, and Ceremonies of the Plains-Ojibway and Plains-Cree Indians." *Anthropological Papers of the American Museum of Natural History* 11, no. 6: 475–542.

———. 1915. "Folklore of the Menomini Indians." *Anthropological Papers of the American Museum of Natural History* 13, no. 3: 216–546.

Skinner, Neil. 1968. *Hausa Readings*. Madison: University of Wisconsin Press.

———. 1969. *Hausa Tales and Traditions*. Vol. 1. London: Cass.

Smith, Anne M. 1974. *Ethnography of the Northern Utes*. Santa Fe: Museum of New Mexico Press.

———. 1992. *Ute Tales*. Salt Lake City: University of Utah Press.

Smith, Edwin, and Andrew Murray Dale. 1920. *The Ila-Speaking Peoples of Northern Rhodesia*. London: Macmillan.

Smith, M. 1940. *The Puyallup-Nisqually*. New York: Columbia University Press.

Speck, Frank. 1915. "Some Naskapi Myths from Little Whale River." *Journal of American Folklore* 28: 70–77.

———. 1925. "Montagnais and Naskapi Tales from the Labrador Peninsula." *Journal of American Folklore* 38: 1–32.

——. 1934. *Catawba Texts*. New York: Columbia University Press.

——. 1935. *Naskapi*. Norman: University of Oklahoma Press.

——. 1985. *A Northern Algonquian Source Book*. Edited by Edward S. Rogers. New York: Garland.

Spicer, Edward. 1984. *Pascua: A Yaqui Village in Arizona*. Chicago: University of Chicago Press, 1940. Reprint, Tucson: University of Arizona Press.

Spier, Leslie. 1928. *Havasupi Ethnography*. New York: Anthropological Papers of American Museum of Natural History.

Stephen, Alexander M. 1936. *Hopi Journal*. Edited by Elsie Clews Parsons. New York: Columbia University Press.

Stephen, Michele. 1987. "Masters of Souls: The Mekeo Sorcerer." In *Sorcery and Witchcraft in Melanesia*, ed. M. Stephen, 41–80. New Brunswick, NJ: Rutgers University Press.

Stevens, James R. 1971. *Sacred Legends of the Sandy Lake Cree*. Toronto: McClelland and Stewart.

——. 1982. "Stories of the Windigo." In *Windigo: An Anthology of Fact and Fantastic Fiction*, ed. John Colombo, 193–200. Saskatoon, Saskatchewan: Western Producer Prairie Books.

Stevens, Phillips, Jr. 1991. "Play and Liminality in Rites of Passage: From Elder to Ancestor in West Africa." *Play and Culture* 4: 237–257.

Stevenson, Matilda Coxe. 1904. *The Zuni Indians*. Twenty-third annual report. Washington, DC: Smithsonian Institution, Bureau of American Ethnology.

Steward, Julian. 1991. *The Clown in Native North America*. New York: Garland.

Stimson, J. F. 1934. *The Legends of Maui and Tahaki*. Bulletin 127. Honolulu, Hawaii: Bernice P. Bishop Museum.

——. 1937. *Tuamotuan Legends*. Bulletin 148. Honolulu, HI: Bernice P. Bishop Museum.

Stoller, Paul. 1977. "Ritual and Personal Insults in Songrai Sonni." *Anthropology* 2, no. 1: 33–38.

——. 1984. "Horrific Comedy: Cultural Resistance and the Hauka Movement in Niger." *Ethos* 12, no. 2: 165–188.

Street, Brian. 1972. "The Trickster Theme: Winnebago and Azande." In *Zande Themes:*

Essays Presented to Sir Edward Evans-Pritchard, ed. Brian Street and Andre Singer, 82–104. Oxford: Basil Blackwell.

Sullivan, Lawrence. 1988. *Icanchu's Drum*. New York: Macmillan.

Swanton, John Reed. 1905. *Haida Texts and Myths*. Bulletin 29. Washington, DC: Bureau of American Ethnology.

——. 1909. *Tlingit Myths and Texts*. Bulletin 39. Washington, DC: Bureau of American Ethnology.

Tayanin, Damrong, and Lue Vang. 1992. "From the Village to the City: The Changing Life of the Kammu." In *Minority Cultures of Laos*, ed. Judy Lewis. Rancho Cordova, CA: Southeast Asia Community Resource Center.

Tedlock, Barbara. 1975. "The Clown's Way." In *Teachings from the American Earth*, ed. Denis and Barbara Tedlock, 105–120. New York: Liveright Press.

——. 1983. "Zuni Sacred Theater." *American Indian Quarterly* 7, no. 3: 93–110.

Teicher, Morton I. 1960. *Windigo Psychosis: A Study of a Relationship between Belief and Behavior among the Indians of the Northeastern Coast*. Seattle, WA: American Ethnological Society.

Teit, James. 1898. *Traditions of the Thompson River Indians of British Columbia*. Boston: Houghton, Mifflin for the American Folklore Society.

Terry, Patricia. 1983. *Renard the Fox*. Boston: Northeastern University Press.

Thomas, Jacqueline. 1970. *Contes, proverbes, devinettes ou enigmes, chants et prières Ngbaka-Ma'bo*. Paris: Editions Klincksieck.

Thompson, Stith. 1929. *Tales of the North American Indians*. Cambridge, MA: Harvard University Press.

——. 1946. *The Folktale*. New York: Holt, Rinehart and Winston.

——. 1955. *Motif Index of Folk Literature*. Bloomington: University of Indiana Press.

——. 1966. *Tales of North American Indians*. Bloomington: University of Indiana Press

Thompson, Vivian L. 1990. *Hawaiian Legends of Tricksters and Riddlers*. Honolulu: University of Hawaii Press.

Tipaya, Maenduan, comp. 1991. *Tales of Sri Thanoncha: Thailand's Artful Trickster*. Edited by Mechai Thongthep. Bangkok, Thailand: Naga Books.

Titiev, Mischa. 1944. *Old Oraibi: A Study of the Hopi Indians of Third Mesa*. Papers of the Peabody Museum of American Archaeology and Ethnology, vol. 22, no. 1. Cambridge: Harvard University Press.

———. 1971. "Some Aspects of Clowning among the Hopi Indians." In *Themes in Culture*, ed. J. Michael Mahar and Henry Orenstein Mario Zamora, 326–336. Quezon City, Philippines: Kayumanggi Publishers.

Todd, Loreto. 1979. *Tortoise the Trickster and Other Folktales from Cameroon*. London: Routledge and Kegan Paul.

Toelken, Barre. 1987. "Life and Death in the Navajo Coyote Tales." In *Recovering the World: Essays on Native American Literature*, ed. Brian Swann and Arnold Krupat. Berkeley: University of California.

———. 1990. "'Ma'ii Joldlooshi La'Eeya': The Several Lives of a Navajo Coyote." *The World and I* 5, no. 4: 651–660.

Towsen, John. 1976. *Clowns*. New York: Hawthorn.

Tremearne, A. J. N. 1910. "Fifty Hausa Folktales." *Folklore* 21.

———. 1970. *Hausa Superstitions and Customs*. 1913. Reprint, London: Cass.

Trigger, B., ed. 1978. *Handbook of North American Indians*. Washington, DC: Smithsonian Institution Press.

Turner, H. J., and H. Edmonds. 1968. "St. Michael Eskimo Myths and Tales." *University of Alaska Anthropology Papers* 14, no. 1: 43–83.

Turner, Victor, ed. 1982. *Celebration: Studies in Festivity and Ritual*. Washington, DC: Smithsonian Institution Press.

Tuutuwutsi, Mumuspi'yyungqa. 1995. *The Bedbugs' Night Dance and Other Hopi Sexual Tales*. Edited by Ekkehart Malotki. Translated by Ekkehart Malotki. Lincoln: University of Nebraska Press for Northern Arizona University.

Twain, Mark. 1965. *The Adventures of Huckleberry Finn*. Reprint ed. New York: Bantam.

Van Den Brink, J. H. 1974. *The Haida Indians*. Leiden, Netherlands: E. J. Brill.

Vathanaprida, Supaporn. 1994. *Thai Tales: Folktales of Thailand*. Englewood, CO: Libraries Unlimited.

Vaudrin, Bill. 1969. *Tanaina Tales from Alaska*. Norman: University of Oklahoma Press.

Vecsy, Christopher. 1993. "The Exception That Proves the Rule." In *Mythical Trickster Figures: Contours, Contexts, and Criticisms*, ed. William Hynes and William Doty, 106–121. Tuscaloosa: University of Alabama Press.

Verboven, Dirk. 1986. *A Praxiological Approach to Ritual Analysis: The Sigi of the Dogon*. Ghent, Belgium: Africana Gandensia.

Vizenor, Gerald. 1990. "Trickster Discourse." *American Indian Quarterly* 14, no. 3: 277–287.

Voegelin, E. W. 1933. "Kiowa-Crow Mythological Affiliations." *American Anthropologist* 35: 470–474.

Walker, James. 1980. *Lakota Belief and Ritual*. Edited by Elaine A. Jahner and Raymond DeMallie. Lincoln: University of Nebraska Press.

———. 1982. *Lakota Society*. Edited by Raymond DeMallie. Lincoln: University of Nebraska Press.

———. 1983. *Lakota Myth*. Edited by Elaine A. Jahner. Lincoln: University of Nebraska Press.

Wallis, Wilson, and Ruth Sawtell Wallis. 1955. *The Micmac Indians of Easter Canada*. Minneapolis: University of Minnesota Press.

Wang, Chi-Chen. 1944. *Traditional Chinese Tales*. New York: Columbia University Press.

Wardroper, John. 1970. *Jest upon Jest*. London: Routledge and Kegan Paul.

Webster-Jain, Sheila. 1988. "Clever Fools." *The World and I* (August).

Wells, Henry. 1963. *The Classical Drama of India*. London: Asia House Publishing.

Welsch, Roger. 1981. *Omaha Tribal Myths and Trickster Tales*. Chicago: Sage Books, Swallow Press.

———. 1990. "Trickster Mythology from around the World: The Laughing Gods." *The World and I* 5, no. 4: 614–624.

Welsford, Enid. 1935. *The Fool: His Social and Literary History*. New York: Farrar and Rinehart Inc.

Werbner, Pnina. 1986. "The Virgin and the Clown: Ritual Elaboration in Pakistani Migrants' Weddings." *Man* 21: 227–250.

Werner, Alice. 1925. *The Mythology of All Races*. Vol. 7: *Africa*. Edited by Canon John Arnott MacCulloch. Boston: Archaeological Institute of America.

———. 1968. *Myths and Legends of the Bantu*. 1933. Reprint, Holland: Frank Cass.

Wescott, Joan. 1962. "The Sculpture and Myths of Eshu-Elegba, the Yoruba Trickster." *Africa* 32, no. 4: 336–354.

Westervelt, W. D. 1910. *Legends of Maui: A Demi God*. Honolulu: Hawaiian Gazette.

———. 1915. *Legends of Old Honolulu*. Boston: Press of Geo. H. Ellis Co.

———. 1979. *Legends of Ma-Ui, a Demi God of Polynesians, and of his Mother Hina*. New York: AMS Press.

Whiteley, Wilfred. 1950. *Bemba and Related Peoples of Northern Rhodesia*. London: International African Institute.

Wilbert, Johannes. 1970. *Folk Literature of the Warao Indians*. Los Angeles: UCLA Latin American Center.

Wilbert, Johannes, and Karin Simoneau. 1982a. *Folk Literature of the Mataco Indians*. Los Angeles: UCLA Latin American Center.

———. 1982b. *Folk Literature of the Toba Indians*. Los Angeles: UCLA Latin American Center.

———. 1983. *Folk Literature of the Bororo Indians*. Los Angeles: UCLA Latin American Center.

———. 1984. *Folk Literature of the Ge Indians*. Los Angeles: UCLA Latin American Center.

———. 1987. *Folk Literature of the Chamacoco Indians*. Los Angeles: UCLA Latin American Center.

———. 1988a. *Folk Literature of the Mocovi Indians*. Los Angeles: UCLA Latin American Center.

———. 1988b. *Folk Literature of the Nivakle Indians*. Los Angeles: UCLA Latin American Center.

———. 1989. *Folk Literature of the Ayoreo Indians*. Los Angeles: UCLA Latin American Center.

———. 1990. *Folk Literature of the Caduveo Indians*. Los Angeles: UCLA Latin American Center.

———. 1992. *Folk Literature of the Sikuani Indians*. Los Angeles: UCLA Latin American Center.

Wilbert, Johannes, and Karin Simoneau, eds. 1978. *Folk Literature of the Ge Indians*. Los Angeles: UCLA Latin American Center.

———. 1986. *Folk Literature of the Guajiro Indians*. Los Angeles: UCLA Latin American Center.

Willeford, William. 1969. *The Fool and His Scepter: A Study in Clowns and Jesters and Their Audiences*. Evanston, IL: Northwestern University Press.

Williams, F. E. 1969. *Drama of Orokolo*. Oxford: Oxford University Press.

Williams, Paul, ed. 1979. *The Fool and the Trickster: Studies in Honor of Enid Welsford*. Totowa, NJ: Rowman and Littlefield.

Wilson, Peter Lamborn. 1991. "The Green Man: The Trickster Figure in Sufism." *Gnosis*, no. 19: 22–26.

Winstead, Richard. 1958. "A History of Classical Malay Literature." *Journal of the Royal Asiatic Society* 31: 5–261.

Wissler, Clark. 1907. "Some Dakota Myths." *Journal of American Folklore* 20: 121–131, 195–206.

———. 1912. "Societies and Ceremonial Associations of the Oglala Division of the Teton-Dakota." *Anthropological Papers of the American Museum of Natural History* 11, no. 1: 1–99.

———. 1913. "Societies and Dance Associations of the Blackfoot Indians." *Anthropological Papers of the American Museum of Natural History* 11, no. 4: 359–460.

Witherspoon, Gary. 1977. *Language and Art in the Navajo Universe*. Ann Arbor: University of Michigan Press.

Wolfe, Tom. 1968. *The Electric Kool-Aid Acid Test*. New York: Bantam.

Wright, Barton. 1985. *Kachinas of the Zuni*. Flagstaff, AZ: Northland Press.

———. 1994. *Clowns of the Hopi: Tradition Keepers and Delight Makers*. Flagstaff, AZ: Northland Publishing Co.

Wright, Pablo. 1986. "Fox Steals the Catch from Tiger." *Latin American Indian Literatures Journal* 4, no. 1: 22–41.

Yu, Anthony. 1980. *The Journey to the West*. 4 vols. Chicago: University of Chicago Press.

Zijderveld, Anton. 1982. *Reality in a Looking Glass: Rationality through an Analysis of Traditional Folly*. London: Routledge.

Zong, In-Sob. 1952. *Folktales from Korea*. London: Routledge.

Zozayong. 1972. *Spirit of the Korean Tiger*. Seoul, Korea: Emille Museum.

Zvelebil, Kamil Veith. 1973. *The Smile of Murugan, on Tamil Literature of South India*. Leiden, Netherlands: Brill.

Index